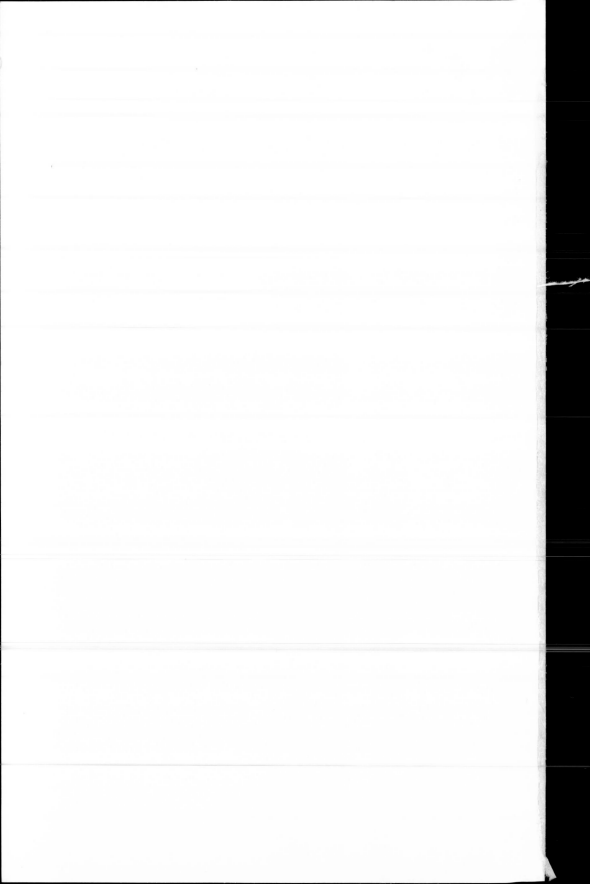

BY DAVID A. JASEN

Recorded Ragtime, 1897–1958
Tin Pan Alley

BY DAVID A. JASEN AND TREBOR TICHENOR

Rags and Ragtime

BY GENE JONES

Tom Turpin: His Life and Music
The Original Dixieland Jass Band

SPREADIN'
RHYTHM AROUND

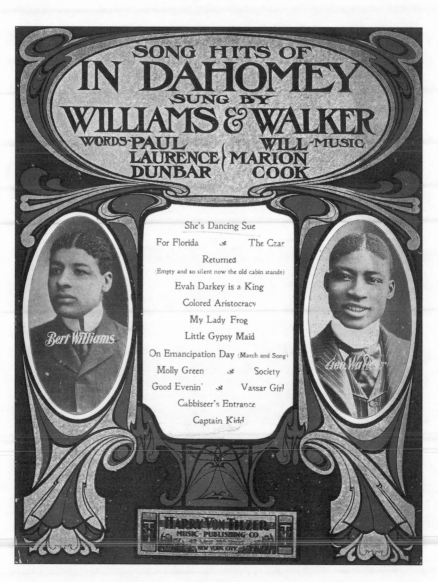

In Dahomey

SPREADIN' RHYTHM AROUND

Black Popular Songwriters, 1880–1930

DAVID A. JASEN

AND GENE JONES

SCHIRMER BOOKS

An Imprint of Simon & Schuster Macmillan
NEW YORK
Prentice Hall International
LONDON • MEXICO CITY • NEW DELHI • SINGAPORE • SYDNEY • TORONTO

Schirmer Books
An Imprint of Simon & Schuster Macmillan
1633 Broadway
New York, New York 10019

BOOK DESIGN BY KEVIN HANEK

Library of Congress Catalog Number: 98-10639
Printed in the United States of America
Printing number

1   2   3   4   5   6   7   8   9   10

LIBRARY OF CONGRESS CATALOGING-IN-PUBLICATION DATA
Jasen, David A.
    Spreadin' rhythm around : Black popular songwriters, 1880–1930 /
by David A. Jasen and Gene Jones.
        p. cm.
    Includes bibliographical references and index.
    ISBN 0-02-864742-4
    1. Composers, Black—Biography. 2. Afro-Americans—
Music—History and criticism. I. Jones, Gene (Gordon Gene) II. Title.
ML390.J26 1998
781.64'092'396073—dc21
[B]   98-10639
                                                   CIP
                                                   MN

This paper meets the requirements of ANSI/NISO Z39.48–1992
(Permanence of Paper).

To three generations of Jasens—
my mother Gertrude,
my wife Susan, and our son Raymond

and

To Annie, Julie, and Christopher

CONTENTS

• •

ILLUSTRATIONS

• •

ACKNOWLEDGMENTS

● ●

W E ARE GRATEFUL TO EVERYONE WHO helped us in the task of assembling materials and information for this book. Many of the careers we trace here are being examined for the first time, and our aim was simply to do right by them all. For years we have collected and enjoyed the music we write about, and we believe that the makers of the music, whether they are well known or not, deserve attention and respect. We appreciate all those who searched for data, those who read early drafts, and those who gave their time and talents to tracking these lives with us.

Throughout the writing process, we were haunted by the "Questions File," which was the ongoing list of things we did not know but wished we did. For a while the Questions File seemed to grow in a direct ratio to the manuscript pages themselves. We "wrote around" missing information, trusting that it would be found somehow. And with the help of friends who took our requests seriously, almost all of it was. We would like to thank those who made particularly large dents in the Questions File:

- Mr. W. W. Law, longtime civil rights leader and president emeritus of the NAACP, Savannah (Georgia) chapter, helped us tell the story of "Lift Ev'ry Voice and Sing."
- John Tillotson, a knowledgeable collector and extraordinary finder of books, was generous in helping us deconstruct and reconstruct the complex career of Clarence Williams.
- Mrs. Janice Cleary and "Ragtime Bob" Darch provided copies of locally published music as well as information regarding Maceo Pinkard's early years in Omaha.
- Christopher Steele collected data—especially song lists—for us, providing information on collaborators and publishers in

the careers of several early writers.

- Eunmi Shim shared information on Chris Smith with us.
- Ms. Gerry Lassiter, library assistant in the Virginiana Collection of the Hampton (VA) Public Library, sorted out the story of the school that Jo Trent attended in Virginia.
- Nan Bostick found the photo of Jo Trent.

Much of the information on the Paramount company and on J. Mayo Williams' years there is taken from research done and interviews conducted in the late 1960s and early 1970s by Gayle Wardlow and Stephen Calt. Their history of the Paramount label appeared as a five-part series in *78 Quarterly* over the years 1988–1992. In a telephone interview, record pioneer Milt Gabler recalled for us J. Mayo Williams' last days at Decca.

Three dealers in popular music have helped us build our collections over the years, and as we worked on this book, they kept our want lists in mind and supplied us with original copies of hard-to-find song sheets. Our thanks to Wayland Bunnell, Beverly Hamer, and Joel Markowitz.

We were lucky to have good writers among the early readers of this book. Lois Battle, a novelist, and Lanny Flaherty, a playwright, offered valuable suggestions as well as encouragement. Their margin notes ranged from meticulous style suggestions to the best question of all: "What do you mean by this?" Their keen eyes and their comments were invaluable to us.

We are extremely fortunate to have a superb and sympathetic editor in Richard Carlin. His enthusiasm for this book and his supervision of the project deserve great thanks.

Several of the major figures in this book have had fine recent biographies. Although these are cited in our bibliography, we would like especially to thank three writers who have treated their subjects with precision and have given us full-length pictures of them. These biographers and their subjects are:

- Reid Badger (James Reese Europe)
- Scott E. Brown (James P. Johnson)
- Barry Singer (Andy Razaf).

Finally, a special thank-you to Ann Steele, producer of the Tom Turpin

Ragtime Festival, who has given us help that is, in Duke Ellington's phrase, beyond category. She has aided our research and has given us critical reading along the way. And with great enthusiasm and skill—as well as endless patience—she prepared our manuscript. Her commitment to this project has been boundless, and she made sure that it was a proper job.

AUTHORS' NOTE

●●

THE CONTRIBUTIONS OF AFRICAN-AMERICANS to American popular music are vast and incalculable. The distinctive sounds of our songs and the rhythms of our social dances over the last hundred years have been the sounds and rhythms of black writers, instrumentalists, and singers. Their legacy is the influential body of writing and performing that put the "American" ingredient into American pop. Their harmonies and rhythmic ideas have made our commercial music generally recognized as the world's best. When makers of music anywhere imitate American music, they are, consciously or unconsciously, drawing on streams that go back to the drummers in New Orleans' Congo Square in the 1820s and to the rich harmonies of plantation church singing. This book is both a study and a celebration of the composers, lyricists, and performers who have, over the years, planted those sounds so deep in our soul.

Each songwriter in this book made his mark on popular music before 1930. Although this statement reads like an explanation of parameters, it is really a reminder of the size of the achievement celebrated here. In the fifty years from the end of the Reconstruction era to the beginning of the Depression, a few hundred people, most of whom were born with great odds against them, transformed America's musical culture. We have chosen to base our book on the published compositions and recorded performances of the African-Americans to whom we are most in debt. Some important early performers are not treated at length only because there is nothing by which we may sample their work. We have nineteenth-century newspaper accounts of the comedy of Billy Kersands, but, despite his popularity during his lifetime, to try to conjure him now would be only speculation. The major figures in our story have left plentiful evidence of their talents—published songs, recordings, and films—that shine with their genius.

All of our subjects came to music-making during a time when the commercial music industry was the epicenter of show business. Show business and the mass marketing of popular music started together and enhanced each other. The music helped to sell the entertainments, and the entertainments helped to sell the music. Minstrel shows, vaudeville, Broadway, radio, and movies served as vehicles for introducing and selling popular music to the public. Classical music, which stayed in concert and recital halls, has not had similar mass appeal in America.

The musical profession has always been a tough one, and for black writers and performers of this time, the chances against success, or even survival, were impossibly high. So this book is as much about perseverance and ingenuity as it is about talent. The list of obstacles overcome by any of these innovators would be many times longer than the list of his or her achievements. Every published song, every hit record, every film appearance was a long shot. The common thread in these lives is the hard climb up—from chitlin circuits, tent shows, mud shows, medicine shows, black and tans, sporting houses, honky tonks and street corners. By necessity, our main characters were mostly hyphenates: singer-composers, writer-publishers, actor-lyricists, and so forth. If one door was closed to them, they built another door or they came in through the window. But they all made it from the ragged edges of show business into the shiny stronghold that was designed to keep them out. Although we will accentuate the positives rather than enumerate the negatives in these lives, the reader should not forget the generations of prejudice and poverty that shadow every success, as well as every failure, in these remarkable careers.

DAVID A. JASEN
GENE JONES

PROLOGUE

. . . .

Before Pop

LTHOUGH THERE WERE MANY KINDS OF music in seventeenth-century America, America was not really a musical nation. Emigrants brought with them the folk songs and church music of their home countries, but the singing and playing of folk songs had to remain private pleasures. The church-centered colonial settlements and towns frowned on the parties and dances that would have been the natural occasions to perform them. And church music had its restrictions, as well. No instruments were allowed in the services. Congregational singing was done from the old, mostly English, hymnals or, more often, "lined out": a leader, usually a deacon, would sing a line and the churchgoers would repeat it or answer it. With concerts, parties, and stage performances forbidden, the only musical need was for an up-to-date hymnal. The first book published in America was the collection that we now know as *The Bay Psalm Book*, issued in Cambridge, Massachusetts, in 1640. The French and Spanish settlers of the South and Southeast were more tolerant of music and dancing, but even in these areas, music was mostly a church activity, and a plain one at that.

With the growing desire for independence and the first stirring toward nationhood in the eighteenth century, America needed a kind of music that it didn't have. Nothing in the canons of church music or folk song could express the specifically American feelings of grievance and defiance that were leading to a revolution. The first pieces of American songwriting that were known throughout the colonies were the pieces that satisfied this need: martial airs. Many amateurs tried their hands at writing them, often setting their fiery messages to melodies borrowed from familiar English songs. The most popular anthem of the Revolutionary era was William Billings' "Chester," which was originally conceived as a religious song by its composer. He fitted his tune with new words ("Let tyrants shake their iron rod . . . "), and the result resounded at patriotic rallies throughout the 1770s. "Chester" joined the dozens of songs written to praise George Washington and the cheeky new lyric for "Yankee Doodle"—another borrowed English tune—to boost the rebellious spirit.

In the mid-eighteenth century, Americans loosened up a bit about the use of instruments and the public performance of music. Instruments, mostly organs, violins, and flutes, began to be imported in the early 1700s, and the first public concert—music for music's sake— was given in Boston in 1731. Thomas Jefferson played the violin for pleasure, and Benjamin Franklin took credit for inventing the glass harmonica. In 1759 Francis Hopkinson, then twenty-two, published his song "My Days Have Been So Wondrous Free," one of the first native efforts that is not about church or war.

As the enjoyment of entertainment grew, along with the prosperity to produce it, America had its first wary contact with opera. The first to see a production was an imported English ballad-opera, *Flora, or Hob in the Well*, performed at the Courthouse in Charleston, South Carolina, in 1735. A contemporary notice hints that it was a lively affair with a fulsome plot, dancing Pierrots, and a pantomime interspersed. The "Wondrous Free" composer, Hopkinson, got up an "oratorical entertainment" called *The Temple of Minerva* in Philadelphia in 1781, but the first real American opera was *The Archers, or Mountaineers of Switzerland*. This adaptation of the William Tell story, with libretto by William Dunlap and music by Benjamin Carr, was produced in New York City in 1796. With three centuries of American subjects to draw on, composers and librettists were looking to England, Switzerland, and (most often) to mythology—anywhere but America—for subject matter.

The most frequently played "serious" music of this time was a curious mix of the borrowed (the Overture to *Iphigenie en Aulide*) and the martial (William Hewitt's *The Battle of Trenton*, which was a piano sonata, and

Benjamin Carr's *Federal Overture*). It would not be until the 1850s that America could boast a composer/performer worthy of international fame, the New Orleans-born Louis Moreau Gottschalk, who was inspired by the Spanish and African-American music of his native city.

By the early nineteenth century, a few regional publishers had begun to issue song sheets for home use. Some were formerly printers of church music, like Oliver Ditson in Boston, and some others, like Atwill's Music Saloon in New York City, had begun to see a vague connection between their customers hearing a song performed and their wanting to play it at home. By the end of the century, the production and promotion of sheet music would be a fine science, developed in the think tanks of Tin Pan Alley.

There were slaves in America before there were Pilgrims. In 1619 a Dutch ship arrived at Jamestown, Virginia, with a cargo of twenty Africans, seventeen men and three women, to be sold as "indentured servants." Their "servitude" would be lifelong and without wages. In 1675 there were 5,000 slaves in the North American colonies. By 1700 there were 28,000; by 1750, nearly a quarter of a million. (The last legal shipment of slaves would be carried on the *Clothilde*, which unloaded its human cargo at Mobile Bay, Alabama, in 1859.)

Like the American settlers who had emigrated by choice, Africans brought their music with them. The songs of the slaves were rightly seen as insidious by slaveholders. Whites were greatly outnumbered by blacks on any plantation, as well as in many small towns and settlements, and although whites held the upper hand, they lived in a state of unease because of their minority. When it was discovered that drumming had been used as communication among slaves who had carried out bloody rebellions in the Southeast, drums were outlawed by several state legislatures. In the deep South, drums were thought of as accompaniment to voodoo rituals. Whites believed that the very sound of polyrhythmic drumming could turn its listeners from docile servants into crazed zombies.

Slave songs were dangerous, too, because they were in a language that whites couldn't understand. Who could know what messages were being conveyed when Africans sang to Africans in their own tongues? In the early eighteenth century, a great missionary effort was made to "convert" slaves and to establish Christian churches for them on plantations. The idea was to tame the slaves, to obliterate the language and culture that the masters couldn't understand, and to replace "heathen" beliefs with a rudimentary version of Christianity. The ring-shout, a holy dance of African origin, was particularly suspect. The ring-shout's blend of the spiritual and the sensual horrified white slave owners. Its improvised call-and-response singing, its dramatic movements and its sophisticated rhythms were unlike anything ever seen or heard in Puritan America. If slaves could be induced to sit in neat rows on simple wooden pews and sing the foursquare hymns of the Christian church, white America could breathe easier.

Work songs were generally permitted, however, because they were useful for coordinating synchronous movement. Cane-cutting songs, rice-fanning songs, pulling songs, hammering songs, rowing songs, chopping songs—all mostly repetitive snatches of rhythmic doggerel—constituted the monotonous repertoires lined out by the gang foremen of slavery days.

Given an institution that supplied endless free labor, the plantation system could only prosper. By the early nineteenth century, many plantation owners could indulge themselves in grand living. The "big houses" grew larger and more ornate, while the adjoining slave quarters just grew, as the numbers of slaves increased. Plantation owners began to pride themselves on their lavish hospitality and gracious homes. Week long parties, often celebrating hunting or harvest seasons, were occasions to show off and share the prosperity of a thriving plantation. And parties needed music. Many slave owners recruited small dance orchestras from their estates' slave populations. Most slave musicians were ear players, of course, as no owner was softhearted enough to provide musical instruction for even the most accomplished of them. But many plantations could boast a champion fiddler as well as a few guitarists or banjoists to accompany him. They were proudly presented at parties and holiday balls to provide the reels, jigs, and galops for dancing.

And on Sunday afternoons, a plantation owner sometimes offered his houseful of guests a concert. The hosts and their company sat on expansive porches and listened to the singing of slaves assembled in the yard to entertain them. The slaves knew what was expected of them—spirituals—and the owners congratulated themselves for indulging the homemade music of the people who made such a pleasant life possible for them.

Given the estimations and expectations of blacks by whites, it is nothing short of miraculous that, by the 1850s, a few African-Americans were trying to make careers on the concert stage. The first was Elizabeth Taylor Greenfield (1824–1876), who was born a slave in Natchez, Mississippi, and was adopted by Philadelphia Quakers. Risking the disapproval of her adoptive family, she trained in voice as a child and began singing at local events. Encouraged by all who heard her, she made her professional debut in Buffalo, New York, in 1851, and thereafter toured the northeastern United States and Canada. In 1854 she sang for Queen Victoria at Buckingham Palace. Thomas J. Bowers (1823–1885), a tenor, studied briefly with Greenfield and made his first professional appearance with her in Philadelphia in 1854. The Luca Family (four singing brothers, one of whom was the piano accompanist) was featured in concert with the Hutchinsons, a white family of singing abolitionists from New Hampshire, throughout the 1850s. Cleveland Luca (1838–1872), the "wonderful boy pianist," particularly stirred the passions of the ladies in his audiences. A writer of the time said that "forgetting often, in their enthusiasm, that he was black, it seemed that they would certainly carry him away."

And some prodigious instrumentalists also took to the concert hall. "Blind Tom" Bethune (1849–1908), who was mentally as well as physically impaired, could dazzlingly replicate the most difficult piano pieces after one hearing and kept a repertoire of 700 classical and semi-classical works in his memory, his managers claimed. Justin Holland (1819–1887), a virtuoso on piano, flute, and guitar, published the first American method book for guitar in 1874. Frederick Elliot Lewis (b. 1846) was a Boston-based performer and arranger of music for piano, organ, and violin.

These performers were precisely in the mainstream of concert music in their time, acknowledged for their renditions of Mozart and

Blind Tom

Beethoven as well as the sentimental songs and instrumental showpieces so loved by the age. But because they were black, there was a taint of freakishness to their accomplishments. They couldn't escape the mention of race, even in their best reviews. They were given racial nicknames that became their billing, even in major concert halls. Elizabeth Greenfield was "The Black Swan"; Thomas J. Bowers was "The Colored Mario" (after a famous Italian tenor). Blind Tom Bethune's press notices usually included a phrase such as "Negro phenomenon" or "colored-boy pianist" in their opening sentences. To the whites who heard them, the wonder was not that these artists performed so well, but that they could perform at all.

The first exposure that most white Americans had to "real" African-Americans singing "their" music came during the tours made by the Fisk Jubilee Singers in the last quarter of the nineteenth century. Fisk University, in Nashville, Tennessee, was a struggling institution from its very beginning. It was established for the education of ex-slaves by the Congregational Church shortly after the Civil War. At the time of the university's opening, the campus consisted of an abandoned army hospital barracks and the grounds surrounding it. Supporting the university became such a strain on its church sponsor, the American Missionary Association, that its closure seemed imminent by 1870.

More in desperation than in hopes of succeeding, the university's choir director, a white New Yorker named George L. White, offered the services of his singers as a fund-raising tool. The eleven-member choir, with their pianist and a chaperone, set out on a tour in October 1871 with the seemingly impossible goal of earning $20,000 for their school. They prepared a program of operatic selections and temperance and "light classical" songs. Over the objections of some of the singers, who didn't want to be reminded of slavery days, it was decided to add some spirituals (such as "Keep Me from Sinking Down" and "O Brothers, Don't Stay Away") to their repertoire. The choir's first performance, in Cincinnati, raised only a small sum, and their Chillicothe, Ohio, concert netted them only $50, which the choir generously donated to the victims of the great Chicago Fire.

Even though they were not attracting audiences in great numbers, the choir and their director noticed that the best response was to the "slave song" part of the program. So the choir renamed itself in midtour and became the Fisk Jubilee Singers ("jubilees" were the up-tempo spirituals of antebellum times). When they sang for the Council of Congregational Churches in Oberlin, Ohio, in December, they greatly impressed the visiting minister, Henry Ward Beecher. Beecher put a large donation into the collection plate and exhorted his fellow churchmen to do the same. The choir made $1,300.

Encouraged by their first success, the choir headed for the Northeast, where they had successful concerts in Massachusetts, Connecticut, and New York. In Washington, D.C., they were received with great acclaim by President Grant. On returning to Nashville in May 1872, the singers presented their amazed school officials with a check for $20,000.

But the best was yet to come for the singers. Immediately after arriving home, they received an invitation from the popular bandmaster Patrick S. Gilmore to sing at the World Peace Jubilee, a huge musical exposition that he was producing in Boston in June. The Jubilee Singers were the hit of the festival. Their performance of "The Battle Hymn of the Republic" brought the audience to its feet and set off thunderous cheering. Gilmore escorted the singers from their choir risers to his own platform, front and center, to perform encores.

The Jubilee Singers' glorious voices and their repertoire of spirituals hit the concert world like a thunderbolt. Here, at last, was the true "American" music that had been hoped for for so long. Audiences loved it, and serious musicians took it seriously. It was unlike any other nation's music; it was ours. By early 1873, a European tour for the choir was underway. They began in London, where they moved Queen

Victoria to tears with their singing of "Go Down, Moses" and "Steal Away to Jesus." Mark Twain, who was then visiting in London, heard them for the first time there, and he never forgot their effect on him. The original Jubilees would make many more tours before the group disbanded in 1878, and Fisk would send out many other groups to follow its first. In seven years, the Fisk Jubilee Singers raised over $150,000 for their school, and they inspired other black colleges to send their choirs out for the same purpose.

In 1897, long after such spiritual-singing groups had become commonplace, Mark Twain heard the Jubilees again, this time in Switzerland. He wrote to a friend:

> Away back in the beginning, to my mind, their music made all other vocal music cheap, and that early notion is emphasized now. It is utterly beautiful to me and it moves me infinitely more than any other music can. I think that in the Jubilees and their songs America has produced the perfectest flower of the ages, and I wish it were a foreign product so that she would worship it and lavish money on it and go properly crazy over it.

But despite the trailblazing done by the Jubilees and the concert artists who preceded them, despite their talent, dignity, and diligence, America, in its heart, preferred another image of the black people in its midst. By the time the Jubilee Singers undertook their first tour, the nation was thirty years into its love affair with the minstrel show.

CHAPTER 1

"IN THE EVENING BY THE MOONLIGHT"

The Minstrel Era and the Beginnings of Tin Pan Alley

THE FIRST STOCK CHARACTER TO RECUR ON the American stage was the "Jonathan" figure, a plain-speaking Yankee who mocked the Anglophiles around him in a handful of plays of the mid-eighteenth century. "Jonathan" was soon joined by another American type, an eccentric "Negro boy," who was by turns comic and pathetic. At first the "Negro boy" was so peripheral to the plots of the plays that he was nameless, but over the years, as audiences began to look forward to his songs and mangled wordplay, he acquired names, "Mungo" and "Sambo" among them. (Lewis Hallam was the first "Mungo," in a 1769 play called *The Padlock*.) He became a dependable source of fun, and by the early 1800s a few American actors had begun to specialize in the blackface delineation of him.

One of these actors was Thomas Dartmouth "Daddy" Rice, a gangly New Yorker who had begun as a spear carrier in plays in his native city. In 1828, his career as one of the first song-and-dance men took him to Louisville, where he devised a bit of material that would change theatrical history. He drew his inspiration from the singing and the shuffling step of a crippled black stable hand who worked near the the-atre. Rice decided to impersonate the old man in his act, and in doing so, he created the first and most devastating of the minstrel stereotypes.

"Jim Crow" arrived full-blown at Rice's next stop, in Pittsburgh. Wearing the stable hand's shabby clothes, which he had purchased to add "authenticity," Rice, in blackface and wooly wig, sprang at his audience, eyes rolling, wagging a finger, and doing a grotesque hop as he sang in a thick dialect:

> W'eel about and turn about
> And do just so,
> Eb'ry time I w'eel about
> I jump Jim Crow.

The onlookers were paralyzed with delight at this spectacle. Then they shot from their seats, screaming their approval. Daddy Rice had, in a stroke, given the American public the performance and the character it had been waiting for. Rice found that Jim Crow was a hit everywhere he went. (In 1833 Rice experimented by giving Jim a partner in the act. The little blackfaced boy he pulled out of a sack that he carried on stage was Joseph Jefferson, who would become one of the most beloved American actors.) After four years of trooping Jim around the South and Midwest, Rice took his misshapen darky to New York in 1832, then to London in 1836. Jim Crow became Rice's signature character, played in every performance he gave until his death in 1860 and often in theatres so crowded that seating had to be placed on the stage around him. Rice's caricature inspired dozens of imitators, and Jim Crow—the shuffling, brainless, eager-to-please black bumpkin—was off on his own career. He would haunt American stages, and black per-formers, for a hundred years.

The second classic stereotype to enter the minstrel pantheon was Jim Crow's opposite number—"Zip Coon," the citified black dandy, overdressed in his "long tail blue" coat and tight silk pants, brash and pretentious, eager to show his country cousins the latest dance steps and to confound them with his jokes and riddles. Zip Coon was the creation of a contemporary of Rice's, the "Negro delineator" George Washington Dixon. Like Jim, Zip had his own theme song (the "Zip

Coon" melody is now known as "Turkey in the Straw"), borrowed from a folk song, as Rice had borrowed his. Between them, Jim and Zip constituted a catalog of human frailties: ignorance, vanity, cupidity, and laziness. Both were harmless, sexless, hopeless. And both were painted black.

Given the enormous popularity of Rice, Dixon, and their black-faced disciples, it was inevitable that someone would figure out how to combine their beloved characters with suitable "darky" songs to make a full evening of fun. The inevitable occurred in New York City in January 1843, when four out-of-work circus performers met in a boarding house and decided to cast their lots together, each in the hope that four unknown entertainers would draw an audience better than one. They called themselves the Virginia Minstrels. In early February they did short sets of their material between the acts of plays in New York, first at the Chatham Theatre, then at the Bowery Amphitheatre. Audiences enjoyed them, so they kept at it. In March 1843, at Boston's Masonic Temple, they gave the first full-length minstrel show.

Dan Emmett, the most versatile of the four, played banjo, violin, and flute. Billy Whitlock was also a banjoist. Frank Brower played the bones (the poor man's castanets—in Brower's case, made of the actual ribs of a horse). Dick Pelham rounded out the rhythm section with his tambourine. They paired off for bits of crosstalk, and they accompanied each other during solo songs. After some success in the Northeast, the Virginia Minstrels began a tour of England. Although they were well received there, professional jealousies among them caused them to break up the act before their tour was over. The original Virginia Minstrels lasted only about six months, but their show concept was quickly taken up by others.

The first important minstrel impresario was Edwin P. Christy of New York. Christy's troupe began small—four people at first, including the producer—but it was more professional than the Virginia Minstrels from the beginning. A better producer than performer, Christy saw the need for a structure and a context in which a minstrel entertainment could happen, a "natural" setting for blackfaced fun and music. Drawing his inspiration from actual slave entertainments he had heard about, Christy envisioned an evening that would represent a sort of festival on a showbiz plantation. Cheerful black neighbors in outlandish

costumes (dressed up and dressed down) would come together to entertain each other—and the audience—with jokes, dancing and songs.
The characters would play off each other's foolishness, and the music
would be strictly "Ethiopian"—that is, the humble banjo, tambourine,
and bones would be the foundation of everything. Devoid of any relation to reality, yet advertised as completely "authentic," the Christy
show—and the dozens that followed it—presented slave life as a nonstop party in a darky Eden. Everybody sang, nobody worked, nobody
got whipped, nobody was sold. The formula was so successful that, in a
time when a one-week booking was a long stay, Christy's Minstrels
were in residence at New York's Mechanics' Hall for ten years.

The public loved the roaring, low-class energy of the minstrel
shows and flocked to see the dozens of troupes that sprang up during the
1850s and 1860s. Any town large enough to have a railroad station and
a hall could host a minstrel show. Any town small enough to have only
a railroad station and a hall usually saw no other professional entertainment except minstrel shows for a generation in the mid-century.

With so much competition on the field, the shows grew grand and
bloated trying to outdo each other. Entire railroad trains were needed
to transport sets and personnel. Producers sent advance men to paste
up garish three-sheets heralding the imminent arrival of "Gigantic
Minstrels," "Mammoth Minstrels," and "Mastodon Minstrels," shows
big enough to shake up any small town and most cities in America. But
no matter how huge or slick the presentations became, the idea of the
"neighborhood party" given by black buffoons did not wear out its welcome for fifty years.

E. P. Christy prided himself especially on his troupe's music. In
September 1847 he discovered the work of a twenty-two-year-old
songwriter from Lawrenceville, Pennsylvania, named Stephen Foster.
Foster, from a middle-class family and self-taught in music, had been
peddling his songs to minstrel performers, Daddy Rice among them,
with no success. But when Christy heard a singer named Nelson
Kneass perform Foster's polka-paced "Oh, Susanna" in a variety show
at Andrew's Eagle Ice Cream Saloon in Pittsburgh, he quickly saw its
possibilities for the minstrel stage. After several hearings, Christy
remembered enough of the melody and words to pass them on to one
of his singers. "Oh, Susanna" became the hit of Christy's show. People

not only wanted to hear the song, they wanted to buy it. A Cincinnati publisher, W. C. Peters, wrote to Foster, asking for the manuscript. Foster, still the amateur, sent it, no questions asked. The composer was delighted when Peters sent him a fee of $100. The song was published with the Christy name all over it (and Foster's nowhere on it). Foster did not know that he had written the hit of the 1848 minstrel season until a friend sent him a copy. Emboldened by the fact that he had written something good enough for Christy to steal, Foster quit his day job in a Cincinnati office and began to think of himself as a professional songwriter.

There is no evidence that Foster and Christy ever met, but the pilfered song began a symbiotic relationship that would last the rest of Foster's life. He would send Christy dozens of songs over the years—along with wheedling letters about payments and composer credit—and Christy used many of them in his various minstrel companies.

This arrangement, one-sided as it was, solved for Foster the nineteenth-century composer's biggest problem: distribution. Songwriters of his time usually had their work published—or they self-published—only to have a small flurry of local sales, followed by the song's disappearance from the printshop window. With Christy behind them, the Foster songs got national attention. They were sold in theatre lobbies after performances, and wherever the Christy troupe went, Foster's songs went, too. Although his mentor and his publishers were neither scrupulous nor punctual with their payments and accounting to him, Foster was at least able to eke out a living as the first American songwriter who was not a performer, teacher, or church musician.

Throughout the 1850s Foster songs enlivened minstrel evenings: "Camptown Races," "Jeanie with the Light Brown Hair," "My Old Kentucky Home," "Old Dog Tray," "Old Black Joe," "Massa's in de Cold Ground," and "Ring de Banjo" were among the nearly 200 published. Foster had a strong melodic gift and a good ear for the banjo-based syncopation of the minstrel stage. His songs achieved the instant status of "folk material," appropriated and unpaid-for by the hundreds of minstrels who sang them.

In 1852, *Uncle Tom's Cabin*, Harriet Beecher Stowe's blockbuster novel, was published, and it was read, discussed, and argued about for years. It presented more fully drawn African-American characters than any novel or play before it, and minstrel producers seized on three of the book's figures to become stock players in the plantation comedy of their shows. The first was Uncle Tom himself—sometimes called Uncle Silas, Jasper, or Eph by minstrel producers—who became a wistful old man longing for the good old days on the plantation and reminiscing about them in song. (The kindly old Uncle began to get more stage time after the Civil War, when the good old days were really gone.) Aunt Chloe—sometimes called Dinah or Jenny—also entered the minstrel scene. She was the bossy peacekeeper and general scold of the shows' antebellum fantasy land. Minstrel pros referred to her as "the wench role," and, to compound the merriment, she was always played by a man. (Aunt Chloe would evolve into the more generic—and gentler—Mammy in the early 1900s.) Mrs. Stowe's Topsy, the sprightly, mischievous pickaninny, provided a role for child actors on the minstrel stage. These three Stowe characters, along with Jim Crow and Zip Coon, completed the cast of archetypes for minstrel humor.

Along with the setting and characters, a proscribed format—a certain and unvarying playing order—for minstrel shows was in place by 1860. We cannot know who, if anyone, deserves the credit for figuring out this framework, but somehow, in the blur of activity of the minstrels' first decade, everyone seems to have agreed on it. As specific as a recipe, this structure was found to be foolproof by troupes of all sizes, however rich or poor in production values or talent. Everyone knew that a minstrel show had to have a First Part, an Olio, and an Afterpiece/Walkaround.

The First Part began with a clattering overture, a medley of songs that would be featured during the evening. The curtain opened to reveal the troupe in all the splendor of setting and costume it could muster. In the center of a semicircle of gaudily dressed blackfaced comedians sat the master of ceremonies, Mister Interlocutor, a dignified, spiffily dressed white man. The two principal funmakers, Mr. Tambo and Mr. Bones—the Jim and Zip figures—were seated at opposite sides of the stage on the ends of the semicircle (hence, called "end men"). All arose to sing a welcome and a promise of a good time. At the finish of the opening song, the Interlocutor gave his ritual cry, "Gentlemen, be seated!" Then the first burst of snappy patter among the Interlocutor and his end men began, laced with local references, of course. The Interlocutor was slightly pompous but patient with the foolery of his fellows, bemused by the ignorance all around him. The puns and conundrums of Tambo and Bones were greeted by the laughter and stylized appreciation of the others on the front row. A synchronized raising and shaking of their tambourines punctuated the jokes. A singer, usually a tenor, stepped forward to perform a sentimental song with all the stops out. Then more jokes, a specialty dance (an early one was the "Virginia Essence," the forerunner of the soft shoe), more crosstalk, and a First Part finale performed by all.

Next came the Olio, a set of various individual specialties usually performed "in one": before the front curtain to allow the changing of scenery for the final part of the show. Instrumentalists, especially those trick players who could manipulate two clarinets, play tuned water glasses, do animal imitations on their horns, and the like, as well as jugglers and comic singers—all got to show their stuff in solo turns. But the indispensable part of the Olio was the stump speech. This was the star comic's feature of the evening: a burlesque lecture, delivered in heavy dialect, on a topic of the day such as temperance or women's rights.

Finally the curtain opened on the setting for the third part of the show, the Afterpiece and Walkaround. Afterpieces began in the late 1840s as sentimental playlets about life on the plantation, but by the mid-1850s they had turned into sharp-edged skits poking crude fun at serious drama. (One was called *Medea, or a Cup of Cold Pizen*.) The conclusion of the show was the Walkaround, a long and elaborately choreographed number that brought the comedians back for one more antic and ended with a strutting parade around the stage by everyone. It was for the Walkaround that Christy had wanted "Oh, Susanna." Another popular Walkaround tune was Dan Emmett's "Dixie," written for Bryant's Minstrels in 1860.

For all its foolishness and the slander of its subjects, the minstrel system of producing, promoting, and booking companies marks the beginning of American show business. The conventions of minstrelsy were tried and proven over many years, so they were ready and waiting for the first free blacks who wanted to be entertainers. Their stage was set. Their stories were written. Their characterizations, costumes, and makeup were laid out. To be in show business, all they had to do was put them on.

JAMES A. BLAND

James A. Bland was neither the first nor the biggest of the African-American minstrel stars, but among the hundreds of black minstrels,

James A. Bland

his name is the only one recognized today. He alone left a body of work that still matters. His small number of copyrights seems to indicate that he thought of himself mainly as a performer rather than as a songwriter, but a handful of his songs were so good that they have survived by a hundred years the institution that they were written for. There are too many parallels for his career not to be compared to Stephen Foster's: middle-class childhood, early infatuation with minstrel shows, success at writing for them, carelessness with money, a pauper's death. The idea of his being "the black Stephen Foster" was prevalent in Bland's own lifetime and must have rankled him, but the point of the comparison, then as now, is that, between them, they wrote the best songs of the minstrel era.

James A. Bland was born on October 22, 1854, in Flushing, Long Island, New York. He was the descendant of freemen on both sides of his family, his father's from South Carolina and his mother's from Delaware. His father Allen was one of the first college-educated blacks in the United States, having received a degree from Wilberforce University in Ohio. Shortly after the Civil War, when James was in his early teens, Allen Bland was offered an appointment as an examiner at the U.S. Patent Office. He accepted the position, and the Blands moved to Washington, where they found a comfortable house at Fifteenth and L streets.

While still a public school student, James took up the banjo and began to play at school functions and parties. After graduation, with music already a rival to his studies, he dutifully enrolled at Howard University. (His father enrolled at the same time and eventually completed a law degree.) During his time at Howard, James noticed the singing of the ex-slaves who were working as groundskeepers, and he tried to compose songs like those he heard.

Bland was a fixture at campus parties. Handsome and gregarious, he was always on hand with his banjo to sing a few of his "refined" songs. Howard was a strict school, requiring uniforms for its students along with mandatory attendance at daily roll calls and drills. Attending entertainments of any kind was strictly forbidden. It was a sign that music was winning the tug-of-war with school when James began to break the "no theatre" rule by sneaking away to see minstrel shows. By 1873, music had won him for life. We can imagine the horror of his respectable parents when he left the university to become a blackfaced entertainer.

His first jobs with minstrel companies were short-term: brief tours to Boston and New York, with Bland always returning to his family's home to await the next producer's call. During his hiatuses he did some street-corner playing, and he sang for a while at a Washington beer garden.

In 1878 the young minstrel's songwriting career began. Bland managed to place one of his ballads with the white minstrel star George Primrose, whose performance of it led to its publication that same year. As soon as the song saw print, other showmen took it up for their own use. The song was "Carry Me Back to Old Virginny," a masterpiece of ballad writing that was immediately compared to Foster's best. It is a serene, graceful song that is nostalgic without being musically mawkish. Its straightforward lyric is set to a one-octave melody, easy to perform and to remember. It was perfectly suited to the Uncle in the Olio, longing for the days before the War.

By the end of the year, Bland was playing in Chicago with Sprague's Georgia Minstrels, one of the most prosperous companies of the time. The company carried eighty performers, and its leading player was Sam Lucas (1840–1916), already on his way to becoming America's most popular black minstrel star. Lucas, in a generous gesture to his promising young colleague, dedicated his 1879 song "Put on My Long White Robe" to Bland.

Bland's reputation as songwriter/performer rose when his "In the Evening by the Moonlight" was published in 1880. This still, hypnotic

Sam Lucas

ballad was another lyric gem and was very easy to harmonize. It remains a favorite of quartet singers to this day. In 1879 Bland's lively pseudospiritual, "Oh, Dem Golden Slippers," became the definitive Walkaround number. After about five years in the business, Bland had become the minstrels' most renowned songwriter. There would be several other Bland songs to have some currency in minstrel shows ("In the Morning by the Bright Light," "Hand Me Down My Walking Cane," "Dancing on de Kitchen Floor," and "Close Dem Windows"), but his name was made by his three early hits. Some claim that the song-buying public of his time didn't know that Bland was black, but a drawing of his face was prominent on several of his song sheets. He is depicted as dreamy-eyed, well-dressed, and contented-looking, the picture of dignity, staring out past the drawings of blubber-lipped stereotypes capering around him.

Sometime in mid-1879, Bland was hired away from the Sprague troupe by Haverly's Genuine Colored Minstrels. Sam Lucas also went with the Haverly company, to costar with the wide-mouthed black comedian Billy Kersands (1842–1915). Lucas performed his own song "Carve Dat Possum," and Kersands's specialty was singing and dancing while holding a cup and saucer in his mouth. James Bland was given some comedy assignments along with his singing, performing a monologue and even taking a turn as Interlocutor. In November 1879 the Haverlys astonished the citizens of Shreveport, Louisiana, by giving a preshow parade with two brass bands marching off in opposite directions, then combining their ranks to meet while playing the same tune in perfect unison.

In June 1881 the Haverly troupe played a week in Boston, their last U.S. engagement before sailing to Liverpool to begin a tour of England. On July 30 they opened at Her Majesty's Theatre in London, where their advertising promised "65 Real Negroes." Kersands was still on the roster along with the singer Wallace King (1840–1903) and the clog-dancing Bohee Brothers. Bland sang his "Golden Slippers" to great applause.

English audiences loved Bland, and the feeling was mutual. When the Haverlys returned to the United States in the late spring of 1882, Bland chose to stay in England. For more than a decade he was the toast of Europe, billed as "The Prince of Negro Songwriters," performing solo in the largest music halls, giving a command performance for Queen Victoria and the Prince of Wales, and seen at society parties all over London. During the 1890s, he made tours of Ireland and Germany, where he was proclaimed one of the three best American composers (the other two were Foster and Sousa). But his home base was always London. He was so comfortable there that he began to do his solo shows without blackface makeup. He was a big spender, but a big earner, too, claiming once to have made $10,000 in a single season.

To keep his reputation in America alive, Bland returned to the United States in the fall of 1886 to work a few months with Hicks & Sawyer's Colored Minstrels. He was back in London soon after the job was over. It was a pattern he would repeat for fifteen years: a short tour with an American company, followed by several years in England.

It was during Bland's globe-hopping years that minstrel conventions began to crumble. The producer Sam T. Jack had the brilliant idea of featuring women prominently in his *Creole Show* in 1890, and the sixteen women on stage were not a battalion of Aunt Chloes. They were beautiful girls, high kickers in slit skirts and skin-colored tights. Of course, such glamorous creatures would not be typical of the old plantation, so Jack scrapped the time-honored setting in favor of an abstract and gaudy facade. There were still some minstrel elements in *The Creole Show*, but even these had been tinkered with. (There was a female interlocutor!) Jack's show was one of several black productions that took steps toward musical comedy in the 1890s. Over the decade sex appeal crept into black shows. More and more, black extravaganzas began to move toward Jack's vision of urban glamor and away from Bland's dream of Old Virginny.

In effecting such drastic changes, the minstrel show was fighting for its life. In 1880 the singer/entrepreneur Tony Pastor had had the idea that frequently changed bills of "clean" variety acts could attract the patronage of families. He tested his theory at his Fourteenth Street Theatre in New York and found it sound: families indeed flocked to see Pastor's varied bills of entertainment. The concept of vaudeville was born, and the days of rowdy, men-only music saloons were numbered. As systems of booking routes and theatre chains were developed by vaudeville producers, the days of the minstrel show seemed numbered, too. Presented with the kaleidoscope of novelties offered by vaudeville, the public tired of the minstrels' frozen format and hoary jokes.

If Bland noticed any of these changes, he did nothing in his writing or performing to accommodate them. Although his act was beginning to ossify, well-paying bookings still came to him. A couple of his songs even found new life through a new medium, cylinder recordings. "Carry Me Back to Old Virginny" was recorded by Len Spencer in 1893, and Silas Leachman recorded "Golden Slippers" in 1894. Both of these cylinders sold well, and it is puzzling that there were no others and that Bland never made recordings himself.

Bland was still earning enough to play the spendthrift star. During his 1890 appearance with Cleveland's Colored Minstrels in San Francisco, a show business paper reported that he had purchased a four and three quarter carat diamond ring. Bland's fellow minstrel, Tom Fletcher (one of the few memoirists of the profession), recalled how Bland kept up his snappy wardrobe:

> Bland would walk into a store and pick out what he wanted. After the clerk had wrapped up the merchandise, Jim would ask for the proprietor, have a short talk with him and walk out of the store with his goods without paying. That evening, during his act, Jim would give the store a big boost. If the show had a two- or three-day stand in the town, Jim would manage, at each performance, to have something different to say about the store, but always plugging it. In some towns, after he had improvised such "commercials," he would receive shoes, suits and other similar tokens of the merchant's gratitude.

Back to England, back to America. W. C. Handy remembered the thrill of meeting Bland in Louisville in 1897. In late 1898, "The Idol of the Halls" worked a few months with Black Patti's Troubadours in the Midwest, and it would be his last good booking. During this period a few Bland songs were published in the United States and in Europe, but there were no hits among them. He had spent his prime years coasting on his early stardom.

By the turn of the century, the game was up: Bland had begun to look old-fashioned on two continents. He left England for the last time in 1901, returning to America to begin a long slide into poverty and obscurity. Unmarried, apparently estranged from his family, and utterly without prospects, he borrowed an office from a lawyer friend in Washington and set to work on a musical comedy. His script, called *The Sporting Girl*, was sold outright to two local comedians who produced it in Washington's Kernan Theatre. It was a quick failure. Bland shuttled aimlessly about the Northeast for several years. Eubie Blake's biographer, Al Rose, quotes Blake on meeting Bland in Atlantic City during this wandering time:

> I suppose he must have been working in some joint around there. Anyway, I met him on the Boardwalk and he says to me, "Hey, Eubie! Lemme buy you a drink." Then he took me for a walk *past* all the places the colored people could go in safely, to this real high-class place. Now there's no colored people in there. Even the bartender is white, see. Well, he orders his drink. I get my Old Overholt. . . . We talk for a while, and he tells me how much he enjoys hearing me play. Then we have another one. Now I got to get to work pretty soon, see, and I suppose he does too. Now he goes to the men's room and he never comes back. Now I got a dollar in my pocket, see. . . . Anyway, this bad-looking bartender gives me a tab for two dollars and twenty cents. Now I ain't got two dollars and twenty cents, so we argue and I tell him I'll pay for my own but I got nothing to do with that other fellow. I was still a dime short, but he let me go. I don't know whether Jimmy Bland ever paid his tab or not, but I know *I* never saw him again.

James Bland died in Philadelphia on May 5, 1911. He was buried in Merion Cemetery in Bala-Cynwid, a Philadelphia suburb. For years afterward, only one performer kept his name alive. The concert soprano Alma Gluck often sang "Carry Me Back to Old Virginny" as an encore, and she recorded it in 1915. W. C. Handy, who had been so impressed at meeting Bland in 1897, programmed a few of his songs in a Carnegie Hall concert of 1928.

The rediscovery of Bland was primarily due to Dr. James F. Cooke, the editor of *Etude* magazine, who found Bland's still-unmarked grave in 1938 and, in 1939, published the first biographical article about him, written by Dr. Kelly Miller, a professor of mathematics at Howard University. As interest in Bland grew, the Virginia Conservation Commission decided to adopt his first hit as the official state song in 1940 and saw to it that his grave got a headstone. The first folio of James Bland songs was issued in 1946.

Around this time, Bland became the first songwriter to become the subject of the "hundreds-of-lost-songs" myth. The wishful thinking began with a bald line in Dr. Miller's article: "Mr. Bland wrote over 700 ballads during his lifetime." Although there are only thirty-eight Bland copyrights registered with the Library of Congress, researchers seemed to want to believe in the 700 "lost songs." The figure recurs in articles over the years, usually with the speculation that Bland gave away songs by the dozens to other performers who published them under their own names and/or that his songs were stolen wholesale by publishers.

Like all songwriters, Bland certainly wrote more songs than he copyrighted or had published. In pre-ASCAP days, it was common practice for publishers to buy songs outright for $10 to $50 each. Royalty agreements were unusual for black and white composers alike, and only the most prolific hit-producing writers could command them. However, any songs bought from Bland would certainly have been issued under his name, because the Bland name would have been the key selling point. From 1880 until the mid-1890s, there was no bigger name in minstrel song. To publish his work under the name(s) of others would have made no sense. And the idea of Bland's letting hundreds of his songs slip away from him is surely without foundation. But the "lost songs" myth dies hard, for Bland and for several other writers, black and white, who followed him.

With three all-time standards among his thirty-eight copyrights, Bland's achievement is impressive enough. When we consider that all of his work was written in a dialect that embarrasses us now, and that it was written for a kind of entertainment that became archaic in his own lifetime, we should be satisfied with the craftsmanship of his two beautiful ballads and the high spirits of his "Golden Slippers." They are timeless proof of his talent.

⬥

The process of making a song into a "hit" in the nineteenth century was a clumsy affair. The main venue for presenting popular songs to the public was the minstrel show, and songs traveled as the minstrels traveled—by train. Blackface performers came to town, sang the songs, then, after the performance, sold a few published songs featured in their show. If a song made a particularly strong impression, a local music store owner could send for more copies from the publisher. If the publisher had copies of the song in stock, they would be sent, sometimes after a wait of several weeks. By the time the new supply arrived, the impetus for the demand had long ago left town. Sales accumulated slowly for even the most successful songs, like those of Foster and Bland.

In the 1880s and 1890s a dozen or so new publishing firms, most of them in New York City, overhauled this system, streamlined it, and made the selling of sheet music the most vital and profitable part of American show business. By the time these aggressive, upstart firms had acquired the collective nickname "Tin Pan Alley," around 1902, they had already changed the lackadaisical music business profoundly. Their successful experiments in creating demand for, and insuring a supply of, their product were unheard of before their time. They proved that there could be untold riches in the selling of song sheets, and would-be songwriters and publishers hurried to stake their claims in the music-publishing gold mines that dotted New York's Union Square.

Creating the demand for songs was the tricky part. Young companies, such as Howley-Haviland, Shapiro-Bernstein, Joseph Stern & Co., and especially M. Witmark & Sons, hired staff writers to turn out songs on topical subjects. To keep their customers visiting music stores, the stock had to be ever-changing. They all wanted songs to celebrate (and make fun of) events and personalities of the day. Newsworthy topics—President Cleveland's White House wedding, the electric light, the financial panic of 1892, and the Spanish-American War—inspired dozens of popular songs. The standby subjects of mother and home were not neglected, but most of the Alley's raw energy went into creating, then satisfying, the amateur's itch for the newest song on the latest subject.

The look of song sheets had to change, too. The old way of decorating sheets with fancy lettering and line drawings on white backgrounds looked stodgy in the new marketplace. Color was the first improvement, then full-page drawings and designs began to catch the eye of the music-store browser. A sub-industry of illustrating song sheets attracted the leading commercial artists of the time.

The most effective visual element, the publishers soon realized, was the celebrity photograph. The music industry hitched its wagon to the stars of vaudeville. The endorsement of a new song by a well-known personality could be a big boost to sales. To provide this piece of insurance for new songs, a new profession sprang up: the "song plugger." The plugger relentlessly pursued vaudeville performers with two goals in mind: to get his firm's songs heard in as many acts as possible and to get the best-known performers to lend their photos to the covers.

No place was off limits to the indomitable pluggers. They wormed their way into dressing rooms, harassed headliners in restaurants, distributed lyric sheets in saloons, strong-armed bandleaders, and pushed their wares into the hands of any performer who would take them. Although entertainers saw the pluggers as nuisances, their efforts paid off. The links they forged between publishers and performing artists would make more hits, and make them faster, than the previous generation's professionals could have dreamed possible.

Oddly, the publishers saw the fledgling recording industry as an enemy rather than as an ally, believing that every sale of a cylinder record precluded the sale of a song sheet. Discographies of the cylinder era reflect little effort by publishers to get their songs recorded. There were many recordings of comedy monologues, medleys of old favorites, light classical material, a few Broadway songs, and, almost coincidentally, it seems, a few recordings of popular songs timed to coincide with their release on song sheets. The publishers couldn't imagine the sale of a cylinder prompting the sale of a song sheet or vice versa, and the idea of "breaking a song" in two media at once wouldn't become commonplace until the 1920s. The biggest vaudeville stars were leery of recordings, too. The earliest pop singers on cylinders were nonentities, like Silas Leachman and Len Spencer, who had no stage careers to lose if the public didn't like their records.

But the nation's supply of printed songs and its access to them were serious business to the young publishers. They sent traveling salesmen around the country to place their products and to create an efficient reorder system in department stores as well as in music stores. These salesmen were especially attentive to the growing "dime store" chains, such as Woolworth's (founded in 1879). They helped stores set up music departments, complete with young women who sat at pianos all day, thumping out the latest songs for shoppers. Through such gimmickry as on-site dance lessons, local songwriting contests, and price wars, they turned the music department into the liveliest and busiest area of the stores.

GUSSIE L. DAVIS

The first African-American songwriter to have hits in this new, nonminstrel world of commercial music was Gussie Davis. Without reference to the minstrel tradition in the music or the lyrics of his hits, he wrote several of the biggest-selling songs of the gaslight era. One of his publishers, Edward Marks, remembered his being so shy and self-effacing that he seemed unlikely to succeed in the rough and tumble world of Tin Pan Alley. Underneath his quiet demeanor, however, was a tenacity that placed more than 200 of his songs—through more than a dozen publishers—before the public.

Gussie Lord Davis was born on December 3, 1863, in Dayton, Ohio. He went to Cincinnati in his mid-teens and applied for admission to

Gussie L. Davis

Nelson Musical College there. When his application was denied because of his race, he suggested that he be allowed to trade janitorial work for music instruction. The college accepted his offer. While working at the school and studying, he held several jobs, with a stint as a Pullman porter among them.

At seventeen, Davis paid a local printer, Helling & Co., $20 to publish his first song, "We Sat Beneath the Maple on the Hill." He managed to peddle enough copies to make a small profit on the song, and this encouraged him to issue other locally published efforts. A white publisher, George Propheter, who was a sometime lyricist, wrote the words for several of Davis' melodies. When Propheter decided to take his publishing business to New York in 1886, he asked Davis to come with him as his staff composer. In 1887 two Davis-Propheter songs were heard on the vaudeville stage. Doing their own plugging, the pair managed to place "Wait 'Til the Tide Comes In" and "My Pretty Mountain Maid" with several performers.

Although Davis had not yet had a nationally known song, he was interviewed about his profession for the New York *Evening Sun* early in 1888. The young writer predicted the decline of the "Negro and jubilee songs" of the minstrel era:

> A woman buys it [a song sheet] and sings it at home. She cannot sing
> a minstrel or Negro song in the parlor, and refined people would not
> allow it in the house.

Davis would be proven wrong about what would be allowed in the house a few years later when the coon song fad began. But he knew precisely the Alley's target audience of 1888.

The kind of song that Davis had in mind for the "refined" home was the tearjerker. This was a commercial descendant of the story-songs, specifically the murder ballads, that had enthralled listeners in the British Isles for hundreds of years. These narratives of gore and revenge, often based on real events, packed the details of the plot into the verse and delivered the moral—or sometimes just a warning—in the chorus.

The modern, commercial "folk songs" had a different purpose—to sell sheet music rather than to pass along traditional lore—so some changes in subject matter were in order. The tearjerkers wove their stories about whatever might disrupt the happiness of the home: a deceased parent or child, a philandering father, an errant daughter, a drunken son, a lost and unforgotten love. Lyricists scoured the daily newspapers for accounts of real-life domestic tragedy. A typical tearjerker strung its plot through three or four verses, each verse followed by a shorter, easier-to-sing chorus that provided the moral. The tearjerkers were almost always written in 3/4 time and were played with a lilting waltz rhythm that gave a pleasing tension and drive to the lugubrious lyrics. The form inspired no great melody writing, the lyric being the reason for the song's existence. The manufactured melodrama of the tearjerkers gave the new pop music industry its first commercially reliable genre of song.

Two of the earliest tearjerker hits came in 1880: "Cradle's Empty, Baby's Gone" and "Why Did They Dig Ma's Grave So Deep?" In this time of tuberculosis epidemics, fevers, fires, unchecked diseases, and generally unsanitary living conditions, the sudden deaths described in these songs were common occurrences, and the song-buying public recognized all too well the agonies described in them. (An etiquette book of the period stressed the importance of making proper farewells to visitors, because the host might never see them again.) In the way that song genres are created, the 1880 hits inspired imitations. Then the imitations inspired imitations, among them Paul Dresser's "The Outcast Unknown" and "The Letter That Never Came"—not a comment on the postal system, but the story of a man who dies after years of waiting for a letter from his childhood sweetheart.

Gussie Davis' first hit was a classic tearjerker, "The Fatal Wedding," published by Spalding & Gray in 1893. Davis wrote the melody, and the lyric was provided by William H. Windom, a black singer. Like most of its kind, the song seems top-heavy now, with three sixty-four-measure verses, each leading into the thirty-two-measure chorus. Windom's lyric pushes the morbidity envelope, even for its time. A poor woman with an infant in her arms interrupts a society wedding to announce that the groom is already married to her and is the father of her child. The child dies on the spot in the church. The bride's parents promise to care for the distraught woman. The groom promptly commits suicide and is buried with the child in a double funeral. A popular cylinder recording of the song was made soon after its release by George J. Gaskin.

Davis' success with "The Fatal Wedding," after seven years of writing in New York, made him a respected figure in the music business. In late 1893 he was elected secretary of the Colored Professionals Club, a charitable organization that gave benefits for black entertainers who were down on their luck. And in 1894 he was invited to join Bob Cole's All-Star Stock Company, a training unit for black theatre professionals that operated out of Worth's Museum in New York City. Davis was one of two composers in the company; the other was Will Marion Cook. Although Cole's company lasted only about a year, it would be remembered as the first source of formal theatrical training for blacks.

More successful Davis songs came in 1894: "Picture 84" (with music by Charles B. Ward), "Only a Bowery Boy" (lyric by Ward), and "Sing Again That Sweet Refrain" (music and lyric by Davis). In 1895 Bonnie Thornton introduced his "Down in Poverty Row" (music by Arthur Trevelyan) in her vaudeville act. That same year, Davis won $500 as second prize in the New York World's songwriting contest for his "Send Back the Picture and the Ring."

In 1896 Howley, Haviland & Co. published Gussie Davis' major *memento mori*, "In the Baggage Coach Ahead." In words and music by Davis, "Baggage Coach" tells the sad story of a crying child on a train. When the other passengers complain to the child's father, he explains that the baby cannot be quieted because the mother is lying in her coffin "dead, in the baggage coach ahead." The chagrined passengers help the father to comfort the child, and then they go their ways, chastened by the glimpse they have had into the blighted lives of the child and its father. Compared to other tearjerkers, "Baggage Coach" is rather compact. It has only two verses, instead of the usual three or four, and its moral (don't judge a situation too hastily) is implied, not stated directly. The song was based on an incident witnessed by Davis during his brief time as a train porter in Cincinnati.

Imogene Comer, a white vaudeville singer, introduced the song and kept it in her act for three years. "Baggage Coach" sold over a million copies of sheet music within a few months of its issue. A cylinder recording by Dan Quinn was one of the best selling records of 1896, and the song had another splash of popularity in 1925, when it was recorded by a country singer, Vernon Dalhart. Davis would have a few more songs with respectable sales, including some attempts at coon songs, but none had the impact of "In the Baggage Coach Ahead."

In 1899, five years after his residency in the All-Star Stock Company, Davis finally tried his hand at writing songs for a musical show. In August of that year, his show, *A Hot Time in Dixie*, began a tour of the Midwest. The show was still on the road when Davis died on October 18, 1899, in the home he shared with his wife Lottie in Whitestone, New York.

Gussie Davis was among the most important of the first generation of Tin Pan Alley writers. He found his genre—the tearjerker—and he stuck to it, with great success. He was a pure product of the publishing industry, sure of his market and of how to write for it. His work is so mired in its time that it is seldom performed any more. The generation that followed him made fun of the tearjerkers, and succeeding generations forgot them altogether. One who remembered was Eugene O'Neill. In the third act of *A Moon for the Misbegotten*, Tyrone's searing memories of bringing his mother's body home for burial are triggered by two lines of an old song:

> *But baby's cries can't waken her*
> *In the baggage coach ahead.*

CHAPTER 2

"STAY IN YOUR OWN BACK YARD"

· ·

Black Songwriters of the Coon Song Era

A FEW YEARS AFTER TIN PAN ALLEY perfected the crafts of creating and selling tearjerkers, the industry found another new genre of song. This was the tearjerker's antithesis, the coon song. The first one was J. S. Putnam's "New Coon in Town," published in 1883. A great vogue for these musical racist jokes lasted from 1895 until around 1905, and they accounted for many of the biggest song sales in commercial music's first booming era. A few of the more rambunctious ones outlived their time ("Bill Bailey," "The Preacher and the Bear," "My Gal Is a High Born Lady"), but the great majority of them are justly forgotten ("You'se Just a Little Nigger, Still You'se Mine, All Mine," "Bake Dat Chicken Pie," "Every Race Has a Flag But the Coon").

At first glance, coon song titles might suggest merely a continuation of the old minstrel stereotypes, but there is a marked difference of attitude in the coon songs. They have an urban, in-your-face toughness that borders on belligerence. The minstrel songs strut; coon songs swagger.

Coon songs also added a new subject to the demeaning list of minstrel cliches. Money—wasting it and needing it—was a preoccupation of coon lyrics to a degree that must have made the robber barons of their era smile. "When You Ain't Got No Money, Well, You Needn't Come 'Round," "Bring Your Money Home," "That's Where My Money Goes," "It Makes No Difference What You Do, Get the Money," "If Money Talks, It Ain't on Speaking Terms with Me"—all denote an obsession that the minstrels would have been embarrassed to admit.

And coon songs added a potent symbol to minstrel images of watermelon, chicken, and possum that supposedly typified the race: the razor as a weapon. "The Bully Song," "Never Raise a Razor 'Less You Want to Raise a Row," and "R-A-Z-O-R" celebrate the possibility of mayhem in playful melody and rhyme. At boisterous parties for dark-town swells and belles, the guests may "hire sharp razors from a barber at the door," or they may bring their own. The rural eccentrics of minstrelsy would never have attended such dangerous events.

Like tearjerkers, coon songs needed no memorable melodies. A coon song's tune was merely a delivery system for the joke. The verse was the setup; the chorus, the punch line. They were usually in easy, 4/4 time, with conversational dotted-eighth syncopation. Within their narrow musical bounds, coon songs ranged from the sentimental ("Mammy's Little Pumpkin-Colored Coons") to the fantastic ("If the Man in the Moon Were a Coon") to the near-provocative ("I've Got a White Man Working for Me").

The popularity of coon songs was sparked by powerhouse performances given them by several white women vaudeville singers. Stella Mayhew, Marie Cahill, May Irwin, her sister Flo Irwin, Clarice Vance, and (later) Sophie Tucker were among the specialists in the genre. They were all hefty, unlikely to be mistaken for leading ladies even in the age that adored the full-figured Lillian Russell. And they were all leather-lunged belters, capable of sending every word of a lyric to the back row of the largest theatre. Their dynamic renditions of this material became known as "coon-shouting." The idea of a white woman assuming black characterizations in song was a new one, and vaudeville audiences loved the novelty. May Irwin was identified especially with coon songs, and her violent "Bully Song" was one of the biggest hits of 1896. When she graduated from vaudeville to the Broadway stage, she took her coon songs along for interpolation into the scores of her shows. Audiences expected coon blockbusters from her, and she delivered them. In their search for material, the coon-shouters often used (and championed) the songs of black writers.

Although they are unsung and unsingable today, coon songs had a profound effect on American popular songwriting. Their constant use of syncopation attuned the public ear for the ragtime that would appear around the turn of the century. And their slangy, "low-class" lyrics took a big step away from politer European/operetta song models. Their commercial success introduced "black" subject matter—and the work of many black songwriters—into middle-class white parlors on sheet music and cylinder records. In this time of families entertaining themselves at home around the piano, part of the fun was the naughtiness of playing at being black. Other ethnic groups also took their lumps in song, but blacks got the worst of it.

The aspiring African-American songwriters of the coon song era were faced with essentially the same proposition as those of the Reconstruction era: they had to sell what people were buying. "Coon" imagery saturated American popular culture in advertising, in magazine and newspaper illustration, in Currier & Ives prints, on song sheets, and in performances from medicine shows to the Broadway stage. It must have been impossible to imagine a time when the darky cartoon would not be the reference point for whites' thinking about blacks. And in the June-moon period of lyric writing, the very word "coon" was a godsend to the hacks of Tin Pan Alley—punchy, up-to-the-minute slang that was very easy to rhyme.

Some black writers and singers transcended the coon song, some subverted it, a few specialized in it. But the verbal slumming of the coon song was Square One, the point of professional departure, for them all. It embodied a set of perceptions that they all had to deal with because they were the same color as the cartoons on the sheet music. Gussie Davis alone sidestepped the taint of coonery, because he was not primarily known as a performer and because he had established his success in an earlier genre. The black talents of this time carried heavy burdens of low esteem and low expectations. Zip Coon had moved to town and the music business had given him a home.

IRVING JONES

Most black songwriters of the 1890s were uncomfortable with the coon song. Its cliches dogged them, professionally and personally. They hated being expected to pour every lyric sentiment through the funnel of its imagery. Even the most basic subjects for song—love, mother, fun—were given the "coon" twist. In 1896 the "white" love song said "I Love You in the Same Old Way, Darling Sue." The "black" expression

Irving Jones

of the same idea in the same year was "I'se Your Nigger If You Wants Me, Liza Jane." As the "white" singer of 1901 missed his "Sweet Annie Moore," the "black" singer yearned for "Maizy, My Dusky Daisy." The "white" singer flirted with "Kiss Me, Honey, Do," and the "black" urged his girl to "Mingle Yo' Eyebrows with Mine." In "white" lyrics, mothers sang lullabies to their babies; black "mammies" crooned to their "pickaninnies" or their "little yaller boys." If a white couple enjoyed a musical stroll down a shady lane "In the Good Old Summertime," blacks seemed to prefer dancing the "Buzzard Lope" at the "Coontown Carnival." Coontown was the worst neighborhood in Tin Pan Alley, and most blacks couldn't wait to move out.

The only exception was Irving Jones. He alone among black writers wrote coon songs exclusively. He was one of the earliest practitioners of the genre, and he rode the fad until its demise. On his list of nearly fifty published numbers, there is not a title that could be mistaken for anything but a coon song.

Irving Jones was born in New York City sometime around 1874. As a teenager, he found work in the first edition of Sam T. Jack's *Creole Show* as a comedian. The reliable minstrel Sam Lucas led the cast, but the show got most of its attention for being the first black company to feature women. During the *Creole's* summer tour of 1890, Jones got married, and his wife Sadie joined the beauties in Sam Jack's chorus line.

Irving Jones didn't have much to do in the *Creole Show*, but the charming and brash young hustler was in his element. The minstrel Ike Simond, in his *Reminiscence and Pocket History of the Colored Profession from 1865 to 1891*, remembered observing Jones while on a train en route to Chicago. Simond "happened to drop into Sam T. Jack's *Creole* car," where he found Irving Jones taking charge of a game of craps. "Irving Jones was holding stakes and by the way he turned flip flaps and growled from the bottom of his bread basket, I could see that he would not get left."

By 1893, after three years with the *Creole* company, Irving Jones was being assigned feature spots in the show. One of these was a comic specialty that he devised called the "Possumala Dance," a parody of the "Pas Ma La," a stately (New Orleans) Creole ballroom dance. Jones' lyric describes the rough doings at a "colored hop" held at "Bad Land Hall." The overdressed guests, several of them toting guns and razors, are full of beer and wine. A bully named "George Good Health" "pulled his gun and began to shoot," and "All the dancers they began to skoot." Policemen break up the dance and haul the miscreant to jail. While he is rolling away in the patrol wagon, George sings, "Nobody knows how bad I am, If you fool with me, you'll get in a jam." The song confirmed the worst suspicions about black folks' idea of a good time, and it was the hit of the show.

In 1894 Jones pitched the song to publisher Willis Woodward, and it became the first of his compositions in print. The coon fad had not caught on yet, and the sales of "Possumala Dance" were not spectacular. But by 1897, after Ernest Hogan's "All Coons Look Alike to Me" had taken off, Tin Pan Alley was ready for Irving Jones, and Irving Jones was ready with the goods. He sold his work piecemeal, one song at a time, to whoever would see him and give him a hearing. Among his repeat purchasers was Edward Marks, a partner in the Joseph Stern Company, which began its association with Jones in 1897 by publishing his "Take Your Clothes and Go." Marks thought of Jones more as a physical comedian than as a songwriter, as this passage in his autobiography, *They All Sang*, indicates:

[H]is contemporaries remember him as one of the most typically comic-strip darkies of the lot. He invented the "Palmer House Walk," the comedy exaggeration of a bowlegged waiter's stride as he carries a tray high above his head. He stuttered engagingly and could make a "bladder face."

"Take Your Clothes and Go" sold about 100,000 copies over two years. Another popular Jones song of 1897 was "Get Your Money's Worth," published by F. A. Mills. Money would become Jones's favorite song subject, as more than a dozen of his titles indicate.

Irving Jones was never in the first rank of comedians, but he worked steadily, going where booking agents sent him and wherever black vaudeville routes took him. He spent 1895 to 1897 with John W. Isham's *Octoroons* company, as the rising tide of coon songs lifted his professional boat. In January 1898 Gussie Davis organized an entertainment in honor of the *Darkest America* company at New York's Douglass Club. It was a prestigious affair, and Irving Jones was invited to be a part of it. Sharing a bill with the Golden Gate Quartette and Williams and Walker, Jones sang "Get Your Money's Worth."

With the popularity of coon songs peaking in 1898–1899, Irving Jones was in his heyday. He published about twenty songs during this time, including "Give Me Back Dem Clothes," "If They'd Only Fought with Razors in the War," and "I'm Livin' Easy." The latter was recorded by Silas Leachman, and years later, it was recalled by Charles Ives in his *Memos* as an outstanding example of "blackfaced comedians . . . ragging their songs." Many of Jones's sheet music covers have photos of him in costume and on stage sets (but not in blackface), in tableaux depicting the situations described in the lyrics. He wasn't writing hits, but he was certainly getting his work—and his face—before the public, under the imprints of more than a dozen publishers.

By July 1898 the *Christian Advocate* had had enough. In one of the earliest outcries against the flood of degradation in pop songs, the *Advocate* concluded:

[A]ll of that class of music is written at the expense of the Negro. Some people's idea of the colored man is based entirely on what they get from the "coon songs" and other "ragged music" of our degenerate day.

Instrumental ragtime's syncopated guilt-by-association with coon songs would deter America's musical establishment from accepting it for years.

Heedless of what the *Christian Advocate* might think, Irving Jones carried on. In 1899 he played a season with the Black Patti Troubadours, plugging his latest, "All Birds Look Like Chickens to Me." That same year, he had his only brush with musical theatre, a brief stint in Will Marion Cook's playlet, *Jes' Lak White Folks*.

In 1900 he was out with a vaudeville act, billed as "Irving Jones and Charley Johnson, Two Cut-Ups." The act later became "Jones, Grant and Jones" (the other Jones was his wife, Sadie). Feist & Frankenthaler published his 1900 song "The Ragtime Millionaire," containing one of the earliest lyric references to having "the blues."

Jones remained one of the most popular acts in black vaudeville, never again overreaching into musical comedy, but always on the circuits with fresh, funny material. His chesty, belligerent stage character masked an offstage shyness as well a surprising ability to laugh at himself. Ed Marks recalled Jones' favorite anecdote about life on the vaudeville road. After a matinee in Ft. Wayne, when his act had not gone over well, Jones took a walk before the evening show. A small boy approached him and said, "I seen you on the stage." Jones stuttered, "Yeah? Whu-whu-whut did I did?" Boy: "You didn't did nothing."

As he traveled, he published. "One More Drink and I'll Tell It All" was issued in San Francisco in 1901, and "You Needn't Think I'm a Regular Fool" in Denver in 1905. But by 1905 the coon fad was passing. The major black writers had moved beyond it, and the public had tired of it. All of the jokes had been made, all of the twists had been done. There would be a few more coon songs published through the decade, including Jones's last song, "Any Old Way You Cook Chicken," in 1910. By the time the Indianapolis *Freeman* published its blistering article entitled "Coon Songs Must Go," in January 1909, they had just about gone.

There would be a few more professional highlights for Irving Jones. The *Freeman* announced in March 1909 that he was in vaudeville, "going it alone, as usual, helped by his big reputation." He was an appealing performer and black audiences loved him as one of their own, a private, and possibly a guilty, pleasure. He kept at it throughout the teens, receiving a good review for his "droll comedy" at Chicago's Grand Theatre in 1919.

And he lived long enough to see several of his songs taken up by black songsters and issued on "race records" in the 1920s. In the late twenties, he was still touring the Radio-Keith-Orpheum circuit. Jones died on March 11, 1932, in New York City.

The passing of the coon song did not mark the end of stereotypes in popular music, of course. The rash of "mammy" songs was yet to come, to be followed by songs about darktown strutters, hot chocolates, lazybones, and "high yellas." There would be sexually explicit blues in the 1920s and dope songs in the thirties, but pop music would not see the coon song's particular combination of race cliches and "badness" again for nearly ninety years.

ERNEST HOGAN

By 1890, New York City, with a population of nearly three million, had become the capital of American show business. Its first-class theatres had not yet clustered in the West Forties to be known as the "Broadway" district, but there were over twenty of them, more than any other city could boast. New York was becoming the hub of vaudeville's "wheels," sending acts out to theatres all over the United States. Tin Pan Alley's young publishing hotshots were already beginning to drive their regional competitors out of business. But as of 1890, there had been no African-Americans in the first-class theatres either as performers or customers, none sent out on the major vaudeville wheels, none regularly writing or publishing in Tin Pan Alley. By 1900 blacks would be involved, as performers and composers, in New York's best

Ernest Hogan

theatres, in big-league vaudeville, and in the music business. After the turn of the century, the doors were still hard to open, but they would never be locked tight again.

U.S. Census figures for 1890 showed 1,490 "actors and professional showmen" among the African-American population, most of them employed in minstrel or black vaudeville shows. There would emerge from this number a handful of genuine "crossover" stars who could headline in white, as well as black, theatres. In the top rank of these was the self-educated, hard-working Ernest Hogan, one of the most beloved comedians of his day.

Hogan's fame would be eclipsed by that of Bert Williams, and the memory of him would be tainted by the notoriety of his biggest song. But it might be said of him that he climbed the highest, because he started nearest the bottom. And several of his contemporaries ranked him above Williams. Like Bert Williams, he was very funny; unlike Williams, his comedy was tinged with pathos. The actor-librettist Flournoy Miller called Hogan "the greatest of all colored showmen." The dancing star Ida Forsyne said of him: "Bert Williams just had one style, but Ernest Hogan was great—he was really *ingenious*." The ragtimer Luckey Roberts remembered him as "the greatest performer I ever saw." He was the picture of confidence on stage, a natural worrier offstage. Hogan's career hit all the highs and lows of the changing black show world of his time.

He was born Reuben Crowders in Bowling Green, Kentucky, some time shortly after the Civil War. He had little, if any, formal education, leaving home in his early teens to work in various small tent shows and minstrel companies touring the mid-South. One of his first jobs was as an anonymous "pickaninny" in a low-rent tent-show version of *Uncle Tom's Cabin*. By 1891 he had taken his stage name and was co-owner of his own show, Eden and Hogan's Minstrels, based in Chicago. His travels must have taken him to Kansas City, as that was where his first song was published. This was an eccentric dance number called "La Pas Ma La," issued by the J. R. Bell Company in 1895. Unlike Irving Jones' "Possumala," Hogan's song did not parody the Creole ballroom dance but tried to describe its steps in the lyric. Hogan was becoming known for his crablike, scuttling dance steps, and his song suggests his knees-bent, backward-hopping style:

> Hand upon yo' head, let your mind roll far,
> Back, back, back and look at the stars,
> Stand up rightly, dance it brightly,
> That's the pas ma la.

In 1896 J. R. Bell issued a piano version of "La Pas Ma La," making it the first pop song to prompt an instrumental spinoff.

In 1896 Ernest Hogan joined the young black talents who were beginning to gather in New York. He collaborated with one of the most promising of them, Bert Williams, on a song called "Ninth Battalion on Parade," which they placed with Witmark for publication.

The next Hogan song, published by Witmark in August 1896, became the first big hit of its kind: "All Coons Look Alike to Me." Hogan showed the song to Isidore Witmark, who was enthusiastic enough about it to give Hogan a royalty agreement (still a rarity in 1896). Witmark doctored the music a bit and tinkered with the lyric of the second verse, then gave it to his arranger, Max Hoffman. Hoffman devised an extra syncopated chorus "with Negro 'Rag' Accompaniment," the first use of the word "rag" on a song sheet. Hogan's song was given a cover drawing of seven grotesque coons and was sent to market.

The chorus lyrics are the parting words of the singer's girlfriend. She has left him for another man, so all coons (that is, *all men*) look alike to her, except her new beau. The words are no more offensive than those of a hundred other coon songs, but the title of Hogan's song struck a nerve. He had accidentally capsulized one of the baser tenets of prejudice, that all blacks are alike and need not be thought of or dealt with as individuals. The black press and clergy were outraged by the song's seeming acceptance of an evil that they were fighting every day. Their anger was directed not so much at Hogan himself as at the explosion of coonery in pop songs that his hit set off. "All Coons Look Alike to Me" sold over a million copies over the next several years, and it became the specialty number of many vaudeville singers.

The song was plainly dangerous. The first few notes of its chorus became an all-purpose, nonverbal taunt when a white whistled it around blacks. It could start fights on streetcars and in saloons. Yet it was heard everywhere—from street corners to the Broadway stage. The formidable May Irwin sang it in her 1896 show *Courted Into Court*. In the same show, Irwin introduced another 1896 coon rage to Broadway, the white Kentuckian Ben Harney's "Mr. Johnson, Turn Me Loose." Len Spencer made the first recording of "All Coons," a cylinder for Columbia in November 1896. A more important recording was Vess Ossman's "Ragtime Medley," made by the banjoist a month later. Ossman's medley consisted of "All Coons Look Alike to Me," "Mr. Johnson, Turn Me Loose," and "A Hot Time in the Old Town Tonight." This package of instrumental syncopation was very popular, and it heralded the ragtime era that was just around the corner. The Ossman recording prompted Witmark to issue an instrumental version of Hogan's hit, a schottische arranged by F. W. Meacham, in 1897.

In later years Hogan would tell his friend Tom Fletcher that he regretted having written the troublesome song that made his reputation in New York. But in September 1897 Hogan was telling the Indianapolis *Freeman*, one of the leading black newspapers of the time, that he was still receiving $400 per month in royalties for "All Coons Look Alike to Me." If his royalty agreement was based on the standard penny-a-copy terms, the song was selling 40,000 copies per month a year after its publication! There would be about thirty-five published Hogan songs, but none as big as his sensation of 1896.

Hogan was out of town while his song was taking off. In October 1896 he began touring with the Georgia Graduates company. He stayed on the road with the Graduates in the Western states until June of the following year.

Immediately after Hogan's return to New York, he was hired as the featured comedian with Black Patti's Troubadours. This year-old touring company, organized by the concert soprano Sissieretta Jones (better known as Black Patti), delivered "Three Hours of Mirth and Melody," from operatic arias to coon songs and sketches. Hogan was

Black Patti

given a solo spot to sing a medley of his own songs, and he was billed for the first time as "The Unbleached American." When his year with Black Patti was over, in the summer of 1898, Hogan came back to New York. His next show would be the one that put him in the history books.

The show was a forty-five-minute musical sketch called *Clorindy, or the Origin of the Cakewalk*, with music by Will Marion Cook and lyrics and libretto by the poet Paul Laurence Dunbar. When it opened at the Casino Theatre Roof Garden on July 5, 1898, it became the first black show to play at a first-class New York theatre. The Casino Theatre, at the southeast corner of Broadway and Thirty-ninth Street, was the first in the city to open an outdoor "roof garden" for summer entertainments. The idea was to generate income during the months when it was too hot to attract audiences for indoor fare. *Clorindy* was one of a series of late-evening variety shows planned for the Casino, and it was an unexpected hit for its creators and its management. The large cast, led by Hogan in his first starring role in New York, dazzled Casino Roof audiences with their energetic delivery of Cook and Dunbar's syncopated score—and especially with its eleven-minute cakewalk finale (see the section in Chapter 3 on Will Marion Cook).

Clorindy ran through the summer, and a touring version—integrated into a Williams and Walker show called *Senegambian Carnival*—was sent out in the early fall. Perhaps remembering his being in the wrong place (out West) to capitalize on the New York success of his hit song, Ernest Hogan chose not to leave town with *Senegambian Carnival*. Instead, he joined John W. Isham's *Octoroons* company for the winter season at Howard's Athenaeum in New York. The Athenaeum was a comedown after the Casino Roof, but Hogan's fortunes were definitely rising. In May 1899 he went to Philadelphia to star in E. E. Rice's *Captain Kidd*—as the only black performer in a cast of 128. Hogan's fame and his appeal to white audiences were beginning to attract more offers for work. The offer that intrigued him most would lead to a year of struggle and calamity halfway around the world.

Hogan was sought out by M. B. Curtis, who was assembling a minstrel company for a tour of Australia and New Zealand. Curtis had lined up some well-known black talent, including the comic actor Billy McClain, Madah Hyers (billed as "the Bronze Patti"), and the magician Carl Dante, but he needed a star. Curtis promised bookings in the best Australian theatres, and he offered Hogan the title of "Director of Amusements," as well as top billing. Hogan signed on.

What Hogan did not know was that Curtis was a woefully inexperienced producer and that there were already two large minstrel companies touring Australia ahead of the Curtis company. (One was O. M.

McAdoo's Minstrels & Cakewalkers, and the other was a group of American expatriates who had remained in Australia after the conclusion of their tour.) M. B. Curtis's Afro-American Minstrels opened in Sydney on July 3, 1899, two weeks after the McAdoo company had been there. Curtis' troupe was well-received, and one of Hogan's reviews called him "the life and soul of the show." But business was never as good as it should have been because they were trailing the McAdoos everywhere, presenting the same kind of show that each city had just seen.

As the show teetered financially, Curtis began to withhold salaries. When members of the company went to him in

Billy McClain

protest, Curtis drew a revolver on them. Billy McClain had had enough. He, along with a few others, quit the show and applied to McAdoo for jobs in early August. McAdoo hired them, and the loss of these players and their specialties was another blow to the Curtis company's box office. In September the trouper's nightmare became reality for Hogan and the others. Curtis absconded with the company's funds (owing salaries, of course) and left his penniless cast of fifty stranded, thousands of miles from home or help.

Although he could have wired American friends for money to get himself home, Ernest Hogan chose to stay with the company and reorganize the show. He had had some experience as a director with the Black Patti company, and now he assumed the duties of producer as well. Hogan cobbled together a new show, using Curtis' leftover sets and whoever would—or had to—stay. If they were successful, they could earn the passage money to get them back to the United States.

They struggled into the winter, finally arriving in Brisbane in mid-January. Ernest Hogan's Minstrels (their new name) opened to excellent reviews. ("Miss Madah Hyers is about the most cultured operatic star that has ever been our lot to hear. . . . Carl Dante, the conjurer, is a marvel. Ernest Hogan is one of the best comedians we have ever seen. . . .") Business was good enough for the company to begin banking some money for steamship tickets. Hogan arranged a mid-March booking at Honolulu's Orpheum Theatre. If all went well there, they could be on their way to America. In anticipation of this, they prepaid a steamship company $1,900 to cover their fares home from Honolulu.

After four successful weeks at the Honolulu Orpheum, Hogan and his company assembled on the wharf, packed and ready, at 5:00 P.M. on April 11 to board the *Miowera*. When they presented their tickets, they were told by the ticket agent that they could not get on the ship. They watched in amazement as other passengers were taken aboard. Through a blatant act of racism, the company was stranded again. Carl Dante, acting as the company's business manager, sent for a lawyer. When the lawyer arrived and sized up the situation, he promised to file a suit against the steamship company. In the meantime, while waiting for justice, the company would have to earn its keep in Honolulu.

The city's audiences had liked their show, but Hogan realized that something new would be needed to keep them coming. He didn't know how long the wait for legal action would be, but he knew that they had to recoup their lost passage money. Determined to create as many new shows as it took to sustain his company, Hogan devised, directed, and starred in three new shows in six weeks. The Orpheum presented each as it was ready: two full-length musical farces and a production of *Uncle Tom's Cabin*, with Hogan as Uncle Tom.

It worked. Audiences came to see each of Hogan's new offerings. The company would not win its lawsuit and be reimbursed for their lost ticket money until September, but they had earned enough to get themselves home by late May. In recognition of Hogan's heroic effort, the manager of the Orpheum presented him with a gold watch on the closing night of his last show there. Standing on a stage draped with leis, Hogan made a farewell speech. He said that he would always remember the city's support for him during his ordeal and that he would like to return someday and make his home there.

Hogan was back in New York by mid-June and he went immediately to work. His new show was another short musical play by Cook and Dunbar, *Jes' Lak White Folks*, presented as a late-evening "roof" entertainment at the Cherry Blossom Theatre off Times Square. But Hogan's homecoming to his New York public was disrupted by a harrowing incident that would shake everyone in the black theatrical community.

On the evening of August 12, 1900, a white man and a black man got into a scuffle on the corner of Forty-first Street and Eighth Avenue. The row escalated when the white man struck the black man with a club. The black man pulled a pocket knife and stabbed his attacker, then disappeared into the night. When the wounded man was taken to the hospital, it was discovered that he was Robert J. Thorpe, an off-duty police officer. White residents of the West Forties were outraged by the stabbing, and when Thorpe died two days later, their rage boiled over. For the next two days, angry whites roved the midtown area harassing blacks, cursing them and shoving them off sidewalks. By August 15, the day of Thorpe's funeral, racial tension was at a fever pitch all over the city.

Late that evening, as Hogan was leaving the theatre after his show, he unwittingly stepped into a howling mob of several hundred whites who were prowling the theatre district. He was recognized by one of them, and the cry went up: "Get Ernest Hogan!" The terrified Hogan began to run down Broadway, the mob at his heels. The pursuit lasted for several minutes until Hogan darted into the Marlborough Hotel, at Thirty-sixth and Broadway. A plainclothes officer, who had been called from his patrol on Thirty-fifth Street, drew his revolver and held the mob at bay while Hogan escaped. The events of that sultry August night were a reminder that, despite the gains made by blacks in the arts and professions, all coons still looked alike to many of their countrymen.

Hogan was rattled by his close call. He accepted a series of vaudeville bookings that took him on the road for eight months. He came back in May 1901 for a long vaudeville run at $300 a week at the New York Theatre, at Broadway and Forty-fourth Street, near the scene of the previous year's madness. In late August, Hogan bought a three-story house at 50 West 134th Street and became the first black star to reside in Harlem.

In the autumn of 1901, Hogan kept his promise to return to Honolulu. He presented a variety company there, and they settled in for a three-month run. His friend Billy McClain, who had come to Hawaii with another show, stayed on with Hogan after his own booking was over, and a brief partnership as actor-producers began.

In November 1902 Hogan and McClain opened in Gus Hill's Smart Set musical, *Enchantment*, at New York's Star Theatre. This edition of the annual Smart Set shows would be remembered as the best. Hogan and McClain recreated their comic dueling scene from the ill-fated Curtis tour; the sketch highlight was Hogan's initiation into the Royal Roosters Lodge. The featured dancer was Ida Forsyne, and the primary singers were Cordelia McClain (Billy's wife) and Mattie Wilkes (Hogan's wife, whom he had met while preparing this show). The Indianapolis *Freeman*'s review of *Enchantment* compared it to Williams and Walker's *In Dahomey*, which was then on its tryout tour before coming to New York. Williams and Walker were just about

Mattie Wilkes

review-proof by 1902, and Hogan got the supreme accolade when the paper said that "they are excelled only by Ernest Hogan's individual performance in . . . *Enchantment*." The Smart Set show toured to Canada and the Midwest after its New York run. Using some of their material from *Enchantment*, Ernest and Mattie Hogan would star together in various short vaudeville musicals for the next three years. In early 1905, Hogan assembled a vaudeville musical group called the Memphis Students, which would play an extended run at Hammerstein's Victoria until the early fall (see the section on Will Marion Cook in Chapter 3).

Late in 1905, seven years after *Clorindy*, Ernest Hogan finally got the musical he had deserved for so long: it was *Rufus Rastus*, produced by Hurtig and Seamon, who had presented the Williams and Walker successes of recent years. The score was mostly by Joe Jordan, with several contributions by Hogan himself. Hogan played a struggling actor work-ing at a series of day jobs, and the role gave him a wider range of comic tones and situations than he had ever had to play before.

Rufus Rastus toured to several cities before opening at New York's American Theatre, on Eighth Avenue at Forty-second Street, on January 29, 1906. The show was Hogan's triumph. His comic ability was well-known before *Rufus Rastus*, but the depth that he brought to his new role took him out of the ranks of "darky comedians" forever. The defining moment for the Hogan character came in a remarkable song (music by Joe Jordan, lyric by Earl Jones) called "Oh, Say, Wouldn't It Be a Dream?" The song is comic, but there is an edge to it. It is half whimsy, half threat. "Coon" imagery haunts the daydreams of the desolate Rufus. He wishes that "Broadway was a garden full of watermelons ripe," but he would also like to see Congress "full of folks as dark as sin" who would "paint the White House black and christen battle-ships with gin." The lyric rides over a stately, marchlike melody that gives a cool, uneasy tone to the song. There was

Rufus Rastus

nothing remotely like it in the repertoire of Bert Williams. In Hogan's later performances, he touched the heart as well as the funnybone, a reach that Williams chose not to make.

After its successful run in New York, *Rufus Rastus* took to the road again, touring through the spring of 1907. After years of being a dependable funnyman, Ernest Hogan was suddenly a hot property. The Hurtig & Seamon company wanted a new show for him, to begin as soon as *Rufus Rastus* had run its course. The producing team began to assemble collaborators for the next Hogan project. Hogan would direct as well as star and, with Will Vodery, would supply most of the melodies; Henry Creamer and Lester Walton would write lyrics. The book was assigned to two bright young men, Flournoy Miller and Aubrey Lyles, just beginning their careers after graduating from Fisk University and having a successful first play at the Pekin Theatre in Chicago. The

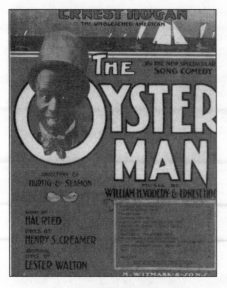

The Oyster Man

result was *The Oyster Man*, which opened at New York's Fourteenth Street Theatre on November 25, 1907.

Although Hogan had been exhausted during much of the rehearsal period, his performance was as energetic as ever, and he gathered another set of good reviews. For some reason, *The Oyster Man* cut short its New York run to begin a tour of the Midwest in late December. In Lima, Ohio, the first stop, Hogan had a physical breakdown and was forced to leave the show temporarily in January. John Rucker, the second comic lead, replaced him for a few weeks. Hogan returned to the show, but collapsed again after a performance in Boston. Hurtig and Seamon, realizing that their star was seriously ill, disbanded the *Oyster Man* company in March.

In June 1908 Hogan's New York theatre friends produced a benefit for him to help cover his medical expenses. Hogan was not indigent by any means, but in the days before theatrical unions, benefits were the way the profession looked out for its own. The star-studded show lasted four hours, and Tom Fletcher remembered it as the "greatest assembly of colored actors ever to appear in the same theater and on the same stage in one night." Williams and Walker, Cole and Johnson, S. H. Dudley, Will Marion Cook, Alex Rogers, James Reese Europe, Joe Jordan, Will Tyers, and James Vaughn—the top echelon of black theatre—all turned out to honor Ernest Hogan.

Hogan's health deteriorated, and further diagnosis revealed that he was suffering from

John Rucker

tuberculosis. Hurtig and Seamon arranged for his recuperation at a sanatorium in Lakewood, New Jersey, but he died there on May 20, 1909.

Hogan's death hit the black show world hard. Besides his talent and his generosity, his star power would be missed. His celebrity was a long time coming, but it was real and it was honestly earned. He was one of the very few black actors around whom white producers could build shows, shows that meant jobs for many others. And his passing was a sharp reminder of how far so many of his colleagues had come in the last ten years. To climb from the mud shows of the Reconstruction era and reach as high as Broadway took more than talent. Ernest Hogan had what it took.

BERT WILLIAMS

In the demi-universe of black entertainment in the early years of our century, Bert Williams was not just a star: he was the sun. All sorts of enterprises revolved around him: musical shows, big-time vaudeville, international touring, music publishing, and recordings. He drew every major black composer, lyricist, and librettist of his time into his orbit. All wrote for him, some wrote with him, and many of them flourished in his light as they never would again. When he moved from the black universe to the white, by joining Ziegfeld's *Follies*, his light shone cooler, being further away, but it still shone brilliantly.

He began his career as the embodiment of a stereotype, as Jim Crow to George Walker's Zip Coon. In the era of fake coons, he and his partner originally billed themselves as "The Two Real Coons." But by the time he was thirty, he had so enlarged and transformed his stage persona that the coon stereotype itself began to crack and fall away. Although he performed in blackface all of his life, the laughter that he generated was the "laughing with" variety, not the "laughing at" that is provoked by cartoons.

Bert Williams

Egbert Austin Williams was born November 12, 1874, in Nassau, the Bahamas, British West Indies, where his father Frederick was a waiter at the Royal Victoria Hotel. In 1885 the Williams family came to America, spending a year in Florida, then moving on to Riverside, California. Frederick Williams was a laborer there, and his wife Julia was a laundress. Around 1890 Bert Williams left high school to join a medicine show. He spent a year or so hawking elixirs in lumber towns and mining camps along the California coast, then settled in San Francisco to work in Martin & Selig's Mastodon Minstrels. When George Walker, a young dancer from Lawrence, Kansas, joined the Mastodons, Williams was paired with him for a few skits. Walker's salary was $8 a week, and Williams' was $9, since he also served as stage manager. It was the beginning of a partnership that lasted twenty years.

George Walker was a year older than Williams. He was handsome, lithe and athletic, a flashy dancer and a glib talker. The contrast with the slow, drawling Williams was a good starting point for comedy. At first, Walker was the comic and Williams his straight man, but during their first two years together, the roles became reversed. They worked in San Francisco as a music hall team for a while, then made their way through the Midwest to Chicago.

John W. Isham hired them for his *Octoroons* company there but dismissed them when they failed to impress Chicago audiences. Working with various agents, they got sporadic bookings out of Chicago, playing in Pittsburgh, Detroit, and Louisville.

In the summer of 1896, Williams and Walker were sent to West Baden, Indiana, to perform for the Show Managers of America, a professional organization that was convening in the spa town. One of the attending managers was Thomas Canary, a coproducer of the upcoming Victor Herbert operetta, *The Gold Bug*. Canary was so taken with the team that he urged them to go to New York to audition for his partner, George Lederer. He promised them that he would write to Lederer on their behalf. Williams and Walker were thrilled with this chance, and somehow they scraped together the money to get to New York.

Lederer didn't think they were anything special. He saw their audition as run-of-the-mill minstrelsy, and he heard his orchestra's difficulty in grasping the syncopation of their songs. And as he admitted in an

interview given to *Variety* years later, he couldn't imagine black performers on the legitimate stage. Williams and Walker got the traditional "we'll call you" that follows a failed tryout.

So when *The Gold Bug* opened at Broadway's Casino Theatre on
September 21, 1896, Williams and Walker were not in the cast. The
show, now remembered only as Victor Herbert's worst failure, tottered
even on its opening night. Perhaps in a desperate move to save his sink-
ing show with an outrageous novelty, Lederer called Williams and Walker. He plunked their vaudeville act into the middle of the second night's
performance. They were unbilled and completely unexpected, and they
stopped the show. The audience called them back for encore after
encore. The team couldn't save *The Gold Bug*—it ran six days—but the
show's flop didn't hurt them. Williams and Walker were on their way.

Through George Lederer, the pair got an immediate booking at
Koster & Bial's, a large music hall on Thirty-fourth Street, just west of
Broadway, the present site of Macy's department store. Within a few
weeks of arriving in New York, they followed a Broadway debut with
star billing at a major vaudeville house. The city went wild for them,
keeping them at Koster & Bial's for seven months. Never had black
performers been so lionized in New York. The high spot of their act was
a comedy version of the cakewalk, the new dance fad that was starting
to move from the professional stage into the ballroom. Williams and
Walker weren't the first cakewalkers in New York, but they capitalized
on the craze as no other act did.

The cakewalk was an exuberant, high-stepping strut, the immediate descendent of the old minstrel show walkaround. The dance seems
to have evolved around the time that women were added to the casts of
black shows. The opportunity for dancing in couples inspired the
improvisational teamwork of the cakewalk and added a sexual frisson
to black variety. Dora Dean and her partner Charles Johnson were
among the first cakewalkers, performing the dance in the early 1890s
editions of *The Creole Show*. In 1893 the first published cakewalk
appeared ("The Opelika Cakewalk"), and in 1895 the dance was used
as the finale of the *Octoroons* show. By 1896, just when New York was
getting its first look at Williams and Walker, social dancers were beginning to try the cakewalk at parties. It was the first black "crossover"
dance, and Williams and Walker crossed over with it.

The idea was to put one's personal stamp on the strutting—to throw the shoulders farther back, to kick higher, to demonstrate more flash and spirit than anyone else. Merely to step out on the floor as the orchestra struck up a cakewalk was to announce that one was about to show off. Williams and Walker's cakewalk was irresistible, celebrating and spoofing the fad at the same time. In early 1897 two women were added to their act, which had by then turned into a cakewalking

Charles Johnson and Dora Dean

jubilee. Walker and his girl threw out the challenge with a few nifty steps, cool and slick, for Williams and his girl to pick up and match. The big, shambling Williams would respond with a slow, loose-jointed grind. Then Walker again, with chest and backside stuck out simultaneously, in a more intricate prancing step. Then Williams, grinning with delight at his own skill, twisting and flailing in mockery of the classy dancing all around him.

The routine was so funny that in 1896 the American Tobacco Company asked to photograph them in dance poses for a series of eight trading cards to advertise their Old Virginia Cheroots cigars. For the photo session, Williams and Walker were paired with two actresses from the Black Patti Troubadours company, Stella Wiley (who was Bob Cole's wife) and Ada Overton (who would soon marry George Walker). The pictures were so popular that the company re-issued them as lithographs and, later, on postcards. A small-town Missouri publisher, John Stark, asked for permission to use one of the poses for a sheet music cover. Permission was granted, and in September 1899, Williams and Walker and their cakewalking ladies appeared on the first edition of a musical landmark, Scott Joplin's "Maple Leaf Rag."

As white society began to negotiate the cakewalk, Williams and Walker were on hand to teach them how. When the team heard that William K. Vanderbilt had been seen cakewalking, they delivered a letter to his home, challenging him to a competition for a $50 prize.

Vanderbilt declined their offer, but when the newspapers told the story, the public enjoyed imagining the tycoon's dance-off against the pros.

The European tours of the Sousa band in the early 1900s made the cakewalk, briefly, an international phenomenon. "At a Georgia Camp Meeting" was an audience favorite in London, Paris, and Moscow. The avant-garde was paying attention, too. Stravinsky's "Ragtime for Eleven Instruments" and Debussy's "Golliwog's Cakewalk" recall the European excitement at hearing this fresh burst of syncopation from America.

The cakewalk was too strenuous to last as a social dance. The frenzy for it had to cool down. And the musical establishment heartily disapproved, as it would disapprove of ragtime, coon songs, and jazz. An 1899 editorial in the *Musical Courier* sniffed:

> Society has decreed that ragtime and cakewalking are the thing, and one reads with amazement and disgust of historical and aristocratic names joining in this sex dance, for the cakewalk is nothing but an African *danse du ventre*, a milder edition of African orgies.

The cakewalk disappeared from society ballrooms around 1901, more a victim of exhaustion than of embarrassment. For a few more years, it remained a feature in the black shows from which it had sprung, always useful as a rousing finale. But while it lasted, the cakewalk craze had done wonders for Williams and Walker, and vice versa.

Bert Williams' first published song was "Dora Dean," a paean to the beautiful dancer in *The Creole Show*. It was issued early in 1896 by Broder & Schlam, a San Francisco firm with offices in New York. As the fame of Williams and Walker grew, it was inevitable that publishers would want their songs and their pictures on song sheets. Williams placed seven songs for publication in 1897, three of them collaborations with Walker. An 1896 song—written by Williams alone—was published by S. Brainard and Sons as "Oh, I Don't Know, I Thought I Was a Winner." Soon after it was issued, the same song was retitled and recopyrighted as "Oh, I Don't Know, You're Not So Warm." The second version was published by Brainard in 1897, with a new rag accompaniment arranged by D. A. Lewis. "Oh, I Don't Know, You're Not So Warm" is usually named as the first song with ragtime accompaniment, but it is really the second: Ernest Hogan's "All Coons Look Alike to Me" beat it into the marketplace by several months.

There would be two dozen songs credited to Williams and Walker, their last written together in 1902. Although there were no real hits among them, the partners' songs sold well enough to keep publishers interested. The song credits on these pieces usually read "By Williams and Walker." Only one of their song sheets makes the music/lyric distinction—"I've Been Living Moderate All My Life" (1901), with "Lyrics by George Walker" and "Music by Bert Williams." But on almost all of Williams's collaborations with other writers, he is listed as composer, so it may be assumed that Williams wrote most of their tunes and Walker most of the words.

Williams never considered himself much of a composer, but he kept at it steadily until 1914. His list of seventy-six published songs puts him among the three most-published black songwriters of his time. (Bob Cole had the most publications, and Rosamond Johnson is a close second to him.) In 1919 Williams analyzed the songwriting craft—and minimized his part in it—in an article for *Theatre Magazine*:

> There are three things that a successful song must have, in my opinion. It must have a humorous situation, it must have a clear story, and a chorus that has a definite trick of words that is funny. The music is the least part of the trouble. The lyrics are the important feature.

Their success at Koster & Bial's led to more, and bigger, vaudeville for Williams and Walker. They headlined at Philadelphia's Bijou Theatre in March 1897, then came back to New York to share a bill with Maurice Barrymore. White vaudevillians still saw them as a novelty, as a fad that might go away. The racism and professional jealousies that would lead to protests against the black team's star billing would not arise for another few years.

In April 1897, Williams and Walker played for a week at London's Empire Theatre. Williams would remember this booking as their only real failure. They followed a ballet troupe on the Empire bill, and Londoners did not know what to think of the team's homemade cakewalk. In the fall of 1897, they joined a touring company headed by McIntyre and Heath, the premier white blackface team. Williams and

Walker got great reviews everywhere they went, turning their East Coast celebrity into a national one.

When Williams and Walker made their hasty move from Chicago to New York in 1896, they had found an apartment to share on West Fifty-third Street, in a neighborhood that was attracting many of the city's black theatre professionals. The dining room of the nearby Marshall Hotel, at 127–29 West Fifty-third Street, was an especially hospitable place for meeting and comparing notes on careers. The Marshall was a four-story brownstone house that had been converted for use as a hotel by its proprietor, Jimmie Marshall. It was small, pricey and fashionable. There was a four-piece orchestra in the dining room, and guests made reservations long in advance for the special Sunday dinners. Bob Cole and Ernest Hogan were regulars there, as were the composers Will Marion Cook and J. Rosamond Johnson. In the manner of all young show people, they had long late-night discussions, planning and daydreaming about shows they would create with and for each other. Within a year or so, Williams and Walker, unlike the others, were actually in a position to realize some of the dreams hatched at the Marshall Hotel. The networking that went on there in the late 1890s would assure the team their pick of material from their talented friends for the next ten years.

By 1898 Williams and Walker were no longer just a vaudeville act but were established stars, ready for full-length shows. Walker felt that a touring company was a logical step for the team. Under his philosophical and managerial guidance, the step was taken, and plans were laid to produce an annual Williams and Walker musical to tour vaudeville houses around the country. There would eventually be four of these vaudeville/musical productions, each adding new names to the Williams and Walker roster of writers and to their company of players.

The first production of the new company was *Senegambian Carnival*, which was essentially the team's vaudeville act with Cook and Dunbar's one-act *Clorindy* grafted onto it. The plot of *Senegambian Carnival* concerned the Walker character's trying to con the Williams character out of the gold he had found in Alaska, and it served mainly as a clothesline to hang songs and dance numbers on. Williams' big song was a holdover from *Clorindy*, "Who Dat Say Chicken in Dis Crowd?" *Carnival* toured for a few months, playing successfully in Boston, Cincinnati, and Washington, D.C. It was during the run of this show that Bert Williams began to court Lottie Thompson, a widowed actress eight years older than he, who would soon become his wife.

The company's second production was *A Lucky Coon*, which began touring the New England states in December 1898. By this time Williams and Walker had entered into a permanent management agreement with the powerful Hurtig & Seamon, which owned several theatres around the United States and, briefly, dabbled in music publishing. Williams and Walker had started at the top in New York, and it was Hurtig & Seamon's job to keep them there. For a black company, even one headed by stars, the danger of sliding back into second-class vaudeville was great.

Williams and Walker, in their different ways, wore success easily. Walker became the offstage counterpart of his onstage dandy. No day was complete for him without a consultation with his tailor. He loved to stroll along Broadway showing just the proper amount of cuff. His array of suits—and their complimentary matching spats—gladdened female hearts during his daily rounds in the theatre district. He was a sport, a flirt, a true swell. The Williams style was more conservative but no less grand. James Weldon Johnson remembered his conviviality during this first flush of fame. He was:

> tall and broad-shouldered; on the whole a rather handsome figure, and entirely unrecognizable as the shambling, shuffling "darky" he impersonated on the stage; luxury-loving and indolent, but highly intelligent and with a certain reserve which at times exhibited itself as downright snobbishness; talking with a very slow drawl and getting more satisfaction, it seemed, out of being considered a great raconteur than out of being a great comedian.

With their third show, *The Policy Players*, Jesse Shipp (1869–1934) began his long association with the team. Shipp, a seasoned librettist and "script doctor," rang some changes on their usual plot device, Walker's trying to swindle Williams, giving Bert Williams a brief impersonation of the "Ex-President of Haiti" and an encounter with New York society, represented by the "Astrobilt" family. Songs were contributed by Will Accooe, Cecil Mack, and Tom Lemonier. *Policy Players* was their biggest show to date, with fifty people in its cast. Lottie Williams and Aida—nee Ada—Overton Walker (1880–1914) danced in the show. Mattie Wilkes, the young soprano who would soon marry Ernest Hogan, was especially admired by the critics.

For *Sons of Ham*, the company's offering of 1900, Williams and Walker recruited the clever songwriter Tim Brymn (1881–1946) and the singer Alice MacKay, the wife of Will Accooe. Bert Williams' feature song was "My Castle on the Nile," by the new team of Bob Cole and the Johnson Brothers (J. Rosamond and James Weldon). In December 1900, smallpox broke out among the cast when they were playing in Pittsburgh, forcing the company to disband temporarily. The show was revived briefly in the spring of 1901, but Williams and Walker were back in vaudeville as a duo by June. They were institutions now, worthy of the highest accolade of show business: blatant imitation. In late 1901, Dan Avery and Charles Hart, a black vaudeville team, opened at Keith's Union Square Theatre billed as "a Williams and Walker act."

In October 1901, Williams and Walker went into the Victor studios in New York to make their first recordings. There were ten of these flat-disc sides: four solos by Williams, three by Walker, and three duets. Because Walker didn't like the sound of his voice on discs, he never recorded solo again. And he

Ada Overton
(Aida Overton Walker)

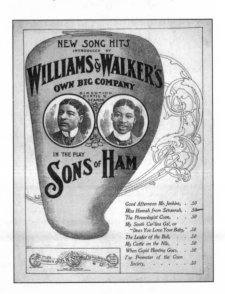

Sons of Ham

Alice Mackay

would record only one other duet with Williams, "Pretty Desdemone," five years later. But for Williams the October sessions were the beginning of a recording career that lasted until his death twenty-one years later. Williams wasn't the first black recording artist (that was George Washington Johnson [1846–1914], with his 1891 cylinder recording of "Laughing Song"), but he was the first to sustain a recording career. His easy, talk-singing baritone is a pleasing contrast to the overwrought vocalizing of his contemporaries, and Bert Williams records are virtually the only ones of the period that are listenable today.

In 1902 Hurtig & Seamon began to assemble the personnel to create a Broadway musical for Williams and Walker. Their four previous shows had been conceived for vaudeville touring, with short stops at New York vaudeville houses. But each show had been more elaborate than the last, moving the stars toward "legitimate" theatre, to be played in "legitimate" theatres. The Broadway project was called In Dahomey, produced by Hurtig & Seamon on a $15,000 budget, a huge outlay for the time. Jesse Shipp concocted the three-act story, involving the attempts of two con men (Williams and Walker) to bilk the leader of a "back to Africa" movement. The nominal composer was Will Marion Cook. (In this age of interpolation, almost any Broadway composer could be called "nominal," as a score without added songs by other writers was a rarity. Theatre scores by one writer or one team were not common practice until the late teens.) As usual with Williams and Walker shows, the interpolations in In Dahomey were top-notch, with con-

Will Accooe

tributions by Williams himself, James Vaughn

(1870–1935), and J. Leubrie Hill (1869–1916). The American publisher of the *In Dahomey* songs, Harry Von Tilzer, predictably placed two numbers that he had written in the show. Aida Overton Walker and Lottie Williams were featured in the large cast, as were two newcomers, the tenor Henry Troy and the soprano Abbie Mitchell.

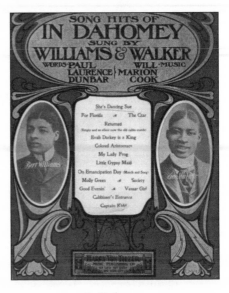

In Dahomey

After a brief tryout tour in late 1902, *In Dahomey* opened at the New York Theatre, on Broadway between Forty-fourth and Forty-fifth streets, on February 18, 1903. Reviews were good, although some critics found too much trivial plot and too few raggy songs. Williams' personal reviews were superlative. *The Theatre* magazine said in its April 1903 issue that he was "a vastly funnier man than any white comedian on the American stage." The show had a middling fifty-three-performance run. Perhaps because the Williams and Walker company had been such a familiar sight on New York vaudeville stages, the landmark achievement of *In Dahomey* was generally overlooked: it was the first full-length show written and performed by African-Americans to play in a first-class New York theatre.

Hurtig & Seamon made immediate plans to take *In Dahomey* to London after its New York run. Williams and Walker at first demurred, remembering their cool reception there in 1897. But the booking of the elegant Shaftesbury Theatre in the West End was too good to pass up. The company set sail for England on the *Urania* on April 28, 1903.

The first-night audience in London was reserved enough in their approval to cause

J. Leubrie Hill

concern among the company. The stars and producer Jules Hurtig sat up all night waiting for their reviews in the morning papers. The critics were generally positive, but several of them complained about the ending ("as flat as a pancake," one called it). Williams and Walker knew what was wrong and they knew how to fix it. They quickly devised a giant cakewalking finale, to be danced around a six-foot set piece shaped like a cake and "iced" with a hundred electric lights. *In Dahomey* never had another lukewarm reception during its seven months in Great Britain.

London society took up Williams and Walker as New York society had seven years earlier. They were invited to give cakewalk lessons in private homes. There was a command performance of *In Dahomey* given at a party to celebrate the ninth birthday of the Prince of Wales (who would become King Edward VIII in 1936). The eighty company members—and their truckloads of scenery hauled from the Shaftesbury—overflowed the improvised stage area in Buckingham Palace. There was a champagne reception afterward, at which Williams gave King Edward VII some tips on the cakewalk and told him some funny stories.

London intellectuals loved Williams and Walker. The critic Max Beerbohm praised their show in print. And George Bernard Shaw toyed with the idea of giving Bert Williams a role in the first production of his *Caesar and Cleopatra*. He wrote to a friend: "By far the best acting now in London is that of Williams and Walker in *In Dahomey*. I shall certainly ask Williams to play 'Ftatateeta.'" (Cleopatra's maid!)

During the company's London stay, the British publisher Keith, Prowse & Co. issued the complete vocal score of *In Dahomey*. This publication is the only printed score of a black show of the period.

Williams and Walker were welcomed everywhere. Oxford students gave a party in their honor. In Scotland, Williams was accepted as a member of an Edinburgh chapter of the Masonic lodge.

They had come to England as curiosities, but they left as international stars. When they made the long, successful American tour of *In Dahomey*, their audiences knew they were seeing the show that had made the king laugh.

During the two-year life of *In Dahomey*, a subtle shift occurred in the working relationship of the starring partners. Reviewers began to single out Bert Williams as the superior performer, as "a particular star" who "must be given the greater part of the night's success." It was not that George Walker had slipped, it was that the Williams stage character was growing in a way that Walker's was not. There was a new dimension to Williams, gradually changing him from a Jim Crow buffoon to a black-faced Everyman. He was funnier than ever, many said. And his comedy was becoming dry, still, almost stoic. It made him an even bigger contrast to his partner, the extroverted song and dance man. Bert Williams was becoming the sort of character who traveled through life alone.

The "new" Williams was encapsulated in the work of a young lyricist from Nashville named Alex Rogers (1879–1930). As had many another black songwriter of the early 1900s, Rogers had made his way to New York, hoping to get a hearing by Bert Williams. And as was often the case with black writers, Rogers' first work in New York was as an actor. He had a small role in *Sons of Ham*, and he was hired again to act in *In Dahomey*. His most important contributions to *In Dahomey*, however, were two songs that he wrote for Bert Williams. Their titles were "I'm a Jonah Man" and "I May Be Crazy But I Ain't No Fool." Taken together, they sum up the character that Bert Williams would play for the rest of his life: the wry observer of his own hard luck, a man who expects the worst and always gets it. The tone of the lyrics is weary and matter-of-fact, just this side of cynical. The singer isn't asking for pity, he is merely making a comment. When we see the "sad" black-faced Williams photos below the titles on the Rogers song sheets today, we invest them with a pathos that is not there in Williams' recorded performances of them. His put-upon character was a comic, not a pathetic, creation. His aim was to get laughs, not sympathy. Contemporary reviewers never mentioned that Williams touched them, only that he made them laugh. Williams' comic persona had no more "poor me" in it than Buster Keaton's.

Williams and Walker's musical material had always been several cuts above ordinary coon song fare. Even in their "Two Real Coons" days, their songs ranged from the topical ("Snap Shot Sal" and Will Accooe and Ernest Hogan's "The Phrenologist Coon") to the gently satirical ("She's Getting More Like the White Folks Every Day"). Their lyrics are dappled with dialect, and their point of view is that of entertainers trying to be entertaining. The Rogers lyrics are slangy— and very light on dialect—and the point of view is one of detach- ment. The audience is allowed to eavesdrop on the philosophical grumbling of a man with very low expectations. It was irresistibly, and universally, funny.

Rogers' masterpiece was "Nobody," written for Williams in 1905. It quickly became his signature song. He recorded it twice, and audiences clamored for it in every vaudeville performance he gave after introduc- ing it. The published version contains ten verses, each of which describes two situations in which the singer is ignored by anyone around him who could offer help or encouragement. "Who soothes my thumping, bumping brain?" "Who says, 'Here's two bits, go and eat'?" "Who says, 'Look at that handsome man'?" "Who took the engine off my neck?" The title provides the answer every time. And when the singer makes his threat that he doesn't "intend to do nothing for nobody notime," we know that nobody will notice his reciprocation.

Rogers would write with and for Williams through 1909, giving him better specialty material than anyone else ever did: "Believe Me," "Fas', Fas' World," "Let It Alone," "My Old Man." And when the Rogers-Williams songs stopped coming, other lyricists had no choice but to write for the Williams character in the Rogers style. Bert Williams couldn't be imagined any other way.

During the In Dahomey years of Williams' artistic growth, Walker's offstage role was expanding. He became the social conscience as well as the managerial watchdog of the Williams and Walker company. Williams' temperament was not suited to either role, and he gladly deferred to his partner in all matters concerning what they should be producing and where they should be producing it.

Walker dreamed of a "national Ethiopian theater in New York," a resident company that would produce plays and musicals by black writ- ers featuring all-black casts. He knew the talents were there. He had met and befriended them in his Marshall Hotel days. The need was for black producers (all of whom were still at the road-show level) and for black capital. Until these could be developed, the Williams and Walker company would have to serve as the way station toward the dream. Walker saw his company as much more than a source of personal glory and wealth. He wrote in the New York *Age* in 1908:

> Our payroll is about $2300 a week. Do you know what that means? Take your pencils and figure how many families could be supported comfortably on that. Then look at the talent, the many-sided talent we are employing and encouraging. Add to this what we contribute to maintain the standing of the race in the estimation of the lighter majority. Now do you see us in the light of a race institution? That is what we aspire to be, and if we ever attain our ambition, I earnestly hope and honestly believe that our children that are to be will say a good word in their day for "Bert and me and them."

Walker knew the problems of black show folk on both sides of the paymaster's window. In 1905, the same year that he bought a life membership in the Black Business Men's League, he began to consider the need for a professional organization for black vaudeville performers. The first attempt at an American performers' union was the White Rats (named for a predecessor British organization), organized by seven vaudevillians in 1900. Although the White Rats claimed that their membership was open to blacks, they supported the "one black act per bill" policy of most theatre managers, and they protested the billing of a black act over any white act. In other words, black Rats were welcome as long as there weren't too many of them and they stayed at the bottom of the bill. When George Walker began to talk about forming the Colored Actors Beneficial Association, he faced the immediate resistance of the White Rats as well as that of white managers. Walker's group barely got beyond the planning stage, and it was soon supplanted by another group with smaller, more attainable goals. This was the Colored Vaudeville Benevolent Association, organized by the actor/manager Robert Slater (1869–1930). The purpose of the CVBA was charity—to provide loans and gifts to black performers who needed them. Needless to say, George Walker was generous in lending his time and his money to help his fellow actors, privately as well as through the CVBA.

Another of Walker's organizational efforts had a longer life. This was a club for black theatre professionals, called "The Frogs." (The name was the title of an Aristophanes play in which a reference is made to "our minstrel frogs.") In July 1908 the Frogs came into being at George Walker's home in Harlem. Walker was elected president, and other officers included J. Rosamond Johnson, Jesse Shipp, and R. C. McPherson, the lyricist and publisher known as "Cecil Mack."

The Frogs

Befitting his degree of activism, Bert Williams was named head of the Art Committee.

The Frogs provided a black counterpart to the all-white Players Club. It was a place for interaction among theatre professionals and leaders in "art, literature, music, scientific and liberal professions." The Frogs flourished into the 1920s, and their annual all-star benefit shows, the Frogs Frolics, were the highlight of many a social season in Harlem.

The organization that figured most in George Walker's goals as citizen and businessman was, of course, the Williams and Walker company. He was a fierce negotiator, as willing to clash with his own managers, Hurtig & Seamon, as with any theatre owner who offered less than the best to his troupe. He knew that the Williams and Walker shows had implications beyond show business for his race. The collection of talents that he had assembled deserved presentation in settings worthy of them. When Hurtig & Seamon refused to fight with him for such a setting, Walker broke his company's contract with them and began looking for other management. Hurtig & Seamon filed a lawsuit to stop him.

The situation arose soon after the triumph of *In Dahomey*. The show had opened well on Broadway, had played an extended run in London's West End, and had toured the United States successfully for forty weeks. Hurtig & Seamon had quadrupled its $15,000 investment on the American tour alone. So Walker made big plans for a follow-up. He wanted to do another show with an African setting—including a mountain, a working waterfall, and live animals—and to increase the company's size to 125. In short, Walker wanted to present the grandest thing that Broadway had ever seen. He went to Hurtig & Seamon and asked for $30,000 to produce it.

He was appalled when Hurtig & Seamon not only refused him the money but also recommended that Williams and Walker's next production be housed at the Majestic Theatre. This was a second-class theatre uptown on Columbus Circle, so far from the main theatre district that it was called "the Arctic Circle" by Broadway wise guys. Walker would have none of it. He put out the word along Broadway that he and his partner wanted new management. In June 1905 Hurtig & Seamon went to court to keep their biggest clients from leaving.

Abyssinia

The matter took two months to make its way to a New York State Supreme Court docket, but at the August hearing, Williams and Walker prevailed. They were released from their Hurtig & Seamon contract and were allowed to seek new representation. The producer who passed Walker's rigorous cross-examination was Melville B. Raymond. The trade papers announced that in early 1906 Raymond would present Williams and Walker's new production, *Abyssinia*.

When the ads for *Abyssinia* appeared, New York theatre insiders must have wondered what the fuss with Hurtig & Seamon had been about. The show was set to open on February 20, 1906, at the Majestic Theatre, the same "Arctic Circle" venue that had so offended George Walker when Hurtig & Seamon had proposed it. Melville Raymond had found the Majestic to be the best that he could get for the Williams and Walker company.

What the stars did not know was the extent to which a producers' cartel, called the Theatrical Syndicate, could manipulate access to theatres according to its members' particular interests in various shows and playhouses. The Syndicate was a theatrical trust, formed in a secret meeting of six powerful producers and theatre owners in 1895 and ruled by Abraham Lincoln Erlanger. Within a few years of its organization, the Syndicate controlled over 700 major theatres across the United States, including almost every theatre in the Times Square area. (The Syndicate's dictatorship over the American theatre would last twenty years, until it was broken by the Shuberts in the mid-teens.)

Abyssinia was produced in a scaled-down version of Walker's grandiose vision. There were a hundred players, some striking scenic and lighting effects, and a few live animals on stage. Jesse Shipp wrote the book and Will Marion Cook got composer credit, although six of the eight published songs were composed by Bert Williams. Reviews were good, but the show could manage a run of only thirty-one performances. As soon as *Abyssinia*'s tour was underway, Walker began to look for management to replace the now-bankrupt Raymond.

"Nobody" was interpolated into the *Abyssinia* score, and it was, of course, Bert Williams' big number. He was called by Columbia Records to record it, along with three other solo songs and what would be his last duet with Walker. Williams would remain a Columbia artist for sixteen years. In 1905 Williams and Walker had signed on as "staff writers" to publish exclusively with a new black firm, the Gotham-Attucks Music Company. Walker's name never appeared on a Gotham-Attucks

Bandanna Land

song, but the company wanted the right to publish anything from the Williams and Walker shows. When Bert Williams went into the Columbia studios over the next several years, he usually brought Gotham-Attucks songs with him.

Despite Melville Raymond's inept management, *Abyssinia*'s tour was profitable. Williams and Walker were still box office, and their projects were still attractive to prospective producers. In March 1907 they signed with F. Ray Comstock, an associate of the Shuberts, to produce their next show, *Bandanna Land*. The team's second management change produced the same result:

Bandanna Land opened on February 3, 1908, at the Majestic Theatre. Williams and Walker had hit Broadway's glass ceiling again.

The familiar creative staff was assembled again for *Bandanna Land*. Cook and Shipp were the main writers, with Leubrie Hill, Chris Smith, and Cecil Mack represented by interpolated songs. George Walker found a definitive solo number in Rogers and Cook's "Bon Bon Buddy," and Bert Williams scored again with "Nobody." Another Williams feature was "Late Hours," a song he composed to lyrics by David Kempner. The comic specialty that followed "Late Hours" was a solo pantomime of a poker game, with Williams enacting the betting, bluffs, exaltations, and disappointments of all the players in a four-handed poker game. Like most of the comedy features and songs in Williams and Walker shows, the poker sketch had little to do with the plot. But the artistry of Williams' acting of the four players proved that he was a world-class comedian. The publisher Edward Marks said in his autobiography:

> In facial expression and pantomime he [Williams] equaled the greatest clowns. Chaplin himself can hold an audience no better.

The poker game would join "Nobody" on the A-list of Williams' inimitable material. It would be part of his comic repertoire for the rest of his life.

Bandanna Land's reviews were better than those for *Abyssinia*, and the show lasted eleven weeks in New York before beginning its tour. While the show was on the road, the company began to unravel. Lottie Williams left, announcing her intention to retire from the stage. Will Marion Cook resigned as music director, to be replaced by Will Vodery (1885–1951). And in August, during a performance at Boston's Orpheum Theatre, George Walker began to fumble his lyrics to "Bon Bon Buddy." It was the first sign of the disease that would kill him.

Walker's diagnosis showed that he was exhibiting early symptoms of syphilis. There

Will Vodery

was no effective treatment at the time, and he knew the outlook was bleak. The symptoms would progress from the embarrassing to the debilitating. Over time, memory loss and slurred speech would be followed by seizures and temporary paralysis.

As he trooped on through the fall, his condition worsened. Finally, in February 1909, during *Bandanna Land*'s run in Louisville, Walker accepted the fact that his days on stage were over. He left the company, pleading "overwork" and promising to return. His wife Aida took over his role—in his costume—until the tour ended, in Brooklyn, two months later.

In May, perhaps in rehearsal for the inevitable, Bert Williams made his first appearance as a solo performer in vaudeville. He tried out his act in Boston and went from there to Hammerstein's Victoria Theatre in New York. *Variety* said that his "songs and talk were highly amusing. Williams was never funnier." The White Rats protested his star billing at Hammerstein's, but the theatre's management held firm. Williams was undeniably the drawing power on the bill, and his name remained at the top of the roster.

In the summer of 1909, Ray Comstock made plans for a new musical to star Williams alone. Aida Overton Walker withdrew from the project immediately, choosing to perform in vaudeville instead of in the company that her husband had led so ably. Will Marion Cook also passed on the show, to be replaced as composer by J. Rosamond Johnson. The show was called *Mr. Lode of Koal*, and it began its troubled life in Toledo, Ohio, on August 29.

Upon arriving in Toledo, Bert Williams was dismayed to learn that Comstock had not yet arranged any succeeding bookings for the fall. This was the kind of mismanagement that George Walker would never have tolerated, and the *Mr. Lode of Koal* company would suffer from it throughout the eight months of the show's existence. A tryout tour was finally pieced together, on a city-by-city

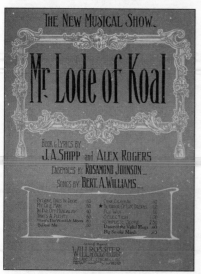

Mr. Lode of Koal

basis, that took the company to St. Louis, Chicago, Kansas City, Indianapolis, and Louisville, with an uneasy wait in each city to confirm the next booking. The legendary Williams patience was sorely tested by Comstock's incompetence and seeming indifference. The last straw was the company's arrival in New York to find themselves booked—for the third time—in their old hard-luck house, the Majestic Theatre.

Mr. *Lode of Koal* opened on November 1, 1909, to begin a five-week run at the Majestic. Williams got his usual glowing notices, but the show could not survive a winter in the "Arctic Circle." It lurched into another half-arranged Comstock tour and finally closed in March 1910. Comstock's predilection for low ticket prices and long-jump bookings had doomed the show. The ticket sales at second-class theatres could not pay for the long, illogical hops on the producer's zigzag railway schedule. Mr. *Lode of Koal*, having played major cities with one of the country's most popular stars leading its cast, closed showing a loss of $11,000.

Bert Williams in blackface

Dejected at the failure of his first solo show, and in debt because of it, Bert Williams accepted the first offer that came his way. This was an April 1910 stint back in vaudeville at Hammerstein's. And the White Rats objected to his star billing again. This time, Hammerstein's management relented and changed the printed program to list Maude Raymond at the head of the printed bill. But in huge electric lights on the front of the theatre, the name "BERT WILLIAMS" lit up Times Square.

Broadway buzzed with speculation as to what Bert Williams would do next. The rumors flew: he would star in a drama produced by David

Belasco; he would move to London to make a music hall career; he would reorganize the Williams and Walker company. There was no question that he would work. But his twenty years with George Walker had taught him that it mattered what he did and where he did it.

Because he was black, there was a fragility inherent in his stardom. Two consecutive flops could hurt him in a way that they could not hurt George M. Cohan or Raymond Hitchcock. He knew that he would not be considered either for straight plays or for standard (white) musical comedy. He had neither the temperament nor the business ability to re-create the Williams and Walker company alone. He could not count on anyone in the Broadway establishment for advice. His three professional managers had all wanted to offer his shows primarily to black audiences at low ticket prices rather than to bet that white audiences would pay top dollar to see him, even after *In Dahomey* had proven otherwise. He had burned his bridges with Raymond and with Hurtig & Seamon. Now his association with the bumbling Comstock was in shambles. Williams had a lot to think through.

And for the first time since his San Francisco days, he had to think it through alone. There would be no more counsel from George Walker. His disease was running its deadly course, and his mind was gone.

Williams' dilemma deepened when Florenz Ziegfeld offered him a three-year contract to star in his annual *Follies*. The salary was good—$500 a week. He could make twice that touring in vaudeville, but if he took Ziegfeld's offer, he could have an easier life at home and enjoy the prestige of Broadway work. The big question raised by the Ziegfeld option was the one that nobody could answer: what was it like to be the only African-American onstage or backstage in a Broadway theatre? No one knew, because no one had been in the situation. The most appealing prospect of the *Follies* was that it would be a chance to break with Comstock. Williams accepted.

Williams and Comstock filed suits against each other on the same day. Williams sought release from the contract that Comstock "had not kept any part of" in his handling of *Mr. Lode of Koal*. Comstock sought to stop Williams from working for Ziegfeld. Charges of mismanagement (Comstock's) and unreasonable demands (Williams') collided in the New York State Supreme Court for eight months. In December a ruling came in Williams' favor. In the meantime, Williams had gone to work, confident of the strength of his case. He had opened on June 20, 1910, at the Jardin de Paris, the roof garden of the New York Theatre, in the *Follies of 1910*.

Some of the expected flap about Williams' hiring materialized, with the white press criticizing Ziegfeld for offering the job, the black press criticizing Williams for taking it. Ziegfeld stood his ground with the press and with the *Follies* company. When several cast members came to him to protest Williams's presence at rehearsals, Ziegfeld called their bluff. He told them that the only irreplaceable member of the company was Bert Williams.

Williams knew that the backstage situation would be touchy. He resolved to conduct himself with dignity at all times, to avoid confrontation if possible, and to stand up to injustice if he had to. It was the pattern of the *Follies* to run through the summer in New York, then to send out a touring version that would play until the following spring. Life would be even more complicated on the road. Railway cars, hotels, cafes, bars, theatres—all would present a maze of unspoken rules about which door to use, which seat, which table, which elevator. And the rules changed slightly in each city. Racism could trump the ace of stardom anywhere. Williams had picked his way through this social minefield for years, and he knew the territory. His quiet professionalism would see him through eight *Follies* and eight touring editions. He was nobody's best pal, but he was a friendly and reliable, if somewhat distant, company member.

Bert Williams' first *Follies*, budgeted at $13,000, was the fourth edition of Ziegfeld's annual revues. The producer would not add his name to the title until the following year, but by 1910 he had already put his personal stamp on the revue form. He used the traditional ingredients—song, dance, and comedy—but the recipe was all his own. Before Ziegfeld, Broadway revues were rowdy affairs, usually built around the antics of their star comedians. The revues of Weber and Fields and the Rogers Brothers masqueraded as musical comedies, but their flimsy, always interruptible, plots were the merest excuses for a hodgepodge of crosstalk, slapstick, songs, and burlesque. Ziegfeld's innovation was to see the revue not as a melee, but as an elegant environment in which to display the hitherto most anonymous person in the musical theatre—the chorus girl. He spared no expense to create an atmosphere of glamorous naughtiness. His chorus girls did not sing, of course. That would be too common. They walked, they posed, they glided, they flew on swings, they descended on plywood moons. Sometimes they even deigned to look at the audience, cool and otherworldly in their perfection. Settings, costumes, and music were all put to service for their enhancement. Ziegfeld's comics and singers were allowed their moments to shine, but they were second-class citizens in this kingdom where beauty reigned.

Besides Bert Williams, the stars of the *Follies of 1910* were Anna Held (Ziegfeld's wife, the first French sex kitten to captivate America), Vera Maxwell, and Lillian Lorraine (Ziegfeld's current girlfriend). A newcomer to the Broadway stage was Fanny Brice, newly risen from neighborhood burlesque and delighted with her $75-a-week salary.

Bert Williams sang six songs, with "Constantly," "Believe Me," and "Play That Barbershop Chord" getting the best response. He played Jack Johnson in a boxing sketch and appeared as a blackbird in a take-off of Edmond Rostand's arty play, *Chanticleer*. The *Follies* ran for eighty-eight performances in New York, then set off on its tour. Williams's New York reviews had been extravagant ("the real star of the evening," "the needed artist in this great assemblage of good-looking nobodies. . . . the Mark Twain of his color"). He would reap similar praise for his work in Chicago, St. Louis, Indianapolis, Detroit—everywhere the *Follies* took him. Columbia Records called him to record four of his *Follies* songs in the summer of 1910.

On the evening of January 6, 1911, bad news arrived for Bert Williams backstage at Teller's Broadway Theatre in Brooklyn. He was informed that George Walker had died a few hours earlier at a sanitarium in Islip, Long Island. The blow was not unexpected, but it was still dreadful. Williams collapsed in grief. Then he pulled himself together and left the theatre without finishing the show.

There were four people at the private funeral on January 9: Walker's mother, his wife Aida, and Bert and Lottie Williams. Williams had often sent money to his partner during his illness, and now he paid for the funeral and for shipping his body back home to Lawrence, Kansas.

The white press noted the passing of the "Bon Bon Buddy" and fondly remembered his cakewalking days. The black press mourned the loss of a champion. He had almost singlehandedly realized the dream of a generation of black show folk: a first-class company that commanded attention and respect. He had tangled with the White Rats over the rights of black performers. Like Ernest Hogan, he had narrowly escaped the violent mob in Times Square on that terrible August night in 1900. He had shrugged off the posturing of the monologist Walter Kelly, who had refused to appear on a bill with Williams and Walker in 1905. ("The man is foolish," Walker had said to the press.) He had been a tireless performer at benefits. He was proud of his company and he insisted on the best for them. George Walker had set high standards for the black showmen who followed him. He was thirty-seven years old when he died.

The devastated Williams rejoined the *Follies* company to finish the tour. After nearly six months on the road, he returned to New York in June, just as rehearsals for the *Ziegfeld Follies of 1911* were beginning.

In addition to Bert Williams, the holdovers from the 1910 cast included Brice, Maxwell, and Lorraine. The comic newcomer to the cast was an eccentric Australian character man named Leon Errol. When he was paired with Williams during rehearsals, they devised a sketch that would be remembered as the funniest scene in any *Follies*. The piece was called "Upper and Lower Level," and it concerned the efforts of a laconic redcap (Williams) to steer a wobbly British tourist (Errol) through the chaos of renovation at Grand Central Station. Errol wants to go to "the upper level," and the two—with Williams carrying Errol's baggage—pick their way higher and higher until they are balancing on steel girders swaying above the terminal. Errol thinks the upper level is just a little further up. So, after several frightening missteps, Williams ties a rope around their waists, mountaineer-style, and they proceed even higher. When Errol offers Williams a nickel tip as Williams is hauling him up from a fall, Williams unties the rope and lets him drop. The act started with only four lines of written dialogue, then gave way to physical and verbal improvisation by the two comics. At twenty-two minutes, it was unusually long for a *Follies* sketch, but it never failed to produce nonstop laughter.

Williams also introduced two new songs—"Dat's Harmony" and "Woodman, Spare That Tree"—and reprised his poker game from *Bandanna Land*. After a respectable eighty performances in New York, the *Follies* annual tour cycle began.

The next *Follies* opened later than usual, on October 12, 1912. It was tamer than its predecessor, despite the reteaming of Williams and Errol. Bert Williams' standout songs were "Borrow from Me" and "My Landlady." The most talked-about feature of the 1912 edition was a huge production number, "The Palace of Beauties." When the show finished its eighty-eight New York performances and its tour, Bert Williams' three-year obligation to Ziegfeld was up. Oddly, it seems not to have occurred to either party to renew their contract. Bert Williams was "at liberty" again.

The three years with Ziegfeld had been good for Williams. They had provided income with which to pay off his debts from the disastrous *Mr. Lode of Koal*. And they had given him new confidence as a performer. He was now routinely acclaimed by reviewers as America's best comedian, black or white.

Several years earlier, Bert and Lottie Williams had brought his parents from California to live with them. Bert took a lease on a barbershop in Harlem, which his father Frederick ran until his death in 1912. Lottie's sister died in the spring of 1913, and the Williams family took in her three daughters. To accommodate their growing household, Williams bought a four-story brownstone at 2309 Seventh Avenue, near 135th Street, in Harlem. Lottie decorated it beautifully, installing built-in bookcases for Williams' large library and designing a small formal garden in the courtyard at the rear of the house. The gentleman clown and his family settled comfortably into their new home.

January 1913 found Williams back in the Columbia studios for his first recording session in three years. Accompanied by Charles A. Prince's orchestra, he caught up on some of his recent *Follies* songs and rerecorded "Nobody" as a dialogue with a trombone.

In August he was the main attraction of the annual Frogs Frolic. This particular edition was remarkable for its gathering of talent from the three generations of black show business up to that time. The venerable Sam Lucas sang a song. Aida Overton Walker, sharing a stage with Bert Williams for the first time since *Bandanna Land*, sang Irving Berlin's "That International Rag" with Jesse Shipp. Bert Williams appeared in drag to sing "Just Because She Made Dem Goo-Goo Eyes" with S. H. Dudley. A young comedian named Billy Robinson was also featured. (He would turn to dancing in a few years and would acquire the nickname "Bojangles.") The 1913 Frolic was so successful at the Manhattan Casino that it was sent on a brief tour. Ticket demand was so great in Richmond, Virginia (Bill Robinson's birthplace), that, for the first time, whites were willing to sit in the "colored" section of the City Auditorium to see the frolics of such distinguished Frogs.

In December, Williams played a solo vaudeville turn at the Palace Theatre in New York. His thirty-three-minute act allowed him the time to sing five songs and to tell a few stories. He was called back to sing "Nobody" and to do the poker sketch as encores. Williams loved storytelling and was very good at it, but Ziegfeld would not have permitted so much "slow" comedy in his *Follies*.

Early in 1914, Ziegfeld engaged Williams for the next *Follies*, the second edition to be presented in the New Amsterdam Theatre. Williams played the long-suffering caddy to Leon Errol's duffer in a golf sketch, and the pair copied their classic "Upper and Lower Level" as workmen on a skyscraper. The comedian Ed Wynn made his *Follies* debut that year, as did the beautiful Marilyn Miller in a small role.

Williams' big song was one that he had introduced at the Palace a few months earlier, "The Darktown Poker Club." He had written the music with Will Vodery, and the lyrics were by a white writer, Jean Havez. It is a strange throwback to the coonery of fifteen years earlier. In the song, a disgruntled poker player serves notice that he has brought along his razor to settle any arguments that might arise during the game. Williams' three published songs from the 1914 *Follies* are the last on which his name appears as composer. (He is one of three writers credited on "The Unbeliever," published in 1920 but possibly written earlier.)

Bert Williams would appear in the next three *Follies*. He made a hit each time, and was always well reviewed, but a malaise was creeping into his work. As all of Ziegfeld's comedians did sooner or later, Williams began to feel constrained by the weak and repetitive sketch material that he was assigned by the *Follies* writers. He was responsible for finding his own songs, and the quality of his musical material remained high. But he fretted about his comedy. With the addition of the stunning Joseph Urban sets in the 1915 *Follies*, Williams began to feel even more like an adjunct to the scenery. He wondered if Ziegfeld were paying attention to his efforts. He would have had his answer if he had known what Ziegfeld admitted to a friend:

You know, I don't have a very quick sense of humor. Half the great comedians I've had in my shows and that I've paid a lot of money to and who made my customers shriek were not only not funny to me, but I couldn't understand why they were funny to anybody.

Once when W. C. Fields was rehearsing for a *Follies*, he asked Ziegfeld how long his sketch should be. The producer asked an assistant, "How long does it take the girls to dress here?" He was told, "Seven minutes." Ziegfeld said to Fields, "Hold your sketch to seven minutes."

A new comic usually made his best showing in his first or second *Follies*, using the material that had got him noticed by Ziegfeld or his scouts. When the "A" material ran out, there was little help from the producer to find more. The feeling among his comics was that Ziegfeld would give more attention to choosing fabric for petticoats that would never be seen than to making sure his comedians had good songs and sketches. He hired the greatest comics of his day—to keep them out of Shubert shows, some said—but he left them adrift in the sea of opulence around them.

During this uneasy time in the mid-teens, Williams suffered from a loneliness that bordered on depression. Occasionally he saw a few old friends like Jesse Shipp and Alex Rogers, but he kept mostly to himself. After his nightly *Follies* performances, he went home to his library, where he would read until the early morning hours. Then, if his insomnia were bothering him, he would slip away to a neighborhood saloon. Eubie Blake remembered:

He spent his time sitting in Matheney's, watching people. He never seemed interested in having company. He'd just sit there and drink. But he wasn't mean. Don't get the idea he was mean. He was *very* kind.

Blake placed some of the blame for Williams' solitary life on Lottie. He said, "His wife was *fierce*, and it seemed like she never liked him to have *any* friends."

Among his *Follies* colleagues, Eddie Cantor and W. C. Fields were closest to Williams. But on the *Follies* tours, Williams was subject to various racial restrictions that made socializing hard for him. The segregation of hotels, restaurants, and bars kept even his friends at arm's length. Usually Williams would accommodate local prejudices simply to keep his life from becoming a series of confrontations with head waiters and hotel managers. But his frustration could boil over. Eddie Cantor told of such an incident in a St. Louis bar. The bartender, trying to discourage his patronage, told Williams that gin was $50 a glass. Williams laid a $500 bill on the bar and said, "Give me ten of them."

In 1915 Williams was joined on the New Amsterdam stage by W. C. Fields, and in 1916, by Will Rogers. A particularly bad piece of obvious casting and coarse writing befell Williams in a 1916 sketch. In a Shakespeare travesty, Williams as Othello whacked his Desdemona (played by a male actor) with a sledgehammer.

The 1917 edition had the strongest of all *Follies* comedy casts: Williams, Fields, Rogers, Walter Catlett, Joe Frisco, Fanny Brice, and a bright young newcomer, Eddie Cantor. Cantor's presence provided the opportunity for a sketch with Williams. The scene was Grand Central Station. Williams played a porter who was meeting the train bringing his son (Cantor in blackface) home from college. The porter has bragged to his friends about his brawny, football-playing son, and they have all gathered to see him. Cantor steps off the train, a mincing fop in a pinchback suit and white horn rims. With every effeminate move-ment and college-bred affectation, he embarrasses his father more deeply. Finally, Williams orders him to carry his own bags and marches him home to what will surely be his comeuppance.

The sketch was not one of Williams' best, but Cantor never forgot the lessons in comedy that he learned by working with him. In his 1928 autobiography, *My Life Is in Your Hands*, Cantor wrote:

> my association with him was a joy and an education, for Bert Williams was not only a great actor, but a great and liberal teacher. . . . He had a unique way of rendering songs, injecting his talk between rests and catching up with the melodic phrase after he had let it get a head start. His knack for rhythmic timing was inher-ent and has never been excelled.

And Cantor remembered Williams' physical comedy: "[H]e was a miser with gestures, never raising a hand six inches if three would suffice."

The only evidence left of Bert Williams' mastery of pantomime is "A Natural Born Gambler," a silent short from 1916, the only one of his handful of films to survive. The film incorporated his poker sketch within a slender story, and Williams showed himself to be much subtler than other film comedians of the period. While the Keystone Cops, Fatty Arbuckle, and even Chaplin registered emotion by jumping, gaping, and popping their eyes, Williams' most eloquent gesture is a shrug.

In the late teens, Bert Williams took steps toward getting out of his gilded rut. In 1918 he chose not to appear in the *Follies*, but to go into Ziegfeld's *Midnight Frolic*, a supper club show on the New Amsterdam roof. Ziegfeld had begun his *Frolic* in 1915 as an adjunct to his *Follies*, a place to break in new talent and to see old *Follies* favorites in a more intimate setting. The glamour quotient was still quite high, but the shows were smaller and the pace was more relaxed. Williams shone there. His material was of the usual type—a few songs and stories—but it was Bert Williams pure and up close. The New York *Evening Journal* reported that he stopped the show, receiving a "storm of applause, which sounded like a barrage and drumfire" and which lasted a full five minutes.

Soon after his *Frolic* debut in April, Williams got in touch with his black audience again by appearing at a benefit for the "Colored Men's Branch" of the YMCA, given at the Alhambra Theatre in Harlem. After his solo turn, he was greeted by an outpouring of love that moved him greatly. His neighbors wanted him to know how much they admired his talent and that they knew what he represented. Willie the Lion Smith said he "had that same kind of class that Duke Ellington possesses."

Williams became a naturalized citizen of the United States in June 1918. He went into the next *Midnight Frolic* the following December, and he played a week at the Palace during the *Frolic*'s run, prouder of his work than he had been in a long time.

Considering the satisfaction that he was finding in other venues, we may wonder what enticed Bert Williams back for the 1919 *Follies*.

Part of the answer must have been that Irving Berlin had been commissioned to write the score. Berlin had recently returned from his service in the army—and from his wildly successful army show, *Yip! Yip! Yaphank*. He was thirty-one years old and at the top of his game. He had already written three successful Broadway scores, and there had not been a year without several Berlin hits since 1911, when his "Alexander's Ragtime Band" had become an instant standard. He and lyricist Vincent Bryan had supplied Williams' big number in the 1911 *Follies*, "Woodman, Spare That Tree," and Williams must have looked forward to Tin Pan Alley's preeminent songsmith writing for him again. After a short rest at an Indiana spa, he began rehearsals for the June 16 opening.

Although there were interpolations by more than thirty other composers and lyricists, the 1919 edition is remembered as the "Berlin *Follies*." Among his fourteen songs were the classic beauty-parade number, "A Pretty Girl Is Like a Melody," and an Eddie Cantor hit, "You'd Be Surprised." But his Bert Williams specialty, a Prohibition song called "You Cannot Make Your Shimmy Shake on Tea," written with a Ziegfeld staffer, Rennold Wolf, was only a mild success. Williams' other songs and sketch material were no better. The centerpiece of the 1919 *Follies* was a ten-minute "minstrel show," a bizarre exercise in nostalgia that reportedly cost $35,000 to design and costume. The segment featured a hundred Ziegfeld girls, Bert Williams and Eddie Cantor as end men, and a chorus of forty-five "Follies Pickaninnies" dancing the shimmy. Van and Schenk sang "Mandy," and Marilyn Miller, in a clinging pants suit and pink satin top hat, did an imitation of George Primrose. With twenty years of New York triumphs behind him, Bert Williams was back on Broadway, in the world's glitziest minstrel show.

Eight weeks into its run, the *Follies of 1919* was closed by an actors' strike. There had been strike talk along Broadway all summer. Actors Equity Association, the six-year-old actors' union, at last had the membership numbers (nearly 6,000), the star power (Ethel Barrymore, Florence Reed, Ed Wynn, Marie Dressler, and Douglas Fairbanks, among many others), the American Federation of Labor's charter, and the public support to demand that producers address their grievances. Equity wanted what actors had wanted for generations:

standard contracts, fair hiring and firing practices, rehearsal pay, reimbursement for costumes and for transportation to out-of-town jobs.

Beginning on August 6, Broadway shows went dark one by one, and Ziegfeld's glittering jewel at the New Amsterdam took on enormous symbolic significance to the union. If Equity could shut down the mighty *Follies*, producers everywhere would realize the actors' strength and determination. Eddie Cantor was Equity's firebrand in the *Follies*. He made evangelistic appearances at AEA fundraisers, and he incessantly talked up the union to the chorus performers in the show. On Wednesday, August 13, Cantor stood on Forty-first Street, at the rear of the New Amsterdam and across the street from its stage door. As cast members arrived for work, Cantor called to each one to join him in a strike. By 8:00 P.M. he had them all. In a pouring rain, they ran jubilantly to AEA headquarters to announce that the *Follies* had fallen. The audience, who had been filing into the New Amsterdam's Forty-second Street entrance, was unaware that the company they had paid to see had fled the theatre. After stalling for a while, the New Amsterdam's house staff accepted the situation—there would be no show. By 9:00 P.M. nearly 2,000 refunds had been given, and the audience had been sent away.

The only *Follies* actor who didn't get the word was Bert Williams. Since his first entrance was nearly an hour into the show, his habit was to arrive at the New Amsterdam shortly after 9:00 P.M. As usual, he entered by the stage door and went directly to his dressing room to get into his blackface and costume. After dressing, he walked out to find an empty house. When a stagehand told him what had happened, he cleaned up and went home. Williams was not an Equity member, and he may or may not have joined Cantor in his crusade, but the company's forgetting him was a hurtful reminder that after eight years of working for Ziegfeld, he was still an outsider.

Over the course of the month-long AEA strike, all of Broadway was shut down, as well as the sixty shows that were in rehearsal in New York. Facing a combined loss of an estimated $500,000 a week, the producers were forced to deal with Equity. The union's gains were relatively small—chorus contracts for Broadway shows, half pay after four weeks of unpaid rehearsals, extra pay for extra performances—but Equity had won its most important point: the right to bargain for the actor. The strike had wrecked Broadway's summer season, but the fall season could go on. The *Follies* reopened on September 10 and ran through December 6. Bert Williams finished the run and the subsequent tour, but he would never work in a *Follies* again.

During 1919 and 1920, Bert Williams concentrated on recording as he never had before. Columbia issued twenty-two Williams sides, a quarter of his total output, in these two years. His taste in choosing songs was as good as ever, and these late recordings are very funny. Among the best are "Eve Cost Adam Just One Bone," "I Want to Know Where Tosti Went (When He Said Goodbye)," and "I'm Gonna Quit Saturday." He also recorded two monologues, called the "Elder Eatmore Sermons," written by Alex Rogers. W. C. Handy claimed that one of these was so hilarious that it cured the pain in his eyes. Prohibition was on everyone's mind in 1919, and it became Williams' favorite subject for song: "Everybody Wants a Key to My Cellar," "The Moon Shines on the Moonshine," "Ten Little Bottles," "Save a Little Dram for Me."

In 1920 Williams signed up for a revue to be produced by Rufus LeMaire. The show would feature the producer's brother, George LeMaire, who had worked with Williams in supporting roles in the *Follies*. Eddie Cantor, who was still on the outs with Ziegfeld for his leading the 1919 strike, also enrolled for the *Broadway Brevities of 1920*. The *Brevities* had its tryout in Philadelphia, then moved to New York's Winter Garden, a Shubert house at Broadway and Fiftieth Street. Despite songs by George Gershwin, Irving Berlin, and Harry Ruby, critics disliked the music nearly as much as they disliked the weak and vulgar sketch material. Nor was George LeMaire an asset. He was not in the Williams-Cantor league as a singer or a comic, yet he got as much stage time as they. (He would have a long career as a costume designer.) The show managed 105 performances, but it did not tour, nor did it spawn the succeeding editions implied by the date in its title. *Broadway Brevities* was merely another in the string of expensive revues in which Bert Williams had too little to do.

He had to break with revue. After seeing Charles Gilpin's triumph in O'Neill's *The Emperor Jones*, Williams began to dream of doing a dramatic role, possibly in London. He made a half-serious search for a script, but he chose instead to play the lead in a book musical, his first since *Mr. Lode of Koal*.

In the summer of 1921, the producer A. H. Woods signed Bert Williams for a new show called *Under the Bamboo Tree*. The project had the backing of the Shuberts, and the Shuberts' house composer, Sigmund Romberg, was assigned to write the score. Williams was to lead an all-white cast, with support from a husband-and-wife dance team, Sammy White and Eva Puck. The slight plot concerned a porter (Williams) and the guests at a resort hotel searching for buried treasure.

Under the Bamboo Tree had built-in problems. Sigmund Romberg was an expedient rather than a thoughtful choice to do the score. He had worked for the Shuberts since 1914. He had contributed songs of all kinds to their revues and shows, but since the success of *Maytime* in 1917, he had been writing in the operetta style that he would stay with through the 1920s. The book and lyrics were assigned to a novice named Walter DeLeon. They were an unlikely pair to write "Bert Williams numbers."

The rehearsal period was rough. Williams worked himself to exhaustion trying to make theatrical gold from the straw of his material. And his health was bad—shortness of breath, stomach aches, and fatigue plagued him throughout his long work days. But Williams had a credo that kept him going. He thought that a star was the person the audience paid to see, the one without whom there would be no show. By that definition, he had not been the star of the *Follies* and the *Frolics*. Those shows could and did go on without him. He knew that, as the star of *Under the Bamboo Tree*, he had his obligations.

The Shuberts canceled a Philadelphia tryout, realizing that the show needed much more work. Will Vodery was brought in to beef up the Romberg score. And there were scattered firings of mid-level staff, a sign of a show in trouble. *Bamboo Tree* finally had its first performance, in Cincinnati, on December 4, 1921. Local critics were generally kind, but word of mouth was not good. The show lost money during its two weeks in Cincinnati. Smelling disaster, the Shuberts began to withhold writer royalties.

Bamboo Tree moved on to Chicago, where it was booked for a twelve-week run. Williams caught a cold that turned into pneumonia, but he slogged on, never missing a performance. Except for his time on stage, he remained in bed. The Chicago critics praised Williams, but business was never better than break-even. Next stop, Detroit.

The Detroit reviews were the best so far, especially positive about the dancing and about Williams' performance. On Monday, February 27, Williams collapsed backstage after his first scene. The doctor who was called forbade him to continue the run. When the announcement was made that Williams could not perform but that an understudy would finish the show, the audience quietly filed out and asked for refunds. Bert Williams had lived up to his notion of a star.

He was taken back to New York by train the next day. Lottie met him at the station and took him home. He was diagnosed as having "degenerative myocarditis," a previously undetected heart condition. The pneumonia was hanging on, and he was weakening fast. A blood transfusion was needed, and Will Vodery volunteered as donor. For several days, Williams lay unconscious. On Saturday, March 4, 1922, he died at home, at age forty-seven.

He had three funerals. There were private rites for his family, a private Masonic funeral, and a public Masonic funeral. His body lay at home from Sunday until Tuesday, when it was taken for the public funeral to St. Phillip's Protestant Episcopal Church in Harlem. More than five thousand people came to say goodbye. Many of them, those who knew Bert Williams only from his stage appearances, saw the color of his face for the first time.

"TELL ME, DUSKY MAIDEN"

• •

The First Black Composers on Broadway

B Y THE MID-1890s, BROADWAY WAS THE last stage venue left for black composers and performers to conquer. There had been black minstrel troupes touring successfully since the black producer Charles Hicks organized his Georgia Minstrels in Indianapolis in 1865. Hicks was soon followed by another black showman, Lew Johnson, who sent out a minstrel company from St. Louis, and, for the remainder of the minstrel era, there had been about half as many black troupes as white ones. There were black vaudeville stars, a few of whom were winning the attention of white audiences by the early 1890s. Blacks were less visible on the concert stage, but they had been there since the 1850s, performing the classical repertoire (since Elizabeth Greenfield in 1851) and concert versions of spirituals and slave songs (since the Fisk Jubilee Singers in 1871). In the mid-1870s two sisters from Sacramento, California—Anna Madah and Emma Louise Hyers— gave up their careers as concert singers to form a touring musical company. The Hyers Sisters shows were extravagant musical melodramas, presenting stories of the black experience from Africa (*Urlina, the African Princess*) to America (*Out of Bondage*).

In 1888 Sissieretta Jones (1869–1933), a black singer from Portsmouth, Virginia, made her first concert appearance. Critics and audiences couldn't find enough superlatives to describe her glorious voice. They could only compare her to the most famous singer of the day, the Italian prima donna, Adelina Patti. So Sissieretta Jones became known as "The Black Patti," and she toured four continents in the first five years of her career. In 1896, on the advice of her managers, she formed the Black Patti Troubadours, a touring company that offered everything from art songs to minstrel numbers to short musical plays. The Troubadours were frequent visitors to New York, playing major vaudeville houses for white and black audiences, but Broadway remained just out of their reach. (However, Black Patti would hire— and train—many of the black talents who would make the leap to "legitimate" theatre.)

The New York musical theatre that so tantalized the young black stage folk of the mid-nineties was a frivolous affair. It still reflected its haphazard origins of 1866, when a French ballet troupe was thrown into a potboiler melodrama called The Black Crook and "musical comedy" was born. The sight of girls in tights leaping about in a papier-mâché Hades had stood New York on its ear, and the vogue for expensive nonsense set to music had continued unabated. There had since been a few productions that stressed content over scenery— notably the rough-and-tumble Harrigan and Hart shows of the 1880s—but thirty years after The Black Crook, Broadway musical fare had the appeal, and the nourishment, of bonbons.

Broadway had long been smitten with operetta, and by the mid-nineties hacks of all nations had gathered in New York to write and produce it. The American stage was swathed in froufrou, musically and scenically, and the task of sweeping it away would take many years. But because musical shows were so expensive to produce, with the most expensive tickets and stars, they represented "class" to composers, black and white. To have written a score for—or even to have an interpolated song in—a flop New York show was prestigious in a way that Tin Pan Alley or vaudeville success was not. Broadway was a glittering prize, and shortly before the turn of the century, a few black writers dared to dream of attaining it.

WILL MARION COOK

The black composer who got there first was Will Marion Cook, a man who by training and temperament probably should never have been involved in the collaborative hurly-burly of theatre at all. Having been stymied in his hopes for a career as a concert violinist, Cook came to musical theatre by default. He was almost thirty years old before he paid any attention to popular song or had any desire to write a show. When he began writing for the theatre, he was without experience in any phase of show business. He had aimed himself like a bullet at the concert stage.

Will Marion Cook

He made his start in 1898, just as the coon song craze was approaching its height. Thus he was given philosophical questions to deal with that he had never dreamed of: questions about how to be true to himself, his talent, and his race in a buyer's market for cartoons. His theatrical contemporaries were wrestling with the same questions, of course, and Cook took them all to task for their answers. He became almost as well-known for his disagreeable nature as for his music. Perhaps this was because the profession itself disagreed with him.

William Mercer Cook was born on January 27, 1869, in Washington, D.C., the second of the three sons of John and Isabel Cook. Both of his parents were graduates of Oberlin College in Ohio, and his father graduated in the first class of the law school at Howard University. John Cook practiced law in Washington and also taught at Howard, so the Cook family led a serene, secure life in their home at Sixteenth and M streets. Their peace was shattered in 1878, however, when John Cook died at age forty of tuberculosis. Isabel Cook tried to manage alone for a while, but by 1881 it had become necessary to send her sons to live with various relatives.

Young Will went to live with his grandfather in Chattanooga, Tennessee. The old man was an accomplished violinist, and his grandson was fascinated by the instrument. Will took up the violin and practiced constantly. In 1884 it was decided that he should be sent to live with an aunt in Oberlin with the hope that he could enroll in the music department of the college. By 1886 he was at Oberlin College studying privately with Professor Amos Doolittle, who was amazed at his progress. After two years of intensive coaching, Doolittle was sure that Cook should develop his talent further. He sent him back to his mother in Washington with a letter recommending that Will study abroad. Isabel Cook had no idea of how to finance the trip until Frederick Douglass, a family friend, organized a benefit to raise Will's traveling expenses at Washington's First Congregational Church, where Will demonstrated his ability by playing classical selections. Nearly $2,000 was raised, and in the fall of 1888, young Will left for Germany. He would be away for two years, studying harmony, counterpoint, and piano with Josef Joachim at the Hochschule für Musik in Berlin.

When Will returned to Washington in late 1890, Douglass came to his aid again. To make use of his young friend's training, he organized an orchestra, and he appointed Cook as conductor. The orchestra made two short tours of the mid-Atlantic states before it disbanded, and Cook—now using the name "Will Marion Cook"—was hooked for life on the feeling of power he had with a large musical ensemble under his command.

In January 1893 the Cleveland *Gazette* announced that Cook, thanks to a third intercession by Douglass, would be in charge of the music for "Colored Folks' Day," August 25, at the Chicago World's Fair. Cook planned a grand premiere for the occasion, a performance of an opera that he had written based on *Uncle Tom's Cabin*. The cast would include "only members of the race," and the leading soprano would be Sissieretta Jones. Rumor had it that the story would be updated to protest a lynching that had taken place in Paris, Texas, a year earlier. Fair officials became uneasy at the prospect of such a controversial event as "Colored Folks' Day" neared, and plans for Cook's opera were scrapped. (None of this score has ever been found.)

On August 25 at the fairgrounds, there was a powerful oration by Frederick Douglass, and Paul Laurence Dunbar (1872–1906), a young poet from Dayton, Ohio, read a new poem called "Colored Americans." The orator's grandson, John Douglass, played the violin, and there were classical selections by various small ensembles. The hit of the musical portion of the program was the Boston tenor, Sidney Woodward, who received five encores for his Verdi arias. But there was no opera by Cook and no mention of why it did not go on as promised.

Cook was elsewhere in Chicago, playing the violin with a group of black classical singers at Bethel Church. At an afternoon concert with this group he met a young baritone, Harry T. Burleigh (1866–1949), from Erie, Pennsylvania. Burleigh, three years older than Cook, seemed well on his way to a concert career. He had been admitted to New York Conservatory on a scholarship a year before, and he thought the Conservatory would be just the place for Cook. Among Burleigh's teachers was the Czech composer (and director of the school) Antonin Dvorak. Dvorak was fascinated by spirituals, and Burleigh had ingratiated himself by sharing his knowledge of them. The maestro thought that "Negro airs" could be the basis for an American school of composition, and, to show the way, he had recently written the symphony that became known as "From the New World." Burleigh had been helping copy the parts for its premiere, which was set for December 16, 1893. He wrote a letter of introduction for Cook to Dvorak, recommending them to each other.

Cook arrived in New York in early 1894, and he began to study with—and to detest—Dvorak almost immediately. He felt that Burleigh was the teacher's pet, and he resented the attention Dvorak lavished on the singer. Cook refused to play in the Conservatory orchestra under Dvorak's direction. His studies in harmony with Professor John White were all that kept Cook at New York Conservatory for the next year or so.

Cook was briefly a member of Bob Cole's All-Star Stock Company at Worth's Museum in 1894, as composer-in-residence, but he felt Cole was as insufferable as Dvorak. Cole saw the company as a school for black theatre and envisioned himself as the teacher. Unlike Cook, Cole had little formal education, and his theatrical knowledge came from his experience in various minstrel and vaudeville companies. Cook mocked Cole's Southern accent and belittled his show-business pragmatism. He quit the company, passing up his best chance to learn something of the profession he was about to enter.

There are varying stories about what occurred in the mid-nineties to turn Will Marion Cook from classical music to theatre. The stories give different settings for the incident (a Carnegie Hall recital, a Boston Symphony audition), but they make the same point. In some professional situation, Cook had played well and had been pronounced (by a critic or by an auditor) "the world's greatest colored violinist." Cook supposedly smashed his instrument in rage and screamed, "I am not the world's greatest colored violinist! I am the greatest violinist in the world!" And he vowed never to play again. At nearly thirty years old, Cook went back to Washington to live with his mother.

Cook still made occasional trips to New York, however, and it was during one of these, in late 1896 or early 1897, that he became acquainted with Bert Williams and George Walker. Their star was in the ascendant, and the fact that they discerned talent in Cook was very flattering to him. He pitched an idea to them, a show about the beginnings of the cakewalk, their specialty dance, set in Louisiana in the 1880s. The team encouraged him to write it and may have led him to believe that they would perform in it. Cook was fired by the possibilities, and he hurried back to Washington to work on a musical play about the cakewalk.

Cook chose as his collaborator Paul Laurence Dunbar. The twenty-six-year-old poet had already had three collections published, and he had flirted with the idea of writing for the theatre. (He had told an interviewer of a possible collaboration with the Indiana poet James Whitcomb Riley.) William Dean Howells was the first to praise his work, and the literary establishment had followed suit. Dunbar was popular with the public, too, especially for his dialect verse. He was already being spoken of as "the Negro poet laureate." For all the acclaim, his poetry was not making him rich, however, and he was working at a clerical job at the Library of Congress. Cook summoned Dunbar to a borrowed room—without a piano—in the basement of a house near Howard University and quickly outlined the story he wanted. Fortified by beer, whiskey, and raw beefsteak, they wrote Clorindy overnight.

The next morning, Cook couldn't wait to play his score for his mother. In a 1944 memoir published by Theatre Arts in September 1947, he recalled her reaction. He had launched into what he called "my most Negroid song," which was "Who Dat Say Chicken in Dis Crowd?" Isabel Cook was crushed. She cried, "Oh, Will! Will! I've sent you all over the world to study and become a great musician, and you return such a nigger!"

His mother had hit a nerve. For the rest of his working life, Cook would think of himself as a champion of "Negroid" music and would believe that he was writing it and that no one else was. Cook's music would always be an uneasy mix of "low-class" materials used in what he thought was a "high-class" way. As fiercely proud as he was of his race, he was oblivious enough to the sensibilities of ordinary black folk—and to the music business of 1898—to confuse coon songs with black expression. He loudly decried the racial stereotypes in popular music, yet many of his early show songs are musically and lyrically indistinguishable from the songs of Irving Jones. And in his later show scores and choral works, he seldom let the innate dignity of real "race" materials—syncopated songs and spirituals—go unadorned. He draped them in the symphonic and operatic trappings of the concert stage. Size mattered to Cook. He liked large choruses, orchestras, and choirs. If he could combine several large ensembles, so much the better. He would spend his life trying to make "art" of something already artful in ways that he did not quite trust.

Undaunted by his mother's remark, Cook went to New York in early June 1898 to find a publisher for his score. He could not have known how unlikely it was that a publisher would be interested in songs from an unproduced show by an unknown composer, but he managed to get an appointment with Isidore Witmark. He went to the Witmark offices prepared to demonstrate his songs. Mindful of his company's success with Ernest Hogan's "All Coons Look Alike to Me," the publisher expressed interest in the *Clorindy* songs. According to Isidore Witmark's autobiography, Cook seized on this and offered to give away all publication rights and to forego royalties if Witmark would help him get a production of the show. Witmark said that he would do his best, but that he would not require Cook to give up his royalties to publish the songs.

Cook heard that E. E. Rice, the manager of the Casino Theatre Roof Garden, was looking for short musical shows to feature in a series of late-evening entertainments, to be called "Rice's Summer Nights."

Merely on the basis of this rumor, Cook sprang into action, casting and rehearsing chorus parts before any contact had ever been made with Rice. Williams and Walker were unavailable (they were touring in vaudeville), but Ernest Hogan heard Cook playing the *Clorindy* songs in a restaurant one day and liked them enough to volunteer himself as lead comic for the show. Cook worked furiously, rehearsing his unpaid actors wherever and whenever he could get a few of them together, and spending every spare hour trying to see Ed Rice. After days of being put off by Rice, Cook finally saw him. Rice promised a tryout for *Clorindy* on Monday morning, June 28. If the show passed muster, it would go on that evening.

The twenty-six member company, plus Hogan and Cook, arrived at the Casino Theatre before Rice did. The Casino's conductor, John Braham, welcomed Cook and began to pass out his orchestra parts. Cook stopped him, saying that his singers could follow only his own direction, and mounted the podium to conduct the score. As the company began to sing, Ed Rice stormed in. He shouted to Braham, "No nigger can conduct my orchestra on Broadway!" Braham shouted back, "Go back to your little cubby-hole and keep quiet! That boy's a genius and has something great!" Braham saved Cook's audition. After hearing the score, Rice grudgingly agreed to let the *Clorindy* company go on that night.

But it rained that Monday evening. The open-air Roof Garden was soaked, and the opening was postponed for a week. The following Monday, July 5, 1898, *Clorindy, or The Origin of the Cakewalk* had its premiere, with Cook conducting. The show went on at about 11:45, playing to an audience of fifty or so, which grew as the *Clorindy* music drifted down to the people leaving the Casino's show downstairs. The departing theatregoers changed their minds and hurried up to hear the music and singing on the roof. By the end of the

Clorindy

opening number, the Roof Garden was packed and the ovation was so deafening that Cook froze, unable to continue. Hogan ran to the footlights to urge him on: "What's the matter, son? Let's go!" Cook struck up Hogan's first number, "Hottest Coon in Dixie," and the show took off like a rocket. The syncopated numbers poured out—"Jump Back, Honey, Jump Back," "Who Dat Say Chicken in Dis Crowd?"—building to the roaring cakewalk finale, "Darktown Is Out Tonight." The Roof Garden exploded with cheering. In about an hour—including the time given to encores—*Clorindy* had made history. The first black show in a Broadway theatre was an indisputable success. Cook remembered that he drank water at the opening-night party, thought it was wine, and got "gloriously drunk."

Clorindy's appeal to its audiences lay in its size and speed. New York audiences had heard syncopation before, had heard coon songs interpolated into Broadway shows, had seen the cakewalk. But never had they heard the full force of a Broadway orchestra playing an entire score of syncopated music. Nor had they experienced syncopated singing done by a twenty-six-member ensemble while they did the cakewalk. (Up until this time, Broadway choruses had kept to a strict division of labor: the singing chorus sang, and the dancing chorus danced.) And Ernest Hogan had put some zip into Dunbar's book. During the extra week of rehearsal that the rainstorm bought for *Clorindy*, Hogan had whittled away at Dunbar's story, keeping only a few lines as song cues and remnants of a plot. Dunbar, who brought his bride of four months to the opening night of *Clorindy*, was mortified. He felt that his libretto had been ransacked to make a coon show. And his dialect verses—which had looked quaint and "characteristic" on the printed page—seemed monstrous when declaimed into the open air over Broadway.

Clorindy was extended through the summer at the Casino, and plans were made for a fall tour. Williams and Walker decided to incorporate *Clorindy*, which was mostly songs anyway, into their touring vaudeville musical, *Senegambian Carnival*. The tour brought Will Marion Cook even greater renown, and it also brought him the company of a girl named Abbie Mitchell (1884–1960). She was a student of Harry Burleigh's and had auditioned for the first production of *Clorindy*, but, at fourteen, she had been considered too young. Cook

Abbie Mitchell Cook

remembered her, though, and when a leading role became available during the *Senegambian Carnival* tour, he sent for her. It is not known exactly when they were married, but by 1900 she was being billed as "Abbie Mitchell Cook." (They would divorce after several years, but would continue to work together well into the 1920s.)

Whether Isidore Witmark did anything to help get *Clorindy* produced, he did keep his bargain to publish seven of the *Clorindy* songs. On these song sheets, and on several other early publications, Cook's last name is omitted and composer credit is given to "Will Marion."

In January 1899 Cook received his first semiannual accounting for royalty payments on the *Clorindy* songs, and he was very displeased. He flew into the Witmark offices with a lawyer in tow, demanding to know why his music had not produced more money. Witmark explained to Cook that a demand for songs often took time to build and that future royalty statements would be better. He also reminded Cook that he had offered to give his songs away and that Witmark had refused to let him. Cook's lawyer was satisfied, but Cook was not. Finally Witmark became exasperated with Cook and told him that, no matter how well the *Clorindy* songs sold, Cook would never publish another number with the Witmark firm. And he never did.

Within a few months of alienating his publisher, Cook also alienated his collaborator. Trying to repeat *Clorindy*'s success, Cook and Dunbar set to work on another musical sketch. The result, called *Jes' Lak White Folks*, played briefly at the New York Theatre's roof garden. Although not as good as *Clorindy*, nor as successful, it would be produced several times over the next year or so. The show marked the end of the Cook-Dunbar partnership. Dunbar had recently published his first novel and his first short-story collection, and his literary future looked bright. The introverted, self-doubting poet hated theatre writing and saw no need to do any more of it. He went to Colorado for a long rest in the fall of 1899, vowing never to work with Cook again. The Cook-Dunbar songs that turned up in later shows were trunk songs or reworkings of material from *Jes' Lak White Folks*. When James Weldon Johnson interceded to persuade Dunbar to write with Cook in 1900, Dunbar said, "No, I won't do it. I just can't work with Cook; he irritates me beyond endurance." The first biography of Dunbar, written shortly after his death in 1906, makes no mention of Cook or of Dunbar's theatre lyrics.

Will Marion Cook, with various collaborators, wrote two vaudeville musicals for Ernest Hogan in 1901. The first, called *Uncle Eph's Christmas*, was produced in Boston in January. The second, *The Cannibal King*, had a short run in a New York variety house. Cook had the idea in late 1901 of overhauling the second Hogan show as a vehicle for Williams and Walker's first Broadway venture. *The Cannibal King*, after much revision of score and less revision of story, became *In Dahomey*, the first full-length musical written and performed by blacks in a first-class house in New York.

In Dahomey opened on February 18, 1903, at the New York Theatre, in the heart of the Broadway district. Cook was in great evidence on opening night, conducting the orchestra with his customary brio. (Will Accooe had conducted during the tryout tour.) The show was highly praised, consolidating the leading comedians' success as well as Cook's. *In Dahomey* set the pattern for Cook's contributions to the Williams and Walker shows to come. His songs were not the published hits nor the crowd-pleasers. In fact, the Williams and Walker show publications rarely included Cook's material. Their hits came from interpolated songs, often with melodies by Bert Williams himself. Cook was a sort of composer-in-chief, responsible mostly for ensemble numbers, opening choruses, and finalettos. In the credits Cook's name led all the rest, but Cook's music was actually the operetta glue that held the vaudeville together.

When *In Dahomey* went to London in the late spring of 1903, Cook and Abbie Mitchell were both in the traveling company, he as conductor and she as a featured singer. Cook's music got the reviews that he wanted in London—"music of the highest class" and orchestrations "full of vivid colour." But his conducting style was disconcerting to some who disliked his facing the audience to conduct the overture and his incessant humming and singing along with the orchestra. Cook added a choral curtain-raiser to the score for the London run, a song called "Swing Along" (with lyrics by himself), which would become one of his most popular works. He and his wife left the show before the tour of Great Britain was over, returning to the United States in August.

Cook's next show was the third of his three Broadway "firsts." He wrote the score for a musical play called *The Southerners*, which opened at the New York Theatre on May 23, 1904. The play was set on a plantation in the 1830s, and it featured a large chorus of black singers as well as a large chorus of whites. Although one of the leads was played by the white minstrel Eddie Leonard in blackface, *The Southerners* was the first truly integrated musical on Broadway. Despite the uneasiness of audiences and management about race mixing on so large a scale, there was no trouble among the cast. *The Southerners* ran for thirty-six performances and had a short tour.

In early 1905, Cook enlisted as music director for an elaborate vaudeville act built around a "singing orchestra" being assembled by Ernest Hogan. The group was called the Memphis Students, and it featured Abbie Mitchell as costar with Hogan. A twenty-five member company sang old and new Cook music, including a long medley that Cook had arranged called "Songs of Black Folk." The Memphis Students had a successful tryout at Proctor's Twenty-third Street Theatre, then moved into Hammerstein's Victoria for an extended run.

Hogan had to leave the company for a while because his new show, *Rufus Rastus*, was in preparation, but he wanted to keep the Memphis Students going. He named a young comedian, Bobby Kemp, as his replacement and turned his attention to other matters. Cook wanted to take the Memphis Students to Europe and began making plans to do so. Hogan tried to stop the tour by issuing an injunction against Abbie Mitchell to bar her from singing in any company other than Hogan's. Somehow Cook wrested—or bought—control of the group from Hogan, and the tour went forward. The black press took Hogan's side in the dispute, some writers even suggesting that Cook was kidnapping the Students to take them abroad. Cook renamed the group the Tennessee Students, in case Europeans didn't know where Memphis was, and in November 1905 a group of sixteen Students—including Abbie Mitchell, Bobby Kemp, and Will Dixon—opened at the Palace Theatre in London. After a successful run there, they played at the Olympia Theatre in Paris and at the Schumann Circus in Berlin.

The Tennessee Students were a multi-talented group. Their drummer, Buddy Gilmore, juggled his sticks as he played, and Will Dixon did a specialty turn as a "dancing conductor." Instrumentalists often dropped out of their section playing to sing in four-part barbershop harmony. But the real novelty was the orchestration itself. The traditional violin section, which had been the heart of Cook's show orchestras, was replaced by mandolins, guitars, and banjos. There was also a saxophone, one of the first used in nonsymphonic music.

Cook had discovered folk instruments in a big way. He would add their colors to his arranger's palette, to be used in orchestra-sized sections, and he would add folk music to his list of styles to be "legitimized" on the concert stage. The melange of musical expression represented by the Tennessee Students was pure Cook—big arrangements of simple songs, a flash of Tin Pan Alley syncopation, and the symphonic mantle of "art" to cloak it all.

Williams and Walker's second Broadway show was *Abyssinia*, which opened in New York in February 1906. Cook's songs were again overshadowed by interpolations ("Nobody" and "Let It Alone"). After *Abyssinia*'s New York run, Cook went to Chicago to work on a Pekin Theatre score, for *The Man from Georgia*, with Joe Jordan. The Pekin's next production, in early 1907, was *In Zululand*, and it featured one of Cook's most successful songs, "Wid de Moon, Moon, Moon" (lyrics by William Moore).

In 1908, for *Bandanna Land*, Cook finally wrote three songs for a Williams and Walker show that could hold their own with the stars' interpolations. One of these was "Bon Bon Buddy" (lyric by Alex Rogers), written for George Walker, who made it Cook's most successful pop tune from this period. The two other outstanding Cook songs, used as ensemble numbers in the show, were "Rain Song" and "Exhortation—a Negro Sermon" (both with lyrics by Rogers).

Cook soon had another short-lived hit with "Lovie Joe" (lyrics by Cook, music by Joe Jordan), written for Fanny Brice's debut in the *Follies of 1910*. Marie Cahill sang Cook's "Whoop 'Er Up" (lyrics by

Andrew Sterling) in *Judy Forgot*, also in 1910. (She had interpolated a
song by Cook and Cecil Mack called "The Little Gypsy Maid" in *The
Wild Rose* in 1902. Mack rewrote the lyric as "Brownskin Baby Mine"
for *In Dahomey*.) In 1911, nearly twenty years after their aborted opera
at the World's Fair, Cook (with lyricist Alex Rogers) finally wrote a
show for Black Patti. It was called *In the Jungles*, and her Troubadours
company toured it successfully to Chicago, Cincinnati, and Louisville.

The watershed year for Will Marion Cook was 1912. A historic
concert and a set of songs published that year would let the world see
him as he saw himself—as the composer who made art music out of
"characteristic" race materials. The concert was presented at Carnegie
Hall by James Reese Europe's Clef Club Orchestra on May 2. Cook was
not a Clef Club member, and he had, in fact, denounced Europe's goals
and his direction of the organization. (Although Europe and Cook had
similar ideas about music, Europe's showmanship and his association
with dance orchestras seemed undignified to Cook.) But by 1912, any
organization that purported to present the music of leading black composers could not omit Cook's work.

In a remarkable feat of diplomacy, Europe not only secured the
rights to perform two of Cook's numbers, he persuaded Cook to play
violin on the program. Cook had sworn off playing years ago, but he
agreed to sit anonymously in the violin section. Cook's two songs, performed by a huge choir and Europe's 125-member orchestra, were
"Rain Song" and "Swing Along." The audience response to them was
overwhelming. The cheering went on and on, culminating in calls for
the composer. Europe walked over to the violin section and acknowledged Cook. Cook arose, unable to speak, weeping with joy (see
Chapter 5 for more on James Reese Europe).

The publication that confirmed Cook's preeminence in "Negro art
song" was "Three Negro Songs," issued by G. Schirmer in 1912. "Rain
Song" and "Swing Along" were published in this set, and they were
taken up by choruses everywhere, as was, to a lesser extent, the third
song, "Exhortation." In these pieces, more than any others, Cook hit
his mark. They are infectious secular songs with a spiritual feel—the
simplest and least affected of his work. They lift the heart as they set
the feet tapping. They remain in the choral repertoire to this day, their
origins as show songs long forgotten.

He was not a tall man, but Cook cut an imposing figure in those days. He cultivated the look of an artist, with his severe black clothing and his lion's mane of steel-gray hair. Eubie Blake recalled that "he never wore a hat because he was proud of his bushy hair. That was all that gave him away so you could know he was a Negro. Most eccentric man I ever met. . . . I believe he was the reincarnation of Richard Wagner—looked like him too. Very proud!"

Still under forty-five years old, Cook was the grand old man of black music in all its "legitimate" forms. He was surely unaware that the first generation of ragtime composers had attained his ideals more completely than he had. (They had used folk materials in a new and entirely sophisticated way, had created new forms, and had inspired new kinds of writing as Cook never did.) And with his lifetime list of about forty published songs, Cook was out-published by almost all of his contemporaries, including the actors Bert Williams and Irving Jones. But nobody was doing precisely what Cook was doing, and in the teens his work seemed very important. In 1913 he was named one of "100 Distinguished Freedmen" at the National Emancipation Exposition in New York City.

He would never repeat the successes of his Williams and Walker shows, but he continued to compose for the theatre. Cook wrote the score for the Negro Players show, *The Traitor*, which had a brief run at Harlem's Lafayette Theatre in March 1913, and reworked *The Cannibal King* in 1914.

There had been no black show on Broadway since S. H. Dudley's *His Honor the Barber*, which opened at the Majestic in May 1911, so in 1915 producer Lester Walton assembled a top-notch black team to try to put one there. Cook shared composer credit with James Reese

His Honor the Barber

Europe; Henry Troy wrote the book; Henry Creamer, the lyrics; and
Jesse Shipp was hired as director. It was to be the first starring vehicle
for a new comedy team, Flournoy Miller and Aubrey Lyles. Abbie
Mitchell and the dancer Ida Forsyne were given large featured roles.
The show was to try out at the Howard Theatre in Washington, then
to take first-class bookings on the road, if they could be secured, and
finally to move to Broadway. Cook was to conduct the orchestra as well
as compose. No expense would be spared for sets and costumes.

The elephantine result was called *Darkeydom*, as offensive a title as
had been given a show in fifteen years. It was the last of the old-line black
musicals, and it was a flop. It was crammed with burlesque and vaudeville
turns that obliterated the sketchy plot. It was off-putting to black audiences and too leaden for whites. It played its week at the Howard in mid-
October 1915, then moved to the Lafayette, where it struggled a few
weeks before closing. And it was to be Will Marion Cook's last musical.
Among Cook's handful of published songs from the show was "Mammy,"
dedicated "To the Memory of My Teacher John White."

In late 1918 Cook formed an aggregation he called the New York
Syncopated Orchestra. His impetus was probably the success of the
Original Dixieland Jazz Band, the five-piece white group from New
Orleans taking the country by storm with their ramshackle syncopation. Although he had published only one syncopated instrumental
himself (a 1914 fox-trot called "Cruel Papa!"), Cook's response was to
assemble a thirty-six-piece orchestra and twenty-voice choir to show
them how jazz was *really* done. The NYSO's instrumentation was modeled on the Clef Club's: violins, mandolins, banjos, guitars, saxes, trum-
pets, trombones, bass horn, timpani, pianos, drums. The program was a
typical Cook mixture: several of Handy's blues, Cook's own choral
numbers, Nathaniel Dett's "Listen to the Lambs," and a medley of
Brahms waltzes. The choir did some a cappella spirituals as well as
singing with the orchestra. The NYSO toured the United States for
four months, only occasionally breaking even under its enormous travel expenses. In Chicago, Cook added to the payroll by recruiting
another player, the clarinetist Sidney Bechet.

Cook had never hired a nonreading musician before, and the fact
that he wanted Bechet indicates at least some curiosity about jazz on
Cook's part. Bechet was hired near the end of the tour, and he went

back to New York with the NYSO. Soon after returning to his home base, Cook saw a chance to recoup his losses on the road and to turn a profit with his group. He contracted with the London revue producer Andre Charlot to bring the NYSO to England for six months. To place his group nearer the supposed geographic roots of syncopation, Cook renamed them the Southern Syncopated Orchestra, and they set sail to make a June opening at Royal Philharmonic Hall.

However, the Original Dixieland Jazz Band got there ahead of them. Since April the ODJB had been doing turnaway business at London's Palladium, and they had been invited to play at the Victory Ball at the Savoy Hotel to celebrate the signing of the Treaty of Versailles. The SSO got good reviews—and Bechet got the first review ever given to a jazz soloist—but the ODJB had stolen their thunder. Cook had the ingredients for jazz but he chose not to make it. The SSO was treated as an enjoyable novelty, which is what it was. King George V asked to hear them—he had enjoyed the ODJB's command performance earlier—so on August 9, Cook took about fifteen of his players to Buckingham Palace, where Bechet scored heavily with his "Characteristic Blues."

Financial disputes arose among the SSO management, and Cook left England to return to the United States in the early fall. A reorganized SSO played two months at the Apollo Theatre in Paris, and a splinter group of vocalists, calling themselves the SSO Singers, performed in the United Kingdom into 1921. Several of the SSO members defected to various small European bands (such as Bechet) or formed their own (Benny Peyton). Cook's personnel scattered across the Continent, and only by its disintegration did the SSO further the cause of jazz in Europe.

Back in the United States Cook fronted a musical company sent out by the Clef Club. Dramatic readings and art songs were presented, as well as syncopated concert music, and the ensemble included Fletcher Henderson, the contralto Georgette Harvey, Paul Robeson, and the actor Richard B. Harrison. Cook was a conductor and choral arranger now, not forgotten as a theatre composer but not actively composing, either. In 1924, long after his most productive years as a writer were over, he joined ASCAP. (Harry Burleigh and James Weldon Johnson were charter members in 1914.)

In 1923 Cook conducted the *Runnin' Wild* orchestra during the show's tryout at the Howard Theatre. In 1924 he organized the Negro Folk Music and Drama Society and produced a concert series, called *Negro Nuances*, to feature the Society at the Lafayette Theatre. The following year his series was called *Virginia Nights*, and it had a brief run in Greenwich Village.

Young Duke Ellington sought out Cook for help with his compositions. After a typically lofty preface ("You know you should go to the conservatory, but since you won't, I'll tell you. . . .") Cook often complied. Ellington described his lessons with Cook as "one of the best semesters I ever had in music." In 1929, when he was coaching the chorus for Vincent Youmans' *Great Day*, Cook took notice of Harold Arlen, the pianist who had been hired to play for dance rehearsals. He encouraged Arlen to experiment with the vamps that he had been improvising to see if there was a song there; and so, Arlen's first hit, "Get Happy," was composed. Cook's real protégé was a young singer named Eva Jessye (1895–1992), who became the first black woman to conduct a professional chorus. In 1925 Cook encouraged her to form her first group, which she called the Original Dixie Jubilee Singers. The group was renamed the Eva Jessye Choir in 1926, when it embarked on its first tour. Jessye supplied singers for several 1930s films, and she served as choral director for Virgil Thomson's *Four Saints in Three Acts* and for George Gershwin's *Porgy and Bess*.

Cook wrote a folk opera, *Saint Louis 'Ooman*, in 1929 with his son Mercer Cook, a professor of Romance Languages at Howard University and a sometime songwriter. Their opera went unproduced, but Cook had one last hit song in the late twenties, with his lyrics for Donald Heywood's "I'm Coming Virginia." Leading a group called Will Marion Cook's Singing Orchestra, he accompanied Ethel Waters on her Columbia recording of the song in September 1926. The song had many recordings, vocal and instrumental; Bix Beiderbecke's May 1927 version, with the Frankie Trumbauer orchestra, is one of the landmarks of twenties jazz.

Will Marion Cook remained a presence in the music world during the 1930s, but, except by school and community choruses, he was more honored in memory than by performance. He died of cancer in New York City on July 19, 1944.

As the first generation of black Broadway veterans passed from the scene, the recollection of the times and the trials that shaped Cook's unique musical vision faded with them. The generation that jitter-bugged knew of Cook only as an old man whose music had somehow been important, a long time ago.

BOB COLE AND J. ROSAMOND JOHNSON

The most successful black musical theatre writers of the early century were the prolific Bob Cole and J. Rosamond Johnson. They delivered the goods—to producers, to publishers, to audiences, to actors—for ten years. Their songs were interpolated into nearly thirty Broadway shows, providing showstoppers for stars and hits for publication. In an age that expected charm in the theatre, they wrote to order. They moved faster and did more than their contemporaries because they carried less weight. Without the philosophical baggage of Cook, or the burden of stardom shouldered by Williams and Walker, they were freer to work, whenever and wherever occasions arose. Their commitment was to show business, not to ideology.

Bob Cole was—with the possible exception of George M. Cohan—the most versatile theatre talent of his day. He was an actor, a librettist, a lyricist, a director, a singer, a dancer, a producer, and a composer. He used all of his gifts when working on his own shows, but amazingly, he also could collaborate easily with others as an employee, wearing one hat at a time. His name is on nearly 120 song sheets as composer and/or lyricist, making him the most-published black writer of his era. Cole and his main partner, the composer J. Rosamond Johnson, were the only black writers of that time to have long-term relationships with a Broadway producer and with a major publisher. Each relationship fed the other: their theatre songs were likely to be published and their published songs were likely to be featured in shows. Cole and Johnson didn't make the rounds, nor did they wait in offices with librettos and lead sheets in hand. They were working pros; they were in demand.

Robert Allen Cole was born July 1, 1868, in Athens, Georgia. His father, Robert Cole, was a carpenter and a sometime local politician;

his mother, Isabella, was a housewife. His parents and sisters enjoyed music at home, and they often organized informal musicales, performing on the piano, banjo, and guitar for their friends. In his mid-teens, young Robert lived with relatives in Jacksonville, Florida, and when his family moved to Atlanta, he moved with them. He was at Atlanta University for a year or so—in the University's prep school, then at the University itself—but he left Atlanta sometime in the mid-1880s for the Northeast to begin a show business career. He formed a vaudeville duo with Lew Henry (later the manager of the S. H. Dudley shows), and by 1890 he was based in Chicago, where he joined the original *Creole Show* company. Another member of this company was the petite singer-dancer Stella Wiley, whom Cole later married.

The *Creole* company was a new organization, and Cole, hoping to make himself indispensable, grabbed off as many jobs as he could. He served the producer Sam T. Jack as singer, dancer, monologist, and stage manager (which meant "director" during this time). He was beginning to try songwriting as well, and in 1893 the Chicago publisher Will Rossiter issued his first two songs: "Parthenia Took a Fancy to a Coon" and "In Shin Bone Alley." Cole and Wiley toured as a song-and-dance duo intermittently during the early 1890s, but kept Chicago, and the *Creole Show*, as their home base.

By 1894, when he was twenty-six, Bob Cole was getting the urge to produce. He and Stella moved to New York, where he started his All-Star Stock Company at Worth's Museum. He brought together a dozen or so young black actors and writers and organized classes and workshops in which to develop their crafts. Worth's was a dime museum at Sixth Avenue and Thirtieth Street, home to the sort of "educational" freak-show exhibits so popular in the Barnum era. (Worth's claimed to have the pickled head of President Garfield's assassin, and the grisly item was on display for several years.) It was an unlikely place to present black theatre in repertory. The All-Star Stock Company was a noble effort, but a doomed one. It folded after a few months of failed shows.

One of Cole's All-Star "students" was Billy Johnson, a minstrel show veteran from Charleston, South Carolina. He was ten years older than Cole, and he had done a bit of songwriting ("The Trumpet in the Cornfield" in 1881). Johnson had been based in New York since his first appearance there, with the Hicks-Sawyer Minstrels in 1887.

When the All-Star Stock Company disbanded, Johnson went to the original *Octoroons* show, assembled by John W. Isham in 1895. Cole and Stella returned briefly to the *Creole Show*. A year later, Cole and Billy Johnson met again as members of the first company of the Black Patti Troubadours.

The Troubadours company was the idea of Sissieretta Jones's white managers, Voelckel and Nolan. "The Black Patti" was enjoying great acclaim as a concert singer, but her managers knew that, to achieve real commercial success, a stage show must be built around her. They envisioned a kind of concert-vaudeville that would feature Jones in a mini-concert of operatic airs. The rest of the evening would be "low-brow," including a vaudeville olio as well as an hour-long musical farce. With the addition of an original playlet, the Troubadours took the final step from minstrelsy to black musical comedy in the 1890s, not long after the *Creoles* and the *Octoroons* had urbanized the minstrel show beyond recognition.

The Troubadours began with a cast of fifty. The first company's soubrettes were Ada Overton and Stella Wiley, and the primary comedians—and writers of the one-act musical—were Bob Cole and Billy Johnson. Cole and Johnson called their elaborate sketch *At Jolly Coon-ey Island,* and they devised two good comic parts for themselves. Billy Johnson appeared as "Jim Flimflammer," a bunco artist, and Cole was "Willie Wayside," a tramp in whiteface and red beard. Their songs included "The Black Four Hundred's Ball," "Red Hots," and "Song of the Bathers." During the winter of 1896–1897, the Troubadours toured

Bob Cole and Billy Johnson

Coon-ey Island with great success. Cole and Johnson would later extract their comic scenes from this show to create a two-man vaudeville act for themselves as the Flimflammer and Wayside characters.

Cole's short musical was the hit of the Troubadours' first season, and he was becoming known as a librettist and composer as well as an actor. *Coon-ey Island* was well-reviewed, and Howley-Haviland published "The Black Four Hundred's Ball." So, in June 1897, during the company's extended run at Proctor's Fifty-eighth Street Theatre in New York, Cole asked Voelckel and Nolan for a raise. When the managers refused him, he took his score and left the company. Voelckel and Nolan had him arrested for theft. In the arbitration that followed, both sides won: the Troubadours retained the right to use Cole's score, but Cole established legal ownership of his music and was awarded payment for the use of it.

The squabble over ownership of his music galvanized Cole. He determined to produce his own show, to write it and star in it, to show Voelckel and Nolan a thing or two. Billy Johnson also quit the Troubadours, in sympathy with Cole. (Ernest Hogan was hired to replace the team as the comedy lead in the company's rewritten version of *At Jolly Coon-ey Island*). Cole and Johnson worked through the summer of 1897 writing the book, music, and lyrics for a two-act musical. They knew they would have to produce it with their own money—that is to say, on a shoestring—but by September they were ready. Despite threats from Voelckel and Nolan to blackball any performer who worked for Cole, the team managed to assemble a cast of eighteen. On September 27, 1897, in a small theatre in South Amboy, New Jersey, *A Trip to Coontown* gave its first performance. The show was the first full-length musical comedy to be produced, written, staged, and performed by blacks.

A Trip to Coontown was a revue-like musical modeled on the "sightseeing" shows of the era (*In Gay New York* and *In Gayest Manhattan, or Around New York in Ninety Minutes*, both in the previous season, and the champ of them all, *A Trip to Chinatown* in 1891). Cole and Johnson portrayed their comic-tramp and con man characters, and the supporting cast included Jesse Shipp, Tom Brown, and Walter Dixon. The score fulfilled the title's promise of an evening of coonery ("When the Chickens Go to Sleep," a gambling song called "4-11-44," and "No Coons Allowed"). There was one successful ballad, "I Hope These Few Lines Will Find You Well." Howley-Haviland published several of the show's songs, including "The Wedding of the Chinee and the Coon," which was added to the score during the show's tour. The innovations of *A Trip to Coontown* lay in its evening-long plot and its bright, urban tone, not in the collection of coon songs that comprised its score.

The company's tour was hampered by the machinations of Voelckel and Nolan. Black Patti's managers put out the word that any theatre booking *A Trip to Coontown* could not expect to book the Troubadours show that season. So the first six months were rough for the Cole-Johnson company. They played a dismal succession of one-nighters in bad theatres, and were finally reduced to touring the Canadian provinces in the winter to escape the far-reaching spite of the Troubadours' bosses. In early April 1898 *A Trip to Coontown* played briefly at Jacobs' Third Avenue Theatre in New York (three months before *Clorindy* opened at the Casino Roof Garden).

Cole and Johnson kept the show going. Their fortunes improved during a second swing around the country, playing better theatres and to bigger audiences than in the previous year. In the spring of 1899, *A Trip to Coontown* was back in New York, this time on Broadway, with short runs at the Casino Roof Garden and the Grand Opera House. It was a success, but not a novelty. By that time New York had seen *Clorindy*, *Jes' Lak White Folks*, and three Williams and Walker shows. Sam Lucas joined the cast in late 1899, providing another star name to attract audiences in a third season. With its creators still leading its company, *A Trip to Coontown* stayed on the road throughout most of 1900. In the show's third year, the partnership of Cole and Johnson began to fray. Some say that there was a financial dispute, others that Johnson's excessive drinking bothered Cole. In any case, Cole seems to have been the dissatisfied party. He may not have been actively looking for new partners in the summer of 1899—there were still vaudeville and theatre commitments with Billy Johnson to be kept—but he was certainly open to the idea of writing with someone else. It was during this time—at the Marshall Hotel, where so many professional matches had been made—that he met two brothers who had come up from Florida to peddle an opera.

The opera's composer was J. Rosamond Johnson, and its librettist was his brother, James Weldon Johnson. At the time they met Cole, neither was seriously looking for a show business career. Both were teachers, highly educated themselves, from a family that had been free, middle class, and literate since before the Civil War. The Johnson brothers were not just strivers, they were achievers. Their trip to New York was a "go-see," made as much out of curiosity as in hopes of getting a production of their work.

Bob Cole and James Weldon Johnson

The Johnson brothers were born in Jacksonville, Florida: James Weldon on June 17, 1871; John Rosamond on August 11, 1873. Their father, James Johnson, was a head waiter at Jacksonville's St. James Hotel (at age fifty, he would receive the call to preach, and he became pastor of Ebenezer Methodist Church). Their mother, Helen Dillet Johnson, was the first black female to teach in a Florida public school. The Johnsons encouraged intellectual pursuits, and their home in Jacksonville's La Villa suburb contained many books as well as a square Bacon piano. James Weldon could play the piano a bit, but he preferred the guitar. John Rosamond was the real pianist in the family, soon surpassing the ability of his mother, who was his first teacher. Both boys attended the Stanton School, and both were obviously destined for education beyond Stanton.

James Weldon left home first, in 1887. He spent his last two high school years at Atlanta University's prep school, then stayed to complete a B.A. at the University. (This school held its first classes in a railroad car in 1865, and within twenty-five years it had become one of the leading black universities. W. E. B. DuBois taught there from 1897 to 1910.) He studied Latin and Greek, took his English composition courses very seriously, and enjoyed the required manual training in the carpentry shop. When he returned to Jacksonville after graduation, he was appointed—at age twenty-three—principal of Stanton School, which he had attended as a child. In 1895, he became founder and editor of the first black daily in the United States, *The Daily American.*

The paper's demise after about eight months of publication didn't leave him without projects. He expanded the Stanton curriculum to make the school into the first black high school in Florida. He studied law by reading on his own in a local lawyer's office. After eighteen months of preparation, he passed the state bar exam, becoming the first African-American admitted to the Florida bar.

Rosamond had left home in 1890 to study at the New England Conservatory of Music in Boston. After six years at the Conservatory, he went on the road briefly in late 1896 with *Oriental America,* the second production of John W. Isham's *Octoroons* company. (Isham had come to Boston to recruit classically trained musicians to compete with those in the Black Patti show.) When Rosamond returned to Jacksonville in early 1897, he began to give private lessons on the family piano, and he was soon appointed music supervisor for the Jacksonville public schools. His brother Weldon had been writing essays and poems, and he wanted to try writing lyrics to some of Rosamond's tunes.

Rosamond found time in the evenings to write with his brother. Their first project was an opera called *Toloso,* a satirical story with a Spanish-American War setting. They got up a local production of it, and Jacksonville theatregoers, black and white, were lavish in their praise. They encouraged the Johnson brothers to seek a professional production and publication of it. In the summer of 1899, after school was out, they took a train to New York.

The Johnson brothers found a room in a boarding house near the Marshall Hotel and planned their rounds. They got in to see Isidore Witmark (as had another beginner, Will Marion Cook), but the publisher thought their project was a curiosity, nothing more. He declined it. Because the attempt was only half-hearted anyway, the brothers were not particularly discouraged. They stayed on in New York for several weeks to mingle with the black show folk of Fifty-third Street.

They met Bert Williams, George Walker, Will Marion Cook, Harry Burleigh, Paul Laurence Dunbar, and Ernest Hogan—the elite of the small world of black theatre in 1899.

They were especially impressed with Bob Cole. Although he was only thirty-one, he was much more experienced than the others, as librettist, performer, and published songwriter. His *Trip to Coontown* had played twice in New York by then, and there had been a Cole and (Billy) Johnson song—"I Wonder What Is That Coon's Game"—interpolated into *A Reign of Error*, the Rogers Brothers show that had come to Broadway in March.

Perhaps as an experiment, perhaps for fun, Cole and the young Floridians tried writing a song together. The result was a gentle love song called "Louisiana Lize." It is an ordinary coon song in sentiment and dialect, but there are musical touches in it that show the hand of Rosamond Johnson. There is a four-bar tag (with lyrics) after the verse and another one after the chorus, making each twenty measures long. There are passing chords in minor keys, making it more sophisticated than anything Cole had written with Billy Johnson. (On songs with Billy Johnson, the composer credit is always given to Cole. The credits on "Louisiana Lize" read: "Composed by Bob Cole, Words and Music Edited by J. W. and Rosamond Johnson," and they probably describe the process of writing the song.) Cole liked "Louisiana Lize" enough to try to get it published. They sold the performing rights to May Irwin for $50, then, able to guarantee a star's plug for the song, they pitched it to the Joseph Stern Company for publication. The $33 shared by the Johnson brothers from the sale to May Irwin did not entice them to change professions, but as they headed back to Jacksonville for the fall school term, they must have been pleased to have sold their first song on the first try.

In February 1900 a song was needed for combined school choirs to sing at a Lincoln's Birthday celebration in Jacksonville. The Johnson brothers wrote a rolling, hymn-like march called "Lift Ev'ry Voice and Sing." Rosamond had professionally printed copies made in New York for the schoolchildren to rehearse with. The song made such an impression on the music teachers that it stayed in the choral programs of the choirs that sang it. From Jacksonville it spread, like a folk song, in handwritten and typed copies to black churches and schools throughout the South. Within twenty or so years, it had become the traditional opening song for school assemblies, graduation ceremonies, and NAACP meetings across the nation. It was finally published in a commercial edition by Edward B. Marks in 1921, long after it had become known as the "Negro national anthem."

The summer of 1900 found the Johnson brothers back in New York, anxious to work with Cole again. The Johnsons' "Run, Brudder Possum, Run" was interpolated into the score of *The Rogers Brothers in Central Park* in September 1900, and the trio had four songs in a May Irwin show, *The Belle of Bridgeport*, in October. By that time, the Johnsons were back in Jacksonville, at school. Stanton School did not know that it had Broadway songwriters on its staff, nor did Broadway know that two of its most promising new writers were teaching black children in Jacksonville.

In the fall of 1900 Paul Laurence Dunbar came to Jacksonville for a public reading arranged by James Weldon Johnson. His trip turned into an extended visit with his host. The poet and the budding lyricist had long evenings of talk about literature and the theatre. Dunbar had been scalded by his experience with Will Marion Cook, and he had vowed never to write for musical shows again. He was also tired of writing the kind of verses that were the most popular of his creations, the dialect-drenched, watermelon/possum/chicken poems that had made him famous. Johnson saw Dunbar's point about stereotypical subject matter, but he disagreed about the use of dialect and slang. Johnson appreciated the strength and vividness of authentic black talk, and he didn't want to give it up. He thought that there must be a middle way, a kind of lyric writing on universal subjects that, without apology or embarrassment, could draw on the richness of real "characteristic" language. Many of the best Cole-Johnson songs over the next ten years would take this middle way.

The Johnsons were a long time leaving Jacksonville, but in the summer of 1901—after a disastrous fire in the spring that had destroyed Stanton School—they left for good, committed to New York and to Bob Cole. They moved into the Marshall Hotel, a block from where Cole lived, and the trio worked steadily at songwriting. Cole's split with Billy Johnson was complete by then, and he was ready to use all of his contacts and energy to place their songs.

Billy Johnson would never again have the success that he had had with Cole. He toured in vaudeville as a single act for several years, and he had about twenty more published songs, with various composers. He wrote and staged several shows for the Pekin Stock Company, then formed his own company with Tom Brown. He died in a fall from the balcony of the Pioneer Club in Chicago on September 12, 1916.

After a few weeks of writing, and of Cole's hustling, the trio's songs began turning up all over town. Cole and Rosamond completed Paul Laurence Dunbar's barely begun libretto and wrote the lyrics for *The Cannibal King*, Will Marion Cook's short-lived show for Ernest Hogan. The Primrose and Dockstader minstrel company was using their "No Use Askin'." They had three songs in Peter Dailey's *Champagne Charlie*, and two in *The Supper Club*, which Cole also staged, at the Winter Garden. Bert Williams recorded their song "My Castle on the Nile."

In late summer 1901, the team gathered about fifteen of their songs, several of which were being used or were slated for use in Broadway shows, and took them to the offices of the publisher Joseph Stern. The Cole-Johnson team was obviously a going concern, and Stern wanted in on the action. The company signed them to a three-year exclusive contract, with a monthly cash guarantee to be deducted from their royalties. With a strong foothold on Broadway and a publisher who wanted first look at everything they wrote, they were suddenly miles ahead of any of their writer friends at the Marshall Hotel. (The team would occasionally publish with other companies besides Stern, probably peddling songs that Stern had turned down.)

Stern's bet on Cole and the Johnsons soon paid off, with two hits among their interpolated Broadway songs of 1901. The team had four songs in *The Little Duchess*, a Ziegfeld production starring Anna Held, which opened in October at the Casino Theatre. One of these was "The Maiden with the Dreamy Eyes," a serene, non-dialect song that became Anna Held's theme and sold well for Stern for several years. In November the producing team of Marc Klaw and Abraham Erlanger presented an English import called *The Sleeping Beauty and the Beast*. The producers thought that this pantomime from Drury Lane would have a better chance on Broadway if it were "Americanized," so they called Cole and the Johnsons to contribute songs to the score. Among these was a beautiful dialect ballad with a habañera feel, "Nobody's

Lookin' but de Owl and de Moon." It is one of the period's prettiest love songs, and it became a staple of the Stern company's catalog.

In his 1933 autobiography, *Along This Way*, James Weldon Johnson described the trio's writing method:

> The three of us sometimes worked as one man. At such times it was difficult to point out specifically the part done by any one of us. But, generally, we worked in a pair, with the odd man as a sort of critic or adviser. Without regard to who or how many did the work, each of us received a third of the earnings. There was an almost complete absence of pride of authorship, and that made the partnership still more curious.

The covers of their songs say that they are by "Cole and Johnson Brothers," but the inside credits are more specific. Rosamond is usually named as composer, James Weldon is always listed as a lyricist, and Bob Cole's name might be in either column—as sole lyricist, as co-lyricist with James Weldon, as sole composer or as co-composer with Rosamond. Because Cole could write either words or music, he was the "odd man" who was "critic or adviser." Many of the "Cole and Johnson Brothers" songs name only two contributors, some name only one. Whatever their system, it worked.

In 1902 they had their biggest hit, an interpolation sung by Marie Cahill in *Sally in Our Alley*, called "Under the Bamboo Tree." Its languid, tango-pulsed verse—with standard English lyric—and its flirtatious, syncopated chorus—in pidgin-English—tell the story of a jungle courtship. ("Down in the jungles lived a maid, Of royal blood but dusky shade . . . If you lak-a-me lak I lak-a-you. . . .") It is one of those rare pop songs that manages to be funny and sexy at the same time, an audacious piece of songwriting without precedent in pop music. The chorus melody is a paraphrase of "Nobody Knows the Trouble I've Seen," supposedly done by Rosamond on Cole's dare. (The inside page of the song sheet credits Cole alone as composer and lyricist.) It was sung by Marie Cahill for years, and it was first recorded by Arthur Collins and Byron Harlan. By itself, it inspired a new genre of pop writing: the "jungle song" ("Down in Jungle Town," "By the Light of the Jungle Moon," "Aba Daba Honeymoon," and many others). It is "catchy" in the best sense; the cleverness sticks in the mind. T. S. Eliot showed his obsession with it when he played with the song's jagged language in his 1927 "Fragments of an Agon," twenty-five years after he first heard it.

There was another remarkable Cole-Johnson song in 1902, but because it was published under a pseudonym, it was not associated with them. This was their reworking of a folk song, "The Darby Ram," which they called "Oh, Didn't He Ramble?" The published song credits the writing to "Will Handy," and it is odd that the Joseph Stern company would not use the real names of its most popular writers on the song. It was introduced by the minstrel George Primrose (who was the first to sing "Carry Me Back to Old Virginny," in 1878). "Oh, Didn't He Ramble?" was rougher and more "lowdown" than any other Cole-Johnson song, and it was taken up immediately by New Orleans bands. It remains a dixieland standard. ("He rambled till the butchers cut him down. . . .")

In early 1902, at the suggestion of a manager who had heard them entertain at a party at Sherry's, Cole and Rosamond decided to shape a two-man vaudeville act for themselves. By June they were headlining at Keith's Fourteenth Street Theatre. They sidestepped all the conventions of musical teams of the day, and in doing so, created the "class act," an idea that would be imitated by black and white duos for thirty years in vaudeville (and in cabaret to this day). They scrapped all of the traditional straight man-comic buffoonery—funny clothes, feigned ignorance, songs with punch lines—that had so long cluttered musical acts. Cole and Johnson's aim was to make the audience feel that they were at a party—perhaps a party at Sherry's—where witty people performed top-drawer, up-to-date songs in an intimate setting for friends who knew quality when they heard it. Cole and Johnson used all of their art to make a half hour or so of seemingly artless, sophisticated charm.

They entered talking, the quick, dapper Cole first, the calm, benevolent Rosamond slightly behind him. They were both in evening dress, discussing the numbers that they would perform at a party to which they were on their way. Crossing the brightly lit stage, they spied the grand piano at center and stopped to make their list. Rosamond sat down at the piano, saying that he would like something classical for their opener. He played Paderewski's "Minuet." Rosamond next suggested an art song, and, over Cole's offhand objections, sang "Still wie die Nacht," in German. Cole said that the partygoers would surely expect something of Cole and Johnson's, then he proceeded to sing their "Mandy." The rest of the act wove together a dozen of their original songs, in medleys and individual pieces, with Cole as the primary soloist and Rosamond occasionally singing harmony as he played. After a song or two, Cole would begin an idle soft-shoe dance. He pulled the white silk handkerchief from his breast pocket and made long, slow arcs with it as he glided to Rosamond's hushed accompaniment. There was no blackface, no cakewalk, no hard sell, no hoary jokes to mar the simplicity of it. There were only two talented men, casually dispensing moonbeams.

By 1903, without yet having written a full score, the Cole and Johnson trio were the hottest writers on Broadway. They had interpolations in seven shows, and audiences heard their songs in performances by Eddie Foy (in *Mr. Bluebeard*), Marie Cahill (who got ten of their songs into her *Nancy Brown*), and Lillian Russell (in Weber and Fields' *Whoop-Dee-Doo*). Dockstader's Minstrels used a Cole and Johnson song, and even Cole's old enemies, Voelckel and Nolan, wanted their work. Cole was hired to write the book for—and to bring about ten Cole and Johnson songs to—Black Patti's musical of the season, *Darktown Circus Day*. Their January 1903 royalty check from Stern amounted to $6,000, and in July the figure doubled.

After the success of *The Wizard of Oz* in early 1903 and *Babes in Toyland* in October, Klaw and Erlanger knew that the market could bear another "children's musical" as an excuse for spectacle. They imported *Mother Goose*, a Drury Lane show, for a December 2 opening at the New Amsterdam. And again, they called on Cole and the Johnsons to give an English show "American" songs. Among the team's interpolations in *Mother Goose* was a set of six songs to make an extended production number called "The Evolution of 'Ragtime.'" Like Will Marion Cook, Rosamond Johnson was only vaguely aware of the work of the classic ragtimers—he called Scott Joplin a "famous dance-hall musician" in his 1937 book, *Rolling Along in Song*—as "The Evolution of 'Ragtime'" proves. The first song in the set is called "Voice of the Savage," and the lyric (by Cole) is written in an invented "Zulu" language ("Jana wana wana woeugh!"). There is a soft-shoe number called "Essence of the Jug" and a plantation hoedown called "Darkies

Delights," which interpolates Sam Lucas' old minstrel ditty, "Carve Dat Possum." Only the last song, "Sounds of the Times" (also known as "Lindy") had a life after the show. The cover of the Stern publication of "The Evolution of 'Ragtime'" calls it "A Musical Suite tracing and illustrating Negro music through all its various forms down to the present day," but it is really a collection of Tin Pan Alley cliches introduced by an arty "African" cliche. Their best work for *Mother Goose* was a simple ballad, "There's a Very Pretty Moon Tonight."

They wrote another moon song in 1903, the gently syncopated "Lazy Moon," the sine qua non of moon songs from an age that was musically moonstruck. The premise of "Lazy Moon" is that the singer's girlfriend will meet him "in the lane tonight, If the sky is bright and clear," and he is urging the moon to shine so that his love will keep her promise. The song aches with anticipation, its verse beginning in a minor key, then slipping into a major, its chorus beginning with a melodic leap that catches the heart, all of it riding over an easy, soft-shoe rhythm. Its lyric is not in dialect (and it doesn't rhyme "June"). It is a masterpiece of pop craft, and it is one of the few Cole-Johnson songs that did not find its way into a show.

Most of the Cole-Johnson Broadway work was done for the producing team of Marc Klaw and Abraham Erlanger, the czars of the theatre around the turn of the century. Klaw and Erlanger had more theatrical real estate, more money, and more power than anyone else in the business. Klaw was the icy but mild-mannered financial overseer of their complicated enterprises, and Erlanger was a crude, explosive tyrant who fancied himself the artistic arbiter of everything that went into the houses throughout their far-flung empire. Besides holding sway over the vast Klaw-Erlanger dominion, Abe Erlanger was the driving force within the Theatrical Syndicate, an association of producers and landlords that controlled almost every major theatre in the country that was not owned by K & E. Between them, for twenty years, Klaw and Erlanger held a stranglehold on the American theatre. To a very great extent, they determined what got produced, and when and where it appeared, how long it stayed, and when and where it toured. (James Weldon Johnson, in his autobiography, says that the Cole-Johnson trio was given a three-year contract by Abraham Erlanger to work exclusively on K & E shows, but he does not give the date of the contract. There was no year from 1901 through 1906 when Cole and the Johnsons did not work for K & E, but there was also no year in which the trio worked exclusively for them.)

In 1904, after a dozen or so interpolation assignments in K & E shows, Abe Erlanger gave the team their first chance to write a full score for a Broadway show. This entailed the complete musical overhaul of another imported Drury Lane extravaganza, *Humpty Dumpty*, which opened at the New Amsterdam on November 14. The cast numbered 250, and the fairy-tale spectacle was lavish. The Cole-Johnson score was pleasant and well-crafted, but no more. The scenery got the reviews, and the show ran for about four months. *Humpty Dumpty* was the first white Broadway show with a score by black writers.

The trio tried again, with even less success, when K & E asked for a complete score in a hurry for their next production, *In Newport*. Fay Templeton led the cast of this show, which opened at the Liberty Theatre on December 26, 1904. *In Newport* was a quick failure, running about three weeks, and the musical team was exhausted from being in Abe Erlanger's crucible for so long.

As a working vacation, Cole and Rosamond took their vaudeville act to Orpheum theatres on the West Coast. Almost immediately upon returning to New York, they were offered six weeks at the Palace Theatre in London. The trio stayed on for a three-month holiday in Europe, taking long sojourns in Paris, Belgium, and Holland. It was during this time that Bob Cole began talking about writing and producing their own show.

Cole knew it would be hard. He and Rosamond were popular and well-paid vaudeville stars, but they were not in the Williams and Walker category. No producers were clamoring to present them in a show, so the seed money would probably be their own. And if they turned down assignments from Klaw and Erlanger to work on their own production, they would be putting their association with Broadway's most powerful producers at risk. Except for a handful of interpolations in Williams and Walker shows, the patch job on *The Cannibal King*, and Black Patti's *Darktown Circus Day*, they had worked exclusively on shows for white performers. There was a question of being able to assemble staff and stars for a black show by Cole and Johnson, and there was a question of whether black theatregoers would support the effort. They had been in the white mainstream, and just outside the black mainstream, since their teaming.

So Cole made a plan. The duo would take as many well-paying—and short-term—vaudeville dates as they could get in the United States in late 1905, then return to London in 1906 for a final vaudeville appearance at the Palace. The income from their published songs and the vaudeville work would give them the freedom to write. The plan went as scheduled through 1905, but by the time the duo left for England for their farewell booking, the writing team had been reduced by one.

James Weldon Johnson had been active in Republican politics in New York City for several years. He was a strong supporter of Theodore Roosevelt, and for TR's no-contest race for the presidency against New York judge Alton B. Parker in 1904, the Johnsons had written a campaign song ("You're All Right, Teddy"). James Weldon's loyalty to Republican causes was rewarded in 1906 when President Roosevelt

appointed him U.S. Consul to Venezuela. The honor was too great to refuse, so in the late spring of 1906, around the time that Cole and Rosamond sailed for England, James Weldon Johnson sailed for South America. Several of his leftover lyrics would turn up in the two succeeding Cole-Johnson shows, but the trio would never write together again.

By late summer of 1906, the first black show by Cole and Johnson was ready for its tryout tour. It was called *The Shoo-Fly Regiment*, and despite the interpolation of a piece of Cole and Rosamond's vaudeville act, it had the

The Shoo Fly Regiment

most cohesive libretto of any black show of the period. It is set in 1898 and it tells the story of a young teacher in an industrial school for Negroes in Alabama. The teacher and his friends are anxious to make up a regiment of soldiers to enlist in the army and fight in the Philippines during the Spanish-American War. The young man's fiancee disapproves of his going, but he goes anyway. In the second act (set in Manila), the teacher shows his bravery by leading a danger-ous—and successful—attack on the Spanish. The Shoo-Fly Regiment returns to its home town for a glorious welcome in Act III, and the teacher and his girl are reunited. There was comedy in *The Shoo-Fly Regiment*, but the black characterizations that it put on the musical stage were more serious, and more interesting, than any that had been there before.

The score was rich in comic numbers ("De Bo'd of Education," "The Ghost of Deacon Brown," and "If Adam Hadn't Seen the Apple Tree") as well as the traditional site-specific numbers of musical come-dy ("I'll Always Love Old Dixie" and "On the Gay Luneta"). The Cole libretto included the first serious, face-to-face love scenes by black stage characters, and one of the love songs was J. Rosamond Johnson's best, "Li'l Gal." The lyric was a Paul Laurence Dunbar poem that Johnson had set to music years earlier, and the song's restless har-monic shifts between major and minor perfectly catch the bittersweet declaration of Dunbar's verse. The melody is rangy, going from the urgency of repeated high notes to a descending calm in the four repe-titions of the title's words. It is closer to art song than to pop or show writing of the time, and it is gorgeous. Another love song, the more earthbound "Sugar Babe," was added to the score during the show's second season.

The characters that Cole and Johnson played in *The Shoo-Fly Regiment* were almost incidental to the plot. The real acting roles went to Theodore Pankey as the teacher, Sam Lucas as a member of the board of education, and Andrew Tribble, a noted female impersonator, in the role of the busybody, Sis Hopkins.

The Shoo-Fly Regiment, carrying a company of sixty, played its try-out in August 1906 in Washington, D.C., then commenced a tour. The going was tough, and the troupe faced many of the road problems that had bedeviled the Williams and Walker companies: long jumps between short bookings, often at second-class theatres, in Texas, Kansas, and Indiana. It is not known whether Klaw and Erlanger were actively hindering the progress of *The Shoo-Fly Regiment* by denying access to good theatres, but they certainly did not help by getting it better ones. (Cole and Johnson were the producers of *The Shoo-Fly Regiment*, not Klaw and Erlanger, but the writers' longstanding association with K & E bought them no favors on the road. Cole surely knew that the Syndicate arm reached into every city with a theatre. Did he ever ask his old bosses to smooth the way?) The creators of the show dug deep into their own pockets to keep it going, and they had to lay off the company for a short time early in 1907 because they ran out of money.

The Shoo-Fly Regiment finally made it into New York, heralded by ads that promised "The Most Beautiful Dusky Chorus in the World." It opened on Broadway at the Grand Opera House on June 3, 1907, and closed almost immediately, probably because Cole and Johnson couldn't meet the payroll. The show reopened on August 6 at the Bijou Theatre (a house belonging to K & E's rivals, the Shuberts), where it lasted two weeks. The stay at the Bijou was long enough to attract a team of professional managers who wanted to put the show out again. The second season on the road, though still hard, was much more successful than the first.

Shoo-Fly's second tour was barely over when Cole and Johnson began work on their next show, *The Red Moon*. This was another innovative project, subtitled "An American Musical in Red and Black." The story concerns a half-Indian, half-black woman named Minnehaha, who is kidnaped from her rural Virginia home by her estranged father, Chief Lowdog, who takes her to rejoin her tribe and to live with him in the West. Her boyfriend, a trickster named "Plunk Green" (played by Cole), and his piano-playing friend, "Slim Brown" (Johnson), set out to find her. To effect her rescue, they impersonate a doctor and a lawyer, and their cleverness wins the day. Chief Lowdog is reconciled with his wife, the wily suitor Red Feather is bested, and Minnehaha is returned to the arms of Plunk Green.

The Red Moon is Cole and Johnson's best score, a fresh amalgam of "Indian" music, Tin Pan Alley syncopation, ballads, and dialect numbers. Ed Marks called *The Red Moon* "the most tuneful colored show of the century," and Eubie Blake was still playing "Bleeding Moon" sixty years after he first heard it. There were no long-lived pop hits from the score, but the published songs show a command of craft beyond that of any other theatre writers of the period. (A few of *The Red Moon's* melodies were by the show's conductor, James Reese Europe.) *The Merry Widow*, which opened at the New Amsterdam in late 1907, had renewed Broadway's love affair with operetta, and *The Red Moon* is American operetta at its best. It is all in a number called "Big Red Shawl"—tom-toms, blue notes, raggy beat, arching melody—pure America, pure Cole and Johnson.

The Red Moon

The writers gave themselves better roles this time. They were the comic leads, not just adjuncts to the plot. It was Rosamond's first comic acting on the stage, and Cole's first since his days as "Willie Wayside." Sam Lucas was cast again, as were Andrew Tribble and Theodore Pankey. Minnehaha was played by Abbie Mitchell.

There are a few scraps of Bob Cole's director's notes from *The Red Moon* at Howard University's Moorland-Spingarn Center. They show a meticulous concern with stage time—"Scene 8:57 - 9:03, Song: 9:03 - 9:06," and so forth—as well as an eye for detail—"Phelps shawl too long," "Tootsie Allen—Green shoes best left out"—and a few line changes that he wanted. He saw and heard—and timed—it all.

The Red Moon gave its first performance in Wilmington, Delaware, on August 31, 1908. Then it began the common pre–New York tour through the Northeast and to the Midwest. It arrived at the Majestic Theatre—the bane of Bert Williams, at Columbus Circle—on May 3, 1909. The score got good reviews, but the show could not sustain more than three weeks at the out-of-the-way Majestic. A second tour was hastily put together, and *The Red Moon* went on the road again.

It was during the brief New York run of *The Red Moon* that producer Ray Comstock approached J. Rosamond Johnson to compose the score for Bert Williams' first solo show, *Mr. Lode of Koal*. Cole was

passed over as librettist-lyricist for Mr. *Lode of Koal*, probably in order
to retain two longtime Williams collaborators, Jesse Shipp and Alex
Rogers. In any case, Cole seems to have ignored the snub and allowed
Rosamond to interrupt their partnership temporarily. Johnson and
Alex Rogers wrote the score, and Williams himself contributed a few
numbers. In August 1909 Mr. *Lode of Koal* began an erratic tour of the
Midwest, and in November it straggled into New York. Like *The Red
Moon*, it stayed a few weeks at the Majestic, then tried the road again.
Johnson's first show without Cole (and Williams' first without Walker)
was an unhappy experience, and Rosamond must have been relieved to
turn his attention again to *The Red Moon*.

But the Cole-Johnson show was struggling almost as hard as *Mr.
Lode of Koal* was. Meeting the payroll was still nip and tuck, and touring conditions were trying. In December James Europe and Abbie
Mitchell left the show (she was replaced by Aida Overton Walker). By
the spring of 1910, the show's creators were tired (which they admitted) and nearly broke (which they didn't). When *The Red Moon*
closed, Cole and Johnson announced that they would not produce a
show in the upcoming season because large shows could not make
money in "popular priced" (read: second-class) theatres. They were
going back to vaudeville as a duo. In October 1910 they were at Keith's
Fifth Avenue Theatre, leading the bill at $750 a week.

On the last night of the Keith's engagement, Bob Cole collapsed
on stage. He was obviously in mental, as well as physical, distress, and
he was first taken to Bellevue Hospital, where he was diagnosed as having paresis. He was moved to Manhattan State Hospital (the mental
institution where Scott Joplin would spend his last days), and he
remained there for several months. After more tests at private clinics,
his diagnosis was revised to the euphemistic catchall, a "nervous breakdown." He needed rest and care, and since he was separated from Stella
by then, he sent for his mother. Isabella Cole came at once and
arranged for her son's recuperation at a boarding house in the Catskills.
He seemed to improve after a few quiet days of sitting on the porch and
swimming in a nearby lake. But one day, while swimming with friends,
he suddenly went still and disappeared under the water. Bob Cole's
death by drowning, on August 2, 1911, was probably a suicide.

Within a period of about two years, the fragile world of black theatre
had lost its most versatile actor (Ernest Hogan), its best businessman

(George Walker), and its most gifted librettist and director (Cole). There were still writing and acting talents aplenty, but none with the drive and tenacity of these three men. Despite the gains made by black talents, black theatre was still a precarious profession in 1911, and without these three—who had made the most happen—there would be a ten-year wait before Broadway saw its next black show. Cole's death marked the end of the first black Broadway era.

Rosamond Johnson found consolation in work. Very soon after Cole's death, he teamed with J. Leubrie Hill to write a short revue called *Hello, Paris*, which ran a week or so at the Folies Bergere, Broadway's short-lived first experiment with cabaret, on West Forty-sixth Street. Next, Johnson formed a vaudeville act with Dan Avery and Charles Hart. The trio's act became the basis of a London revue, *Come Over Here*, in early 1912. Johnson was appointed music director of London's Grand Opera House after the revue closed, and he remained in England for more than a year. While there, he sent for his Jacksonville sweetheart, Nora Floyd, and they were married.

In 1914 Rosamond Johnson became music director for Harlem's Music School Settlement for Colored People, a position he held until his service as a second lieutenant with the National Guard's Fifteenth Infantry during World War I. He performed in various musical acts throughout the twenties, notably with the tenor Taylor Gordon in a concert evening of spirituals. (Johnson had arranged the spirituals heard in Ridgley Torrence's set of three one-act plays, presented at the Madison Square Garden Theatre in 1917 under a collective title, *The Rider of Dreams*. This was the first Broadway drama about black life.)

In 1925 Viking Press issued *The Book of American Negro Spirituals*, edited and introduced by James Weldon Johnson, with musical arrangements by J. Rosamond Johnson. This important collection sold well enough to justify another spirituals book the following year. James Weldon was well into his distinguished career as civil rights activist by then—as a national field secretary, then as National Executive Secretary of the NAACP—as well as being a popular essayist and poet.

God's Trombones, his set of Negro sermons in verse, appeared in 1927 and his memoir, Black Manhattan, in 1930. James Weldon became a visiting professor of literature at Fisk University in 1930, and was appointed to the same post at NYU—becoming the University's first black professor—in 1934. He held both positions until his death in an automobile accident in Wiscasset, Maine, on June 26, 1938.

J. Rosamond conducted the forty-voice choir for Bessie Smith's two-reel film, St. Louis Blues, in 1929, and he wrote the score for the 1933 United Artists film version of The Emperor Jones, which starred Paul Robeson. The director, Dudley Murphy (who had directed the Bessie Smith short), may have recommended Johnson for this assignment. In any case, The Emperor Jones is the first feature film to have a score by a black composer. (There would be occasional film scores by African-Americans—including Duke Ellington's for Anatomy of a Murder, in 1959—but no black writer would have a solid career as a film composer until Quincy Jones, in the mid-1960s.)

Johnson had a few songs interpolated in Broadway shows (Brown Buddies in 1930 and Fast and Furious in 1931), but he was known in the thirties primarily as an arranger and anthologist of spirituals. Lew Leslie's Rhapsody in Black (1931) featured his vocal arrangement of Gershwin's Rhapsody in Blue, and Leslie appointed him music director of his Blackbirds of 1936—a London edition of his revue, which starred Jules Bledsoe and the Nicholas Brothers—and Blackbirds of 1939, the last of the producer's Broadway Blackbirds.

Rosamond Johnson appeared in a short-lived revue, Americana, in 1928, and in 1935 he took an acting role, his first since The Red Moon. He appeared as "Lawyer Frazier," the shyster who peddles cheap divorces, in the original production of Porgy and Bess. Four years later, he appeared with Ethel Waters in Dubose Heyward's drama, Mamba's Daughters. Also in 1939 he took a small part in the film Keep Punching, which starred Henry Armstrong, the only boxer to hold titles in three weight divisions simultaneously. His last stage role came in 1940, when he appeared (again with Waters) in Cabin in the Sky, for which he also directed the chorus.

J. Rosamond Johnson died on November 11, 1954, at his home at 437 West 162nd Street, in Harlem. The kind of theatre that he wrote for died long before him. Our century's two world wars, linked by the Depression, changed the pace of popular entertainments. Modern life took on a nervous edge, and shows were expected to deliver their delights faster. Charm remained a theatrical commodity, but it couldn't dawdle any more. There was no time for watching actors basking in the light of Fresnel moons and commenting on their beauty in song. We expect our shows to get on with it. But in getting on with it, generations of theatregoers have been denied the chance to see anything like the graceful arcs of Bob Cole's handkerchief.

CHAPTER 4

"BUSINESS IS BUSINESS WITH ME"

● ●

The First Black Publishers of Popular Music

MANY OF THE SUCCESSFUL SONGWRITERS of the early twentieth century were also commercial music publishers. From the time of Tin Pan Alley's first smash hit, Charles K. Harris' self-published "After the Ball," in 1892, it was obvious that it was more profitable for a composer to publish his own songs than to sell them outright to publishers for a few dollars or to rent them to publishers at a few cents a copy (the standard royalty). So several songwriters used royalty income from their first hits to begin their own firms. Some were good business-men, some were not, but they all knew that the age-old songwriter complaints against publishers—rejection of their songs, little or no royalty payments, poor distribution, indifferent plugging—could be dealt with only by becoming publishers themselves.

Some composers, like Charles K. Harris, issued their own work almost exclusively, publishing everything that they ground out, much of which would have never seen print otherwise. Other songwriter-publishers, like Harry Von Tilzer, saw publishing as a business, not as the primary outlet for their own work. Von Tilzer, a proven hit writer by 1900, was invited to become a partner in the Shapiro, Bernstein company that year. By 1902 he had his own Twenty-eighth Street firm, enjoying the profits from his own hits as well as the income from successfully acquiring and plugging the songs of others. He was the most prolific and versatile (and the best businessman) among the publishing writers of his time. The Alley would not see his like again until Irving Berlin founded his publishing empire in 1919.

The two necessities for going after riches in the pop song market were money and nerve. Competition was brutal, and a publisher had to be able to issue enough products for the law of averages to work toward his having a hit. He had to be aggressive in pushing his products at the public, and he had to have a cushion of capital to see him through the indefinite wait between hits. The Alley's rule of thumb was that one song out of two hundred made money above the cost of its production.

One plugger of the era recalled that it took about $1,300 to launch a song properly: $50 for lithographing a singer's photo for the cover; $250 for the printing of 10,000 copies; $500 for a year's advertising in professional journals; and a $500 advance (payola) for the singer who introduced the song and featured it in a vaudeville act. The expense of acquiring the song was usually minimal. Most songwriters sold their work outright for $50 or less; those who were in a position to demand a royalty agreement could rarely bargain for more than a penny or two per copy sold. And the publisher did the bookkeeping, reporting the sales of a song in semiannual statements to its writers. A publisher's overhead expenses were for rent, administrative staff, in-house arrangers and demonstrators, New York pluggers, and out-of-town salesmen to get the product into music and dime stores across the country. Some of the smaller publishers, who couldn't afford the space and the staff, chose to farm out the production and shipping of their songs to jobbers—another expense, but cheaper than maintaining a full office and warehouse. It was a complex and risky way to bet that the browser in an Omaha music store—who was probably earning about thirty cents an hour—would lay out fifty cents to take home a song he had heard once in a vaudeville show or, as was usually the case, had never heard at all. But if you could sell *enough* songs to *enough* browsers in Omaha, San Francisco, Chicago, Des Moines . . . you could get rich. Music publishing was more an enterprise for pirates than shopkeepers.

Black songwriters had had alliances with major New York publishers since the earliest days of Tin Pan Alley. Gussie Davis's most frequent publisher during the 1890s was Howley, Haviland (which also published most of the songs of Bob Cole and Billy Johnson). F. A. Mills issued much of Irving Jones' work. M. Witmark and Sons published Ernest Hogan's first hit and several of his later songs. Joseph Stern and Company, guided by its silent partner, Edward Marks, made its niche in the Alley by catching the black musical fads of the late nineties—coon songs, cakewalks, and rags—and by frequently publishing the work of black writers in these genres. Stern's chief arranger, Will Tyers, was black, and the house was especially amenable to giving black vaudevillians (such as Williams and Walker and Chris Smith) a hearing. From 1902 through 1908, Stern was the primary publisher of the Cole-Johnson Brothers songs. With "black" musical styles and subject matter the rage, it made sense to go to the source, and most of the major publishers—including Harris and Von Tilzer—did.

In 1904 Shep Edmonds, a black vaudevillian and entrepreneur, opened the first black publishing firm. Soon afterward, in that same year, John H. Cook, a black businessman, opened the second. When the two firms merged in late 1905, the Gotham-Attucks Music Company was created. During its six-year life, Gotham-Attucks was steered by the lyricist Cecil Mack. The company started small and didn't get much beyond the struggling stage. Their larger, more established competitors could outspend them, outproduce them, outplug them, and outwait them. The black publishers who would come along in the teens would be much more successful than this pioneer firm, but for a few years in the early century, Gotham-Attucks was the shining hope of black Alleymen.

SHEP EDMONDS

Shepard N. Edmonds was born on September 25, 1876, in Memphis, Tennessee. He spent his early childhood in Columbus, Ohio, and received his only musical training in the public schools there. He played the piano a bit, but he was more interested in percussion. He was the showoff of his school bands and orchestras, a flashbang drummer who could solo on xylophone, bells, and tympani. After high school, he took some business courses at Ohio State University, but in 1895 he succumbed to the lure of show business by becoming a percussionist for Al G. Fields' Minstrels.

The Fields company was large and prosperous, flaunting an entire drum corps and four drum majors in their street parades. Edmonds gave drumming exhibitions in front of the theatres where they were appearing, then dismantled his contraption to hurry inside and set up to play in the orchestra. In his second season with Fields, Edmonds began to be assigned songs and comedy bits on the stage.

In 1897 Edmonds went with the *Darkest America* company, a high-class black vaudeville troupe that presented everything from "scenes of slave life" (a fanciful excuse for a corn husking bit and a barn dance number) to operatic selections. The stars of *Darkest America* were Black Carl, the magician, and the comic John Rucker ("The Alabama Blossom"). Edmonds wound up in New York after his season with *Darkest America*, and he began to create a succession of vaudeville acts for himself, including a brief teaming with two English girls, the Beaumont Sisters.

One of Edmonds' vaudeville partners of the late nineties was the white singer-dancer Charles B. Ward, who billed himself as "The Original Bowery Newsboy." Ward had collaborated on two songs with Gussie Davis in 1894 and had had a hit with his 1895 composition, "The Band Played On." Ward was trying to get started as a publisher. One of his few publications was a comedy number written by the duo for the Ward-Edmonds act, "Since Malinda Hinda's Joined the Syndicate." It was Edmonds' first published song and one of his few collaborations with another writer.

As Edmonds' vaudeville career advanced, he enlarged his act. He surrounded himself with six girls and called their turn "Shep Edmonds—Stepping Out." As a solo performer—"The Only Shep Edmonds"—he played at Koster & Bial's and shared bills with Weber and Fields. In 1898 he placed a song, "There Are Those Who Do Not Think That Way," with Witmark, and the following year his "That Will Bring You Back" was featured by Marie Dressler.

In 1901 Joseph Stern published the best of Shep Edmonds' songs: "I'm Goin' to Live Anyhow, Till I Die." It was "Respectfully dedicated to Ernest Hogan," and its lyric tells the story of churchgoers who try to coax a backslider to meetings and then refuse to associate with him when he finally goes. It is a wry, syncopated song with a hymnlike melody, and it is one of the very few pop songs on its subject, the hypocrisy of do-gooders. The song was introduced by Eddie Leonard, then the star of the Primrose and Dockstader Minstrels. Edmonds told an interviewer in 1947 that "I'm Goin' to Live Anyhow" sold over a million copies. In 1903 Edmonds followed it up with another common-sense song, "You Can't Fool All the People All the Time," which was introduced by Marie Cahill and was also published by Stern.

Using the income from his hit and his handful of other songs, Shep Edmonds became a publisher in the summer of 1904. He named his firm for Crispus Attucks, the black seaman who was the first casualty of the Boston Massacre in 1770, and he opened the Attucks Music Publishing Company at 1255–57 Broadway, at Thirty-second Street, in New York City. Attucks was near, but not on, Tin Pan Alley (Twenty-eighth Street, between Broadway and Sixth Avenue). Edmonds did not create the firm as a vanity press for his own songs. (In fact, Attucks seems never to have published an Edmonds song.) He did the most sensible thing a new publisher of that time could do: he went after some songs he could put Bert Williams' picture on.

Williams and Walker were riding high on the success of their first "legitimate" show, *In Dahomey*. The show had received reams of publicity during its tour of the United Kingdom, and it was still touring the United States successfully in mid-1904. Harry Von Tilzer had sewed up the exclusive publication rights to the show's songs—and had published several of them in 1902–1903—but Edmonds managed to find three interpolated numbers that weren't committed to Von Tilzer. He couldn't use the show's title on his covers, but he could, and did, use photos of the show's stars. In 1904 Edmonds issued the three orphan songs from *In Dahomey*. "When the Moon Shines" (by James Vaughn and Alex Rogers) had portrait photos of Williams and Walker framed by decorative lettering reading "Introduced with pleasing effect in WILLIAMS & WALKER'S BIG PRODUCTION." He issued Alex Rogers' "Why Adam Sinned" with a prominent photo of Aida Overton

Walker (everyone knew whose show she was in). The biggest seller of the three was Rogers' "I May Be Crazy But I Ain't No Fool." This sheet shows a blackfaced photo of Williams and a line at the top that says "The Song That Made The King Laugh"—and everyone knew which American show King Edward VII had just seen. (Only one of the popular *In Dahomey* songs escaped both Von Tilzer and Edmonds: "I'm a Jonah Man," which was published by Witmark.)

Edmonds got Williams himself to contribute a song to the Attucks catalog, "Miss Georgia," with lyrics by Alex Rogers. Then, in January 1905, he landed a big one: "Nobody." Alex Rogers had written the song for Williams, who introduced it in vaudeville. It was to be interpolated into the scores of *Abyssinia* and *Bandanna Land*; Williams recorded it twice; and it was the star's most-requested number for the rest of his life. But in early 1905, the song was unattached to a show. Edmonds knew that it would find its way into a production—but it was just lying around loose. Shep Edmonds grabbed it. (It was not issued until after the sale of Attucks Music, but Edmonds secured the copyright.)

The Attucks catalog was small—about a dozen numbers—but because it was almost all Williams-related, it was worth something. Within a year or so, without pluggers or jobbers, Shep Edmonds had, through his canny acquisitions, brought his business to the point of being attractive to a buyer. In September 1905, Edmonds was made an offer by Gotham Music Company, and he sold Attucks Music. (Edmonds later claimed that the selling price was $55,000, which seems beyond the means of the fledgling Gotham Music.) The new Gotham-Attucks Music Company continued Edmonds' strategy of publishing songs performed by Bert Williams. His new show songs—added to the ones already in the Attucks catalog—would be their most valuable copyrights.

Edmonds used his money from the sale to set himself up as a publisher again. He issued his own 1905 song "I'm Crazy 'Bout It," which was introduced by May Irwin. He soon lost interest in the business, however, and he sent the few songs that he would write over the next four years to Remick, Haviland, and F. A. Mills.

In 1907, drawing on his experience as a detective in Philadelphia during his vaudeville layoffs, he opened the National Detective Bureau in New York. This was the first black detective agency, and Edmonds would continue as its head until 1925.

In the late thirties, he tried publishing again, opening the Shepard N. Edmonds Music Publishing Company at 1545–47 Broadway. He issued a couple of songs on which he shared credit with Chris Smith, Freddie Johnson, and Freddie Brown ("Harlem on Saturday Nite" and "Toot'n"). Neither publication went anywhere. In the early forties, he retired to his home town, Columbus, Ohio, and opened another publishing house at 169 Hamilton Avenue. In his old age, Shep Edmonds for the first time ran a vanity press, issuing only his own songs, in small quantities, just enough to impress his friends. In December 1947 he was the subject of a "rediscovery" article by Roy Carew in *The Record Changer*. Carew set Edmonds up as another subject for the "hundreds of lost songs" myth by asserting that he had written "over 2,000 songs." Shep Edmonds' name is on fewer than thirty published songs.

Edmonds died in Columbus on November 24, 1957. His importance to popular music is that he took Attucks Music seriously. He ran it in a businesslike, not a self-serving, way. And in doing so, he set its successor, Gotham-Attucks, on a businesslike course. The merged firm would have its struggles, as Edmonds had, but the lessons of publishing, including the hard ones, would be learned. He paved the way for the more viable black publishing enterprises that would follow him. He was careful to amass copyrights that could compete in the marketplace, not songs published to assuage the vanity of himself and his friends. He put together something that was worth having. Because of Shep Edmonds, Gotham-Attucks could begin with more than a dream.

CECIL MACK

In its August 23, 1908, issue, the *American Musician and Art Journal* ran a short feature on Cecil Mack, the president and "guiding hand" of Gotham-Attucks Music Company. It is a typical piece of trade-journal boosterism, but its optimism didn't seem misplaced at the time. Gotham-Attucks looked like a growing concern; it had songs from three Williams and Walker shows in its catalog by then. Mack himself was writing at the top of his form, with his name as lyricist on nearly a dozen successful songs. A half dozen or so of the top black writers were publishing regularly with Gotham-Attucks. The article praises the smooth-running operation: "The entire staff of the house is colored, girl bookkeepers, stenographers, etc., and very efficient they are." It cites the performance of Gotham-Attucks songs by white vaudevillians as "another evidence of the compelling success of this firm." Of course, the travails of the first black firm to stay afloat in the shark-infested waters of commercial music are not mentioned. Hard work and a good product seemed to be winning the game. By the end of the decade the struggle would take its toll on Mack and his company. By 1911 Gotham-Attucks would be gone.

Richard C. McPherson was born on November 6, 1883, in Norfolk, Virginia. He attended Norfolk Mission College for a short time, and in 1899 he transferred to Lincoln University, the nation's oldest black college, in Pennsylvania. McPherson spent his summers in New York, working to earn money for each upcoming year at Lincoln, and in the city he began to meet show people, among them the black vaudevillian and songwriter Tom Lemonier (1870–1945). They wrote a few songs together—Lemonier the music, McPherson the words—and Lemonier arranged for four of them to be interpolated into the score of Williams and Walker's *Sons of Ham*. Three of them were per-formed by George Walker in the show, and Aida Overton Walker won encores with the fourth, "Miss Hannah from Savannah"; two of the four were published by Joseph Stern. Another McPherson song, "Josephine, My Jo," with music by Tim Brymn, was later added to *Sons of Ham*. It was published by Shapiro, Bernstein and Von Tilzer in 1901, and it was a minor success. By the time "Josephine, My Jo" was released, McPherson had left Lincoln University (in his junior year) and was in the songwriting game. His previous plans to enter the University of Pennsylvania Medical School were put on indefinite hold.

McPherson's first real hit came in 1901 with "Good Morning, Carrie" (music by Chris Smith and Elmer Bowman). It is the gentlest of dialect songs, a delicate, early-morning serenade with a folk song's purity and directness in music and words. It was published by Windsor Music, and it was chosen by Williams and Walker as a duet for their first recording session, in October 1901.

In 1902 R. C. McPherson's nickname ("Cecil Mack") began to appear as his pseudonym on sheet music. His song "The Little Gypsy Maid," written with Will Marion Cook and Harry B. Smith, was interpolated into *The Wild Rose*, and the published version credits "Cecil Mack" as co-lyricist with Smith. Another success of 1902 was his "Please Let Me Sleep," written with Tim Brymn. The lyric makes a neat pun by a contented sleeper: "I don't mind no summer heat or win-t'ry storm, When I turn in bed I feel the spring. . . ."

Cecil Mack

"The Little Gypsy Maid" led to two lyrics for the *In Dahomey* score, both written with Cook. In 1904 there came another hit for Mack, "Teasing," written with Albert Von Tilzer—Harry's brother—and published by York Music Company (Albert Von Tilzer, president). The York connection was important to Mack, because this company handled the distribution of music for the John H. Cook Publishing Company, the second black music firm and the forerunner of Gotham Music.

John H. Cook was the brother of Will Marion Cook, and in 1904—probably because of his brother's stormy relationships with mainstream publishers—he set up a company, at 42 West Twenty-eighth Street, to issue Will's songs. There were only a few John H. Cook publications, all published in 1904 and all with music by Will. John Cook's short catalog included three songs from the 1904 show *The Southerners* (with lyrics by "Richard Grant," a pseudonym of the white lyricist Harry B. Smith), as well as "There's a Place in the Old Vacant Chair" (music and lyrics by Will Marion Cook) and "Mandy Lou" (lyrics by Cecil Mack). With the publication of "Mandy Lou," Mack was placed squarely in the sights of John Cook. Mack had money from hit songs; he had worked successfully with the thorny Will Marion; he had collaborated with Albert von Tilzer, a rising (white) star of Tin Pan Alley who happened to own a distribution business.

When John Cook decided, in late 1904, to turn the vanity house for his brother into a broader commercial venture, Cecil Mack, at age twenty-one, seemed eminently qualified to run the enterprise.

The step was taken in February 1905, when the John H. Cook Publishing Company was phased into Gotham Music Company. The company was incorporated at $10,000, and its directors were Will Marion Cook, B. D. Wilkins, and R. C. McPherson. (B. D. Wilkins was better known as Barron Wilkins. He was already successful as an owner of various cabarets in the Tenderloin district, and he probably contributed a large piece of the incorporation money. He would move his club activities to Harlem in the early teens and would thrive as one of the most respected business leaders in that community until his death in 1924.) The Gotham offices kept John Cook's address.

Gotham Music issued two unsuccessful Bert Williams songs ("Lorraine" and "Little Moses," both with lyrics by Earle C. Jones) and kept pushing the *Southerners* pieces. But it soon became obvious that Gotham needed more and better copyrights. Shep Edmonds had them. Attucks hadn't published much, but Edmonds had acquired more wisely than John Cook had. Gotham made him an offer, and in September 1905 the deal that created the Gotham-Attucks Music Company was done.

Cecil Mack's first coup at the helm of the new company was to sign up Bert Williams and George Walker as "staff writers" for Gotham-Attucks. Mack knew that a new Williams and Walker show was imminent, and he wanted his pick of songs from the score. Walker wrote nothing for Gotham-Attucks, but Williams would be the firm's most loyal and most-published writer. Mack issued most of the published songs from Williams and Walker's *Abyssinia* and *Bandanna Land*, and Williams did his part in promotion by choosing several of them for his Columbia recordings.

Cecil Mack published nothing of his own in 1905. (While organizing the publishing business, he probably wrote little.) He began to make up for it in 1906 by renewing his collaboration with the composer who brought out the best in him, Chris Smith. Smith would be Mack's main writing partner over the next ten years, and their songs are the best-crafted musical jokes of the time, several of them having punch lines as titles. They are musically and lyrically laid-back, slangy and full of low-key observations and tongue-in-cheek advice. The writers convinced Marie Cahill to sing "He's a Cousin of Mine" in *Marrying Mary*, and Bert Williams recorded their "All In, Down and Out" in late 1906. These songs, along with "Let It Alone" from *Abyssinia*, got Gotham-Attucks off to a good start.

Gus Hill asked Cecil Mack and James Reese Europe to write the score for his Smart Set Company's touring musical of 1907, *The Black Politician*. The show starred the up-and-coming comedian S. H. Dudley, and it offered a great opportunity to get Mack's songs around the country. It was Mack's first full score, and five of the Mack-Europe numbers were published from it. The trouble was that they weren't published by Gotham-Attucks. The Chicago publisher Will Rossiter issued the *Black Politician* songs, probably by arrangement with the show's producer in exchange for backing the show. However Rossiter got the songs, the situation with *The Black Politician* was one that would plague Gotham-Attucks throughout its existence. None of the company's regular writers, because of producer or collaborator commitments, could publish exclusively with Gotham-Attucks. The company's directors (Mack and Cook) and its star composers (Bert Williams and Chris Smith) all published with other firms during this time. Another problem was that Gotham-Attucks could not afford to pay competitive advances to its writers. The list of black writers who got better deals elsewhere and never published with Gotham-Attucks includes Bob Cole and the Johnson Brothers, Irving Jones, Shep Edmonds, Ernest Hogan, and Al Johns.

To complicate the bind, the larger publishers—such as Remick, Haviland, and Stern—plugged their black writers' work more effectively than Gotham-Attucks could. Mack's company had no out-of-town salesmen, so its distribution was mainly in the Northeast. Gotham-Attucks never printed an annual catalog, as did Whitney-Warner and Remick, and it couldn't afford ads in trade journals to announce its new titles. The company occasionally recycled its songs in dance folio collections, but its main form of advertising was the ads on the back of its music. The music store owner and his browsers had to see a Gotham-Attucks song to know what other Gotham-Attucks songs were.

The songs from *Bandanna Land* brought some bounty to Gotham-Attucks in 1908. Cook's "Bon Bon Buddy" and "Red Red Rose" sold well, as did Williams' "I'd Rather Have Nothin' All of the Time Than Somethin' for a Little While," "Late Hours," and "Fas' Fas' World" (and the interpolation of "Nobody" prompted a reissue of the company's biggest copyright). Cecil Mack and Chris Smith had two successful songs in the show: "It's Hard to Love Somebody" and a surprise hit, "You're in the Right Church But the Wrong Pew." Another big-selling Smith-Mack song of that year was "Down Among the Sugar Cane," written with Avery and Hart, the vaudeville team. The company, encouraged by some steady sellers, took over new office space at 136 West Thirty-seventh Street in the autumn of 1908. (They had spent about a year at 50 West Twenty-ninth Street.) Cecil Mack was invited to become a founding member of the Frogs, and he served as the first secretary of the organization. Gotham-Attucks seemed to be making it.

Actually, Mack was putting up a brave front for the trade press. He told the *American Musician and Art Journal* in early January 1909 that the last year "had not been as good as we had hoped," but he was "confident we have a very good year before us." He admitted that the company was giving away its band and orchestra music—"only to recognized artists in the profession"—but he said that things were picking up enough to stop the practice soon. Mack cited the plugging given to his songs by Williams and Walker, and he predicted a coup soon: "Next year they are going to star in *Near the Nile*. We will publish most of their new songs." Mack must have known by then that Walker's performance in *Bandanna Land* was already being impaired by the disease that would kill him, but he could not have known that, a month after his *AMAJ* interview appeared, Walker would withdraw from the show and retire from the stage. *Near the Nile* would never happen, and Gotham-Attucks could not pin its hopes on Williams and Walker much longer.

Cecil Mack contributed lyrics to *His Honor the Barber*, Gus Hill's Smart Set production of 1909. The music was mostly by Tim Brymn and Chris Smith. Gotham-Attucks published the Mack-Brymn "Porto Rico" and "That's Why They Call Me Shine" (written by Mack and Ford Dabney and interpolated late in the show's tour). But the hit of the show was "Come After Breakfast" (by Smith, Brymn and James Burris), and it was published by Joseph Stern. Gotham-Attucks missed out entirely on the Bert Williams songs from 1909's *Mr. Lode of Koal*, which were issued by Will Rossiter. The loss of the company's star writers' hits to other publishers was a bad sign. Gotham-Attucks needed product in 1909, it needed hits. The company was not publishing enough, or distributing widely enough, to keep its writers out of the hands of its competition.

By 1910 there was outright defection among the Gotham-Attucks regulars. Chris Smith was publishing more often with Stern and Remick, and Will Marion Cook's "Lovie Joe" went to Harry Von Tilzer. Even Bert Williams was publishing with other companies. He gave one of his 1910 *Follies* songs ("Chicken") to Gotham-Attucks, but his bigger ones, "Constantly" and "You're Gwine to Get Somethin' What You Don't Expect," went to Remick and Feist respectively. Each of the old-line firms was issuing six or eight songs a month during this time, enough for a handful of hits to offset the cost of the flops over the course of a year. Gotham-Attucks played it very close to the bone, publishing about ten songs a year throughout its existence. The firm was in the untenable position of being unable to plug competitively or to afford flops.

Mack responded to the crisis by signing up songs by unknown writers, including some white ones, L. Wolfe Gilbert among them. The company published its only rags in 1911: "Mutt and Jeff Rag" by M. C. Rowe and "Volcanic Rag" by Leah Monks Robb. Neither the rags nor their writers were ever heard of again. There is the sad suspicion that Gotham-Attucks became a sometime vanity house in its last year, publishing songs that beginning songwriters paid to have issued. Williams and Smith gave the house one last song in 1911 ("Next Week! Some Time!! But Not Now!!!"), and Cecil Mack issued his last with Gotham-Attucks that year: "What Makes Me Love You the Way I Do?" (the composer credit went to "Barney Barber," possibly a pseudonym of Will Marion Cook, who is listed as the original copyright owner).

By mid-year in 1911, it was time to go. Mack and his backers probably felt as much relief as regret when they closed the doors of Gotham-Attucks. The company's copyrights were bought up, by Stern first and later by Robbins-Engel, and the best of the Gotham-Attucks songs saw reissues in various folios over the years.

Cecil Mack was a freelance songwriter again. He wrote mostly with Chris Smith in the mid-teens, and they had one more success with

"Never Let the Same Bee Sting You Twice," published by Broadway Music in 1916. They placed their "My Country Right or Wrong" in the *Ziegfeld Follies of 1915*.

In 1923 Mack had his most successful show score, written with James P. Johnson for *Runnin' Wild*, which opened on Broadway in October. The best known of the Johnson-Mack songs is "The Charleston," but even in its day, it was known as an instrumental number. Few of the song's recordings have featured the lyrics. Mack's best lyric writing for the show is a ballad, "Old Fashioned Love." Johnson and Mack collaborated on *Mooching Along*, which had a brief run at the Lafayette Theatre in 1925, but this score yielded nothing like the riches of *Runnin' Wild*. That same year Mack briefly reunited with Chris Smith, with the delightful "The Camel Walk" among their small output.

In the late twenties Cecil Mack organized a show choir for Lew Leslie, the producer of the *Blackbirds* revues. Mack's singers appeared in four editions of *Blackbirds*, as well as Leslie's 1931 *Rhapsody in Black*. The last show to feature lyrics by Cecil Mack was a WPA production of 1937, *Swing It*, with music by Eubie Blake. Cecil Mack died in New York City on August 1, 1944.

Cecil Mack had big songs. For a while, during his early collaboration with Chris Smith, he even showed a distinctive lyric voice. "Good Morning, Carrie" is one of the finest ballads of its time. The best of his joke songs—"He's a Cousin of Mine" and "You're in the Right Church But the Wrong Pew"—can still bring a smile by the way they tell their stories of domestic deception. And the ballads and the jokes of his youth sound like they were written by the same person, a friendly raconteur who knew that both punch lines and sentiment needed a light touch. Would his list of sixty-five or so published songs be longer if he had not had the six-year headache of running Gotham-Attucks? But then, would Gotham-Attucks have run six years without him?

"LIVIN' HIGH (SOMETIMES)"

$$\bullet$$

Black Songwriters of the Teens and Twenties

T HE FREELANCE SONGWRITER OF THE EARLY century was in a risky business, without the safety net of guaranteed publication. The work of songwriting, for him, was not in the writing but in the selling. Like the actor of the time, the songwriter made rounds, getting into the offices that would let him in. Like the salesman from time immemorial, if he could get his toe in the door, he presented his wares. His resume was his list of hits. He didn't have to print it up for presentation to publishers; everyone knew who had written the big ones. Songwriters often wrote in—mostly impermanent—teams, and they demonstrated their material by the composer's playing the accompaniment while the lyricist sang to the (usually poker-faced) publisher.

If Remick wouldn't take it, maybe Feist would; if not Feist, maybe Fred Fisher; if not Fisher, maybe Charles K. Harris. If New York possibilities were exhausted, maybe it was time to pitch the song out of town: to Rossiter in Chicago; Setchell in Boston; Presser in Philadelphia. The song-peddling business ran on gossip, rumor, and luck. Was Jolson looking for new material? Did the house arranger at Shapiro need a lyric for something he had written? Was the Avon Comedy Four in the market for parodies? Would Nora Bayes want an interpolation for her next show?

By 1920 a sale to a publisher usually involved the offer of a contract with a stipulated royalty percentage in it. Not every transaction
involved a contract—publishers were still quick to suggest buyouts—
but every composer knew about contracts by then and had some idea of
what "standard terms" were. When ASCAP was organized in 1914, the
idea of licensing the use of music was born. Hotels, restaurants, and
bars—and later, radio stations—paid ASCAP a flat fee per year for
their use of ASCAP members' compositions. The recording industry
was harder to organize, but by the late teens, ASCAP had put language
into standard contracts concerning songwriter payments for "mechanical use" on records and piano rolls. The songwriter received no royalties for use of his song in a folio or for professional copies (which were
printed by the hundreds and given away to performers and bandleaders). Even though there were "standard terms," everything was nego-
tiable, with songwriter and publisher haggling over each blank space to
be filled in the contract.

Contracts offered to James Brockman and James Kendis, two white
songwriters who worked together with middling success in the late
teens, illustrate the shifting sands of songwriter reputation and publisher
interest. Brockman had a big song in 1915 when he wrote the lyric to
Abe Olman's "Down Among the Sheltering Palms," published by Leo
Feist. Kendis wrote the lyrics and music for a mildly successful novelty
of 1916 called "Nat'an! Nat'an! Tell Me for What Are You Waitin',
Nat'an?" Either achievement would have been enough to get them into
a publisher's office for a few years, but in early 1919 they cowrote a
smash: "I'm Forever Blowing Bubbles," which was published by Remick.

Naturally, Remick wanted to keep Kendis and Brockman. On July
2, 1919, they signed Remick's standard contract for the sale of "I'm
Climbing Mountains." They got a $2,000 advance against their three-
cents-per-copy royalty, plus a 50 percent royalty on all money received
by Remick for sale of mechanical rights. These were generous terms for
the time. About ten weeks later, lightning struck again for Kendis and
Brockman. They signed a standard contract with Broadway Music
Corporation—a smaller firm that obviously wanted to steal them away
from Remick—for a $5,000 advance against a three-cents-a-copy roy-
alty on "I'm Like a Ship Without a Sail." Neither of these 1919 songs
was a success.

On May 26, 1925—with no hits since "I'm Forever Blowing Bubbles," James Brockman (now split with Kendis) signed a contract with Irving Berlin, Inc., for a mother song called "Silver-Head." Berlin took "Silver-Head" with no advance to Brockman and with contract amendments that called for a penny-a-copy royalty on printed copies and one-sixth of all mechanical royalties. Berlin wanted "Silver-Head," but not much. The Brockman stock had dropped in six years. Publishers' memories could be very long or very short, as was convenient, but they were always precise at dating a writer's last hit. The trick was to guess when his next one might be.

Songwriting, like acting and selling, was a young man's game. Most pop songwriting careers lasted about twenty years; four or five hits in that time was a good batting average. Connections to shows and stars could extend a professional life span, but for most songwriters, twenty years was long enough on the high wire.

The songwriters profiled here were not primarily theatre writers. They all had interpolations in shows, and several of them wrote a score or two, but their milieu was the outer offices of Tin Pan Alley, not the inner sanctums of Broadway producers. Their white counterparts were not the Kerns, Gershwins, and Rombergs, but the journeymen, making rounds and hoping for hits: men like Egbert Van Alstyne, Richard Whiting, Con Conrad, Gus Kahn, and Jimmy Monaco. Nor were these black writers analogous to the publishing Von Tilzer brothers. Several of them would try the publishing business, but none would stay with it. Like actors and salesmen, they stormed the offices that would let them in, pitched as hard as they could, and took the best deals they could get.

Through their work, their songs peddled one by one, these writers profoundly influenced the sound and feel of American popular music. Black songwriters had followed existing genres in the nineteenth century—minstrel songs, tearjerkers, coon songs—but from 1910 on, they took the lead, creating the forms and fads, the songs and dances that mark the years of twentieth-century pop.

CHRIS SMITH

Chris Smith belongs on the short list of the best songwriters of the teens. His first hit was a ballad, in 1901, at a time when he was known for his mastery of the rag-song. But no writer, black or white, made the transition from the rag-song to the jazz-song as well as he did. He was primarily a composer, but he could also write a funny lyric. He wrote the biggest dance hit of a dance-mad decade. His list of collaborators ranges from old (white) lions of Tin Pan Alley (Jack Drislane and

Chris Smith

Arthur J. Lamb), to black theatre pros (Will Marion Cook and Bert Williams), to blues masters (W. C. Handy and Clarence Williams), to Harlem piano giants (Luckey Roberts and Fats Waller). He changed with his times, never staying too long with a style just because he liked it or was good at it. Musical fads came fast in the teens, and Chris Smith rode them like waves.

Christopher Smith was born on October 12, 1879, in Charleston, South Carolina, the son of Henry M. Smith, a shoemaker, and his wife Clara. Young Chris was apprenticed to a local baker, and the black minstrel Tom Fletcher remembered the boy bringing pies and cakes around to the theatre to sell to the actors in the touring shows there. Occasionally he could talk his way into employment as an extra in crowd scenes at fifty cents a performance. He and his friend Elmer Bowman (ca. 1879–1916), both still in short pants, ran away with a medicine show as assistants to a quack who was selling axle grease as a rheumatism cure. When the "doctor" withheld their wages on the road, they walked the seventy-nine miles that it took to get back home.

Somehow Smith and Bowman made their way to New York in the late nineties hoping to get into vaudeville. They concocted a song-and-dance act which they showcased in Tenderloin clubs until their first paying job: a week in Utica. They began to write songs together, and in 1898 they managed to place one of them, "A Coon's Day in May," with F. A. Mills for publication. Their first hit came in 1901 with "Good Morning, Carrie,"a gentle wooing song with a tender lyric by Cecil Mack. Also that year they wrote "I've Got de Blues," which is not musically blueslike but is among the first pop songs to describe a bad feeling as "the blues."

Smith and Bowman were frequent, but not exclusive, writing partners at this time. Elmer Bowman began a sometime collaboration with Al Johns ("I've Got Chicken on the Brain" and "Go 'Way Back and Sit Down"), and Chris Smith in 1903 published his first song with Jim

Jolly John Larkins

Burris, who would eventually replace Bowman as Smith's main lyricist. Around 1905 the Smith-Bowman vaudeville act broke up, and Smith teamed with Billy Johnson. The parting with Bowman must have been amicable, since Smith-Bowman songs continued to be issued into 1912.

Smith was writing ordinary coon songs at this point, nothing as musically good as "Good Morning, Carrie." But his work was sharp enough to attract the attention of prominent performers such as May Irwin, Lew Dockstader, Ernest Hogan, and Jolly John Larkins. He began to write with the black vaudevillian Harry Brown, with Billy Johnson, and especially with Cecil Mack. The Smith-Mack "He's a Cousin of Mine" was interpolated into *Marrying Mary* in 1906. The song was published with Silvio Hein, the show's composer, credited as cowriter, the sort of cut-in that was often imposed on the writers of promising interpolations. Smith had three songs with Cecil Mack in *Bandanna Land* (and one with Alex Rogers and Will Marion Cook), all published by Gotham-Attucks.

Smith quickly learned his craft as a songwriter, taking as his specialty the joke-song. There was a musical wittiness in him that helped his lyricists deliver their punch. He could fashion a matter-of-fact lilt for a deadpan line ("Come *af*-ter *break*-fast, *bring* 'long your *lunch* and leave be-*fore* sup-*per* time. . . .") or a square-on-the beat stress for key words in a setup ("You're in the *right church* but the *wrong pew*. . . ."). He and Burris made a lyric in the "Nobody" vein ("Constantly," which Bert Williams used in the *Follies of 1910*), and he could suggest the monotony of a relationship with a repeated note ("But there *ain't nothin' doin' at all with* the undertaker *man*. . . ."). When writing a tune for a word-centered song, Smith enhanced the words in musically clever ways. The Smith tunes of the early 1900s actually swing.

The wild success of "Alexander's Ragtime Band" in 1911 gave ragtime songs a second wind. The genre had cooled in the preceding few years, winding down to lightly syncopated niceties like "Every Little Movement" and "Put Your Arms Around Me, Honey." Irving Berlin's song wasn't very raggy, but it had the zing of a bugle call. It was joyous and rowdy, and it outsold everything else that year. The rag-song was mother's milk to Chris Smith, and he quickly reboarded the ragtime bandwagon. In 1911–1912, rag-songs poured out of him: "Barnyard Rag" (with Billy Johnson); his own "Monkey Rag" (which was also published as an instrumental, "Honky-Tonky Monkey Rag"); "When Mother Plays a Rag on the Sewing Machine" (with Joe Goodwin and Joe McCarthy); and "The Snake (That Sneaky, Snakey Rag)" and "That Puzzlin' Rag" (both with Elmer Bowman), all of them unforced and full of syncopated surprises.

His pop songs got raggier, too, during this time. "Bean, Beans, Beans" (his last success with Elmer Bowman) sold well in 1912, as did his own "I Want a Little Lovin' Sometime" and "My Little Loving Aero Man" (lyric by Charles McCarron and Ferd Mierisch). He also wrote a real blues in 1912 ("I've Got the Blues But I'm Too Blamed Mean to Cry," with Tim Brymn), but his exploration of that form would wait until the twenties. A new social fad was in the making, and a Chris Smith song would encapsulate it.

In 1911 Jesse Lasky and his partner, Henry Harris, opened a new kind of theatre on Broadway, the Folies Bergere. Their idea was to evoke the elegant naughtiness of bohemian Paris in a place that provided food and drink along with intimate variety entertainment. In imitation of their Parisian models, they called their hybrid a "cabaret," and it was the first upscale attempt at this kind of entertainment in America. (The black social clubs of the Tenderloin had combined the "cabaret" ingredients for years, but the white world did not know they existed.) The Folies Bergere was more theatre than club—fewer than half of its 1,100 seats were at tables, the rest were in rows—and its policy of two "shows" a night made the customers feel that someone was holding a stopwatch over their fun. The enterprise soon failed, doomed by its theatrical setting, but the cabaret idea was seized on by the theatre district's older restaurants. The so-called lobster palaces, such as Rector's, Shanley's, and Louis Martin's, could actually provide the feast for all the senses that the Folies Bergere had promised.

By 1911 all the large midtown restaurants had added dance floors. Exhibition dance teams were hired to perform before, during, and after the supper seating. Strolling singers serenaded individual tables; house orchestras kept long hours. All of these places were renowned as restaurants long before they were cabarets, so the patrons were assured of good (and expensive) food. But it was the dancing that gave them their new character. The exhibition teams tricked up old dances. A sudden stop in a waltz made a "hesitation step." They presented exotica from foreign lands—the apache, the tango—and they literally trotted out the flashiest of new fads. When cabaret patrons began to try the new dances, the public social lives of men and women, which had been separate before this time, came together in glorious union on the dance floor. The customers felt the call to get with it, to express themselves in this thoroughly modern and sophisticated way.

Before 1912 it was considered scandalous to dance in a public place; the mere proximity of bodies was unseemly. Dancing at private balls had been mostly confined to the old figured patterns of reels and polkas. Waltzing consisted mainly of whirling together at arm's length. Cakewalks were merely prancing side by side. But the new dances allowed real physical contact, sometimes a lingering contact, with one's partner. Moralists were horrified by the cabaret scene. They had their first glimpse of emancipated women, and they didn't like the look of them. These new women painted their faces, flirted, even chose their partners, didn't wait to be asked, and often paid their own way.

Some of them couldn't wait until evening to dance, so several places—
Bustanoby's among the first—instituted a 4:00 P.M. *the dansant* to tide
them over. Males who frequented these afternoon dances were looked
down upon by hard-working husbands and boyfriends who could not
leave the office in time to be two-stepping by 4:00 P.M. They called
them "tango pirates," these strange, idle men who danced with others'
wives and girlfriends in the daytime. And the husbands had an oxy-
moronic uneasiness that their women were in the arms of some sort of
unmanly Lotharios.

The explosion of interest in social dancing required new dances—
there simply weren't enough old ones. In the years 1912–1914 about a
hundred new dances were introduced to (and faded from) the cabarets.
The dances came from everywhere: Argentina (the tangos and rhum-
bas); society teachers (the politer glides and trots); Paris (the maxixe);
and the exhibitionists themselves (Maurice Mouvet's "The Maurice
Walk," "The Castles' Half and Half," Rosa Mantilla's "Two in One—
Maxixe Tango").

Most striking of all were the American "animal dances," several of
them with moves borrowed from black vernacular dance. The first one
was the Grizzly Bear, a San Francisco import celebrated in an Irving
Berlin lyric of 1910. This was quickly followed by the Turkey Trot,
which put face-to-face partners to pumping and flapping their arms.
After these, animal dances poured out in delirious profusion, each
accompanied by a song lyric intended to be both insinuating and
instructive: "The Angle Worm Wiggle," "The Bull Frog's Glide,"
"Buzzin' the Bee," "The Bunny Hug," "The Peacock Strut," "The
Kangaroo Hop," and "The Pigeon Walk." Only the Fox Trot, the simplest and least ridiculous of them, survived the era.

No black dance was taken up whole by the cabaret dancers. They
took bits and pieces, individual moves and postures, to flavor their
steps. And the names of the moves they took would have been considered vulgar, so they went unheard. No respectable matron, no matter
how free and expressive on the dance floor, would have admitted that
her dancing had been informed by the Monkey Hunch, the Georgia
Grind, or the Buzzard Lope. The Texas Tommy and Stewin' the Rice
made their way downtown a step at a time. An important source of
black dance for white audiences and teachers was the 1913 edition of

The Darktown Follies, written and produced by J. Leubrie Hill, at Harlem's
Lafayette Theatre. Hill's show featured many steps inspired by black
social dance. The circle-dance finale
of *Darktown Follies*—along with Hill's
song "At the Ball, That's All"—was
purchased outright by Florenz Ziegfeld
to become the centerpiece of his
Follies of 1913.

Jim Burris

The time was ripe for a dance-
song to capitalize on this highly visible
curiosity about black dance. Not
another silly animal dance, but something in the know. It couldn't be
overtly "black," but it might tease its
listeners with black musical and lyric
references. In 1913 Chris Smith and Jim Burris created that song, a
perfect marriage of words and music called "Ballin' the Jack."

The Chris Smith melody has tantalized generations, and the Jim
Burris lyric is so good that it is the only set of dance-song words to out-
live its time. The chorus lyrics are more specific than those of other
dance songs. Most of the dance-song lyrics tell you what fun you'll have
learning a new dance; this one tells you how to do it. All of the
dancer's major body parts are accounted for:

> *First you put your two knees close up tight,*
> *Then you sway 'em to the left, then you sway 'em to the right,*
> *Step around the floor kind of nice and light,*
> *Then you twis' around and twis' around with all your might.*
> *Stretch your lovin' arms straight out in space,*
> *Then you do the Eagle Rock with style and grace,*
> *Swing your foot way 'round then bring it back,*
> *Now that's what I call "Ballin' the Jack."*

Anyone who can't make something interesting out of that has no business on the dance floor. If you put your knees together and sway, your

hips will follow and you will be doing a modified grind. Stepping "nice and light" implies a cat-walk. The "twis' around" (with knees unlocked) is a hip roll. The "Eagle Rock" is an arms-out, head-back posture named for the Eagle Rock Baptist Church in Kansas City, known by blacks since the Reconstruction era for the ecstatic, trance-like dancing during its services. When you "Swing your foot way 'round then bring it back,"you are beginning to Stew the Rice. The song's title phrase is said to come from black railroad slang. The engine was called the "jack"—the jackass that pulled the load—and the trainman's hand-twisting gesture was a signal to "highball it," to rev it up and get moving. The signalman's finger-up, swivel-wristed pose was carried over into Trucking in the thirties.

Chris Smith's music invites good-time movement. The chorus is loose and playful, leaving room for a dancer or singer to improvise with a built-in two-bar break—when you "twis' around and twis' around with all your might"—and giving four straight-on-the-beat accents— "Swing your *foot way 'round then*"—to heighten the ending. The verse is also musically deft. It builds intensity harmonically in its first six bars by rising from the tonic to a flatted third to a flatted fifth. The ascending blue notes in the verse lift the song, and the opening of its chorus lets it swing down gently in a new key. "Ballin' the Jack" is very savvy songwriting.

"Ballin' the Jack" was already a dancers' favorite by the time it was interpolated into the score of The Girl from Utah in 1914. One of the musical's stars, Donald Brian, was a better dancer than singer, and he chose "Ballin' the Jack" as a feature number for himself. The song regularly stole the thunder from another interpolation in the show, Jerome Kern's "They Didn't Believe Me." Prince's Orchestra recorded "Ballin' the Jack" that year, and the huge sales of this recording proved that people were dancing at home as well as in cabarets. Joseph Stern published "Ballin' the Jack" in 1913 and, inspired by its success, got Chris Smith and Ferd Mierisch to supply a lyric for Luckey Roberts' "Junk Man Rag," the company's most successful one-step. In a reversal of the usual order, the song version of "Ballin' the Jack" prompted Stern to release a piano version one year later.

Smith stayed with dancing as a song subject for a couple of years. With Jim Burris he wrote "At the Fox-Trot Ball" in 1914, the year of his own "Jungle Ball" and his instrumental "Piping Rock." Smith's other dance pieces of this time were "Keep It Up" (1915) and "Shoot the Rabbit" (1916). Smith showed these off when he tried a vaudeville act again in the mid-teens, pairing briefly with the dancer George Cooper, who had recently dissolved his long partnership with Bill Robinson.

By 1916 Chris Smith and Charles McCarron could spell out in song exactly where the new musical excitement was coming from: "Down in Honky Tonky Town" ("Down where the gals are brown, that's where music grows. . . ."). Smith dabbled with blues again that year with "If You Don't Want Me, Send Me to My Ma" (lyric by Cecil Mack) and his instrumental "San Francisco Blues." The 1917 publication of "Farmyard Blues" pictures Smith back in vaudeville, this time with a new partner, the singer Henry Troy. Their photo on the cover shows the slender, half-smiling Smith seated at an upright piano and Troy seated on top of the piano, his feet hanging over the keys. They are casually dressed, Troy in a double-breasted business suit, Smith in a sport coat, with high-collared shirt, narrow tie, and white socks. They are posed to seem bemused by a barnyard scene drawn opposite them. They are sharing space with a cartoon, but they are not cartoons themselves.

Smith and Burris wrote a jazzy song, "Coolin' the Coffee Pot," in 1917. The genre seemed just right for Smith, and the song promises hot numbers to come. But for two years nothing came: He did not publish in 1918 or 1919. Was he ill? Was he written out? Was he away in the army? (He was forty years old at the time, beyond the reach of the new Selective Service Act. None of the black songwriter veterans mentioned Smith as having been in their units.) Whatever the reason for his absence from the publishing scene, he was away too long. Until the late teens he had published twelve to fifteen numbers a year, most of them with major publishers, but he would never again have this kind of momentum in his career.

Smith came back with five songs in 1920. One was the very funny "I Want to Know Where Tosti Went When He Said Good-Bye," which Bert Williams featured in his *Broadway Brevities*. He wrote the bleak lyric for "The Unbeliever," with music by Bert Williams and Frederick M. Bryan. It is a "Nobody" song turned sour. (The verse tells us that the singer "don't believe in nothin' at all," then the chorus lists several Bible stories that the singer doubts are true. The last line of the chorus is a chiller: "I'm not rich but I'm willing to give away a bundle of dough, If anybody can wash me and make me whiter than snow.") His 1920 story song about a bold bank robber from Bowling Green ("Long Gone," with music by W. C. Handy) was used in *Shuffle Along*.

In 1921 Smith came back even stronger when he began to write with Jimmy Durante. They did four numbers together, all with Durante's music and Smith's words, none issued by a major publisher. They are the best sort of Tin Pan Alley jazz: rhythmic, inventive, and full of ginger. The finest of them is "I've Got My Habits On," on which Smith's lyric credit is shared with Bob Schafer. (Schafer was a self-styled songwriter's "agent," a matchmaker between writers and small publishers. His name is on thirty or so songs, probably all of them cut-ins, with black writers of the twenties.) Durante's breakthrough as a comedian had not yet come, so he was in no better position to command a publisher's attention than was Smith.

Smith tried a novelty piano solo in 1922 called "The Missing Link." He was writing well in the early twenties, but he wasn't being published well. He wasn't getting in at Haviland, Remick, or Witmark any more, and Joseph Stern had left the business in 1920, turning over his catalog to Edward B. Marks. Smith's pieces were now being issued by second-tier publishers, such as Goodman & Rose, Stark & Cowan, Metro, and Skidmore. It had been a while since "Ballin' the Jack."

Smith wrote some good blues in the mid-twenties, most of them bought by Clarence Williams. Bessie Smith recorded the 1924 Smith-Williams-Troy "Cakewalking Babies from Home." Smith also wrote his last solo effort that year, "If You Sheik on Your Mamma, Your Mamma's Gonna Sheba on You." In 1927, he wrote with Handy again ("The White Man Said 'Twas So"), and he had a song in *Bottomland* ("Shootin' the Pistol," with Clarence Williams). With Fats Waller, he wrote "Come On and Stomp, Stomp, Stomp." But none of Smith's 1920s songs got the push they deserved. Most of his publishers were too small to push anything very far. He published nothing in 1928 or 1929, and only one number in 1930. Then there is another blank in his writing life—one that was eight years long. His name is on two songs from the late thirties and two from 1943, listed in a "committee" credit with three other writers. Chris Smith died on October 4, 1949, in New York City.

Like the teens and twenties songs of that other gifted musical illiterate, Irving Berlin, Chris Smith's songs are full of musical surprise and delight. No matter how trite the subject or genre, Smith could find a musical twist to freshen it. He became primarily a lyricist after his odd silence in midcareer, and his words were fresh, too. But he was already sliding by then. He had been too long between hits.

SHELTON BROOKS

One way of coping with the vagaries of the freelance songwriter's life was to treat songwriting as one's secondary profession. A natural professional combination of the vaudeville era was that of the singer-songwriter. The vaudeville stage offered a platform from which to introduce one's writing efforts, and if the writer had a hit song, he became more bookable as a performer. Shelton Brooks was a vaudeville and revue performer who wrote some of the best songs of the teens. Two of them became instant standards, receiving many recordings and sporadic revivals. Brooks published almost exclusively with his first Chicago publisher, Will Rossiter. By automatically giving Rossiter the first look at his work, Brooks escaped the grind of peddling his songs. Brooks' name is on about forty published songs—as compared with Chris Smith's more than

Shelton Brooks

200—and as good as many of them are, he was thought of in his day as an entertainer who happened to have a knack for words and music.

Shelton Brooks was born on May 4, 1886, in Amesburg, Ontario, Canada. His father was a minister. When Shelton was a child, his family moved to Cleveland. In his mid-teens, Brooks began to adapt his self-taught keyboard style—acquired at his family's pump organ—to the piano, and he was soon hacking out a living as a cafe and theatre pianist in Detroit. By the time he was twenty, he had settled in Chicago and was playing at clubs and theatres there. He attained a bit of local vaudeville fame as a Bert Williams imitator, and he was good enough to get his subject's approval when Williams saw his act. He wrote himself a "Williams song" (with lyrics by Mat Marshall) called "You Ain't Talking to Me," which Will Rossiter published in 1909. The song didn't set the world (or Chicago) afire, so Rossiter passed on Brooks' next one.

The next one was "Some of These Days." It was an odd song for 1910, but Brooks believed in it enough to contribute $35 toward getting it published. (The first publisher was William Foster, who would soon make his name as a pioneering black film producer. He began issuing his all-black comedy shorts in Chicago in the early teens.) Brooks also had enough faith to try to get a plug for the song, and he used the best show-business connection he had: his friendship with Sophie Tucker's maid, Mollie Elkins. Tucker was headlining a bill at Chicago's Orpheum Theatre, delivering her trademark repertoire of raunch ("There's Company in the Parlor, Girls") and pep ("The Angle-Worm Wiggle" and "That Lovin' Two-Step Man"). She was an established vaude-

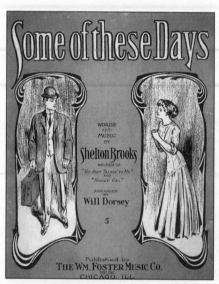

"Some of These Days"

ville star, she had made a few recordings, and she was already tired of songwriters hounding her. At Elkins' insistence, she granted Shelton Brooks a few minutes to play and sing his song. Tucker was bowled over. She took the song into her act immediately, made it her theme, and sang it at practically every performance she gave until her death in 1966. In her 1945 autobiography, entitled *Some of These Days*, she marveled at the song's staying power:

> It had everything. . . . I've turned it inside out, singing it every way imaginable, as a dramatic song, as a novelty number, as a sentimental ballad, and always audiences have loved it and asked for it. "Some of These Days" is one of the great songs that will be remembered and sung for years and years to come, like some of Stephen Foster's.

"Some of These Days" packs more honest emotion than any other song of its time. Its lyric is a stream-of-consciousness mix of defiance and hurt set to the music of a cantor's wail. It is solid and well-made, but cleverness is not its object. There are only two rhymes in its chorus, both of them internal. The song is not about wordplay, it is about the contradictory feelings of a jilted lover:

> *Some of these days, you'll miss me, honey,*
> *Some of these days, you'll feel so lonely.*
> *You'll miss my hugging, you'll miss my kissing,*
> *You'll miss me, honey, when you go away.*
> *I feel so lonely just for you only,*
> *For you know, honey, you've had your way.*
> *And when you leave me, I know 'twill grieve me,*
> *You'll miss your little baby, yes, some of these days.*

The verse has a generic feel. It ambles through a conventional narrative of a couple's parting. ("Two sweethearts courted happily for quite a while, Midst simple life of country folk. When the lad told girlie he must go away, Her little heart with grief 'most broke. . . .") It is musically and lyrically ordinary, and it is a perfect setup for the surprising, minor-keyed outburst of the chorus. The square lyric in the verse of the second (Rossiter) edition is a revision of the folksier original version, and it is just right.

Knowing that Sophie Tucker would promote the song, Will Rossiter bought its copyright from William Foster. "Some of These Days" sold over two million copies over the next few years, becoming one of those songs that would always be available in a recent reprint. Brooks tinkered with the lyric of later editions, but the idea and the architecture of the song remained the same. (He substituted "I'll miss my little dad-dad-dad-dy" for "You'll miss your little baby" in 1922, finally committing to print the words that Tucker had always sung.) "Some of These Days" has spoken to generations of the lovelorn. Sophie Tucker recorded it four times—the first in 1911 for Edison— and jazz greats from Louis Armstrong to Django Reinhardt to Coleman Hawkins have enjoyed improvising on its changes.

Shelton Brooks was at a fork in his professional road. The success of "Some of These Days" could have launched him as a New York songwriter, but he chose not to leave Chicago. He remained a popular vaudevillian, a local star with a hit song. He appeared in two shows at the Pekin Theatre in 1911: *Dr. Herb's Prescription* and *The Lime Kiln Club*. In 1912 he had moderate success with another good song, "All Night Long," published by Rossiter.

In 1913 Shelton Brooks wrote the sly and salacious "I Wonder Where My Easy Rider's Gone." This tale of Miss Susie Johnson's itch for a jockey named Lee was performed in vaudville by Sophie Tucker, and she also recorded it. (Mae West would use it in her film *She Done Him Wrong*, and she would record it for Brunswick in 1933.) The song is slangy and bluesy, and it was notorious enough to provoke a musical "answer." W. C. Handy's 1914 "Yellow Dog Blues" finds Miss Johnson still waiting for news from Lee.

As the dance craze continued through the teens, Shelton Brooks contributed three fine numbers to it. The first was his "Walkin' the Dog," in 1916. Like "Ballin' the Jack," it begins with a verse that promises to teach a new dance followed by a chorus that gives directions. The chorus lyric implies that by 1916 dancers knew how to execute the Texas Tommy, the Slow Drag, and Get Over Sally, because these figures are merely named, not described. "Walkin' the Dog" became the specialty of Johnny Fogarty's Dancing Review, a white company that took black dances onto cabaret stages such as Reisenweber's in New York.

In 1917 Shelton Brooks created another standard that soared as quickly as had "Some of These Days." This was his irresistible two-step, "The Darktown Strutters' Ball." It was introduced in vaudeville by a white trio (Benny Fields, Jack Salisbury, and Benny Davis), and its catchy tune was taken up by dance bands of all sizes. Leo Feist bought the copyright from Will Rossiter and issued the three million copies of sheet music that were sold. "Darktown Strutters'" had three important recordings in 1917 alone: the first to be released was by a saxophone sextet called the Six Brown Brothers, the next was by the Ford Dabney Orchestra, and the third and best was that of the Original Dixieland Jazz Band. The ODJB made their recording for Columbia on May 31, 1917, but it was not released until the fall. It remained in the company's catalog for years.

"The Darktown Strutters' Ball" is an invitation to a dance, and it makes the listener want to go. The chorus opens with four bars of a basic boogie melody ("I'll be down to get you in a taxi, honey, You bet-ter be ready about half past eight. . . ."), and the lyric is a syncopated match. The chorus is twenty bars long—a length that usually indicates a tagged-on four-bar coda—but in this case the extra bars are hidden away in the tune. The "extraneous" measures are "Goin' to dance out both my shoes, When they play the 'Jelly Roll Blues.'" The song could scan melodically and lyrically without them, but they send the song home in a very satisfying way.

Brooks' third great dance song of the decade was "I Want to Shimmie," a collaboration with a white lyricist, Grant Clarke. As the wildness of improvised music struck America in the late teens, social dancing took on a manic quality. The decade that began with cabaret patrons cautiously slipping into trots and glides ended with the brazen shoulder-shaking and breast-wiggling of the shimmy. (Knees, elbows, and rear ends would soon get their workouts in the Charleston and the Black Bottom of the 1920s.) The shimmy was mentioned in the lyrics of black dance-songs as early as 1910, but it was not discovered by white social dancers for nearly ten years. In a noisy ongoing feud, both Mae West and Gilda Gray claimed to have introduced the movement to polite society.

Bee Palmer sang and danced to Shelton Brooks' "Shimmie" in the 1918 summer edition of *Ziegfeld's Midnight Frolic*. The melody is full of built-in breaks for the shaking ("I don't want no waltz for mine, *I want to shimmie, I want to shimmie*, Pavlowa's dance may be divine, But *I'd rather shimmie, I'd rather shimmie*. . . ."), and the Clarke lyric puts down Brooks' own previous dance hit ("I've 'Walked the Dog' and 'Balled the Jack,' but they don't seem to have the knack. . . ."). "I Want to Shimmie" was published by Leo Feist in 1919, the same year that Brooks, Ernie Erdman, and Benny Davis placed their ballad "Jean" with Waterson, Berlin & Snyder.

A Brooks song was the hit of a New York revue, and he had made inroads to New York publishers, but he remained a figure of Chicago's show business scene. From August through October 1920, Shelton Brooks contributed songs to and performed in three musicals for Chica-go's Panama Amusement Company. They were all revivals of white shows, presented previously in Chicago and/or New York, that were rewritten for black audiences. He was the leading man in each of these (*Canary Cottage, Miss Nobody from Starland*, and *September Morn*) opposite Alberta Hunter, a rising star of Chicago cabaret. *Canary Cottage* ran for only two weeks at the Avenue Theatre, but Hunter never failed to receive encores for singing Brooks' "Wake Up with the Blues."

In 1922 Shelton Brooks finally made the move to New York, but he came as a performer, not a songwriter. He was hired by the producer Lew Leslie for Leslie's first Broadway effort, *The Plantation Revue*. Leslie had lately begun a producing career by assembling talent for the Plantation Club, a downtown rival of Harlem's Cotton Club, at Fiftieth Street and Broadway. Leslie's club shows were enormously successful, largely because of the presence of a luminous young singer named Florence Mills (1895–1927). He decided to select the best numbers from his Plantation floor shows and present an evening-long black revue at the Forty-eighth Street Theatre. Besides Brooks and Mills, the cast included Edith Wilson and the dancer U. S. Thompson.

The following year, Leslie produced a revue in London, which he called *Dover Street to Dixie*. The "Dover Street" half—all British variety acts—opened the bill, and the "Dixie" half was an abbreviated *Plantation Revue*, again with Brooks and Mills. The American company was popular with London audiences, and they were invited to give a command performance for the royal family. Reworking his material yet again, Leslie added numbers to his London show and brought it to New York's Broadhurst Theatre for eight weeks in 1924 as *Dixie to Broadway*. Shelton Brooks was given a feature in which to sing his own songs in this edition, and a reviewer called him "the bright spot of the show," quite an accolade for someone sharing a stage with Florence Mills. In 1926 Brooks and Mills were teamed for the fourth time by Lew Leslie, in the first of his *Blackbirds* revues. *Blackbirds of 1926* tried out at Harlem's Alhambra Theatre and traveled to London and Paris. (The first Broadway *Blackbirds* would come in 1928.) The songs for the Lew Leslie shows came from a long list of writers, black and white. But it seems never to have occurred to Leslie to use the proven songwriting talent of Shelton Brooks for his black revues of the mid-twenties.

Brooks made a few recordings in the 1920s. The first were two vocal duets with the blues singer Sara Martin, made for OKeh in April 1923 ("I Got What It Takes to Bring You Back" and "Original Blues"). In February 1926 he provided the piano accompaniment for Ethel

Waters' recordings of "After All These Years" and "Throw Dirt in Your Face" for Columbia.

Brooks was never in great demand as a studio singer or as an accompanist, but he remained highly employable as an actor and revue player. He produced and performed in *Nifties of 1928*; he made a short film comedy for Vitaphone in 1929 ("Gayety," with Hamtree Harrington); and he had a twice-a-week radio show on CBS in 1930 with Bird Allen—as the stars of "Egg and Shell." He was working but he wasn't writing much. In 1930 he had a small Broadway role in *Brown Buddies*, in which he placed one song ("Don't Leave Your Little Blackbird Blue," written with Joe Jordan and Porter Grainger). In the 1930s he pieced out the waning years of vaudeville as a singer. He had a supporting role in, and wrote two songs for, a black film called *Double Deal* in 1939, and he played the Apollo Theatre in 1942.

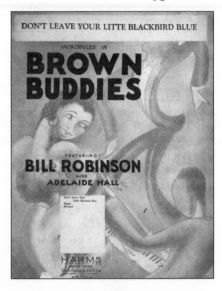

Brown Buddies

In the early 1940s Brooks moved to California. He became a mainstay of Ken Murray's *Blackouts*, a salute to burlesque that ran for seven years in Los Angeles but only seven weeks in New York. He was one of ASCAP's grand old men during this time, honored as a writer of standards that Sophie Tucker was still singing and Dixieland bands were still playing. But his songwriting days were long behind him. Shelton Brooks died in Los Angeles on September 6, 1975.

JAMES REESE EUROPE

The career of James Reese Europe is unlike any other in pop music. He was primarily a leader and organizer of bands and orchestras, and although he never wrote a hit song or had a hit record, he was arguably the most influential musician of his time. The music he made—and the places at which he made it—raised the visibility of and respect for black instrumentalists and composers everywhere. As composer and conductor for the preeminent dance team of his era, the Castles, his polish and professionalism shone in theatres and society ballrooms across America. As leader of the "Hellfighters" Band in war-torn France, he displayed the same grit and stamina as did the Hellfighters themselves. As founder and president of the Clef Club, he made equitable employment possible for hundreds of black musicians in a time when most American Federation of Musicians locals would not accept them as members. Europe was a serious man who loved popular music and the people who created it. He served both of his loves with a large mind and heart.

James Reese Europe was born on February 22, 1880, in Mobile, Alabama. His father, Henry Europe, held jobs as a teacher, reporter,

James Reese Europe

barber, and customs house official, and he provided a solid, middle-class life for his wife Lorraine and their four children. Henry Europe was a self-taught player of several instruments, and his wife was an accomplished pianist. One of their daughters and both of their sons would make careers in music.

In 1889 the Europe family moved to Washington, D.C., where Henry Europe took a job as supervisor in a city post office. Young James went to Preparatory High School for Colored Youth (which later became Dunbar High), and he studied violin with Joseph Douglass, grandson of the orator Frederick Douglass. In 1894 James Europe was a student at M Street High School, enjoying his status as a cadet in his school's drill corps as well as his musical studies with the violinist Enrico Hurlei, then an assistant conductor of the U.S. Marine Band under John Philip Sousa.

Henry Europe died unexpectedly in June 1899, and although James was already serious about beginning a music career, he knew where he was needed. He stayed at the family home at 310 Oak Street for several years, taking various jobs in order to help his mother financially.

James Europe moved to New York during the winter of 1902–1903. Some time in 1904, during a period when he was playing piano and mandolin in Tenderloin clubs, he met John W. Love, the private secretary to the John Wanamaker family. Love recommended Europe to provide a string quartet for a Wanamaker party. It was Europe's first job for the society clientele who would soon rely on him almost exclusively to provide their music.

He was making some theatrical contacts, too. John Larkins hired Europe as chorus and orchestra director for the tour of *A Trip to Africa*. It was on this tour that Europe did his first song-peddling. He placed five of his songs with the Sol Bloom company in Chicago, and they were all published in 1904. The Setchell company in Boston issued a Europe-Larkins song that same year.

In 1905 Europe was a member of the Memphis Students show orchestra, formed by Ernest Hogan and led by Will Marion Cook. When a dispute between Hogan and Cook arose, Europe remained loyal to Hogan and passed up the chance to go with Cook's splinter group to London and Paris. For the next three years James Europe led vaudeville orchestras in and around New York.

Europe's reputation as a leader was made in the four years from 1906 to 1910. As musical director for Cole and Johnson's *The Shoo-Fly Regiment* and *The Red Moon*, S. H. Dudley's *The Black Politician*, and Bert Williams' *Mr. Lode of Koal*, Europe worked closely with the major black composers and stars of the period. He contributed several songs to the Cole and Johnson shows, and six of his collaborations with Bob Cole were published. As he was earning the attention and respect of the creators of black theatre, he was nominated to be a charter member of the Frogs in 1908.

His assembling orchestras and groups of all sizes for various shows and occasions put Jim Europe in contact with ordinary musicians as well as with stars. In train cars, dressing rooms, and segregated cafes, he heard them talk about the prejudice, degradation, and dishonesty they were subject to in the pursuit of their careers. Most American Federation of Musicians locals refused to admit blacks, and the strict segregation of bands kept black players from proving their skills to contractors and white leaders. Because there were no union-regulated wage minimums, black players were at the mercy of their employers. At the end of a job, they were paid what the employer thought they deserved, and this was always less than white players would have received for the same work. To accept employment under these conditions meant paying one's travel expenses to get to a job, on the outside chance that you would not be cheated out of wages when the evening was over. It was common practice for black musicians to be hired for menial jobs at a club or hotel, then to be called in from the kitchen to the main room to play for dancing. At the end of their sets the musicians would be permitted to pass the hat and solicit "contributions" from the dancers and guests. Jim Europe heard the horror stories—and had some of his own to tell. He couldn't remake a prejudiced society, but he determined to change the band business in New York.

Europe realized that the strength of the musicians' union lay in its numbers and in the assurance of quality that it could offer to the employers of its members. It could offer, in any number and combination, players who performed well, read well, dressed well, and were dependable. If you hired union players, there were standard fees and procedures required for their payment. If the A F of M refused to allow blacks onto this two-way professional street, then blacks needed their own organization to function like a union for them. Jim Europe decided to create the kind of organization they needed.

In early April 1910 Europe began to discuss his idea among New York's busiest black bandleaders: Joe Jordan, Ford Dabney, Tim Brymn, and James Vaughn. He sought the advice of writers (Henry Creamer, Tom Lemonier, and Al Johns), arrangers (Will Tyers and Will Vodery), and teachers (among them, his brother John Europe). They agreed on the need for Europe's plan. They made an organization that they called the Clef Club, and there was only one person proposed to be its president: James Reese Europe. By the end of April, as word of what Europe was doing spread, the Clef Club had a membership of 135. The first musicians to join were mostly string players, but within a few months the club could make good on its promise to supply expert players on any instruments that a job required.

The Clef Club needed funds for its administration, and its members needed visibility in the New York music scene. Contractors, club owners, and party hosts had to hear proof that black players were as competent as whites. Europe decided that both needs could best be served by a gigantic fundraiser concert, something big enough to make the papers, to showcase his cause and his players. The idea of a symphony-sized Clef Club Orchestra was born, and the idea alone was newsworthy. There had never been a large black orchestra before, and there was great curiosity about how they would sound and what they would play.

The answers came on May 27, 1910, when Europe led a hundred Clef Club players in a concert at Harlem's Manhattan Casino. The program was what we would now call a "pops" evening, including some vocal numbers, Paul Lincke's "Beautiful Spring" and Joe Jordan's "That Teasing Rag," and it was a huge success. In October the Clef Club presented its (pickup) Orchestra at the Casino again, in a program promising "Sixty Minutes with the Popular Colored Composers." Europe's "Clef Club March" was debuted on this occasion. The long tradition of semiannual Clef Club concerts began in the club's first year.

There is a wide-angle photo of a tuxedo-clad Clef Club Orchestra from this time. They are in a ballroom, and there are about a hundred faces looking at the camera. A small, raised stage at the rear is overflowing with musicians, including a row of tambourine players and a solitary trombonist, all sitting beneath a sign that spells out "Clef Club" in lights. On the floor level below the stage are the string players, dozens of them, seated in a formation as wide as the room, a phalanx of banjos, violins, cellos, mandolins, and guitars. Most of the players are holding their instruments at rest, a few are pantomiming playing them. Europe is front and center, with a baton in his hands. He is tall and handsome and tense-looking, his serious gaze intensified by round, wire-rimmed glasses. He looks as if he is ready to spring.

In December the Clef Club moved into its first headquarters, at 134 West Fifty-third Street, directly across from the Marshall Hotel. Fed by the growing white curiosity about black music and black dance—and by the growing celebrity of Jim Europe—the Clef Club prospered. The phones rang on Fifty-third Street, ensembles of all sizes were put together, and Clef Club players were sent out nightly to parties and dances. Salaries were agreed upon in advance. Travel expenses were subject to negotiation. A dress code for Clef Club musicians was established: tuxedos for advance bookings, dark suits for pickup dates.

The organization is remembered now mostly for its historic concerts, but the importance of the Clef Club in its time was that it accomplished what it was created to do: it placed black music and musicians into the everyday venues of New York's musical life. On a given night in 1911, there might be a dozen or more Clef Club orchestras playing throughout the city, in clubs, hotels, and private homes. Europe's name was synonymous with his organization's, and since employers thought they should get Europe when they booked a Clef Club group, he would dutifully bustle around the city every night, showing his face, checking in, conducting a few numbers with as many of the Clef Club ensembles as he could get to. It was exhausting, but his plan was working wonderfully.

In 1912 Europe had another bold idea: he would raise money for his favorite charity, the Music School Settlement for Colored People, *and* he would demonstrate the variety of African-American music in America's highest bastion of high culture, Carnegie Hall. Others may have dreamed of showcasing black music so grandly, but in 1912 only Jim Europe could pull it off.

Europe assembled a huge orchestra and a choir and set to work, rehearsing players in sections, accommodating their schedules of dance jobs as best he could. He loved strings as rhythm instruments, and his 125-man orchestra was full of them: over forty mandolins, two string basses, eleven banjos, and a few bandores (a banjo-mandolin hybrid). The base of his string-rhythm sound was his section of nearly thirty harp guitars. The harp guitar was a large, cumbersome, double-necked instrument that was a turn-of-the-century invention. Despite its size, it had almost no resonance; Europe needed a lot of them to get the instrument's sound! (There were a few recordings made using the harp guitar. Among these were the sides made by the Ossman-Dudley Trio for Victor in 1906–1907. Even in an ensemble of only three people, the presence of the harp guitar is felt, rather than heard.) Europe found the thrumming of various string voices hypnotic, and his object was to hypnotize, to take the Carnegie Hall audience where it had never been before. He asked for fourteen upright pianos, and he booked fourteen pianists to play them.

He planned a program to include his own "Lorraine Waltzes" (written for his mother), two of his own marches, songs by Rosamond Johnson and Will Marion Cook, a new spiritual by Harry Burleigh, Samuel Coleridge-Taylor's "By the Waters of Babylon," his own composition "Hula," Will Tyers' "Panama," and, to show that a black singer and orchestra could handle the classics, an aria from Saint-Saens' *Samson and Delilah*.

The concert was heavily advertised, and on May 2, 1912, Carnegie Hall was packed to overflowing, its nearly 3,000 seats and all of its standing room taken by an integrated audience. The experiment was a great success. The audience was, if not hypnotized, enchanted by it all—the Cook numbers were the favorites—the reviews were respectable, and over $5,000 was raised for the Music School Settlement. Best of all, the points were made that there existed a rich body of work by black composers; that black instrumentalists were technically competent and exciting players; and that black music and musicians could make credible showings on the concert stage as well as at the dance hall. The idea of African-Americans making "serious" music would never seem ridiculous again. The Clef Club would be back at Carnegie Hall, on Lincoln's birthday, the following year.

On January 5, 1913, James Europe got married. He and his bride, Willie Angstrom Starke, settled into the Europe home at 67 West 131st Street. However, he never broke off his long-running liaison with Bessie Simms, a chorus girl he had met in *The Shoo-Fly Regiment*. Simms would bear his only child, a son, in 1917.

Throughout 1913 the Clef Club and Jim Europe dominated the New York musical world. Their second Carnegie Hall concert solidified the success of the first. As the dance craze heated up, Clef Club ensembles proliferated. Socialites everywhere trotted to Clef Club music. In the fall, a hand-picked Clef Club Orchestra made a triumphal tour of Eastern cities, including Philadelphia, Baltimore, Richmond, and Washington.

It was during this busy year that jealousies arose among the club's hierarchy. To the public, Jim Europe was the personification of the Clef Club, and his celebrity began to be resented by his peers. They said he was taking the best jobs, promoting himself, and plugging his own compositions at their expense. Their envy was first expressed in gossip, then in complaint, and finally in confrontation. On December 30, 1913, Jim Europe turned over the presidency of the Clef Club to Daniel Kildare. Europe kept his membership in the club, and he went peacefully, believing that the club was strong enough to survive without his leadership, choosing not to risk the damage that political infighting might do.

Europe's decision to resign as president was both generous and wise. And his assessment of the strength of the Clef Club was accurate. New York's A F of M Local 310 voted in 1914 to admit black musicians. The Clef Club had created such a demand for black orchestras and leaders by then that they were preferred over whites and could charge more than whites for their services. The union needed them. The Clef Club would remain a force in New York's musical life until well into the 1930s.

The particular source of the Clef Club membership's resentment of Europe must have been the appointment that he received in late summer of 1913. Through a chance meeting, he got the job that any conductor, black or white, would have wanted. He was conducting the orchestra for a posh party at Mrs. Stuyvesant Fish's Newport mansion. The most enthusiastic couple on the floor was a professional dance team, Vernon and Irene Castle. The Castles loved the rhythms and rich textures of Europe's music, and they hired him as their music director.

The Castles were the most famous couple in the dance world by 1913, but they were not as famous as they would become. Vernon Castle was an Englishman, born in Norwich in 1887. When he was twenty, he came to New York to visit his sister, who was a chorus girl in a London import called *The Orchid*. A small role opened in the show, and Vernon took it. After several more Broadway appearances, including a few as a featured dancer in Lew Fields shows, Vernon met Irene Foote at a swimming party in 1910. She was six years younger than he, and she was slim, pretty, and stagestruck. Vernon got her an audition with Lew Fields, and when Fields lost an actress, Irene joined Vernon in the cast of *The Summer Widowers*.

They were married in May 1911, and about six months later, were invited to perform in a revue in Paris. Their revue failed, and they were stranded. They began to hang out at the Cafe de Paris, trying to wangle an audition for the floor show there. While they waited, they danced. They had always loved to dance together, and because they were bright, blithe, and dressy, the aristocratic patrons of the Cafe mistook them for a dance team. When the customers asked for demonstrations of the Grizzly Bear and the Texas Tommy, the Castles gladly obliged. The host of the Cafe noticed the excitement they caused among his guests and hired the couple to fake "impromptu" exhibitions of new steps several times a night.

During their eight weeks of dancing at the Cafe de Paris, the Castles created great demand for their services as dance teachers in the homes and hotels of the Cafe's elite customers. Some of their wealthy students were Americans who went home and told their friends about the wonderful dancing pair. When the Castles returned to New York in May 1912, the cabaret world was breathlessly awaiting them. They were clean-cut and classy—and married—just the pair to heighten the excitement of the growing dance craze and to take the taint of sin off of it. By the time the Castles met Jim Europe, they were setting social trends, not just reflecting them. They were beginning to create their own steps and to define a personal stance and style. They needed their own music to complement their creations, an orchestra that sounded as classy and modern as they looked. They hired Jim Europe to translate their style into musical terms.

In late 1913, the Castles were preparing for the opening of two dance emporiums that would carry their name. Jim Europe's first project as a Castle employee was to create an orchestra to play at these halls. It would have to be smaller and more streamlined than the famous Clef Club ensembles that he had presented at Carnegie Hall and Manhattan Casino. And the rhythm section had to be its heart. Europe hired the drummer Buddy Gilmore, a flashy player with rock-solid time, who was an alumnus of the Memphis Students. He chose as his cadre two of his Clef Club associates, Will Vodery and Ford Dabney (1883–1958), both adept at arranging and conducting. Europe experimented with ensembles of various sizes and decided that a group of about twenty was right.

He called his new aggregate Europe's Society Orchestra, and he took thirteen of his men into the Victor studios to make his first recordings on December 29, 1913, the day before he left the Clef Club. They made four sides, all of them from the Castles' dance repertoire: "Too Much Mustard," "Down Home Rag," "Amapa—Maxixe Bresilian," and "El Irresistible—Tango Argentine." Europe's burst of specialty writing for the Castles had not come yet, but when the group made its next session six weeks later, there were three Europe numbers, along with one by Jerome Kern.

Europe's Society Orchestra was in great evidence at the 1913 openings of both Castle ventures. The first to open its doors—on December 15—was Castle House, an extravagant *palais de danse* in an East Forty-sixth Street townhouse that had been "classed up" with marble, plants, and mirrors by the society decorator Elsie de Wolfe. Castle House charged $2 a head ($3 on Fridays) for the privilege of dancing in either of its two ballrooms, one large and fancy-ceilinged, the other smaller, with mirrored walls. A complimentary glass of tea or lemonade came with the ticket. Irene didn't like to teach, so she left the Castle House ballroom instruction to Vernon—at $100 an hour for a private lesson.

The second Castle venture opened a few days later. This was Vernon and Irene's supper club, called the Sans Souci, at Broadway and Forty-second Street. The price of admission to Sans Souci was $100 a head, and it was the moneymaker of their two enterprises until it was closed by the fire department after being in operation for about six months. The unspoken reason to go to either club was, of course, to get a glimpse of, or possibly even to dance with, one of the Castles.

In the spring of 1914, over a two-month period, the Joseph Stern Company issued ten of James Europe's specialty pieces for the Castles, eight of them written in collaboration with Ford Dabney. This remarkable set of dance numbers attests to more than Europe's capacity for work and the popularity of his employers. Taken together, the Europe-Castle pieces catch the spirit of the dance craze better than any other publications of their time. They are a catalog of the Castles' dances, old and new. They are variously playful or romantic, with no hint of the somber or the arty. The Castles were in the joy business, and Europe's music is the bright proof of it. The two dances written by Europe alone are "The Castle House Rag" and "Castles in Europe." The Europe-Dabney works are "Castles' Half and Half" (in 5/4 time!), "The Castle Walk," "Castle Innovation Tango," "The Castle Combination" (a waltz-trot), "Castle Lame Duck Waltz," "Castle Maxixe," "Castle Perfect Trot," and "Enticement: An Argentine Idyl" (the last jokingly credited to "Eporue and Yenbad" on the sheet music). Never before or since did a publisher issue so many new pieces by a popular (nonthe-atre) composer in so short a time. Of Europe's seventy or so publications, these were the best-known.

During this intense work for the Castles, Europe found time for other professional activities. Soon after leaving the Clef Club, he organized a similar organization, the Tempo Club, and in March 1914 he presented a group he called the National Negro Symphony Orchestra at Carnegie Hall. Neither of these efforts monopolized him as had the Clef Club. The NNSO was, in fact, an ad hoc organization, coming together occasionally to keep Europe's hand in symphonic music.

On April 8, 1914, the Castles were featured performers at a benefit for the NNSO at Harlem's Manhattan Casino. Everyone knew who they were, had read of their glamour, and had tried to do their steps from diagrams printed in magazines; but most of their devotees had never actually seen them. Oddly, the pair had not danced in public very often. (Their 1912 musical, *The Sunshine Girl*, was their only stage teaming since their popularity as a dance team had begun.) But they were soon to change all that. They were about to embark on a thirty-city, twenty-eight-day tour to spread their Terpsichorean gospel outside of New York. The NNSO benefit was their sendoff.

James Reese Europe and his eighteen-piece orchestra occupied one of the Castles' three private railroad cars as they made their dash through the Northeast and the Midwest. The orchestra was seated prominently on stage during the Castles' show, and the sight of the golden couple whirling to the music of nineteen black men lingered in the minds of their audiences long after the show had left town. If they had never seen anything like the Castles, they had never seen anything like the dignified and sophisticated Society Orchestra either. The Castles were tastemakers: Irene was the first female star to bob her hair; Vernon popularized the wristwatch. They were arbiters of the latest and finest things. So if the Castles preferred a black orchestra, it could only mean that black music makers were the best.

Irene Castle said in her memoirs that it was during this tour that the Castles invented the Fox Trot. She recalled a rehearsal break at which Jim Europe began playing W. C. Handy's "Memphis Blues" on the piano in slow, steady 4/4 time. The team got up to try some steps to the music and liked them enough to refine them for stage use. The "Memphis Blues" routine went into their show. The Fox Trot was the slowest and simplest of the Castle dances, and it was programmed mainly as a contrast to the flashier numbers that surrounded it. But, surprisingly, audiences loved it. Because of its relaxed tempo and its easy basic figure—four slow steps, followed by eight quick ones—the Fox Trot allowed couples less proficient than the Castles to learn it quickly and to improvise in the ballroom. The Fox Trot was originally a combination of a walk and a run, and most social dancers could look good while doing it. Arthur Murray's later slow-slow-quick-quick step simplified the Fox Trot even further.

The popularity of the Fox Trot lay in the appeal of its tempo. It replaced the stiff staccato of mid-teens dance music with the relaxation that is the germ of swing. The Fox Trot began as a fad, but its simplicity gave it staying power. As had all of the other fad dances, the Fox Trot inspired songs and instrumentals with its name in their titles. These pieces quickly vanished from the band books, but the Fox Trot refused to leave the floor. Within a few years of its introduction—and its identification with the Castles—the Fox Trot had become simply what one did when a ballad was played. The easy, slightly swaggering feel of the Fox Trot—the pulsating, steady four—is immediately recognizable as an "American" rhythm. It is as distinctive as the intense beat of the *chansons parisiennes*, the 6/8 bounce of English "light music," or the scuffling tempi of the Latin American dances. The orchestra that first showed the world how it went was that of James Reese Europe.

The dance had other claimants besides the Castles. One of these was the black pianist Hughie Woolford, who said that his playing at the Trouville Restaurant on Long Island inspired the trotting of the vaudeville dancer Harry Fox, who created the classic step. But Woolford's own "Trouville Canter," published in September 1914, pictures Wallace McCutcheon and Vera Maxwell on its cover as

"Originators of the Famous Fox Trot." The first publication to include the dance's name in its title was Will Vodery's "Carolina Fox Trot," issued by Joseph Stern in early July 1914. The Vodery piece names Billy Kent and Jeanette Warner as originators. James Reese Europe's "Castle House Rag" is labeled a Fox Trot on its cover, but the first page of the music more accurately calls it a "Trot and One-Step." Europe's "The Castle Doggy Fox Trot" of 1915 is his only publication in this genre.

After their tour, the Castles went to the Continent for a rest, and Europe's Society Orchestra went to the New Amsterdam roof, to play for dancing at the behest of Florenz Ziegfeld. When the Castles returned to the United States, they began rehearsals for a Broadway show designed to capitalize on their fame: this was *Watch Your Step*, with songs by Irving Berlin. The show opened on December 8, 1914, to begin a 171-performance run. Europe's Society Orchestra was passed over in favor of a traditional Broadway pit band, but the Europe-Castle association continued with the team's new enterprise, Castles-in-the-Air. This was a cabaret located on the top floor of the Shubert Theatre on Forty-fourth Street. Jim Europe conducted the twenty-piece Society Orchestra for the December 1914 opening, and he alternated with Dabney as conductor thereafter. (The Castles would also lend their names to another club, Castles-by-the-Sea, on Long Island.)

During the *Watch Your Step* tour in early 1915, Vernon Castle felt stirrings of patriotism as he read the war news from England. By late spring he had made up his mind to get into his country's fight. He announced his plans to leave the show to take flying lessons at Newport News, Virginia, to train for a commission in the Royal Air Force. The Castles danced to Jim Europe's music for the last time at a Tempo Club benefit in late April, and Vernon Castle left for Virginia a few weeks later.

Castle completed his training as a pilot and received his R.A.F. commission. He flew several successful missions over France, and after these, he became a military flight instructor. He was killed in February 1918 in a training accident at Benbrook Field, near Fort Worth, Texas.

Europe's enforced hiatus from accompanying the Castles did not leave him idle. He cloned his Society Orchestra—as he had done that of the Clef Club—nightly sending out a dozen or so ensembles bearing his name to dances around New York. In late 1915 he had his first professional failure, as cocomposer of the unfortunate musical revue *Darkeydom*, but even this could not dim his luster as New York's preeminent musical name.

Early in 1916 a young man named Noble Sissle came to Jim Europe bearing a letter of introduction from a socialite who had heard him sing at a party in Palm Beach. Europe was impressed enough with Sissle's voice and professional polish to hire him as a singer for the various Society Orchestras. Sissle ingratiated himself with Europe and quickly became a close ally of the busy conductor. The singer recommended a Baltimore pianist—and Sissle's songwriting partner—named Eubie Blake to join the orgainization. Blake was sent for, and he was soon working with the Europe orchestras as pianist and conductor. Their association with Europe was a professional boost for Sissle and Blake, and their talents as musicians and administrators were invaluable to the Europe organization.

On September 18, 1916, Jim Europe enlisted in the Fifteenth Infantry Regiment (Colored) of the New York National Guard. Eight days later, Noble Sissle followed his lead and joined up, too. (Eubie Blake stayed behind to supervise the various Europe orchestras while Europe and Sissle were away.) Jim Europe trained as a machine gunner and was on his way to a first lieutenant's commission when he received a call from Colonel William Hayward, the white officer in command of the Fifteenth.

Hayward asked Europe to defer his imminent leadership of a gunnery unit to create "the best band in the U.S. army" as a recruitment tool and morale booster. It was not what Europe had envisioned as his military duty, but he took it on. Because the band was the army's idea, and not Europe's, the leader could dictate his terms. He wanted an increase in band personnel from the army's regulation twenty-eight to forty-four. He wanted the privilege of recruiting and auditioning his players. He wanted decent instruments, administrative support, and rehearsal time. He got everything he asked for. On June 22, 1917, about ten weeks after the U.S. declaration of war against Germany, Jim Europe's Fifteenth Infantry Band gave its first public performance, a celebration of itself in concert and dance music, at Harlem's Manhattan Casino.

On New Year's Day 1918, after a two-week ocean voyage, the 2,000 officers and men of the Fifteenth Infantry, its band playing the

"Marseillaise," strode ashore at Brest, France. During their first few weeks in France, the "best band in the U.S. army" did everything except make music. The entire regiment was assigned massive work detail, building bridges and docks, laying railroad track, preparing the way for the American incursion into the French interior. Finally, in late February, the band was asked to reassemble for "goodwill" concerts at a YMCA camp at Aix-les-Bains, where American personnel had been sent for R and R. The strains of "The Stars and Stripes Forever," "Memphis Blues," and "Over There" so energized war-weary soldiers and their beleaguered French hosts that the band's assignment was extended, for public concerts at Nantes and Chambery. By mid-March, the engineering and goodwill details were over; it was time to fight.

Every American soldier was needed at the front, but in the segregated U.S. army, there was no black division into which the Fifteenth Infantry Regiment could be put. To get them into action, the Fifteenth was temporarily assigned to a French combat unit—the first American unit to be so ordered—and renamed the 369th Infantry Regiment. Jim Europe became a machine gunner again, the first black officer in the trenches in the Argonne Forest. The mission of the 369th was to secure a small patch of the Argonne, to outlast anything the Germans might throw at them, and to hold their ground. The 369th was under fire for ten weeks. In mid-June Lt. Jim Europe, ill from his prolonged exposure to poison gas, was hospitalized. When he returned to his unit in August, he came back as a bandmaster.

The bravery of the 369th earned them the nickname "Hellfighters." They had held their little piece of the Argonne, and in late summer they took an offensive role as part of the Allied push to rid the region of every vestige of German occupation. Victory seemed possible now, and the "Hellfighters" Band would do its bit to stiffen Allied spines for the final effort. The band turned up everywhere soldiers and civilians gathered: in town squares, hospitals, rest areas, even at the Théâtre des Champs-Elysées in Paris. If the bone-tired soldiers could not see America, they could hear it in the Cohan bugle calls and the Handy blues that the band performed. The 369th underwent its last trial in late September in the town of Sechault, a speck on the map that they held under a brutal siege of artillery that lasted forty-eight hours. The unit suffered many casualties, but its survivors were covered with glory. The Allied victory came on November 11, 1918, and six days later the 369th entered Germany, the first American forces to occupy German soil.

The 369th arrived back in New York in early February 1919. The surviving 1,300 men of the regiment had received the Croix de Guerre in December, and on February 17 they were to be honored with a victory parade that stretched seven miles from Twenty-fifth Street into Harlem. At the beginning of the parade, with drum major Bill Robinson leading the way, Europe's Hellfighters Band played their stirring marches, but when they hit 130th Street, they struck up "Here Comes My Daddy Now." Harlem exploded with joy and pride; their heroes were home.

Some of Jim Europe's musical enterprises had waned in his absence, but now he was back, ready to present the band that Americans had been reading about for two years but had never heard. Pat Casey, Europe's manager, easily booked a ten-week tour for "Lt. James Reese Europe and His Famous 369th U.S. Infantry Band," to begin in mid-March. After the tour, Europe intended to work on a Broadway project with Sissle and Blake.

But first there were recordings to make. Pathe Records wanted sessions with the Hellfighters Band as soon as it could get them. In early March Europe took a scaled-down ensemble into the Pathe studio and made eighteen sides, including three Handy blues, current pop fare ("How Ya Gonna Keep 'Em Down on the Farm?," "Ja-Da," and "Indianola"), and several Europe-Sissle songs that they had written in France ("Mirandy," "On Patrol in No Man's Land," and "All of No Man's Land Is Ours"). The Hellfighters recordings, while not really jazz, are looser and less frantic in tempo than those of the Society Orchestra six years earlier.

The Hellfighters Band tour was an enormous success. Many of the original musicians made themselves available to Europe after their military service, and the ensemble was complemented by a singing quartet, the Harmony Kings. Noble Sissle was also a featured vocalist. The first engagement was at Hammerstein's Manhattan Opera House, followed by appearances in cities in the Northeast and Midwest, including Philadelphia, Boston, Chicago, and St. Louis. Because "jazz" was the musical catchword of the day and jazz was primarily seen as a black idiom, several reviewers called Europe's large group a "jazz orchestra." Whatever one called it, it was vastly enjoyable. Pathe couldn't wait until the tour was over to record them again, so on May 7 the Hellfighters Band returned to the studio to make six more sides, including "The Dancing Deacon," "My Chocolate Soldier Sammy Boy," and a cover of the Original Dixieland Jazz Band's hit, "Clarinet Marmalade."

On May 9 the Hellfighters Band returned to Boston. They had sold out their first concerts there a few weeks earlier, and so were rebooked in Mechanics' Hall. Several times during the tour, band members had noticed the erratic behavior of one of the drummers, Herbert Wright, but no one could have foreseen what he would do on that opening night in Boston. During the concert's intermission, Jim Europe was heard in his dressing room having a minor argument with Wright. The members of the Harmony Kings rapped on his door. When Europe rose to let them in, Wright screamed at him. Europe grabbed a chair to defend himself. As the four singers froze in the doorway, Wright bolted over the chair and stabbed Europe in the neck with a pocket knife. Noble Sissle heard the commotion and came running. He seized Wright and hustled him outside. Europe's wound seemed insignificant at first, but the blood wouldn't stop flowing. An ambulance was called, and Europe was taken to City Hospital. The audience was told that Europe was ill and that his assistant conductor would lead the band for the second half of the program. As soon as the concert was over, Sissle and a few others went to check on their leader. Within minutes of their arrival at the hospital, they were told that Europe was dead.

Jim Europe was the first African-American to receive a public funeral in New York City. In the long, sad procession through Harlem on May 13, the new Fifteenth Infantry Regiment Band played, and Europe's Hellfighters Band marched silently behind them. After the service at St. Mark's Episcopal Church on West Fifty-third Street, Europe's body was taken by train to Arlington National Cemetery for burial. About four weeks later, Herbert Wright pled guilty to manslaughter and was sentenced to ten to fifteen years. He was paroled in 1927.

The Hellfighters Band lasted for a year without Europe. America was ready to forget the war by 1920, and part of forgetting meant putting away its music. The national economy was beginning to surge, and the country was about to embark on a ten-year spree, to be accompanied by smaller, hotter ensembles than any ever dreamed of by Jim Europe.

In the early teens, when "ragtime" was the vogue, Europe's ensembles were sometimes called "ragtime orchestras." He accepted the label and obligingly grappled with interviewers' questions about ragtime and the African-American's place in it. A few years later, when the "jazz" label stuck to him, he accepted that, too. He was open-minded and curious about many kinds of music, believing that all types of music had their place, that they all deserved presentation with taste and zest, and that those who played and composed the music should get a fair and decent wage.

SPENCER WILLIAMS

For a few years, in the late teens and early twenties, no one made much distinction between blues and jazz. Both were new, loose and wild-sounding, and "Negroid." Both meant fun on the dance floor, the blues inspiring a slower, more "low-down" movement than the brisk jazz sound did. Blues entered the commercial music scene first, shepherded by W. C. Handy's "Memphis Blues" of 1912. The Handy blues had lyrics, but almost nobody sang them. The few recordings that Handy's work got in the teens were instrumentals, performed by large dance-orchestra ensembles and by military bands. The wildly popular recordings of the Original Dixieland Jazz Band compounded the confusion between the genres. Their scrappy, vigorous sound was indisputably jazz, not to be mistaken for the politer syncopations of a pop orchestra, but their first hits included many uptempo blues tunes: "Livery Stable Blues," "Mournin' Blues," "Satanic Blues," "St. Louis Blues," and

Spencer Williams

"Bluin' the Blues." These records welded blues and jazz in listeners' minds, and the ODJB's delirious, improvised free-for-alls made the perfect accompaniment to America's giddy reel into the twenties. During this careless time of jazzy blues and bluesy jazz, there was no more inventive pop songwriter than Spencer Williams.

Spencer Williams was born on October 14, 1889, to Bessie V. Williams, a twenty-year-old New Orleans prostitute who was running a house at 3 South Basin Street with the help of her sister Loula. The Williams sisters had been raised in Selma, Alabama, and at the time of Spencer's birth, both seemed on their way to prosperity in New Orleans' sin industry. Bessie Williams died when Spencer was around eight years old, and he was taken in by his Aunt Loula. By then, she was advertising herself as "Lulu White, the Octoroon Queen," and as the proprietress of a grand, four-story whorehouse at 235 Basin Street, which she called Mahogany Hall.

Young Spencer spent several years as the pampered child of Storyville's most notorious madam. He didn't exactly have the run of the house, but he was free to wander the neighborhood in search of music. He listened to the visiting professors who manned the parlor pianos, and he heard ragtime bands play in his aunt's saloon next door. By the time he was sent to live with other relatives in Birmingham, in his mid-teens, he was a passable pianist himself, and his head was full of the rocking New Orleans piano sound that he would put into his songs. After a desultory year or so of public school in Birmingham, he headed for Chicago in 1907.

Williams was not a good enough pianist to compete with the sharks who got the sporting house jobs in Chicago's "Levee" district, but he played occasionally at San Souci, an amusement park. He augmented his San Souci wages by stints as a Pullman porter. He tried peddling some songs to local publishers, and finally sold one, "Baby, Please Don't Shake Me While I'm Gone" (lyrics by Rose Cohen), to Will Rossiter in 1912. There were several more Spencer Williams songs issued over the next few years, and in 1916 his name appeared on "I Ain't Got Nobody," a song that had been kicking around since 1914.

The story of Spencer Williams' first hit is a tangled one. In August 1914 "I Ain't Got Nobody" was copyrighted as an unpublished work by Charles Warfield and David Young. In January 1915 Spencer Williams and Dave Peyton copyrighted the extremely similar "I Ain't Got Nobody Much" as their unpublished work. Williams must have peddled his version of the song, because it somehow came to the attention of Roger Graham, the owner-manager of a small publishing house, Craig & Company. Craig published the song in February 1916, crediting the music to Spencer Williams and the lyric to Graham himself.

Later that year, Frank K. Root, another Chicago publisher, bought the Craig & Company version and reissued it with the Williams-Graham credits, using the Craig plates. Then Root must have somehow learned of the existence of the 1914 Warfield-Young version and smelled potential legal problems, so he bought the Warfield-Young copyright and issued this version also, using the same cover—with photos of Bert Williams and Sophie Tucker—as that on the Williams-Graham edition. Now, Root had *two* versions of the same song out in 1916, each credited to a different set of writers.

The two versions of "I Ain't Got Nobody" were sent to market on equal footing, but the Williams-Graham version is the one that caught on, because it is the better song. Both choruses begin with the famous wailing fifth and the three descending chromatic notes ("I- - - - ain't got no-. . . ."), then the Williams melody departs from Warfield's in a small but significant way. It syncopates by putting a rest on the first beat of measure three. The remainder of the Williams chorus is spiked with syncopations that aren't in the Warfield song, making it musically more interesting. And the Roger Graham lyric is smarter than David Young's. (The Young verse begins "I had a sweetheart once I loved, And I was happy as could be . . . ," while Graham opens with the laconic "There's a saying going 'round, And I begin to think it's true. . . ."). The Warfield verse is melodically busier than Williams', which opens on a series of nine repeated notes with shifting harmony underneath them. The Williams-Graham song is more compact and more sure of itself. Spencer Williams' songwriting career obviously began with a petty theft, but his reworking of the purloined song earned its staying power. "I Ain't Got Nobody" would have dozens of recordings over the years, both instrumental and vocal, and it remains one of the best-known standards of the teens.

Spencer Williams' first blues, "Paradise Blues," with lyrics by Walter Hirsch, came in 1916. His first hot dance number, "Shim-Me-Sha-Wabble," followed a year later, as did his "Steppin' on the Puppy's

Tail" and the driving "Tishomingo Blues," named for a small town in northeast Mississippi. Williams was starting to write his own lyrics, which often combined authentic Southern references with current slang. ("Way down in Mississippi, among the cypress trees, They get you dippy with their strange melodies. . . .") The last strain of "Tishomingo" is lush with Williams' characteristic deep-dish harmonies, which make his songs richer than those of any other writer of commercial blues.

In 1919 Williams really hit his stride. He began to write with and publish with Clarence Williams—another transplanted Louisianan working in Chicago, but no relation—who would issue much of his work throughout the 1920s. (Spencer Williams would never have a long-term association with a mainstream publisher, but his two most frequent publishers, Clarence Williams and Joe Davis, were both relentless promoters of their copyrights. Clarence Williams made use of dozens of Spencer Williams songs in his recording sessions, and, in the late twenties, Joe Davis got literally hundreds of radio plugs for his Spencer Williams numbers.) Clarence Williams published three Spencer Williams songs—and shared writer credit on them—in 1919. Each was a hit and each was a gem of songwriting craft.

There was "I Ain't Gonna Give Nobody None o' This Jelly Roll," a galloping piece of double-entendre that was recorded by the Wilbur Sweatman and Ford Dabney bands in the fall of 1919. The Williams-Williams "Yama Yama Blues" was recorded by Anton Lada and his Louisiana Five for the Emerson label in March of that year. Best of all was their "Royal Garden Blues"—named for a black Chicago nightclub—which is perhaps the first popular song based on a riff. (This is a melody that achieves its effect from a repetitive rhythm, rather than from an interesting sequence of notes. "Twelfth Street Rag" and "In the Mood" are examples of riff-based writing.)

"Royal Garden" is an indomitable romp, impossible to deliver offhandedly; its heat is built-in. It is made of two twenty-four bar strains cleverly joined by a four-bar "belt" that allows for a tempo shift between the two main themes. The first theme is lazy and its harmony—but not its melody—is dotted with blue notes. After the four-bar breather, the rat-a-tat riff cuts loose. The melody of the second strain spans only six notes, and it bursts with energy. "Royal Garden Blues" didn't break until 1921, when it received its first spate of recordings.

It was first done as a vocal (by Daisy Martin, Ethel Waters, and Noble Sissle), then as a hot small-band number (by the ODJB, Bix Beiderbecke and His Gang, and the Original Wolverines), then as a staple of the swing bands of the thirties (by Tommy Dorsey, Benny Goodman, and Glen Gray). If there is such a thing as a surefire jump tune, it is "Royal Garden Blues."

Clarence Williams sold the copyrights of all three of these 1919 songs to Shapiro-Bernstein—in a contract that contained a royalty clause—and their success enabled him to move his publishing company to New York in 1921. He issued two more Spencer Williams collaborations from Chicago before he left ("The Dance They Call the Georgia Hunch" and "Roumania"). Spencer Williams, his star writer, soon followed him to New York. There would be several more Spencer Williams songs issued by other Chicago publishers in 1921 (songs that he had previously sold), among them the pumping "Arkansas Blues," published by Frances Clifford. This collaboration with the Chicago drummer Anton Lada is a blues that wants to boogie. It has a restless, rocking accompaniment that moves from the bass clef in its verse to the treble clef in its chorus.

Spencer Williams' name was known in New York by the time he arrived. He was asked to contribute songs to a revue, produced by Irvin C. Miller, a 1921 show that began its life as *Chocolate Brown* and was renamed *Put and Take*. During rehearsals, Williams met the blues writer and publisher Perry Bradford, who also contributed to the score, and he had several of his show songs published by Miller. *Put and Take* ran briefly at the Town Hall Theatre on West Forty-third Street, then toured during the fall of 1921.

Williams also met another publisher around this time. He was Joe Davis, an ex-song plugger and lyricist who had started a small house called Triangle Music in 1916. Davis (who was white) had scraped along for several years issuing his own songs and whatever else came his way. In the early twenties he had decided to specialize in the work of black songwriters, to cash in on the blues/jazz boom. Davis served as an A&R man for several record labels, and he was usually able to get his company's songs onto recording schedules. He was a tireless chaser of plugs and a shameless promoter of his publications. Like any publisher, he drove tight bargains with his writers, but he issued work by almost all of the black songwriters of the twenties, and he pushed his products hard. Davis published his first Spencer Williams song in 1920 ("California Blossom," written with Anton Lada) and another in 1921 ("You'll Want My Love But, Honey, It Will Be All Gone," written with blues singer Lucille Hegamin). Within a few years Davis would be Spencer Williams' primary publisher.

Spencer Williams placed a song, "Got to Cool My Doggies Now," into a Shubert revue, *The Passing Show of 1922*, and Fats Waller made it his first piano roll in 1923; Waller also made Williams' "Haitian Blues" and "Snakes Hips" that same year. Williams and Waller were cut from the same convivial cloth, and they would be occasional collaborators and lifelong friends. In 1924, they wrote together for the first time. Probably to kid the "low-down" imagery of blues lyrics, they assembled "Bloody Razor Blues" and "Bullet Wound Blues." Neither was published, but each got a recording. When Waller was asked to contribute songs for a Lafayette Theatre revue called *Tan Town Topics*, he chose several of his tunes that had Spencer Williams lyrics, including "Senorita Mine" and "Charleston Hound." However, by the time the show was produced, in 1926, Spencer Williams was half a world away.

In 1924, in collaboration with a white lyricist, Jack Palmer, Spencer Williams produced the rambunctious "Everybody Loves My Baby," published by Clarence Williams. It is a minor-keyed exultation that invites breakneck rendition. Its first recording was by the Georgia Melodians in April 1924, and it caught on with dance bands immediately. By June the song was popular enough to be a feature number in *The Ziegfeld Follies*, and, because its popularity continued through the summer, it was put into *Earl Carroll's Vanities* in September. Jazz players and singers loved it. In November 1924 it received recordings by the Red Onion Jazz Babies (with an Alberta Hunter vocal), the Fletcher Henderson Orchestra (with a Louis Armstrong vocal), and Eva Taylor and Clarence Williams. Trixie Smith made two vocal recordings of the song in January 1925, one with the Original Memphis Five and the other with Fletcher Henderson.

"Everybody Loves My Baby" was still going strong in the spring of 1925, and it brought Spencer Williams to the attention of a Chicago socialite who made him an offer that would change his life. Like many rich white people in the mid-twenties, Caroline Dudley Reagan was fascinated by the black music, art, and literature that were sparking the cultural explosion that was labeled the "Harlem Renaissance." She was sure that the time was ripe to introduce African-American culture to her friends in Europe, and that the best way to do this was to take an arty sampling of jazz and black dance to France. Although she had never produced a show before, she had connections in Paris, and she was able to arrange a booking for her production, which she was calling *La Revue Negre*, for the fall. She came to New York to assemble talent, and she chose Spencer Williams as her composer. She hired the band-leader Claude Hopkins, the choreographer Louis Douglas, and, to design the sets, the Mexican artist Miguel Covarrubias. She needed a feature dancer, and Spencer Williams thought he knew just the girl, a cutup he remembered clowning on the end of the chorus line in Sissle and Blake's *Chocolate Dandies*. Williams took Reagan to the Plantation Club to see Josephine Baker (1906–1975).

Baker was nineteen at the time, and she had spent most of her years scrabbling for survival amid the grinding poverty of East Saint Louis. As a child, Josephine MacDonald had pilfered vegetables from local markets for food and had earned a few pennies by selling lumps of coal she had gathered off railroad tracks. At age eleven, she had barely escaped with her life during a horrific race riot in which nearly a hundred of her neighbors were killed by marauding whites. At thirteen Josephine endured a brief marriage, and at fourteen she had taken a job as a waitress in a black St. Louis restaurant frequented by show people. Among Josephine's regular customers were a father-mother-and-daughter act who billed themselves as the Jones Family Band. They took a liking to her and let her try a bit of eccentric dancing during their act at Charles Turpin's Booker T. Washington Theatre. Josephine's dancing was more mugging than movement, but the audience found her funny. When the Jones Family Band moved on after two weeks in St. Louis, Josephine went with them.

Josephine went from vaudeville dancing to black stock shows with the Russell & Owens Company, headed by Clara Smith. She was in Philadelphia in early 1921 when *Shuffle Along* came through on its try-out tour. Baker auditioned to be a replacement in the show, but she failed to impress Noble Sissle and was turned down. Later that year, still in Philadelphia, she met and married Will Baker. This marriage was as short-lived as her first, but she kept her husband's name, the one by which the world would know her.

After the enormous success of *Shuffle Along* in New York, the obligatory road company went out. Baker auditioned again, this time in New York, and was hired to join the touring company in Boston in August 1922. *Shuffle Along* boasted the prettiest and peppiest chorus of its time; one reviewer said they could "wiggle and shimmy in a fashion to outdo a congress of eels." Even in this lineup of beautiful firecrackers, Josephine Baker stood out. At the end of the line, she was all knock-knees, flailing elbows, and crossed eyes, a chuckleheaded Topsy in a bevy of high-stepping Circes. By the end of the year-long tour, Baker had been given billing—as "That Comedy Chorus Girl"—and she had attracted so much attention that she was assured a role in Sissle and Blake's next show. Their *Chocolate Dandies* did not make her a star, but in providing her several solo turns—including a blackface number and a Charleston parody—it made her the most talked-about chorus girl in New York. She was billed among the leads on Broadway and on the tour, in early 1925. When the *Chocolate Dandies* tour was over, Josephine Baker joined the floor show at the Plantation Club. She was on the brink of stardom now, and she knew it. She was coasting, biding her time and keeping herself visible while waiting for the chance that was sure to come.

After Caroline Reagan saw Baker's uninhibited shenanigans at the Plantation Club, the chance came. Spencer Williams' hunch was right; Josephine Baker was the obvious choice to provide the flash that *La Revue Negre* needed. Reagan's first salary offer to Baker was for $150 a week. Baker haggled it up to $250 before she accepted. There were sporadic rehearsals in New York over the summer of 1925, and on September 21, Reagan and her troupe, including Spencer Williams, Claude Hopkins, and a five-piece jazz band that featured Sidney Bechet, sailed for France on the *Berengaria*.

La Revue Negre was to play at the Théâtre des Champs-Elysées, a historic house that had seen the debut of Stravinsky's *Le Sacre du Printemps* at its opening in 1913. The theatre had been closed during the war years, and it had been struggling since its reopening. In April 1925, its managers, Andre Daven and Paul Achard, instituted a series of "artistic" music hall performances designed to attract attention in a crowded theatrical market. Daven's friendship with Caroline Reagan led to his booking her show before it was written or cast. All Daven and Achard knew was that Reagan was bringing them black performers, and that was enough.

Paris was mad for jazz, and French aesthetes of all stripes were besotted with African art. The Cubist painters had been the first to prescribe a "primitivist" point of view as a tonic for a new century already seeing itself as jaded. European sculpture and painting borrowed freely from the long-faced totems and the stolid household objects of Africa. The borrowing let them see the world with new eyes and reclaim the mysticism and power of art itself from the mannerly work of the nineteenth century. The avant-garde composers came next—Debussy, Stravinsky, Satie, and Ravel—infatuated first with the simple syncopations of the cakewalk, later with jazz, which they used to suggest the chaos of the modern world. By 1923 an important ballet score—Darius Milhaud's *La Création du monde*—was paraphrasing "Royal Garden Blues." The intellectual ferment over things African and African-American was at its height in 1925, and Paris was the center of it. The managers of the Théâtre des Champs-Elysées expected *La Revue Negre* to fuel the aesthetic debate, to push the envelope, to become the must-see show of the season.

What Daven and Achard saw in rehearsals appalled them. A week before its opening, *La Revue Negre* was an overlong hodgepodge of tap dancing, band numbers, and indifferently sung blues and spirituals. As producers will when a show is in trouble, they called in a rival to help them revamp it. Jacques Charles, the producer-director of the Casino de Paris, came to a run-through and sized up the situation immediately. There was nothing original in *La Revue Negre*. Paris had seen tap dancing and had heard jazz. If notoriety was the object of the upcoming production, there was nothing vaguely notorious on display in the rehearsal hall. The show needed sex and plenty of it. Charles chose Josephine Baker to deliver the commodity.

He sent her to an illustrator named Paul Colin, with instructions that Colin design a poster and program cover featuring her form. Colin was inspired by Baker's beauty and sassiness, and he set to work. On Colin's first poster, a drawing of Baker is center and slightly behind two cartoony black men, who are mostly eyes, lips, and teeth. She is slant-eyed, with sleek bobbed hair, posed in a short fringed dress with her hands on her hips. On the program cover, Baker is topless and barefoot, dancing on a Cubist stage floor, surrounded by four musicians. Colin's drawings were sexy, but they were also nonspecific to the show. Only days before the opening, no one knew exactly what Josephine Baker would do to fulfill the provocative promise of the poster.

Jacques Charles and Louis Douglas decided that "primitive" was the way to go. They hired a Caribbean expatriate named Joe Alex to partner Baker in something that they would call "Danse Sauvage," a sort of jungle pas de deux that would allow both to appear nearly nude. They threw out many of the vocals and band numbers and placed their hopes for the success of *La Revue Negre* squarely on the bare back of Josephine Baker.

La Revue Negre opened on October 2, 1925, and it made a scandalous sensation. The opening scene, called "Mississippi Steamboat Race," gave Paris its first look at Josephine Baker, a dynamo in cutoff pants who tumbled into the action patting a rhythm on the stage floor with her hands while singing a Spencer Williams scat song called "Boodle Am." This was startling enough, but when the "Danse Sauvage" number began, the roar that arose from the house was deep and primal. Baker was carried on stage, slung over the shoulders of the muscular Joe Alex, her legs waving in a split. Both were naked except for bracelets, anklets, and tiny loincloths. Their dance consisted mostly of erotic posing to the slow, plodding accompaniment of the band. It was an image that would burn in the minds of Parisians for years afterwards: two beautiful black bodies writhing in the heat of "jungle" passion to the sound of jazz. The finale of *La Revue Negre* was a Williams number called "Charleston Cabaret," in which Baker danced frenetically, wearing only a strategically placed flamingo feather. The opening-night audience went crazy. Baker had shocked the unshockable city and had given it an almost orgasmic pleasure. *La Revue Negre* was only about an hour long, but it began the love affair between Paris and Josephine Baker that continued until her death.

Even before their historic opening night, the cast and creators of *La Revue Negre* had felt good about being in Paris. The city welcomed and accommodated them, and seemed blind to their color as no place in the United States did. They loved the absence of the racism that they had known in their home country. In Paris they could go anywhere, hail any cab, drink from any fountain, stay in any hotel, and sit in any theatre without being turned away or ordered to the "colored" section. It was the first taste of everyday freedoms that most of them had known, and it was intoxicating. After their triumph on October 2, the city did more than accommodate them; it adored them. Nobody wanted to go home.

After its sold-out run at the Théâtre des Champs-Elysées, La Revue Negre played for another ten weeks as an independent production at another Paris house, the Théâtre de l'Étiole. In the first months of 1926, the show had extended runs in Brussels and Berlin. By late summer of 1926 Josephine Baker was headlining at the mecca of music halls, the Folies Bergère. It was in her first Folies show that she wore the famous banana skirt and that she began to sing in French.

Spencer Williams stayed on in France with her, acting as her mentor during her rapid ascent. They did their partying at the Music Box, a small club on the Rue Pigalle run by a black American expatriate from West Virginia, Ada "Bricktop" Smith. Bricktop's club attracted everyone from European nobility to black show folk, all of whom came for the soul food and the chance to hear Spencer Williams, Cole Porter, and Leslie Hutchinson spell each other at the piano. The free-and-easy atmosphere at the Music Box seemed to embody the essence of sophisticated, color-blind Paris.

Spencer Williams made his first trip abroad last nearly three years, from 1925 to 1928. He was writing songs during this time, and keeping his hand in Tin Pan Alley by mail. In the August 21, 1926, issue of Variety, the new staff of the reorganized Clarence Williams Music Publishing Company was announced, with Spencer Williams listed as the company's "Band and Orchestra Manager." This was most likely Clarence Williams' way of providing his friend with a U.S. mailing address and a clearing house for his musical business.

Spencer Williams even had an American hit while he was away: "I Found a New Baby," an uptempo, minor-key followup to "Everybody Loves My Baby," written with lyricist Jack Palmer. The song was used in the 1926 Tan Town Topics, and it was recorded several times that year. He began to write songs with Josephine Baker and sent them to

Clarence Williams for publication, including "Black Bottom Ball," issued in 1927, and "Lonesome Lovesick Blues," appearing the following year. There were also three Spencer Williams interpolations in Clarence Williams' show, *Bottomland*, published in 1927.

Sometime in mid-1928, Spencer Williams returned to New York, and he took up headquarters in the Clarence Williams office, even though Joe Davis was by then issuing most of his songs. Major jazz artists recorded his work that year: Louis Armstrong made his "Fireworks," "Skip the Gutter," and "Basin Street Blues," and Duke Ellington did "Tishomingo Blues." Bessie Smith recorded his "I'm Wild About That Thing" and "You've Got to Give Me Some" in May 1929, two months after Armstrong's majestic treatment of his "Mahogany Hall Stomp."

On February 15, 1929, Spencer Williams had his second recording session as an accompanist. (He had played piano as Lizzie Miles sang his "Black Man, Be on Yo' Way" for Brunswick in June 1923.) He backed Phil Pavey, who sang four of his songs for OKeh. He recorded three vocal duets with Lonnie Johnson for OKeh in January 1930, and four smutty songs with Teddy Bunn in June 1930 for Victor; both of his 1930 sessions are notable only for James P. Johnson's piano accompaniment. None of these records sold well, and Williams confined his performing mostly to parties and small clubs in the future.

In 1929 Spencer Williams wrote his best ballad, the soulful "Susianna." It was published—and heavily plugged for radio play—by Joe Davis, and Bing Crosby had the first and best recording. Davis's successful radio plugs for "Susianna" meant that he was feeding the monster that was reputed to be devouring Tin Pan Alley.

By late 1929, the music industry was ailing, and radio was seen as the cause of the ailment. Tin Pan Alley insiders believed that free music available on radio had displaced the piano as the source of home entertainment. Sales of big-ticket musical items—pianos, player pianos, and phonographs—were sluggish, and sales of musical "software"—sheet music, piano rolls, and records—had dropped accordingly. The stock market crash in October 1929, which heralded the coming of the Depression, nearly finished the job. Although the free music on radio was not displacing records (it was live, not recorded) the record industry was in a particularly bad way. Record sales dropped from a high of 104 million in 1927 to 6 million in 1932.

The race series of the major record companies cut back on their product. A few labels folded, and those that remained in business desperately fought for a slice of the shrinking market by issuing the dirtiest songs they could get their hands on. (Spencer Williams wrote some of these—"The Bull Frog and the Toad," "My Man o' War," and "The Monkey and the Baboon," all in 1929.) Music publishers generally chose to play it safe, sticking with the tried-and-true subjects: love, the states, Hawaii, and the like. (Spencer Williams wrote some of these, too. In the early 1930s Joe Davis published his "Hawaiian Lullaby," "Springtime, Lovetime, You," "My Home in Oklahoma," and "The Hills of Tennessee Are Calling Me.")

The real villain in the Tin Pan Alley story was not radio, but musical films. And the sea change in the music industry was the buying up of publishing businesses by Hollywood studios. Entire companies and their catalogs were purchased, not primarily for the purpose of issuing sheet music, but to own songs—and their copyrights—that would be quickly available for use in films. Warner Brothers purchased Witmark in 1929 and soon added the catalogs of Harms and Remick to its music collection. MGM bought out Leo Feist in 1934 and took over Robbins Music the following year. Paramount created its own Famous Music Corporation in 1928, but for several years, most of the "famous" music in its vault was from the Spier & Coslow catalog.

When the revamped publishing companies issued new sheet music, it was mostly film music, not freelance pop. If a song was not an active tie-in to a current film, there was little use for it and no reason to plug it. The major Broadway composers, most of whom were already signed with publishing houses, were placed under contract by movie studios to do work for hire on musical films. During the worst years of the Depression, the transplanted songwriters were guaranteed salaries of $12,000 to $35,000 a year as well as royalties on their film songs.

The black songwriters, even those with Broadway successes and pop hits like Eubie Blake, Fats Waller, and Spencer Williams were not on Hollywood's hiring list. If Hollywood was not calling to Spencer Williams, Paris was. By 1932 he was back in his favorite city, this time with Fats Waller in tow. Waller stayed only a few weeks; Williams would not live in America again for twenty-five years.

When Williams returned to Paris, Josephine Baker was riding high as an international music-hall star, and Continental composers and lyricists were supplying her repertoire, most of it written especially for her use. Although she would not feature Spencer Williams songs, the two remained friends. She recommended him to write English lyrics to a few of her French songs, such as "Sous le Ciel d'Afrique" and "Le Chemin du Bonheur," both written for her film *Princesse Tam Tam* in 1935. But these were for publication only. She preferred to sing the original French lyrics in her performances.

Bricktop was still going strong. She had opened a new club, called Bricktop's, at 66 Rue Pigalle in 1931, and when she gave a party for the Duke Ellington band in 1933, Spencer Williams was there, escorting Josephine Baker. Williams basked in the adulation of the French jazz community. The pianist Alain Romains remembered that he "had a big round face like sunshine. He was always smiling and had a little cigar." In the summer of 1933, Williams was a "guest artist" with the Freddy Johnson-Arthur Briggs All-Star Orchestra, singing two songs on Brunswick recordings made in Paris.

Williams tried to keep in touch with the American music business as he had done before, by mail, but it was not so easy to do any more. The number of his publications dwindled, and most of these were hack work, such as "Chimes of Honolulu," "Hawaiian Kisses," and "By the Calm Lagoon," written for quick sale to Joe Davis. In 1933 Davis began issuing his series of "naughty song" folios, to which Williams was a frequent contributor.

Williams had one more hit when his "Basin Street Blues" was rediscovered and recorded for Columbia by a Benny Goodman band called the Charleston Chasers in 1931. Glenn Miller, a Chasers trombonist, did the arrangement of "Basin Street Blues," and the vocal was assigned to another trombonist, Jack Teagarden. Teagarden claimed that he and Miller wrote both the verse and the lyric to "Basin Street Blues" while preparing for the February 9 session. Williams seems never to have disputed this, and there is neither verse nor lyric on the 1928 Armstrong recording. Armstrong scats a vocal, but there are no decipherable words. The song was published by Joe Davis in 1933 with Williams' name alone on it. "Basin Street Blues" became Teagarden's signature song, and in 1937 it was a hit again, as a Bing Crosby-Connee Boswell duet on Decca Records.

In 1936 Williams married Agnes Castleton, an Englishwoman he had known for nearly ten years, and the couple moved to

Sunbury-on-Thames, a London suburb. That same year, Williams began issuing songs, including a few collaborations with his new wife, under his own imprint in England. (He was not new to the publishing business. In 1923 he had run his own music company in New York.)

He played host to old friends as they came to London, offering invitations to "tea"—passion fruit juice and gin was Williams' teatime libation—to Josephine Baker in 1937 and Fats Waller in 1938. During Waller's visit, they wrote "A Cottage in the Rain" together after a sumptuous supper of fried chicken prepared by Williams. Before he left England, Waller recorded "All Pent Up in a Pent House," tailored to him by Williams and the British pop writer Tommie Connor. Williams also wrote with Benny Carter ("When Lights Are Low," in 1936) and with Django Reinhardt ("It's the Bluest Kind of Blues," in 1942) during his years in England.

New Orleans was much on Williams' mind in the 1940s. He turned out a remarkable series of mood pieces, vigorous and richly harmonic, including "Mahogany Hall Mood," "Farewell to Storyville"—this reworking of his "Good Time Flat Blues" was used in the 1947 film *New Orleans*—and "Basin Street Ball."

Perhaps the nostalgia for his home city was brought on by the hard life in postwar England. In 1947 Williams wrote to Joe Davis that "things are very grim here." He said that he was trying to get money together to leave England, and he offered to sell the U.S. rights to a group of his songs to Davis for $150. He was finally able to move in 1951, not to America but to a suburb of Stockholm, Sweden. Williams had a difficult recuperation from an eye operation in 1954, and in 1957 he returned to the United States. He moved his family—Agnes and their two daughters, Della and Lindy—to a house on Newburg Street in St. Albans, Queens. His health began to fail, and he became something of a recluse in his last years. Spencer Williams died in Queens on July 14, 1965.

MACEO PINKARD

The career of Maceo Pinkard is that of songwriter as journeyman. Except for a few years when he was a teenager, he was never a performer—and he was a publisher only when he had to be. Soon after arriving in New York, he set up his own company, but it was more a repository for his copyrights than a competitive publishing house. He issued a few of his own songs, but not before major publishers had had a look at them. The great majority of his 150 or so published songs are not Pinkard publications. As a composer, Pinkard was a traditionalist—he neither created nor followed musical fads. Although there are many recordings of his songs by jazz players and singers, he was not really a jazz or blues writer. Working squarely in the center of 1920s pop thinking, he made songs that long outlived his era.

Maceo Pinkard

Maceo Pinkard was born on June 27, 1897, in Bluefield, West Virginia, a town that abuts the Virginia line, in the southwestern part of the state. After a few years of schooling at Bluefield Institute, he left home to tour the Midwest with a small dance band that he had organized. In 1915 his travels took him to Omaha, Nebraska, and he settled there, tired of the road by age eighteen.

Although the dance band business held no attraction for him, Pinkard was intent on making a career in music. To sustain himself while he peddled his songs, he gave music lessons and ran a talent agency out of his rooming house at 2512 Lake Street. Not long after Pinkard arrived in Omaha, he sold a lyric to Dick Bruun, the most prosperous of the local publishers. In 1915 Bruun issued the first Pinkard song, "When He Sang That Baritone," with a lyric by Pinkard and a melody by Bruun himself. The following year Bruun published the first song with words and music by Pinkard, "I'm Goin' Back

Home," and another Omaha firm, Independent Music, issued "I Want to See My Girl in London" (music by Pinkard, lyrics by "Con" T'lam).

Pinkard's handful of songs had some regional success with vaudeville performers, and in 1917 he started his own firm to publish his work. The first publication of Maceo Pinkard Music was "The Blue Melody," one of his few instrumentals, featuring a photo of Sophie Tucker's Five Kings of Syncopation on the cover. "The Blue Melody" sold for fifteen cents in its piano version, but an ad on the first page says that a "Regular Orchestration" was available for twenty-five cents and that a "Jazz Band Orchestration" could be had for fifty cents. At nineteen, Pinkard was on his way as writer and as businessman. His small successes in Omaha inspired him to look beyond local (and self-) publication.

Pinkard began to send his songs to out-of-town publishers. In 1916 his first blues song, "Chattanooga Blues," was published by Isadore Seidel of Indianapolis, with a lyric by Pinkard and music by Seidel. The following year, he had songs coming out of Chicago ("I'm a Real Kind Mama," published by Frank K. Root) and New York ("Those Draftin' Blues" from Joseph W. Stern and "Stockyard Blues" from Leo Feist). Pinkard hadn't had a hit yet, but he was getting noticed by mainstream publishers. Sometime in late 1918, he was asked to become a staff writer with Shapiro, Bernstein & Co. in New York. This firm would publish his first hit the following year.

"Mammy o' Mine" is a raggy song on a sentimental subject. Despite the title, it is not a "black" song, and the sprinkling of slang in the lyric is only slang, not dialect. The original cover shows an elderly white woman (who somewhat resembles Woodrow Wilson) staring pensively over the knitting needles poised in her hands. This song is sometimes confused with Al Jolson's signature song, "My Mammy," written in 1920 by Walter Donaldson, Sam Lewis, and Joe Young, but "Mammy o' Mine" is far more musically interesting than the Donaldson number. Jazz players were quick to see it as more than another mother song. Pinkard's trademarks as a composer—a simple but surprisingly wide-ranging melody winding around a constantly shifting harmonic base— arrived full-blown in "Mammy o' Mine," and the song inspired several recordings by jazz bands. The first was by Yerkes Jazzarimba Orchestra in August 1919, and the best was the ODJB's British recording of

January 1920. The lyric to "Mammy o' Mine" was written by William Tracey, a white songwriter who would be Pinkard's most frequent collaborator. (Unlike most black composers, Pinkard wrote primarily with white lyricists. Besides Tracey, he shared credit on his twenties songs with Sidney Mitchell, Bud Green, Jack Yellen, Nat Vincent, Lew Brown, Billy Rose, Roy Turk, Archie Gottler, Sidney Clare, Abner Silver, and Charlie Tobias, among others. These collaborative matches were made by publishers, and they attest to aiming Pinkard songs beyond the "race" market.)

Another 1919 Pinkard song that made a stir was his "Jazz Babies' Ball," which was interpolated into the *Shubert Gaieties* that year. Its lyric, by Charles Bayha, contains the up-to-date couplet "Oh! There ain't no waltzin' allowed/It ain't that kind of a crowd," and there is an extra patter chorus made of a string of two-bar breaks. Sissle and Blake recorded it in the summer of 1920. (It would be used as the theme of Abbott and Costello's television show in the early 1950s.)

Also in 1919, a song called "Granny" was published, with lyrics by its publisher, L. Wolfe Gilbert, and composer credit attributed to "Alex Belledna." Tin Pan Alley was a small world in which everyone knew everyone, but no one knew "Alex Belledna." The following year "Belledna" composed "It's Right Here for You" (with a lyric by Marion Dickerson), which was published by Perry Bradford. In 1921 "Belledna" shared credit with Maceo Pinkard and William Tracey on "'Tain't Nothing Else But Jazz." To put the speculation about the mysterious composer to rest, *Variety* reported on June 3, 1921, that "Alex Belledna" was a pseudonym for Maceo Pinkard, and Pinkard did not—and would never—deny that he was "Belledna." The matter seemed to be settled, and no one asked why, if the pseudonym had been invented to mask Pinkard's identity, the Pinkard and "Belledna" names began to appear on the same songs.

What the trade paper apparently did not know was that Pinkard had recently married an aspiring songwriter named Edna Belle Alexander, and that she was the more likely candidate to be "Alex Belledna." (Pinkard became an ASCAP member in 1921, and Alexander in 1946. The seven songs that she chose to list in her entry in the ASCAP *Biographical Dictionary* included three Alexander-Pinkard numbers—one of them unpublished—three "Belledna" collaborations

with Pinkard, and one other song—the "Belledna"-Gilbert "Granny.")
Edna Alexander's name appears on two Pinkard songs ("Make Those
Naughty Eyes Behave," in 1925, and "Sugar," in 1926), and the
"Belledna" alias appears on six unpublished songs with Pinkard.
"Belledna" also shared credit with Andy Razaf on the raunchy
"Kitchen Man," which Bessie Smith recorded in 1929. A dozen or so
songs do not make a major career, but Edna Belle Alexander seems to
have been the only black woman to have even this many published
songs before the rock era.

Maceo Pinkard's most active year of theatre writing was 1922. He
was signed by the black producer Irvin C. Miller to write the score for a
show called Bon Bon Buddy, Jr. The death of Bert Williams on March 4
of that year hung heavily over the black theatre community, and
Pinkard's score reflected this preoccupation in such songs as "Just
Another Barbershop Chord" and "The Day Bert Williams Said
Goodbye," as well as the title song. Perhaps too funereal to be successful, Bon Bon Buddy, Jr. closed after a brief run in Harlem.

Another producer, Al Davis, saw possibilities in Pinkard's score,
however, and arranged to present a revamped version of the show,
which he would call Liza, at Daly's Sixty-third Street Theatre, the site
of Sissle and Blake's success with Shuffle Along. Liza opened there on
November 27, 1922, and it racked up a respectable 172 performances.
Liza was the first black Broadway show to be backed by black capital,
and its investors increased their earnings by sending out a tour. The
show stayed on the road well into 1924.

Most of Bon Bon Buddy, Jr.'s songs were thrown out, and the few
that remained were overhauled by the lyricist Nat Vincent. A new
song, "The Charleston Dancy," was written for Liza by Pinkard and
Vincent, and the sequence that featured it gave white New York its first
look at the dance that would typify the twenties. Audiences did not
find "The Charleston Dancy" particularly noteworthy, and the song
was not chosen for publication with the other show numbers. James P.
Johnson's "Charleston" of 1923 would be the number that stuck in the
public mind.

Pinkard had a song ("My Dixie") in Spice of 1922, but it was overshadowed by two other interpolations, "Way Down Yonder in New
Orleans" and Gershwin's "Yankee Doodle Blues." Pinkard's most suc-

cessful song of the year was the trickily syncopated "I'm Always Stuttering," undoubtedly inspired by the success of Zez Confrey's "Stumbling." Confrey made a dazzling piano roll of the Pinkard song.

On August 27, 1923, Maceo Pinkard made the first of his three recordings. He provided the piano accompaniment for Gertrude Saunders, the *Liza* star, who sang his "Potomac River Blues" for Victor. Pinkard had set up a recording session for Duke Ellington and his Washingtonians about a month earlier. If these sides had been released, they would have been the first Ellington recordings.

In 1925 Pinkard turned out four big songs and became a major presence in Tin Pan Alley, scoring a hit per month in July, August, and September. July's hit was "Does My Sweetie Do—And How," written with "Alex Belledna" and Sidney Holden. The chorus opens with four bars of relentless syncopation, relieved by four legato bars, making a combination of musical pepper and sugar. "Does My Sweetie Do" went into dance band books immediately upon its release. In August, Pinkard's best Charleston number, "Sweet Man"—which evoked Roy Turk's smartest lyric—was recorded by Lee Morse. Jazz bands, including the California Ramblers and the Goofus Five, picked it up; Frank Banta made a hot piano version for Victor; and Ethel Waters recorded it in October. The irrepressible "Sweet Man" was followed in September by "Desdemona" (music and lyrics by Pinkard). The tempo marking of "Desdemona" is "Charleston Swing," and it is truly a song that straddles two musical eras. The strong accents of the Charleston are there, but there is also a bounce that foreshadows the big band sound too. "Desdemona" was first recorded by Bailey's Lucky Seven on September 11, 1925.

Pinkard's monster hit of 1925, however, came in the spring: "Sweet Georgia Brown." Pinkard was serving a brief stint as a staff writer for Remick when he wrote it, so it was not necessary for him to sign the company's standard contract for the song. The document is dated February 11, and Pinkard's name is typed in at the top as cocomposer with Kenneth Casey. The contract calls for a $225 advance to the composers, a two-cents-a copy royalty on sheet music sold, and one-third of any sale of mechanical rights. The first—and boldest—signature at the bottom is that of the bandleader Ben Bernie, whose name would be the first listed on the published song. He had obviously had an advance look at "Sweet Georgia Brown" and smelled a potential hit. He cut himself in on the sale and royalties of the song in return for making and plugging a recording of it. "Sweet Georgia Brown" received the first of its scores of recordings, by Bernie and His Hotel Roosevelt Orchestra, on March 19, 1925.

"Sweet Georgia Brown" is surprisingly complex, and it is one of the most melodically and harmonically imaginative songs of the twenties. Its tune is so infectious that singers and players simply sail into it, unaware that they are negotiating anything tricky. "Sweet Georgia Brown" is based on an ordinary "circle of fifths" idea, but the "circle" doesn't start in the expected place. The published song is in the key of G, but a tonic (G) chord is not heard until measure thirteen. The song winds through E7, A7, and D7 to get there, and the melody is studded with interesting intervals and leaps from "accidental" to "accidental" along the way. The chorus is thirty-two bars long, but it eschews the usual AABA pop-song structure. The melody keeps turning unexpected corners: the second eight bars and the fourth eight are nothing alike, and the first eight recurs where the bridge would ordinarily be. "Sweet Georgia Brown" is a masterful piece of songwriting that sounds as offhand as an improvisation by an idle whistler. (A recording of "Sweet Georgia Brown," with the melody whistled over a scuffling rhythm, has been used for years in the warmup show of the Harlem Globetrotters. It is the perfect accompaniment to their casual magic.) There was only one cloud over Pinkard's wonderful year of 1925. This was the failure of *Broadway Rastus*, another Harlem revue written for Irvin C. Miller.

Maceo Pinkard's string of hits continued into 1926. "I Wonder What's Become of Joe?" (with lyrics by Roy Turk) was a sort of flapper's answer to "I Wonder What's Become of Sally," a waltz hit of 1924. The Pinkard-Turk song is as pert as "Sally" is sentimental, and it includes a "Charleston chorus" that carries the syncopation of its first chorus even further. Another 1926 song that had a brief vogue was "Gimme a Little Kiss, Will Ya, Huh?" The Pinkard tune is better than the Roy Turk-Jack Smith lyric, but the song is cloying and childish compared to Pinkard's previous string of firecrackers. Jean Goldkette had the best 1926 recording, but "Gimme a Little Kiss" became the signature song of "Whispering Jack" Smith. It remained in the sweet-band repertoire through the thirties and forties.

Pinkard's best work of 1926 was the lazy-sounding, musically hip "Sugar" (lyrics by Sidney Mitchell and Edna Alexander). This song ambles through a sophisticated chain of harmonies that has fascinated jazz players ever since its writing. Like "Sweet Georgia Brown," "Sugar" never goes where it seems to be going, yet its harmonic destinations are always satisfying. Ethel Waters made the first recording of "Sugar," on February 20, 1926, for Columbia. Pinkard provided her piano accompaniment during this session, at which she also sang "I Wonder What's Become of Joe?"

In 1927 a Pinkard trifle called "Here Comes the Show Boat" (lyrics by Billy Rose) began its surprisingly long life. It was sung by Ethel Waters in *Africana*, a Broadway revue of that year, and it was interpolated into Jerome Kern's score in the 1929 film version of *Show Boat*. For several years it was used as the theme of *The Maxwell House Show Boat*, a radio variety program.

In 1928 Helen Kane recorded Pinkard's "Don't Be Like That," and Waring's Pennsylvanians had a hit with his "Lila." Also in 1928 an early sound film melodrama, *The Phantom in the House*, used Pinkard and Abner Silver's "You'll Never Be Forgotten" as its theme, making the composer one of the first—and few—black writers of the time with a film song credit.

Maceo Pinkard tried theatre again in 1929, this time as producer as well as

Africana

composer and lyricist. The result was a shockingly bad college musical called *Pansy* that featured Bessie Smith. It played the first of its three performances at the small Belmont Theatre, on West Forty-eighth Street, on May 14, 1929. There was no way to integrate Smith into the frivolous story line, so she made only a brief appearance in the second act—singing Pinkard's "If the Blues Don't Get You"—and came back for a small role in a sequence that parodied O'Neill plays, "A Stranger Interlude." Audiences and critics hated *Pansy*, and the show would be Pinkard's last.

There were two more Pinkard hits, both coming late in 1930. The first was "I'll Be a Friend with Pleasure" (lyric and music by Pinkard), a flowing ballad that reveals its harmonic beauties in a way that is simultaneously delicate and deliberate. It is the simplest of Pinkard's hits, and Bix Beiderbecke and His Orchestra—including side men Benny Goodman, Jimmy Dorsey, and Gene Krupa—made a glowing recording of it for Victor on September 8, 1930. In November "Them There Eyes" (lyrics by William Tracey and Doris Tauber) strode into the jazz repertoire. This is another Pinkard song that seems to be more ordinary than it is. The published version is in the key of C, yet the song keeps flirting with B-minor chords, and it springs an octave drop in the melody of a two-bar break. Louis Armstrong and His Orchestra made a definitive early recording in April 1931, and Billie Holiday made it hers on a Vocalion recording of 1939.

All of the black pop writers were hurt by the changes in structure and attitude that occurred in Tin Pan Alley in the late twenties, but Maceo Pinkard's professional decline was more abrupt than most. As early as 1931 he began to have trouble getting publication. He had only four published songs that year, two of them issued by Pinkard Publications. His contacts with major houses withered through the thirties, and after 1937 there were no more Pinkard songs except those he published himself. In 1939 he sent out a promotional flyer—obviously hand-typed—from Pinkard Publications, at 762 St. Nicholas Avenue, with his list of "hits" taking up most of the page. He lists eight new songs ("The Very Latest") from his company, and offers them by mail order at "35c. Ea. 3 For $1.00." The same year, on October 2, Maceo Pinkard and his wife were given a one-song slot on ASCAP's Silver Jubilee program at Carnegie Hall. The song that they chose to perform was "Mammy o' Mine."

There is a photograph of Maceo and Edna Pinkard at home. Wearing a sleek-looking suit, he is sitting in a chair, his hands spread over a piano keyboard. He is a plumpish man, smiling broadly enough to show his gap-teeth, and he is gray-haired and bespectacled, looking his fifty years. His wife is standing behind him, her left hand on the back of his chair. She is a strong-looking woman with a wise smile. The latest Pinkard songs, all issued by Pinkard Publications, are spread across the music rack on the piano, carefully aligned so that their titles show. The scene is half Christmas card, half publicity shot. The Pinkards look like the grandparents every child wishes for.

Pinkard songs continued to trickle out under his imprint throughout the 1950s, until the last one appeared in 1959. Maceo Pinkard died in New York City on July 21, 1962. He should be remembered as having fulfilled the tag line on his 1939 flyer: he wrote "Songs That Sing. Songs That Swing. Songs That 'Sell.'"

JO TRENT

Some of the most elemental and enduring popular songs are those that evoke the idea of "home." America, the nation built by immigrants—some of whom had no choice in their emigration—and the busiest and most restless society of modern times, has always been full of people who wanted to go home. American music has reflected this yearning for the old days, for simpler times and places, throughout our history. One of our first drinking songs, performed by Yankee songsters shortly after the fervent years of the Revolution, was called "In Good Old Colony Times." Nineteenth-century settlers, pushing west, missed the "Red River Valley" and "The Little Old Sod Shanty on the Plain." Minstrel show audiences wallowed in the wishful thinking that black folks missed the old days, too (in "Carry Me Back to Old Virginny," "Dixie," and "Old Black Joe").

Jo Trent

The early Tin Pan Alley writers, many of whom had never been south of Fourteenth Street or west of the Hudson River, turned out generic "home songs" by the dozens. The lyrics mooned over girlfriends left behind and teared up at the thought of gray-haired mothers waiting at firesides, hoping for the return of their errant children. ("Father" is the subject of a few of these early songs, too, but he is generally treated as someone who drinks too much and doesn't work enough.)

Songwriters had "Sweet Thoughts of Home" and missed their "School Days." They pondered on objects around the house ("The Mottoes Framed upon the Wall," "A Flower from Mother's Grave"). They recalled scenery that they had never seen ("Down Where the Cotton Blossoms Grow," "Where the Silv'ry Colorado Wends Its Way") and states they had never visited ("My Old New Hampshire Home," "I Want to Go Back to Michigan," "Alabama Jubilee"). Paul Dresser tried to cover all his bets with an 1899 song, "We Came from the Same Old State," in which the home state is never specified.

Despite the phoniness that crept into commercial "home songs," the emotions that they tapped were real. The subject of homesickness never lost its appeal; the market remained steady, even for bad songs. In the late twenties and early thirties, a handful of composer-lyricists began to write honestly in this basic genre of song. They were not yokels. All of them were hip-deep into jazz, and they were sophisticated enough to thrive in the New York music scene. But none of them came from New York, and they were all sensitive enough to remember the sights, language, and feel of small-town life and to recall them in a true and evocative way. They were Willard Robison (from Shelbina, Missouri), Hoagy Carmichael (from Bloomington, Indiana), and, later, Johnny Mercer (from Savannah, Georgia). There is another songwriter who did as much as anyone in the late twenties to get it right: the nearly forgotten black lyricist, Jo Trent. He was not an anachronism: he had had his ears skinned by jazz and his eyes peeled by city life. He lived in his own time. But unlike many of his Alley compatriots, he had obviously been outdoors, had noticed real birds, real skies, real weather. The imagery in his songs struck a chord with all Americans, black and white. And he knew how ordinary people spoke. He was a perceptive observer and a lyrical reporter to be trusted.

Biographical details about Jo Trent are maddeningly sketchy. The primary sources of them are his brief entries in the four editions of *The ASCAP Biographical Dictionary*, and the few facts about him there tantalize more than they satisfy. In looking at the parameters of his songwriting career, and considering his birth date and death date, it is obvious that he had a professional life before and after his Tin Pan Alley years. ASCAP says that he was a "Prof. mgr., music publishing houses" (but we don't know which ones), that he was a "Staff writer, asst. Dir., film cos." (unnamed). "After several years of study in tropics, became specialist and author of book on *Modern Adaptation of Primitive Tones.*" Was this before, after or during his "Educ." at "Collegiate, Hampton, Va.; Univ. of Pa.; Coll. of City of New York"? (There is no record of his being at the University of Pennsylvania. The ASCAP entry error probably comes from the fact that the school near Hampton Virginia, was the Pittsylvania Industrial, Normal and Collegiate Institute. This institution was founded in 1903 by the Cherrystone Baptist Association, and it was the first opportunity for education beyond the elementary level for the rural black children of Pittsylvania County.)

If, as ASCAP says, Joseph H. Trent was born in Chicago on May 31, 1892, how did he happen to attend "Columbus, Ohio, public and high schools"? And when—and why—was he in school in Virginia? Besides ASCAP, no other reference books list him, and only one memoirist, Duke Ellington, recalled him. He is merely a name on song sheets and in the appendices of the biographies of his collaborators. Jo Trent is over thirty years old when we get our first glimpse of him, beginning to peddle songs in New York.

Jo Trent's name is on five songs published in 1923, and we don't know which of them was first to see print. He was either an exceptionally lucky beginner, or, more likely, he had shown promise before that year, because two of his 1923 songs were collaborations with established writers (Will Donaldson and Clarence Williams) and two of them were issued by major publishers (Harms and Fred Fisher). The first recording of a Jo Trent song was "Outside of That, He's All Right with Me," written with Clarence Williams and sung by Esther Bigeou for OKeh in March 1923. Bessie Smith recorded "Outside of That" with Fletcher Henderson's piano accompaniment for Columbia in April. Trent and Roland Irving sold a song to Fred Fisher that year, the steamy "Sweet Pain" ("Oh! Mister Doctor, I think you're great, Go ahead and operate. Sweet pain is in my heart tonight, such blissful misery. . . ."), published with Mamie Smith's photo on the cover, although she did not record the song.

The producer Nat Nazarro hired Trent to write words, music, and libretto for a touring musical, *Hot Chops*, to star Buck and Bubbles, in 1923. A revised version of *Hot Chops*, called *Raisin' Cain* and featuring

Donald Heywood's music, opened at the Lafayette Theatre on July 9. The Trent-Heywood title song was published by Jack Mills. A better theatre credit for Trent came a few months later, when he placed three interpolations into the successful *Runnin' Wild*, which opened in October. One of these, "Heart Breakin' Joe" (written with Porter Grainger), was published by Harms.

As short as the list of Trent songs was in 1923, to the wide-eyed Duke Ellington, recently arrived in New York from Washington, Trent seemed like an old Tin Pan Alley pro. Ellington wrote of their brief collaboration in his 1973 book, *Music Is My Mistress*:

> During my first few months in New York, I found out that anybody was eligible to take songs into the music publishers on Broadway. So I joined the parade and teamed up with Joe Trent, a nice guy who was familiar with the routines of the publishing world. He liked my music and he was a good lyricist, so he took my hand and guided me around Broadway. We wrote several songs together and auditioned every day in one publisher's office or another and, as was normal, had practically no success, until one day when we demonstrated a song for Fred Fisher. . . .
>
> "I like it," he said, after listening to our song. "I'll take it."
>
> "You know, of course, that we want a fifty-dollar advance," Joe said.
>
> "Okay," Fred Fisher replied. "Give me a lead sheet and I'll sign the contract."
>
> "Give the man a lead sheet," Joe said, turning to me.
>
> I had never made a lead sheet before, nor tried to write music of any kind, but it was 4:30 P.M. and I knew the checkbook would be closed at five. So, in spite of ten pianos banging away in ten different booths, I sat down and made a lead sheet. It was satisfactory. We got the money, split it, and then split the scene. . . . The next day, and for many days to follow, we were back in our old rut—peddling songs and failing to find any buyers.

The song they placed with Fred Fisher that day was "Blind Man's Buff," the first Ellington song to sell.

In 1924 Jo Trent sold twelve of his collaborations with Fats Waller to Clarence Williams, but only one ("In Harlem's Araby") was published and recorded. Trent and Duke Ellington also placed their "Pretty Soft for You" with Williams. That year, Trent wrote lyrics for a tab show for Miller and Lyles, the stars who had gotten to know his work in *Runnin' Wild*. The show was called *Honey*, and his collaborators on the score were Porter Grainger and Bob Ricketts. In November 1924, Trent made his only recording, singing "Deacon Jazz." The Blu-Disc label read "Jo Trent and the D'C'Ns." Duke Ellington played the piano accompaniment and provided the D'C'Ns from his own band: Otto Hardwick on alto sax, Freddy Guy on banjo, and Sonny Greer on drums.

Ellington recalled Trent's running up to him on the street in late 1924 and saying that they had to write a show immediately. Trent had had a tip that someone was in the market for a revue. Ellington—"not knowing any better," he said—sat down with Trent and wrote the score for *Chocolate Kiddies* overnight. The next day they took their work to Jack Robbins, a struggling publisher, who wanted to buy it. Trent asked for a $500 advance and, again according to Ellington, Robbins pawned his wife's ring to get the money. *Chocolate Kiddies* was never produced in the United States, but as tailored for the Sam Wooding band, it played two years in Europe, beginning in mid-1925. The revue opened at Berlin's Admiral Palast, and its subsequent tour included performances in the Soviet Union. The ongoing European royalties for the *Chocolate Kiddies* numbers helped Jack Robbins establish himself as a publisher. He issued three of the *Chocolate Kiddies* songs in the United States ("Jig Walk," "Jim Dandy," and "With You"), but none was a success. The Robbins connection helped Ellington more than Trent; the house would issue many more of the composer's numbers than the lyricist's. There was one more Trent-Ellington song, "Yam Brown," published by Frazer-Kent in 1926.

Trent wrote with Fats Waller again in 1926. Their "Georgia Bo-Bo" received a handful of recordings in the spring of that year, the best one by Lil Armstrong's Serenaders (with a Louis Armstrong vocal), made in May for Vocalion. In late 1926, probably in a pairing made by Will Von Tilzer—the owner of Broadway Music Corporation—Jo Trent was teamed with the composer who would be his main collaborator, Peter DeRose. Their first song was a hit, and their five-year association brought out the best in each of them. Trent dug deeper lyrically than he ever had before, and he struck a vein of Americana that stands among the richest in popular song.

Peter DeRose was a white songwriter, born in New York City in 1900. At the time the two writers met, DeRose was married to May Singhi Breen, a songwriter and ukelele instructor, and the couple were three years into a radio career. They had been NBC's "Sweethearts of the Air" since 1923, with their own musical program. Breen had convinced several major publishers to include ukelele chords on their song sheets, and in 1926 she was working for them, filling the demand she had created for ukelele arrangements. DeRose had had a few published songs, including two mild successes: "When You're Gone, I Won't Forget," in 1920, and "Suez," a popular "Oriental Fox-Trot" of 1922. DeRose's early work showed competence, nothing more. He had certainly never composed anything like "Muddy Water."

"Muddy Water," the first Trent-DeRose song, is subtitled "A Mississippi Moan," and it is a "home song" that wails like a blues. DeRose's melody is studded with blue notes and melodic leaps of more than an octave, over a relentless, four-on-the-floor beat. Trent's lyric is simple, and his ear for American speech is true. ("Muddy water 'round my feet, Muddy water in the street, Just God's own shelter down on the delta. . . ." "I don't care it's muddy there, but still it's my home. Got my toes turned Dixie way, 'round that delta let me lay. My heart cries out for muddy water.") "Muddy Water" is informed by black music, but it isn't a "black" song. It can speak to anyone who has had emotional ties to rural life. It has had recordings by black singers and by white singers through the years. The only requirement for putting over "Muddy Water" is to be as honest as the song itself is.

The nightclub singer Harry Richman cut himself in as cocomposer of "Muddy Water" with DeRose, and he made the first recording of it, in January 1927. In March "Muddy Water" got two fine treatments, one by Bessie Smith on Columbia and the other by the Paul Whiteman Orchestra (with a Bing Crosby vocal) on Victor.

Harry Richman claimed in his 1966 autobiography, *A Hell of a Life*—which mentions neither Trent nor DeRose—that his recording of "his" song, "Muddy Water," sold over 300,000 copies. Whether or not this is hyperbole, "Muddy Water" certainly announced Trent and DeRose as a team to watch. In early 1927 they got recordings of their "I

Just Roll Along, Havin' My Ups and Downs," including one in February on which DeRose provided the piano accompaniment for Annette Hanshaw. In May the California Ramblers made a successful Columbia recording of the Trent-DeRose song "Lazy Weather." This song catches the hypnotic stasis of a small-town summer day. ("All the kids look for shade, 'Cause the swimmin' hole went dry, All the birds fluff their wings, Just too doggone hot to fly. . . ."), the contented feeling of "Just layin' around close to the ground." "Lazy Weather" is a pop song that is purely a mood piece. The Trent lyric pulls off the trick of sustaining interest in a song which is nothing but description.

Jo Trent songs were featured in four Broadway shows in 1927, two black and two white. He wrote the lyric for the title song in *Bottomland,* a show produced and com-posed by Clarence Williams, which opened in late June. Trent and Ford Dabney wrote the score for a Miller and Lyles musical called *Rang-Tang,* which opened on July 12 at the Royale Theatre. The plot of *Rang-Tang* was clichéd by then—a pair of con men flee to Africa to escape their creditors—but the stars had enough drawing power to sell 119 performances. Eight of the *Rang-Tang* songs were published by Leo Feist.

Rang-Tang

The most successful of the 1927 shows with Trent songs was the acclaimed production of Arthur Hopkins' drama with songs, *Burlesque.* This was a play in three acts, starring Barbara Stanwyck and Hal Skelly, which began its 372-performance run at the Plymouth Theatre in September. The show-business setting of this story about the long-suffering wife of an alcoholic burlesque performer provided the excuse for three songs—and for the presence of Oscar Levant, appearing as a grind-house pianist. The songs seem to have been written by a committee—credit is shared, with DeRose, a lyricist named Edward Grant, and an old pro of pop, Albert Von Tilzer—but one of them, a torchy ballad called "I'm Wonderin' Who," is very much in the

Trent-DeRose style. ("Who's gonna fret, who's gonna frown, Who'll be unhappy if I don't come around?") Trent and DeRose also got their "Pack Up Your Blues and Smile" into the short-lived *Yes, Yes, Yvette*, which opened in October.

Trent and DeRose continued in their vernacular groove in 1928. Annette Hanshaw recorded their "'Cause I Feel Low-Down" in March, with Peter DeRose as her accompanist. This song perfectly captures the ragged edge of a jilted lover ("Got a mean and don't-care notion, "'Cause I feel low-down"). The Dorsey Brothers Orchestra had a successful recording of the duo's "Dixie Dawn" in the early summer of that year. And there were three hot recordings of a song that Trent wrote with J. Russel Robinson—using his pseudonym "Joe Hoover"—the blue-tinged "Rhythm King." This was Trent's celebration of jazz ("It makes you rock like a chair, heats up the air, It's just like wine"), and jazz players quickly returned the compliment. Bix Beiderbecke and His Gang made it first, for OKeh in September; Paul Whiteman's version— with a scatty Rhythm Boys vocal—was released in November; and the Coon-Sanders Orchestra got to it in December.

Two Broadway shows used Jo Trent songs in 1928. The first was a comedy-heavy edition of the *Earl Carroll's Vanities* that featured W. C. Fields and Joe Frisco. The Trent-DeRose song in the score was "Watch My Baby Walk," which was recorded by a Ben Selvin group, the Bar Harbor Society Orchestra, with a vocal by Robert Wood, for Harmony Records. In October a song by Jo Trent and Louis Alter went practically unnoticed in the flop revue, *Americana*: it was "My Kinda Love." However, within a few weeks, it received the recordings that would establish it as one of Trent's biggest hits. Alter's stair-step melody for "My Kinda Love" is more interesting than the Trent lyric, which combines the slangy and the stilted ("My kinda love, your kinda love, Keeps me believing although you're deceiving. . . ."). Bing Crosby made a very popular recording of it in March 1929, but the lyric is not Trent's best.

Earl Carroll called on Trent again in early 1929. An amateur composer named George Bagby had come to Carroll offering him a large chunk of his aunt's money to produce an operetta that he had written. Carroll took Bagby's offer and quickly proposed a leading actress for the show, Carroll's current girlfriend, Dorothy Knapp. Bagby's choice for

lyricist was another unknown, Grace Henry. Carroll was an oppor-
tunist, but he was no fool. He knew that he needed some professionals
among the neophytes in this well-heeled venture. To support Knapp in
her starring role, Carroll hired Fanny Brice and Leon Errol. To enhance
the Bagby-Henry songs, he hired Jo Trent. The result of their labors
was the anachronistic *Fioretta*, which opened at the Earl Carroll
Theatre on February 5, 1929. The low comedy of Brice and Errol kept
the show running for 111 performances, but the score was an embarrassment. The Henry-Trent lyric to the show's big song, "Dream Boat,"
is full of "Stars glistening on high / Through the blue velvet of sky,"
"Soft summer breezes that blow," "Our souls afire with one desire," and
the like. The *Fioretta* songs, probably edited by Trent rather than written by him, are the only empty lyrics with Trent's name on them.

But during the run of the bloated operetta, another Trent lyric
began to get its first recordings. It was "Wake Up! Chill'un, Wake
Up!," and it is one of the most original conceptions in popular song.
Trent's collaborator was Willard Robison, the Missouri songwriter and
orchestra leader who had made a specialty of small-town songs. They
had written together once before ("Ploddin' Along," in 1928, with
Peter DeRose as co-composer), and Robison had recorded a few Trent-
DeRose songs ("I Just Roll Along," "Lazy Weather," and "Easy Goin'").
Trent and Robison were a perfect match.

The song is a parent's exultation in life, and it expresses the wish
to share that overwhelming joy with one's children. The singer urges
the listening children to get up and greet the new day, which will surely be marvelous. The Robison melody swings gently—but is surprisingly wide-ranged—and the Trent lyric urges it along with a soul-deep
optimism. The love of life is so intense in "Wake Up! Chill'un" that
Trent's imagery suggests a sort of countrified acid trip. ("The sunbeams
are dancin' and laughin' with glee, The leaves on the trees wavin'
'howdy' to me, It seems like the whole world's a big jubilee, Wake up,
chill'un, wake up!") It is one of the most satisfying of pop songs, and it
is one of those that, over the years, became a standard without ever
being a hit.

The success of the Trent-Alter "My Kinda Love" in early 1929 led
to film assignments for the writers. They contributed "Gotta Feelin' for
You" to MGM's *Hollywood Revue of 1929*, and they wrote "One for All,

All for One" (with Hugo Reisenfeld) as the theme for *The Iron Mask*, a 1929 Douglas Fairbanks feature. Although Trent's 1929 film songs were among the first such assignments given to a black songwriter, they were not enough to establish Jo Trent in Hollywood. His songwriting career, like that of the other successful black writers, began to wane when the music business moved west.

In 1930 Trent and DeRose wrote songs for *From Broadway to Paris*, a club revue built around Irving Aaronson and His Commanders. Also that year, Chappell published "Pinin' for Dat Freedom Day," one of the few songs with music as well as lyrics by Trent. It is an art song with ghosts of nineteenth-century work songs in it—in repetitions of the words "diggin'" and "haulin'." There is an archness to the melody and a hopelessness in the lyric ("Keep on tryin' but it ain't no use") that would deter a singer from programming it.

Jo Trent had a small success with "Linda," written with Peter DeRose and Charlie Tobias. It was recorded by Red Nichols and His Five Pennies (with a vocal by Harold Arlen) in November of 1930, and the record sold well into the following year.

Trent must have had high hopes for *Sugar Hill*, the musical that he wrote with James P. Johnson in 1931. A vehicle for the comedy team of Miller and Lyles, it opened on Christmas Day 1931 at the Forrest Theatre. There was a streak of melodrama in the comedy involving Harlem gangsters, and audiences didn't like it. *Sugar Hill* lasted for just eleven performances, and only two of the Trent-Johnson songs saw publication. Neither was a hit, and the show would be Trent's last.

Trent had a brief collaboration with Hoagy Carmichael in 1932 that produced only two songs. Their first was a ballad called "In the Still of the Night," in which both writers seemed to be exhibiting their company manners. The result was somewhat pretentious, and only the Casa Loma Orchestra plugged the song. The second Trent-Carmichael effort was better. This was the sexy "Sing It Way Down Low" ("Singin' way down low, singin' easy and slow, Honey, how I love you singin' way down low"). Carmichael himself made the first recording of it, on September 1, 1932, for Victor.

The last hit for Jo Trent was "Here You Come with Love," written with Harry Tobias and Neil Moret in 1933. It is an earthy lament on the realization that love alone won't pay the bills. ("Rent's overdue, telephone's dead, Icebox and kitchen both in the red. When I need gravy, cryin' for bread, Here you come with love.") Ted Lewis had the big recording of it.

Jo Trent had one more chance to place a song in a film. "Sweet Like You" (written with Newell Chase) was featured in a 1937 Phil Harris short called "Harris in the Spring." The song went nowhere, and even Harris did not record it.

Was Jo Trent written out after fifteen years in the business? Was he writing but not selling? His best collaborators, black and white, were still at it in the late thirties, and most of them wrote through the forties. Did they not ask him to write? Did he not ask them? Why does Trent's list of nearly a hundred songs end in 1937? Did Trent simply move on, go to live in the tropics, write his book? Whatever the reason for his disappearance from the popular music business, we must be glad that he was in it. His words caught the way we talked and the way we used to live. There is one more mystery about him in the *ASCAP Biographical Dictionary*: Jo Trent died on November 19, 1954—a long way from home, in Barcelona, Spain.

ANDY RAZAF

The career of Andy Razaf, which began to bloom in the late 1920s, should have come to full flower in the following decade, but it did not. At the beginning of 1930 he had a string of hits behind him, some of them already on their way to becoming standards. He had had successful songs in three Broadway shows. He had demonstrated the most desirable qualities of a professional songwriter: he was versatile, industrious, fast, and easy to work with. In short, he seemed to be just what Hollywood was looking for during the busy years of early musical films. But because he was black, the Hollywood door did not open to him. And as the Depression mired the music business, the New York door began to close on him as well. By the end of 1930 he had written his last Broadway show, made his last commercial recordings, and done his last radio program. He would have hits in the 1930s, but because of one-sided publishing deals made when he was desperate for money, the hits never paid off as they should have. Although racism loomed over

Andy Razaf

every career in this book, its effect was particularly poignant in Razaf's case. The timing of its sting was devastating. Just as he was poised for greater things, creatively and professionally, he began to slide. He was held back, not because he "wrote black," but because he was perceived as a "black writer."

No black freelancer struggled more valiantly than Andy Razaf did to stay afloat in the mainstream of the music business in the 1930s. He took the opportunities that were offered him, and he created opportunities for himself. He wrote whatever was salable when he needed money, from dirty songs to children's rhymes. He wrote with unknowns, sharing credit on music sheets with instrumentalists who each had one tune needing a lyric. He wrote for club revues that he knew would go nowhere, several times providing full scores for flat fees. This scramble for survival stunted his development as a lyricist. His 1940s songs are no deeper or more polished than those of a decade earlier. When paralysis struck him, at age fifty-five, he kept at it, grinding the songs out and sending them around. The last twenty years of his life were spent in physical pain and professional frustration. He soldiered on, never quite getting anywhere but never giving up either.

None of the turmoil and disappointments of Razaf's life are reflected in his 450 or so published lyrics. His songs mostly radiate contentment, and the heartache quotient is very low. Many of his lyrics sound facile, as if they were written in a hurry (which they were). But there is playfulness in them, as well an instinct for dead-on rhyming and a surety of meter. He seldom wrote, and never sang, the blues. The best Razaf songs are bemused and flirtatious, like a wink from an attractive stranger.

Andy Razaf was born on December 15, 1895, to a fifteen-year-old widow living in Washington, D.C. His name at birth was Andreamentania Paul Razafkeriefo, and his recently deceased father was a nephew of Queen Ranavalona III, of Madagascar. John Waller, his mother's father, had been a hard-working Republican party regular in the Midwest in the 1880s and had delivered the black vote in Kansas for Benjamin Harrison in the presidential election of 1888. As a belated reward for Waller's efforts on his behalf, President Harrison named him U.S. Consul to Madagascar in 1891. Waller took his family, including his eleven-year-old daughter Jennie, to the large island nation off the southeast coast of Africa when he assumed his duties there. John Waller became close to the royal family and gave them his wholehearted support when the threat of French incursion into Madagascar arose. Jennie Waller became close to Henri Razafkeriefo, the queen's nephew, and her father allowed them to marry in early 1895.

Not long after their wedding, France carried out its threat of invasion, and in October 1895 John Waller sent his wife and their pregnant daughter back to the United States for their safety. Soon after Jennie's return, she learned that her young husband had been killed by the French and that her father had been imprisoned in France for his loyalty to the queen. John Waller was released by the French in 1896, and he returned to the United States to collect his family, including his infant grandson, from Baltimore and move them to Kansas City.

Waller began a law practice there, but he was an adventurous man who dreamed of bigger things. He organized a company of black soldiers for the Spanish-American War in August 1898, and took his family along to Cuba when he left to command his troops. In 1900 the Wallers returned to New York. They lived for a while in Yonkers, where John Waller was editor of a local newspaper. In 1907 Waller died of pneumonia, around the time that Jennie Waller remarried and moved to Passaic, New Jersey. When her second marriage dissolved after a few years, Jennie Waller and her son moved back to New York City. She became a stenographer and tried to earn enough to keep her son in high school. He was a good student, an avid reader who liked to tinker with writing verses. Despite her desire to see her son finish his education, Jennie could not stretch her meager income far enough to keep him in school. At sixteen Andy dropped out and went looking for work.

He found a job running an elevator in a building full of publishers and theatrical offices on West Twenty-eighth Street, the street that had been dubbed "Tin Pan Alley" about ten years earlier. He watched the show-business traffic come and go in his building for a year or so, then he decided to put his in-house contacts to good use. Razaf talked his way into an office—probably that of Oscar Radin, a musical director—and pitched a song he had written the words and music for, a jauntily syncopated piece called "Baltimo'." By some miracle, his song was picked up for use in *The Passing Show of 1913*, a Shubert revue already running at the Winter Garden, and it was well enough received to attract a publisher. The composer-lyricist's full name was misspelled in two different ways on the song sheet, and the publisher, James Kendis, suggested that it be shortened on succeeding songs.

There would be no succeeding songs for years. Razaf kept peddling, but no one was buying. He had a dreary succession of day jobs through the teens: in other elevator cars, at a telephone switchboard, in a dry cleaner's, massaging floors at the U.S. Appraiser's Building. In April 1915 Razaf married Annabelle Miller, and she got him a job as a butler in the house where she worked as a maid. In the late teens he hawked radical publications (*The New Negro* and *The Crusader*) on the streets of Harlem. *The Crusader* occasionally published his political verses, and in February 1919 Crusader Music issued a Razaf song, "The Fifteenth Infantry," as a single sheet. Razaf peddled it on the streets along with his papers.

The only recreation that Razaf allowed himself during this time was baseball. He had a neighborhood reputation as a pitcher, and when a new semipro Negro team started up in Cleveland, he was called to come and pitch for them. He and Annabelle moved to Cleveland in May 1920. His baseball career lasted about eight months before restlessness overtook him. He returned to Harlem, more determined than ever to become a songwriter.

Razaf made the rounds of Harlem clubs, offering specialty material to singers. He knew that he was not a great melodist, so he began to cultivate potential composers. One he particularly pursued was a bumptious seventeen-year-old named Fats Waller. Razaf, nearly ten years older than Waller, sought out the young man after watching him win a piano contest at the Roosevelt Theatre in 1921. He introduced himself to Waller on the street outside the theatre and began to sound him out on the idea of their writing songs together. The two hit it off, and although Waller had no particular ambition to be a composer, he agreed to try writing with Razaf.

Waller was much more interested in going to parties than he was in learning the discipline of songwriting, however, and his collaboration with Razaf began as (and would always remain) a catch-me-if-you-can affair. Razaf had great patience with Waller and valued him as a friend, but he couldn't depend on him as a writing partner, and he couldn't wait. In late 1922 Razaf wrote the lyrics for a touring burlesque show, *Joe Hurtig's Social Maids*, to melodies by the pianist Hughie Woolford. One of the *Social Maids* songs, "My Waltz Divine," was published by Remick in early 1923, giving Razaf his first commercial publication since "Baltimo'." Also in 1923, Razaf and Edgar Dowell placed a song into Lew Leslie's *Plantation Revue*, called "He Wasn't Born in Araby (But He's a Sheikin' Fool)." It was published by Rainbow Music, the "race" division of Irving Berlin, Inc.

The first Razaf-Waller song to be recorded came in 1924, "When You're Tired of Me," which was recorded by Clarence Williams (its copyright owner) and his wife, Eva Taylor, in May. In December, Maggie Jones, accompanied by Louis Armstrong on cornet and Fletcher Henderson on piano, recorded the first of many Razaf-Waller songs that would dance along the line between innocence and naughtiness, "Anybody Here Want to Try My Cabbage?" Clarence Williams published it in April 1925, making it the first Razaf-Waller song to see print.

Razaf appeared as a singer in the spring and fall editions of *The Creole Follies* at the Club Alabam on West Forty-fourth Street. The fall 1924 edition of the show featured a song called "Honeysuckle Rose," with music and lyrics by Razaf. Razaf was a great recycler of titles and lyrics, and this idea would be put to use in a better song, five years later.

Recommended for a radio job by Clarence Williams, Andy Razaf made his broadcast debut in 1924, crooning to his own ukelele accompaniment on WGCP. By 1925, Williams had bought several Razaf songs, had written with him, and had helped him get recordings of his work. Razaf was obviously on his way to becoming a fixture on Clarence Williams' roster of black songwriters. But something happened to chill their relationship. Possibly the trouble was with "Squeeze Me." Although Razaf was usually tight-lipped—at least in public—about the machinations of the music business, he began to claim, years later, that he had written "Squeeze Me" with Fats Waller. The song was bought by Williams in 1925 and was recorded by Williams' Blue Five in October of that year. The Bessie Smith recording, made in March 1926, put the song on the map. It was the first Waller song to break, and when it was published in July 1925 (with Aunt Jemima's photo on the cover), Razaf's name was not on it. It was credited to Williams and Waller. Whatever happened with "Squeeze Me," Razaf would rarely publish with Clarence Williams after 1926. Even during his leanest times in the mid-thirties, Razaf took his songs elsewhere.

In late 1926 Ethel Waters recorded an Andy Razaf song called "My Special Friend Is Back in Town." It became one of her most popular numbers, and it was Razaf's first real hit. Waters' recording held its popularity into the following summer, so she featured it in her first Broadway revue, *Africana*, which opened in July at Daly's Sixty-third Street Theatre. The melody of "My Special Friend" was written by J. C. Johnson (1896–1981). Johnson had trained as a pianist in his native Chicago, but when he arrived in New York in the late teens, he was so awed by the Harlem piano giants that he turned to songwriting (often as a lyricist) to escape comparison with them. Johnson and Razaf hit a streak of success in the late twenties, and they remained friends and wrote together occasionally into the early 1940s.

Songwriting was going well for Razaf, but he couldn't quite make a living at it. In October 1926 he took three jobs—as lyricist, singer, and advance man—in a touring tab show called *Desires of 1927*. The Irvin C. Miller production featured a score by Razaf and J. C. Johnson. It toured in the Northeast for four or five months. Back in New York after the tour, Razaf went into the Vocalion studios to sing two songs with Rex Stewart's Serenaders on April 4, 1927, but these sides went unreleased. Razaf would make about a dozen commercial recordings as a singer. None of his records were successful, but several are interesting for their accompaniments. In November 1927 he was backed by Fletcher Henderson's Collegians, as well as by J. C. Johnson's piano. In 1928 he made two sides with Fats Waller, and in the 1940s Eubie Blake played for him on two songs for Asch Records.

In 1928 Razaf and J. C. Johnson followed up "My Special Friend Is Back in Town" with three more hits. The first was "Louisiana," a song more interesting for its harmonies than its lyric. Paul Whiteman made the best-selling recording in April, featuring Bix Beiderbecke on cornet and a Bing Crosby vocal. Beiderbecke liked the tune so much that he recorded it again with His Gang in September. The second hit was the cliché-ridden "Dusky Stevedore" ("See his ragtime shuffalin' gait, Happy 'cause he's handlin' freight"), which had two successful recordings, Nat Shilkret's and Frankie Trumbauer's, in the summer. In August Ethel Waters sang their "Guess Who's in Town?" for Columbia. Razaf must have enjoyed writing to this bright, rhythmic Johnson tune. The published version includes four sets of lyrics for its chorus, and it is packed with delicious wordplay. ("When she goes by, Weak eyes cry out for glasses, Who can deny, She really does know her molasses. . . ." "Some honey child, I want you all to meet her, I'll put it mild, When she's around, don't need a heater. . . .")

The Waller-Razaf partnership had been only half-serious in the mid-twenties, but in late 1927 James P. Johnson recommended them for a writing assignment that would energize it. Johnson was asked by producer/songwriter Con Conrad if Johnson (with his lyricist Henry Creamer) would write a musical score for the comedy team of Miller and Lyles. Johnson was busy with various projects at the time, so he suggested to Conrad that Johnson and Creamer provide half of the score and that the other half be written by Razaf and Waller. The show was called *Keep Shufflin'*, and it opened at Daly's Sixty-third Street Theatre in late February 1928. Creamer and Johnson had two well-received songs in the show, "Give Me the Sunshine" and "'Sippi," but the most striking piece in the score was the deeply melancholy "Willow Tree," by Razaf and Waller.

After their success in *Keep Shufflin'*, Razaf and Waller threw themselves into the selling of their songs. Their names on song sheets were a valuable commodity. They had always seen the casual chicanery of the music business as something of a joke, and they realized that they were now in a good position to play the game. They were out for quick money, and they knew how to get it. They prowled professional buildings along Broadway, dropping in unannounced to delight publishers and their staffs with demonstrations of their latest songs. They sold well enough when Razaf did the singing, but when Waller began to sing, at Razaf's insistence, every song looked like a winner. They could write fast and they could write anywhere: in taxis, over lunch, on the street, in the hallways outside the offices they were about to burst into. Their songs were committed to paper only as jots on the napkins, menus, and scraps that Waller had stuffed in his pockets, just enough to remind Waller of a tricky chord change that he had hummed in a taxi or to recall a rhyme that Razaf had just made on a streetcorner. They blew in like a cheerful breeze, all smiles and sass, demonstrated their goods, took the money, and ran. Sometimes, as soon as they had clinched a sale, they would huddle in a hallway to make a slight change in the song that they had just sold before selling it again to another publisher a few doors away.

The Razaf-Waller songs that were written in haste were also sold that way. Sometimes they were offered contracts with standard rights and royalty provisions in them. Sometimes they were offered a flat fee for a song, with no royalties provided for. Some of these "flat-fee" songs were intended for issue under their names. But sometimes a publisher didn't want their names, he just wanted a song. Waller and Razaf were quick to accommodate. Razaf drove a harder bargain than did Waller in such cases, but any deal was worth their consideration. They sold many songs anonymously and outright, to be issued under the names of other writers. Razaf and Waller shared the attitude that their creative well would never run dry, that they were a boundless source of supply for a demand that would be endless.

Of course, the risk they were running in these hasty deals was that of selling a potential hit for peanuts. If such a thing happened, there was no recourse. And the embarrassment of having been taken could only remain a private matter. For years the rumor circulated throughout the music industry that Razaf and Waller were the writers of "I Can't Give You Anything But Love" and "On the Sunny Side of the Street," both credited to Jimmy McHugh and Dorothy Fields. McHugh was the professional manager of Mills Music throughout most of the twenties as well as being a Mills writer. The Mills office, where McHugh was in charge, would certainly have been a stop on the Waller-Razaf selling sprees, and the two hits could have been bought in a flat-fee deal. Waller never publicly claimed to have written either of them, but his son Maurice remembered his father going into a rage upon hearing "On the Sunny Side of the Street" on the radio. Months before he died, Razaf said to a friend that "I Can't Give You Anything But Love" was his favorite of his own lyrics.

Despite any regrets that may have come from his wheeling and dealing, life looked bright to Andy Razaf in late 1928. He had written songs for a successful show, had lyrics on hit recordings and had several talented collaborators. His professional horizons seemed vast. He took an apartment at 55 West 129th Street. (He had slowly phased himself out of his marriage to Annabelle over the last few years.) It would not be long before the beautiful soprano Minto Cato would move in with him. Razaf was coming up. He had worked hard, and it was paying off.

Did a freelance songwriter ever have so magnificent a year as Andy Razaf had in 1929? His lyrics were featured in an acclaimed Broadway revue score. He had six solid hits that year, all of which would become standards, as well as a dozen more that were recorded by major artists, black and white. Publishers, producers, and singers all wanted a look at any new Razaf song.

Razaf's wonderful year began with *Hot Feet*, a revue that opened at Connie's Inn in late February, for which he provided lyrics to tunes written by J. C. Johnson and "Alex Belledna," among others. *Hot Feet* ran for ten weeks in Harlem, and its success led George and Connie Immerman, the club's owners, to dream of a full-fledged Broadway revue. If whites would venture to Harlem to see black talent in their club, a midtown revue featuring the same black talent could turn a profit and advertise their club at the same time. They wanted a show that was more elaborate, and longer, than *Hot Feet*, but something that conveyed the rowdy fun of an evening at Connie's. With the blessing of their primary backer, the gangster Dutch Schultz, the Immermans hired Andy Razaf and Fats Waller to write the songs for their Broadway venture. The brothers and their underworld angel were in a hurry, so the pianist Harry Brooks was brought in to cocompose with Waller.

The show was called *Connie's Hot Chocolates*, and it opened at the Hudson Theatre on June 20, 1929. In the cast were Margaret Simms,

Paul Bass, the tiny-voiced ingenue Baby Cox, and Edith Wilson. The score included "Say It with Your Feet," "Off Time," "Can't We Get Together?" "Dixie Cinderella," "Sweet Savannah Sue," and "Rhythm Man." But the producers and writers knew that the standout song would be "Ain't Misbehavin'," so it was wound throughout the show and reprised several times.

Critics didn't think much of "Ain't Misbehavin'" on first hearing, but audiences loved it. It is quintessential Razaf and Waller: an insinuating, catchy melody buoying a lyric that is almost diffident in its slyness. The point of the song is that love has made a stay-at-home out of a rake—and that the ex-rake would be great fun to stay at home with. The song was first performed by Paul Bass and Margaret Simms, but when Bass was replaced in the show by the insouciant Cab Calloway, the song exuded even more mischief. About six weeks into the run at the Hudson, Louis Armstrong was added to the pit orchestra, and another opportunity for displaying the song presented itself. Armstrong was given an entr'acte specialty in which he appeared in a white tux to play and sing "Ain't Misbehavin'." The Charleston Chasers were the first to record the song. Their Columbia record, with a vocal by Eva Taylor, was made only eight days after *Hot Chocolates* opened, and it was followed by a spate of recordings over the next few months. The charm of "Ain't Misbehavin'" always came through, and it didn't seem to matter who sang it.

Another song from *Hot Chocolates* received almost as much attention in the theatre, if not in the recording studio: the stark and powerful "Black and Blue." Razaf said that the song was written at the request of—that is, after a threat by—Dutch Schultz. Schultz thought it would be funny if there were a scene in which a dark-skinned woman was discovered in an all-white room in a white-sheeted bed. She would sing a funny song about being too black, about losing her beaux to lighter-skinned women. Schultz ordered Razaf to write this bit of hilarity, and the mobster got more than he bargained for when Razaf and Waller produced "Black and Blue." Razaf stood the comic notion on its head by making a strong statement on racism, and by making it in the context of a pop song. "Black and Blue" has a deceptively casual feel, and there is nothing declamatory about it. It sneaks up on you, cataloging the effects of racism in dribs and drabs of phrases, making an accretion that is finally overwhelming. Razaf's lyric is verbal pointillism, done in nothing but shades of blue. Waller's melody is simple and offhand, sparing in blue notes, using them where they count—the first one is fifteen measures into the chorus, on the word "black." Edith Wilson's performance of the song drew chuckles during the verse, which is about the threat of "browns and yellers" to a darker woman's courtships, but when she finished the first chorus, Razaf's missile hit its mark. *Hot Chocolates* audiences knew that they had been taken somewhere they didn't intend to go. They were caught by the power and simplicity of the song, and their cheering brought encores for "Black and Blue" at every performance. It was fortunate for Razaf that his gamble on a serious song paid off. Even though he had perverted his backer's joke, Dutch Schultz wouldn't harm him for producing a hit. "Black and Blue" didn't get many recordings; Louis Armstrong, Edith Wilson, and Ethel Waters were the only major artists to sing it on records.

Hot Chocolates was a solid success on Broadway, running 228 performances. The Immermans wanted another show from Razaf and Waller, and, as had been the case with *Hot Chocolates*, they wanted it quickly, for presentation in the fall at Connie's Inn.

Razaf knew that Waller would likely be in the mood to party, rather than to work, after the run of *Hot Chocolates*. So, using the bait of home cooking, he enticed Waller to Asbury Park, New Jersey, for a weekend of writing at Razaf's mother's house. Waller accepted Razaf's invitation to a nonstop meal and hied himself to Asbury Park. He reveled in Jennie Razaf's cooking, pausing at his repast only occasionally to sit at the piano and play a few snatches of tunes. In the course of an evening, he and Razaf turned out "My Fate Is in Your Hands" and a rhythm number called "Zonky." They were near to getting a handle on the requisite soft-shoe number when Waller abruptly excused himself and said he had to get back to Harlem. Razaf's hopes sank as his partner fled. With some effort, Razaf was finally able to reach him later by telephone, and "Honeysuckle Rose" was completed with its writers separated by a state line. The three new songs—along with some *Hot Chocolates* leftovers—went into Connie's new floor show, called *Load of Coal*. The club had a $15 cover, but the stiff tab did not deter customers. *Load of Coal*, its stars (Louis Armstrong and Dewey Brown), and its songs packed Connie's Inn.

"Honeysuckle Rose" was the slowest to catch on of all the Razaf-Waller classics written in 1929, however, because of mistreatment in its radio debut. Paul Whiteman wanted to premiere the song on his *Old Gold Program*, but for some reason, he chose to present the song at a galloping tempo. The off-the-cuff charm of "Honeysuckle Rose" was buried under a cascade of notes, and the song did not seem attractive to recording artists. Even Louis Armstrong did not get around to it until 1938, four years after Waller's belated first recording.

Another Razaf song began to catch on during the summer of 1929, "S'posin'," which he had written with a white composer, Paul Denniker. The story of "S'posin'" illustrates the precarious position of black writers in Tin Pan Alley, and the conditions of its sale foreshadowed Razaf's slide from his professional heights.

Razaf and Denniker had been occasional collaborators for several years. Denniker was a bright young Englishman who settled in New York in 1919. He was leading the orchestra at Shanley's Restaurant when Razaf met him in the early twenties. He was taken with American music, especially jazz, and he was very pleased to be given a chance to collaberate with Razaf. They placed a song called "She Belongs to Me" with Triangle Music in 1925, and thus began their writer-publisher relationship with Joe Davis.

Davis, who was white, was one of the two preeminent publishers of black writers in the 1920s (the other was Clarence Williams). Black songwriters generally liked Davis. He seemed to be without prejudice, and they knew that he was more accessible and easier to deal with than the major publishers. A visit with Davis usually resulted in a sale. And he plugged his products fiercely, winning radio play and recordings for his efforts. Davis' relationship with Razaf soon became personal as well as professional. He let Razaf use his office as a writing space, even leaving Razaf there alone if he needed to work past the end of the business day. He occasionally made small loans to Razaf to tide him over, and he began to suggest repayment of these loans in the form of song rights. Razaf had trafficked in rights before and saw nothing wrong with this arrangement.

"S'posin'" was written for use in *Hot Feet*, which had opened in February 1929. The song had gone over well in the show, but it had made no great stir. Nobody was clamoring to record "S'posin'" after its debut. Joe Davis bought the publication rights—probably with a small advance—and Razaf was shocked to learn after the fact that Davis had cut Rudy Vallee in on the writers' royalties for "S'posin'" in return for Vallee's recording it. Before the Vallee version had taken off, Davis made the suggestion to Razaf that he could cancel the debt of a small loan to Razaf in return for all rights to "S'posin'." Razaf agreed. In the summer Vallee's record began to sell, along with those by the Georgians and Seger Ellis. The song would become Razaf's first big "crossover" hit, but he reaped none of the profits from it. If Razaf was bitter about it, there was nothing to do but keep his mouth shut.

In July another deal, even more calamitous, robbed Razaf of the riches he should have earned from the *Hot Chocolates* songs. The entire score, plus several other Razaf-Waller songs—twenty in all—was sold outright to Mills Music Company for $500. There is no first-hand account of this transaction, nor is there a surviving document that explains it. The blame for this foolishness has always been placed on Fats Waller, who supposedly cut the deal without Razaf's knowledge. Waller was always broke, and he no doubt wanted some quick money, but Razaf's name was also on the songs (as was Harry Brooks'). If Waller had acted without Razaf's knowledge or consent, why did Razaf not sue Mills to get his rights back? Or why did he not sue Waller for playing fast and loose with copyrights of which half belonged to him? Razaf had been the negotiator in song-selling sprees with Waller for five years, and neither of them had recently fallen off a turnip truck. Both were wily practitioners of the Tin Pan Alley crapshoot, always willing to bet that instant cash was worth more to them than future royalties would prove to be. The Mills deal was the dumbest ever made by professional songwriters, and it would take a saint to forgive a partner who made it by himself. The Waller-Razaf friendship remained a close one. They were injured parties, but they injured themselves.

Razaf had lost "S'posin'" and the *Hot Chocolates* songs, and possibly "Squeeze Me" and the Jimmy McHugh hits, and he was reeling from these calamities. He needed time to think, a place to be. In September 1929 he turned to the publisher he knew best for sanctuary, signing a two-year exclusive contract to go on staff with Joe Davis. "Exclusive" contracts were seldom really exclusive, and Razaf's was not either. He published with others over the next two years, but his signing with

Davis—and Davis' trumpeting of the fact—marked him for the rest of his professional life as a "black writer." Despite the occasional crossover hit, Razaf would be seen by the industry as a source of black revue material and of dirty songs (published in several 1930s Joe Davis folios). In late 1929 he was accepted for ASCAP membership, and recordings of his year's harvest of hits were still pouring out. But Andy Razaf was broke, and his future was not nearly so bright as it had looked a year before.

Instead of crying over lost copyrights, Andy Razaf went to work. The first big song that came during his tenure with Joe Davis was "Blue, Turning Grey Over You," written with Fats Waller and published by Davis in January 1930. In the spring came "On Revival Day" (music and lyrics by Razaf), which Razaf recorded with the Luis Russell Orchestra for OKeh in May.

The first show opportunity to present itself to Razaf in 1930 was to collaborate with James P. Johnson on *Kitchen Mechanic's Revue*, which opened on March 17, 1930, at the well-known Harlem club Smalls' Paradise, at 2294-1/2 Seventh Avenue. The show was a salute to the service workers of Harlem, and the best-known song was the metaphor-crammed "A Porter's Love Song to a Chambermaid" ("I will be your dust pan, if you'll be my broom. . . ."). The song had one successful recording, Fats Waller's in 1934.

In late April 1930 a show called *Shuffle Along of 1930*, purportedly starring Miller and Lyles, and featuring a few Razaf-Johnson songs from *Kitchen Mechanic's Revue*, opened at Werba's Theatre in Brooklyn. A Brooklyn critic, who knew Miller and Lyles when he saw them, exposed the comedy team on Werba's stage as impersonators. The ensuing scandal closed the Irvin C. Miller production.

About six months later, Razaf's name was attached to a more prestigious show, the one that would be his last on Broadway. This was Lew Leslie's revue, *Blackbirds of 1930*, with a score by Razaf and Eubie Blake. *Blackbirds* opened at the Royale Theatre on October 22, with a powerhouse cast that included Ethel Waters, Flournoy Miller, Broadway Jones, and Buck and Bubbles. Blake himself conducted the Blackbird Orchestra.

Blake composed rangier melodies than Waller, and his tunes inspired Razaf's most mature lyrics. Ethel Waters sang the serene ballad

"You're Lucky to Me," with its simple, sturdy Razaf rhyming. She also introduced a recycled Razaf idea in "My Handy Man Ain't Handy No More." (Razaf had written words and music to a similar song, called "My Handy Man," in 1928. The Razaf-Blake "Handy Man" is musically and lyrically superior to Razaf's earlier one.) The big ballad of the show, "Memories of You," was written for and introduced by Razaf's current flame, Minto Cato. It is a first-class song, among the best from an age of great ballad-writing. Louis Armstrong had the first big recording of it, and the Ink Spots had another, ten years later. Blake loved working with Razaf on *Blackbirds*, and he was in awe of his lyricist's professionalism. He told his biographer, Al Rose: "He never had to change *anything*. His meter was always *perfect*, and he could write the words nearly as fast as I could whistle the tune. God, he was smart!"

Because of Lew Leslie's association with Shapiro-Bernstein, the *Blackbirds* songs were issued by that company instead of by Joe Davis. After a desultory and hitless year, Razaf's contract with Davis expired in late 1931. But as often as not, throughout the 1930s Razaf would publish with Davis and would occasionally collaborate with him, always on Davis' terms.

Fats Waller's career was on the upswing as Razaf's was treading water. Waller was in demand as a radio performer, and in March 1931 he made his first record as a singer. As his fame grew, he became even harder to pin down for songwriting sessions with Razaf. But their batting average was high, considering the little time they had together. They wrote "Concentratin' on You" in 1931, "Keepin' Out of Mischief Now" in 1932, and "Ain'tcha Glad?" in 1933. There would be a few more Razaf-Waller songs in the late 1930s, including "The Joint Is Jumping" in 1938, but their partnership was essentially over by 1934.

With or without Waller, there was a living to make. In the spring of 1932 Razaf got another assignment for a Connie's Inn show called *Hot Harlem*, which starred the Mills Brothers backed by the Don Redman Orchestra. Razaf's only lasting song from this score—written with various composers—was "Stealin' Apples," with a melody by Fats Waller. But the song did not get a hit recording until Benny Goodman's version appeared in 1939.

The Immermans called on Razaf and James P. Johnson for their fall show, *Harlem Hotcha*. This assignment began the dead-end parade of

Razaf's black club revues of the 1930s. He placed a song in the twenty-third edition of *Cotton Club Parade* in 1933 and composed two full scores for revues at Chicago's Grand Terrace Cafe in 1934, *Rhythm for Sale* and *Chicago Rhythm*, with Paul Denniker. There was *Round and Round in Rhythm*, written with Alex Hill for the Ubangi Club, then editions of *The Ubangi Club Follies* with Eubie Blake and Paul Denniker. Razaf was doing piecework now, on shows with interchangeable titles and interchangeable destinies. They all were produced to fill dates on nightclub calendars, and no more. By the time he and Denniker wrote the music for *Hot Chocolates of 1935*, he was getting paid a flat $400 for a full score and splitting his royalties on published songs with the Immermans. Razaf's time was almost as well spent on the five children's songs that he wrote for a Joe Davis folio the following year.

In early 1936 Joe Davis heard a tune played on the radio by the Fletcher Henderson band. He thought it had possibilities as a pop song, so he secured the rights and called in Razaf to write a lyric. Davis published it in the spring of 1936 as "Christopher Columbus (A Rhythm Cocktail)," credited to Razaf and Leon "Chu" Berry, the saxophonist who had created the original riff. "Christopher Columbus" became a favorite novelty for big bands that year, and it received recordings by Bob Crosby, Benny Goodman, Andy Kirk, Teddy Wilson, and Fats Waller (who did the only good vocal).

The song's popularity started a vogue for issuing big band novelties with added lyrics. The lyrics seldom got onto recordings, but it was thought that words provided an extra reason to buy the sheet music. Razaf became an instant specialist in this kind of song that was seldom sung. He wrote words to "Big Chief De Sota" (also known as "Grand Terrace Swing"), "Yancey Special" (a boogie by Meade Lux Lewis), "William Tell" (with Chu Berry), and to "Stompin' at the Savoy" (which had been a Benny Goodman specialty since 1934). Judy Garland had one of the few vocal recordings of "Stompin' at the Savoy," accompanied by the Bob Crosby Orchestra, made for Decca in June 1936.

As "Christopher Columbus" began to take off, Joe Davis had the idea that he could sell theme songs to radio DJs. He put Razaf and Paul Denniker to work writing a song "inspired by" Martin Block's program on WNEW in New York. Block used the Razaf-Denniker "Make-Believe Ballroom" as his theme for years. WNEW's late-night DJ, Stan Shaw ("Stay-Up Stan, the All-Night Record Man"), wanted a theme, too, so Razaf and Denniker wrote "The Milkmen's Matinee" for him.

The most famous of these instrumentals-with-words was "In the Mood," and its story is another sad one. The tune had been around for a long time before Razaf was called to put a lyric to it in 1939. It was an ancient riff that was first recorded by Wingy Manone in 1930 as "Tar Paper Stomp." Fletcher Henderson next recorded it, as "Hot and Anxious," and in 1939, the pianist Joe Garland took out a copyright on it as his own composition, calling it "In the Mood." When Glenn Miller decided to record it in the summer of 1939, he anticipated a hit with his distinctive arrangement. Although the Miller record version would have no vocal, Miller thought that a lyric would boost sheet music sales. Joe Davis made arrangements with Shapiro, Bernstein, the copyright owner, for Razaf to do the job. Razaf was sent to the Victor studio where Miller was preparing to lay down "In the Mood" for release on the Bluebird label. Razaf worked quickly, fitting the recycled tune with a recycled lyric, reworking his words to "There's Rhythm in Harlem." At the finish of the session, he was handed $200, which he assumed to be his advance. He later learned that Davis had promised his lyric to Shapiro, Bernstein as a work for hire, for a flat fee of $200. "In the Mood" was Glenn Miller's biggest hit, and it has proven over time to be the single most valuable copyright owned by the Shapiro, Bernstein company. Razaf saw no more from his lyric. As "In the Mood" was climbing the charts, he was writing naughty songs ("Sell Your Proposition While It's Hot," "Small Size Papa—Big Size Mama") for inclusion in Joe Davis' *For Men Only* folio for a few dollars apiece.

In the summer of 1939 Andy Razaf married Jean Blackwell, a Harlem librarian. They lived for a while at the Dunbar Apartments in Harlem, then moved to Englewood, New Jersey, in the spring of 1940. He was becoming bitter about his fortunes now, writing letters railing at black bandleaders for not programming songs by black writers, venting his rage at 20th Century-Fox for a scene in their 1940 film, *Tin Pan Alley*, which depicted two white men in jail composing "Honeysuckle Rose."

Razaf had high hopes for *Tan Manhattan*, an Irvin C. Miller revue for which he wrote lyrics to Eubie Blake's music. The show's creators had dreams of Broadway, but after a short tryout in Washington's Howard Theatre in January 1941 and a brief run at Harlem's Apollo the following month, *Tan Manhattan* was no more. Two songs from this score are still programmed occasionally. "We Are Americans Too" proclaimed blacks' loyalty to the United States as the nation edged toward involvement in the war in Europe. Razaf wrote a recitation for use with the song, each stanza a reminder of black patriotism during previous American wars. The other song to have a life longer than the show is a beautiful ballad originally called "I'll Take a Nickel for a Dime." The singer wants change for the jukebox, for music to feed the sweet ache for a lost love. The song has a late-night, barroom feel that is haunting. Razaf reworked it in the 1950s, and renamed it "I'd Give a Dollar for a Dime."

In 1941 Luckey Roberts had a hit song in "Moonlight Cocktail," and in 1942 Andy Razaf wrote a lyric for Roberts' "Massachusetts," which was also a hit. He was credited with "special lyrics" to Mike Jackson's "Knock Me a Kiss," as published by Kaycee Music. (There is another 1942 edition of "Knock Me a Kiss," with precisely the same lyric, published by Leeds, that omits Razaf's name and credits the song to Jackson alone.) Razaf also added a lyric to "Twelfth Street Rag," another instrumental that didn't need one. The tune had already had two previous sets of words added to it over the years by two other lyricists. All three of the "Twelfth Street" songs went unsung and unrecorded.

Singers liked the Razaf lyric to William Weldon's "I'm Gonna Move to the Outskirts of Town," however. The song was recorded by Jimmy Rushing and by Louis Jordan, who had his first hit with it in the winter of 1941–1942. It is the only real blues lyric of Razaf's career, and there is a down-and-dirty grittiness to it, surprisingly so, since Razaf never took the blues very seriously, even during the blues boom of the 1920s.

Razaf wrote a few songs during the war years for the U.S. Treasury Department to encourage the buying of bonds. He tinkered, he recycled. He mourned for Fats Waller, who died in late 1943. He tried to stay in the music business. And his persistence would bring him two more hits. In 1944 he reworked the lyric to a 1929 Don Redman song, renaming it "Gee, Baby, Ain't I Good to You?" It was one of Nat King

Cole's most successful recordings of the mid-forties. And in 1947 Phil Harris found an old Andy Razaf tune—written for a *Cotton Club Parade* in 1933—called "That's What I Like About the South." It was one of Harris' biggest hits, and the singer was so fond of it that he claimed to have written it until a blazing letter from Razaf squelched him.

In 1948 Razaf divorced Jean Blackwell, and shortly afterward he married Dorothy Carpenter. They moved to Los Angeles, taking a house at 3429 Country Club Drive. As he had seen his world of popular song displaced by the coming of the big bands and the departure of the old-line publishers, he now saw the big bands being displaced by rhythm and blues. He didn't publish with Joe Davis any more after the war, but the two kept in touch, exchanging cranky letters about the stranglehold that DJs and A&R men had over the record business.

In January 1951 Andy Razaf was stricken with a violent pain and later a paralysis. The diagnosis was that he had tertiary syphilis, a variety of the affliction that was not immediately life-threatening but which would inevitably destroy his spinal column. Razaf had never suffered from an illness of any kind, but he knew that illness was expensive. He began to write pitch letters, the first of his career, imploring publishers to take a look at his newest songs and to take another look at his old ones in their files. He began to write with and for anyone who asked him. His main collaborator throughout the fifties was a young man named Johnny Finke. They got a few publications but had no hits. One of their tunes, published by Handy Brothers in 1953, was "Grab Him!" There is a photo of Razaf on the cover, not quite smiling, square-jawed and cool in a small-checked sport coat and dark tie. There is a brick wall behind him, and, two years into his illness, he looks as solid as the wall.

In 1953, probably for the salary, he began writing a weekly column for the Los Angeles *Herald-Dispatch*. It was called "Time Out for Thinking," and it was a generally positive, free-associative ramble through whatever was on his mind, from politics to New York reminiscences. There were no hard-luck stories about the music business. He would keep up his column into 1955.

Razaf divorced Dorothy and lived alone for a while, tended by around-the-clock nurses, before he remarried in 1963. His fourth wife was Alicia Miller, whom he had met years before, when she was a teenager. He was a paraplegic by then and shot through with pain. In 1972 Razaf was inducted into the Songwriters Hall of Fame, and he made one last trip to New York to accept the honor. He died in Los Angeles on February 3, 1973.

Although Razaf's career seems to have been ruled by expedience, there is an individual voice and point of view in his best songs. His love songs are not of the "churning, yearning, burning" variety. They are flip and jaunty reminders of the small satisfactions of commitment. Being in love is fun, and the loss of a love can be endured best by realizing that another love, and more fun, may be just around the corner. The boulevardier Razaf didn't get serious very often, and even his most powerful lyric is leavened by a light touch. When the Razafian attitude was removed, the song was gone. In 1957 a "new" Razaf-Waller song was issued by Mills Music, called "Alone and Blue." It was "Black and Blue" with a new lyric—possibly by Razaf. All of the references to race had been removed to make a generic ballad about being lonesome. The words express nothing except self-pity, and it is not at all the song it used to be.

CHAPTER 6

"AUNT HAGAR'S CHILDREN"

● ●

The Black Entrepreneurs of the Blues

I**T IS NEARLY IMPOSSIBLE TO IMAGINE A TIME** when American popular music did not draw strength from the blues. The sound, form, and subject matter of the blues are so deeply ingrained in us that they seem to be among the most basic elements of our cultural vocabulary. We know the blues when we hear them, and we hear them—sometimes pure, sometimes diluted—everywhere: in all kinds of rock; in songs on the country charts; in clubs where nothing but the blues is played; in the concert music of contemporary composers; in the most modern of modern jazz.

In the first decade of our century, the blues were hidden in plain sight throughout the South and Midwest. They went unclaimed, even by sharp-eyed regional publishers, performers, and songwriters who were always on the lookout for something new. Those who noticed them at all considered them merely the low-class diversion of a low-class people. The people who created the blues, as well as those who first enjoyed them, didn't buy sheet music. The blues were heard mostly on the street corners of small Southern cities and on the porches of backhouses on large Southern farms. If a Tin Pan Alley firm had done market research to determine whether it was profitable to publish the blues in 1910, the demographic would have been dismal: those who responded to the blues were black, poor, and rural. So, the treasures of the blues remained untapped until a handful of African-American writer-publishers brought them, or rather pushed them, into the main-stream of commercial music.

The word "blues" was used as a name for a melancholy feeling long before there was a music called "the blues." Among the earliest written references to the blues is an entry in a diary kept by a young black woman. Charlotte Forten had been raised and educated in the North, and in 1862 she had come to Edisto Island (between Charleston and Beaufort, off the southeast coast of South Carolina) to start a school for the handful of free blacks in the area and for the few slaves whose mas-ters would let them attend. She was appalled at the living conditions of those who went to her school, and she grew depressed and homesick under the weight of her charge. On Sunday, December 15, 1862, she wrote after coming back from church: "Nearly everybody was looking gay and happy; and yet I came home with the blues."

More as a hobby than as a serious study, Forten tried to describe and notate the work songs and church songs of the Edisto Island slaves. But their singing seemed to her "a very strange wild thing," without form or meter or accuracy of pitch. She was fascinated by slave songs, but she wrote, "of the manner of the singing it is impossible to describe." "Wild" was also the word used to describe slave singing by two other observers of plantation music, the English actress Fannie Kemble (who married a Georgia plantation owner) and the Massachusetts poet William Cullen Bryant (who traveled in the Southeast in 1849). Many whites were impressed by black song, but it was hard to catch on paper.

The first attempts made by white performers at approximating black songs were by minstrel men—the singers, actors, and producers who needed this material for their business. However, white minstrel songs, for all their claims to "authenticity," boiled down complex African rhythms to one or two of the simplest syncopations. The har-monies in minstrel songs were as foursquare as those in the Methodist hymnal. Their lyrics were merely crude, tin-eared burlesques of black speech. The musical conventions of the minstrel show were so firmly in place by the time black minstrel troupes could enter the field that there was nothing to do but carry them on. The songs of black minstrels were neither more complex nor richer than those of whites.

In 1867 the first scholarly attempt was made at notating black singing, in a collection of 137 songs called *Slave Songs of the United*

States. Most of the songs in the book were spirituals, and many were collected on the Sea Islands off Georgia and on South Carolina's St. Helena Island. *Slave Songs* is invaluable for its documentation of lyrics and melodies, but there is the characteristic nineteenth-century stiffness in the notation of harmonies and syncopations in the songs. One of the editors, William Francis Allen, admitted:

> The best we can do . . . will convey but a faint shadow of the original. The voices of the colored people have a peculiar quality that nothing can imitate; and the intonations and delicate variations of even one singer cannot be reproduced on paper. And I despair of conveying any notion of the effect of a number of people singing together. . . . There is no singing in *parts*, as we understand it, and yet no two appear to be singing the same thing. . . . There are also apparent irregularities in the time, which it is no less difficult to express accurately.

Various troupes of jubilee singers in the late nineteenth century made white America aware of the black spiritual tradition, and although white audiences respected its fervor and admired its beauty, it was still a separate and exotic thing. No proper white church choir could, or would want to, sing that way.

The streams of African-American spiritual and secular song rolled on in the last third of the nineteenth century. All-black towns and settlements began to dot the South and Midwest, and black neighborhoods fringed almost every American city. The clustering of African-Americans in great numbers created a market for professional entertainment that had not existed before: black audiences who wanted to see black shows. In the larger settlements, the annual visits of black minstrel companies were not enough to satisfy this demand. Black vaudeville houses opened to offer a platform for acts of all kinds, and rudimentary touring circuits were explored. Black military-style bands were organized in even the smallest towns, as were semiprofessional vocal quartets and dance bands.

Street singers occupied the lowest rung of the musical ladder. These nomads, many of whom were blind and had no other way of earning a living, could be called "professionals" only because they hoped to hear the clink of coins in their tin cups as they played and sang. The street singers didn't offer polished "acts" of the kind seen in the vaudeville houses. They dealt in raw emotions and they expressed them in a raw way. A few simple chords and an impassioned delivery were enough to convey their stories of hard luck, loneliness, and survival. The stories were the important part, as they had been since the ancient days of ballad-making. If the story were good enough and if the singing of it forceful enough to stick in the mind, a listener could go home and make his own version of it, musically and lyrically, then pass it on to his neighbors around the porch.

By 1900 the street singers' accompaniment of choice was the guitar, an instrument which had only recently become affordable. In the mid-nineties various makers began offering guitars for sale in department stores and through mail order. (The Martin guitar company had been in business in the United States since 1833, but Washburn's and Lyons & Healy's instruments were much less expensive and more accessible.) Several companies began selling guitar-making kits that were cheaper than the cheapest ready-made models, and within a few years the guitar had displaced the banjo as the poor man's instrument.

There was a musical as well as an economic reason for preferring the guitar. The hard sound of the banjo did not complement singing. The banjo was fine for clanging out a rhythm for dancing, but one had to sing over it rather than sing with it. The guitar's sound was softer and more flexible, and it allowed for subtlety and shading within a sung line. The guitar could practically sing back to the performer. And if the strings were fretted by a knife blade or the neck of a bottle, a guitar could bend a tone as a human voice could. The streetcorner bard had long ago found his voice in churches and cotton fields, and now, with the guitar, he found his sound. The "talking" guitar was the perfect accompaniment to his singing. His subject matter was all around him, and his audience had the same history of bad times that he had. They had all survived great repression and were there to sing about it and to hear it sung. Around the turn of the century, street singers and their listeners began to share the blues with each other.

W. C. HANDY

W. C. Handy was over seventy years old when he found out that he was not the first person to put a blues on paper. His instrumental "Memphis Blues" was issued in late September 1912, but it was not until the late 1940s that Handy learned—and acknowledged—that Hart A. Wand, a white writer who self-published his instrumental "Dallas Blues" in Oklahoma City, had beaten him to the marketplace by two or three weeks. Ragtime scholars in the 1960s and 1970s dug up other claimants to the "first blues" title. They found that "Baby Seals Blues"—with words and music by the black vaudeville comedian H. Franklin "Baby" Seals, published by John Stark in St. Louis—had been issued in August 1912. More digging led to more discoveries. They saw that Robert Hoffman's "I'm Alabama Bound"—published in New Orleans in 1909 as a "Rag Time Two

W. C. Handy

Step"—is really a folk blues strain. The lyric version of "I'm Alabama Bound," issued in 1910, seems to be the first published blues vocal. At this writing, another New Orleans composer, Antonio Maggio, is ahead in the "first blues" race with his instrumental "I Got the Blues," published in 1908.

For all of Handy's pride of authorship of his "Memphis Blues," the research done since his death would probably have pleased him rather than deflated him. The discoveries have confirmed all of his theories about the musical origins and the dissemination of the blues. Hart Wand said that the whistling of a "colored porter" inspired his "Dallas Blues." Baby Seals sang his blues in vaudeville and sold his song sheets in black theatres after his performances. "I'm Alabama Bound" is an upbeat blues made up of sixteen-bar—not twelve-bar—phrases. "I Got the Blues" is a mixture of twelve- and sixteen-bar strains. So the blues turns out to be what Handy always said it was: it was patterned on black song, of Southern origin, a personal expression rooted in folk music but adaptable to theatrical performance, not necessarily melancholy and not constricted to twelve-bar patterns. Handy was not the first composer of a blues, but he was first to be sincerely interested in where the blues came from. He paid close attention to his folk sources, and his sturdy transcriptions of—and additions to—them put the blues into the mainstream of American music. He believed in the blues, and he stuck with them. (Each of his four predecessors published only one blues composition.) Handy may not have been "The Father of the Blues," but he was indisputably their emancipator.

William Christopher Handy was born on November 16, 1873, in a log cabin built by his grandfather on the western edge of Florence, Alabama. Handy was the son of freed slaves, and his father and his paternal grandfather were both Methodist ministers. The Handy family made its way by hard work and by using what was available to them in their patch of northeast Alabama. It was a life of berry picking, home remedies, and serious gardening. When he was about nine years old, Handy learned to make lye soap from bones that he found in the woods, and his father taught him to plow with a mule.

The Handys didn't hold with music much. There was hymn singing on Sundays at his father's church, but they were proper Methodist hymns—accompanied by a staid organist—not spirituals. Handy's fiddling Uncle Whit was the only family member who, when he joined the church, did not renounce the fun of making music, and Whit sometimes let the boy beat rhythm with knitting needles on the fiddle while he played. Handy was always curious about music, and he enjoyed the obligatory note-training and sight-singing conducted by Professor Wallace at the Florence District School for Negroes. Handy tried to make a bugle out of a cow's horn, and when this experiment failed, he saved up his money to buy a guitar. When the boy proudly brought his new guitar home, his parents were outraged by his purchase. They made him take it back to the store and exchange it for a dictionary.

Handy's musical interest intensified in his early teens. He bought a used cornet for $1.75 from a local musician—paid for in installments—

and defied his parents by playing with a local band and singing with a quartet. He eavesdropped on the method classes led by a circus band-master who had been stranded in Florence, and when he earned $8 for playing the alto horn at a local dance, the idea of a musical career was planted in him. At fifteen, he ran away with a regional minstrel troupe, but when the company dissolved, he came back to Florence to finish high school.

After graduation the only constant in Handy's life was the struggle for money. He worked a year at an iron furnace; he tried teaching for two terms, but found the pay too low to live on; he left teaching for a job in an iron works at $1.85 a day. And he began to trade on his musical skills. He organized a brass band in Bessemer and a vocal quartet in Birmingham. The Birmingham four, called the Lauzetta Quartet, were so emboldened by their local fame that they decided to bum their way to Chicago, hoping to sing at the World's Fair, which was set to open in 1892. When they got to Chicago, they found that the opening of the fair had been postponed until the following year, so there was nothing to do but bum their way back home. They rode the rails as far as St. Louis. There they hit bottom.

In St. Louis the group split up and each singer was left to fend for himself. Handy sang on street corners, and if he made enough money for food, it was rarely enough to pay for a room as well. He often slept outdoors, under railroad trestles, and on the cobblestone walkways that led to the Mississippi River. His St. Louis days were the lowest of his life, and his situation was as grim as that of the drunken woman he saw stumbling through the streets late one night. He listened as she expressed her woe in a one-line song that she sang over and over: "My man's got a heart like a rock cast into the sea."

Manual labor was once more the temporary solution for Handy, but music would once again rescue him from a dead-end situation. He took a job paving the streets of Evansville, Indiana, and in the evenings he played in Evansville's Hampton Cornet Band. Handy was scouted by a bandsman from Henderson, Kentucky, who asked him to come to Henderson to lead their town band. After a few months at Henderson, he received a letter from Chicago. A musician friend had recommended him as a cornetist in the Mahara's Minstrels band, and the letter offered him the job. The pay was $6 a week plus "cakes" (room and board). When Handy joined the troupe in Chicago, his laboring days were over, and his long career as a bandsman began.

On August 6, 1896, Handy arrived in Chicago, where Mahara's was preparing its show for the upcoming season, to begin in Belvidere, Illinois, a month later. Handy made himself useful in many ways: he doubled on several instruments, he wrote orchestrations, he trained a vocal quartet, whatever needed doing.

Mahara's was a large troupe, carrying nearly thirty performers and a fifteen-piece band on the company's private train. The busiest day for the bandsmen was opening day in a new town. The first order of business was the noon parade that showed off the splendor of the company and stirred up the population to buy tickets. If the company had spent the previous night in the town, the parade began in front of their hotel. If not, it began at the train station. When the troupe hit Belvidere, on September 6, they had a new wardrobe to show off. W. A. Mahara, the white owner of the show, led the parade, resplendent in top hat and tails, his St. Bernard dog by his side as they rode in an open carriage pulled by Shetland ponies. Next came six drum majors, dressed in spangled mariachi outfits, then six "walking gents" in Prince Albert suits with white silk hats, kid gloves, and canes. The band in their uniforms, half operetta and half military in design, followed with plumed hats on their heads, their instruments glinting in the light. Following the band were more walking men, in satin suits with lace peeking out of their sleeves. Banners everywhere blazed the Mahara name.

When the rest of the company dispersed after the parade, the band formed in the town square and played a short concert of light classical selections, always including "William Tell Overture" and "Poet and Peasant." The band played again for half an hour or so in front of the theatre just before the show. This second outdoor concert was peppier than the first, usually featuring such numbers as "El Capitan," "Rastus on Parade," and "A Hot Time in the Old Town Tonight." At a few minutes before eight, the band quickly closed shop to hurry inside the theatre and begin the overture.

Handy was a featured cornet soloist during his first season with Mahara's, and in his second season he was put in charge of his own splinter band to play for parades. The following year he was named bandmaster, leading twenty-six players. A portrait photograph from this time shows Handy in his Mahara's uniform. With a gilded cap on his head, he is sitting in an ornate, high-backed, claw-footed chair. His cornet is held at rest in his left hand; his baton is lying across his right knee. His uniform is covered with buttons and braid. He is mustachioed and aloof-looking, like a young prince, new to the throne but with firm ideas about how to run his kingdom.

Handy's music would always reflect the style of a show band of the late nineties, but there are no surviving recorded samples of Handy's band music from this time. In his autobiography he recalled in some detail making a cylinder recording of "Cotton Blossoms" for the Edison company with Mahara's band in Helena, Montana, in 1897. But it is highly unlikely that the Edison company would have been making commercial recordings in Montana in 1897. The band probably played into an Edison machine in a Helena music store and heard their tune played back to them.

When Mahara's route took the troupe through Kentucky, Handy married his Henderson sweetheart, Elizabeth Price, on June 19, 1898. The new Mrs. Handy disapproved of her husband's minstrel career, but she occasionally joined him on the road or met him in cities where there was a long stopover. Handy's first three years with Mahara's took him to Wisconsin, the Midwest, the West, the Pacific Coast, and Canada. For a few weeks in the winter of 1899–1900, the company, with Elizabeth Handy along, went to Havana. Handy never forgot the Cuban rhythms that he heard there—and the sensuous dancing that they inspired—and several of his compositions would be seasoned with them.

As Mahara's fought for its share of a declining minstrel market in the late century, the show became more circus-like. An act featuring thirty trained dogs was added, as well as one with ten performing ponies. Handy's band—featuring a female trombonist, Nettie Goff—became one of the troupe's most popular elements. The band moved up to become the second unit in the parade (after Mahara and his St. Bernard), and Handy's cornet playing was said by some to rival that of the eminent P. G. Lowery.

Touring was hard—Mahara's suffered a smallpox epidemic among the company, and a Texas mob once shot up the band's train—but Handy seemed to thrive on the minstrel life. After the Handys' first child, a daughter, was born in Florence, Alabama, in the summer of

1900, Elizabeth began to urge her husband to leave the road. So in September he resigned from the company to accept a job as bandmaster at Alabama's Agricultural and Mechanical College, a training school for blacks, near Huntsville.

Handy's A&M band program was a good one, but college life didn't agree with him. He chafed at the snobbishness of some of his colleagues who didn't like the popular numbers Handy put into the band's repertoire, and campus politics dismayed him. The Handys had a second daughter while he was working at A&M, and he struggled to support a family of four on his $40-a-month salary. In 1902 Mahara offered him $50 a week to come back and lead the minstrel band. He returned to Mahara's for one more season, but minstrel life had lost its charm for him. He knew that his future lay in music, but he had to try again to settle down.

In the summer of 1903 he accepted a job as leader of a black Knights of Pythias band in Clarksdale, Mississippi, a small town in the northwest part of the state, about fifteen miles east of the Mississippi River. He had had another offer, from a town band in Michigan, but in choosing Clarksdale, he set himself down in the area that we now know as the home of the Delta blues.

Handy's K of P band soon made its mark. It was a semiprofessional group, usually carrying a dozen or so members, and its band book contained numbers for any occasion, from fish frys to funerals. They worked up some dance music, and they were hired by both blacks and whites for parties throughout the Clarksdale area. During his travels to and from his home base, Handy began to pay attention to the music around him. He heard the work songs of roustabouts moving cargo on the levee, and he noticed that street singers could hold a crowd long enough to sell a few of their "ballets," crudely printed song lyrics on cheap paper. Handy wrote in his autobiography of an eerie experience he had while waiting for a train to pick up the band in Tutwiler, Mississippi, late one night. As Handy dozed, he was roused by the singing of a lone guitarist sitting by the railroad tracks. The man sang a lament that consisted of the same line sung three times: "goin' where the Southern cross' the Dog." Handy was haunted by it and he remembered it forty years later as "the weirdest music I ever heard."

Handy's real awakening came at a white dance that the K of P band was playing in Cleveland, Mississippi. Handy's band had done well that evening and had kept the floor crowded with dancers. The man who had hired them asked Handy if his band knew any "Negro music." Handy obliged by calling "Peaceful Henry"—which he described as "an old-time Southern melody"—as the next number. This was all right, but it was not quite what was wanted. The host asked Handy if he minded whether a local group played a tune. The band welcomed a chance for a smoke break and filed out as the local band entered. They were a motley trio, led by "a long-legged chocolate boy," and they made their way to the bandstand carrying "a battered guitar, a mandolin and a worn-out bass." Handy recalled:

> They struck up one of those over-and-over strains that seem to have no very clear beginning and certainly no ending at all. The strumming attained a disturbing monotony, but on and on it went, a kind of stuff that has long been associated with cane rows and levee camps. Thump-thump-thump went their feet on the floor. Their eyes rolled. Their shoulders swayed. And through it all that little agonizing strain persisted.

When the homemade music ground to a halt, the listeners screamed their appreciation and showered the trio with quarters, halves, silver dollars. The cheering crowd wouldn't stop throwing money at the boys. Handy, with a minstrel's eye for estimating the take, saw that the "spasm band" had made more money with their one ungainly tune than Handy and his men would make for the entire evening. He said, "That night a composer was born, an *American* composer."

An arranger was born, really. Handy's first attempts at getting this new kind of music down were the dance arrangements that he made of black folk songs. It was a beginning. Handy's reputation as a bandleader spread beyond Clarksdale, and in 1907 he took on a second job, two days a week working with a black Knights of Pythias band in Memphis.

As his second band became popular, Handy began to see a greener pasture in the larger town. In 1908 he moved his family (now at five, including a baby son) to Memphis.

In Memphis Handy met a young black man employed as a cashier at the Solvent Savings Bank, Harry Herbert Pace (1884–1943). Pace was an amateur singer and lyric writer, and he was a great fan of Handy's band. Pace and Handy decided to try writing together, and they sent their first song to George Jaberg, a Cincinnati publisher, who issued it in 1907. The song was "In the Cotton Fields of Dixie," one of those "old-time Southern" melodies, not a blues.

The social scene was livelier in Memphis than in Clarksdale, and Handy's band flourished. The K of P band played for all sorts of local functions and dances—including some in the red-light district—and Handy began to act as a booking agent for other bands as well as his own. In 1909 a local politician, Edward Hull Crump, found himself in a tight three-way race for mayor of Memphis, and he sought advice about how to get the black vote. A ward heeler named Jim Mulcahy, who owned a saloon, suggested that Crump hire W. C. Handy to write a Crump campaign song and to perform it with his band. Handy came up with a composition called "Mr. Crump," the tune that was his first blues.

"Mr. Crump" was an instrumental with three melodic strains—two of twelve bars each and a middle one of sixteen bars. Handy's original version had no lyrics, but the black electorate, who enjoyed dancing to it, found that they could they could adapt the words of the old "mama don't 'low" folk rhyme to the sixteen-bar strain. Crump was running on a law-and-order platform, and the audience's improvised words made fun of him:

> Mister Crump won't 'low no easy riders here,
> Mister Crump won't 'low no easy riders here.
> I don't care what Mister Crump don't 'low.
> I'm gwine to bar'l-house anyhow—
> Mister Crump can go an' catch hisself some air!

Edward Crump won the election of 1909, thus beginning a career in Memphis politics that spanned more than fifty years. (He would hold twenty-three elective offices and would serve as mayor three more times.) However much or little Handy's piece had to do with this first victory, it remained popular long after the occasion for its writing had passed. Dancers continued to call for it, and Handy decided to try to get it published. He knew that the tune's title was dated, even if the tune wasn't, so he renamed it "The Memphis Blues." He sent it to various publishers in New York and Chicago as well as in Memphis, but they all turned it down. Several of the publishers said in their rejection letters that the tune was missing eight bars—four in each of the twelve-bar strains. But because his audiences never seemed to tire of it, Handy felt that there must be a market for it. He peddled it for three years, with no success, so he decided to publish it himself in the late summer of 1912.

With only one published song to his credit—and an unsuccessful one, at that—Handy knew that he needed help getting his "Memphis Blues" into the marketplace. He turned to a white clerk at Memphis' leading department store, Bry's. L. Z. Phillips was well aware of the local popularity of Handy's composition. He offered to arrange for the printing and copyrighting of the piece as well as the placing of it at Bry's music counter. Handy gave Phillips $32.50 for the cost of printing a thousand copies, plus a dollar for the copyright fee, and left the matter in Phillips' hands. Phillips sent the manuscript to a Cincinnati printer, Otto Zimmerman & Son.

During the wait for the printing to be done, Theron C. Bennett, a Denver music publisher who often dropped in on his retailers, made a visit to Bry's. He met with Phillips and Handy there, and Phillips told Bennett about "The Memphis Blues." Bennett had an idea: if the piece were as good as Phillips said it was, he would like to act as Handy's sales agent. Bennett offered to talk up "The Memphis Blues" whenever he visited the stores that were stocking Bennett's own numbers and said that he could get it placed in music departments all over the country. Handy had never expected a chance at national distribution, and he jumped at Bennett's offer to represent his tune.

On September 27, the thousand copies of "The Memphis Blues" arrived from Ohio bearing the imprint "Published by Handy Music Co." Phillips, Bennett, and Handy delivered them to Bry's. A week later Handy went to Bry's to check on sales. Phillips and Bennett sadly reported that there had been almost none, and they pointed to a large stack of copies sitting on Bry's counter. Handy couldn't understand it. Everyone in Memphis seemed to like the piece, but no one had bought it. Bennett generously offered to help Handy recoup his investment in "The Memphis Blues." He said that he would pay Handy $50 in cash for the copyright and the printing plates. (Handy would retain writer credit.) The discouraged composer agreed to the sale, and when Theron Bennett left town, he was the sole owner of "The Memphis Blues."

Handy did not learn the precise nature of Phillips' and Bennett's scam for more than twenty years. When the printer's business records were checked in the 1930s, it was discovered that Phillips had placed an order with Zimmerman for a second thousand copies. The first thousand copies had sold out at Bry's by mid-week, and when Handy came in a few days later, Phillips and Bennett put the second thousand on the shelf as evidence that the tune was not selling. On October 7, 1912, Bennett ordered 10,000 more copies of "The Memphis Blues," as "Published by Theron C. Bennett Co.," from Zimmerman & Son. Not long after their collusion, L. Z. Phillips became wholesale manager of Theron Bennett's publishing company.

After it was his own, Bennett carried through on his promise to plug "The Memphis Blues." He got wide distribution for the sheet music, and within a few months the copyright had become quite valuable. Bennett sold it to the Joe Morris Company (of New York) in 1913, and Morris' instrumental reissue was so successful that a vocal version seemed like a good idea. Morris hired George A. Norton to write a lyric, and to drive the thorn further into Handy's heart, Norton's lyric described the fun one could have in Memphis while dancing to the Handy band. ("They had a fellow there named Handy with a band you should hear.") Of course, Norton had never actually heard the Handy band, so he got the instrumentation wrong. His sophomoric lyric mentions a "big bassoon"—an instrument that Handy never used—playing "seconds to the trombone's croon."

Two instrumental recordings of "The Memphis Blues" became hits in 1914—one by the Victor Military Band, and one by Prince's Orchestra—and there was a hit vocal version in 1915, a duet by Arthur Collins and Byron Harlan. By the summer of 1914, Vernon and Irene Castle were using "The Memphis Blues" as the accompaniment for their new dance sensation, the Fox Trot. And Ted Lewis would have a big recording of it in 1927. Although Handy shared in the song's fame as its writer—and as the subject of its lyric—for nearly thirty years, Handy did not make a cent from "The Memphis Blues."

With the success of "The Memphis Blues," Handy learned a bitter lesson about song thievery, but he also learned that he was going in the right direction as a composer. He determined never to let a copyright get away from him again, and toward that end, he and his friend Harry Pace formed a partnership. (Their company would be the third music publishing company owned by African-Americans.) The Pace & Handy Music Company issued its first publication, a Handy instrumental called "The Jogo Blues," in 1913.

Just before "Jogo Blues" was ready for sale, Pace moved from Memphis to Atlanta to become secretary-treasurer of the Standard Life Insurance Company there. He left Handy a check to cover the printing costs of "Jogo Blues," as well as those of a song that they had written together, "The Girl You Never Have Met." Pace would take a hands-off role through most of their partnership, acting more often as financial lifesaver than as guiding force.

The new Pace & Handy company couldn't get much distribution for "The Jogo Blues," but the writing of it was an important step for Handy. There was one theme in it that he couldn't get out of his head. He knew he was onto something with his blues, but he felt an urge to write something more elemental than "Memphis," with more varied rhythms than "Jogo," with better words than George Norton's. The call was strong—"I could feel the blues coming on" he said—but he needed a place away from the noisy Handy home on Janette Street to answer it. He did something he had never done: he rented a room on Beale Street to work in for one night. The next morning, when the forty-year-old bandmaster stepped out into the sunlight, he had in his hand the most influential American song ever written, "The St. Louis Blues."

Handy knew the song was good and he couldn't wait to get it into print. Without telling Harry Pace, Handy put up the money for its printing and began pitching it to his contacts at the Kresge's and Woolworth's chains. By mid-September 1914 "The St. Louis Blues" was in the stores. Compared to "Memphis Blues," "St. Louis Blues" was a slow starter. (Pace & Handy couldn't command as many plugs as

Theron Bennett could.) But it found its way into vaudeville performances and onto recordings in the mid-teens, and it took root as
"Memphis Blues" did not. The piece was so satisfying to audiences that
it remained in the repertoires of almost everyone who performed it.

The first of many hit recordings of "The St. Louis Blues" was made
by Prince's Orchestra—without a vocal—in December 1915. By 1916
it had become a staple of Sophie Tucker's vaudeville act and it was a
standard dance number in band books. By 1920 it was the most famous
blues in the world. By 1930 it was the best-selling song in any medium—sheet music, recordings, and piano rolls. In 1950 a study conducted by a music trade magazine found that it had had nearly a thousand
recordings in America alone, making it the most-recorded song up to
that time. "The St. Louis Blues" was something new under the sun, and
it was welcomed everywhere it went. The distinctive words and music
of "The St. Louis Blues" changed the way popular songs were written,
sung, and played.

The lyric of "The St. Louis Blues" was Handy's first attempt at writing words for a song, and the language, imagery, and point of view he
chose were unlike anything else of the time. The lyric is in dialect, but
it is not minstrel or coon speech. The words do not convey ignorance,
helplessness, or foolishness. The song is the plaint of someone who is
hurting, but there is a frankness and toughness in the telling about it.
In the first edition, there are three sets of words for each of the first two
musical themes and two sets of words for the third ("chorus") theme.
Because of the time constraints on recordings made before the LP era,
the entire lyric has seldom been recorded, but there is a shift from
melancholy to resolution when all the words are sung. This dual package of pain and strength is the essence of the blues. The few vocal blues
before it had caught one or the other of these moods, but no single song
had caught both.

The words are sparing in their use of simile, and there is nothing
about them that calls attention to lyric "craft." The comparisons are as
plain and direct as the rest of the song. ("I loves dat man lak a school-
boy loves his pie, Lak a Kentucky Col'nel loves his mint an' rye. . . .")
There were plenty of other "Southern" songs pouring out of Tin Pan
Alley in the mid-teens, including some ephemeral hits, but "The St.
Louis Blues" makes them all sound phony. Here is the first, and most
familiar, set of words:

I hate to see de ev'nin' sun go down,
Hate to see de ev'nin' sun go down,
'Cause ma baby, he done lef' dis town.

Feelin' tomorrow lak ah feel today,
Feel tomorrow lak ah feel today,
I'll pack my trunk, make ma git-away.

St. Louis woman, wid her diamon' rings,
Pulls dat man roun' by her apron strings.
'Twant for powder an' for store-bought hair,
De man ah love would not gone nowhere, nowhere.

Got de St. Louis Blues jes' as blue as ah can be,
Dat man got a heart lak a rock cast in the sea,
Or else he wouldn't have gone so far from me.

In the era of "We'll Have a Jubilee in My Old Kentucky Home," "How's Every Little Thing in Dixie?," and "Mammy's Little Coal Black Rose," Handy's song was more than a breath of fresh air. It was a new wind blowing.

If the "St. Louis Blues" lyrics were innovative, its music was revolutionary. Its harmonies literally put new notes into the pop music scale, and its structure showed writers a new way to build popular songs. The analogy may be made in terms of art: it was like giving painters a new set of primary colors and showing them shapes they had never seen before.

Handy's harmonic discoveries were the result of his trying to solve the old problem of notating black singing. The thing that Charlotte Forten and others in the nineteenth century couldn't get down was the bending of notes. The tones of black singers were true, but they were not hit head-on nor were they held steady when they were sung. African song wandered into quarter-tones, went into places that a guitar could go but a piano couldn't, creating a sound that was somewhere between major and minor. Handy, a skilled arranger, could have written his song for the guitar, but he chose not to. He wanted to find the closest approximation of these variegated tones that could be applied to standard (that is, band) instrumentation. He knew that this major/minor sound often came on the stressed notes of a melody and, therefore, that it was neither an incidental nor a casual effect. The sound was primary. It happened at certain basic and recurring intervals on the scale. Handy decided to approximate this ambiguous major/minor sound by flatting the third note—making a minor note—in a major scale. And he saw that the occasional flatting of the fifth and seventh tones could deepen the minor ("blue note") effect, without changing the "major" sound of the melody. The use of upward-slurring grace notes could indicate a vocal slide to the home note. These grace notes are written into the vocal line as well as into the accompaniment of the first strain of "St. Louis Blues." The slurring effect is achieved in the second and third parts by the use of eighth notes, the first one flatted and sliding up to the second, marked as being tied together. Handy's system of flats and slurs couldn't replicate every nuance of black singing, but it was certainly enough to get the idea across to those who learned their blues from a song sheet. Blue notes had occurred in popular music before—as syncopation had occurred before ragtime—but Handy was the first to use the blue-noted scale as a basis for a body of composition.

The most important innovation of "The St. Louis Blues" was its structure. It is made in an AABC pattern, the A's and the C each being twelve bars long. (The twelve-bar length was Handy's way of imposing form on—and varying—the "over-and-over strains" that he had heard sung by the St. Louis woman and the Tutwiler guitarist. The trio that had showed up his band at the white dance in Cleveland also played a music that sounded formless to him.) Each twelve-bar strain has three lines of four bars each. The melody is sparse. It takes up only two of each four bars—leaving two bars to play with on the end of each line. The "unoccupied" bars may be filled with whatever one has the imagination to put there ("I hate to see de ev'nin' sun go down _ _ _ , _ _ _ _"). The empty bars invite the singer to interject spoken words or vocal ornamentation, and they invite the accompaniment to provide a musical phrase that answers the singer. The twelve-bar form led to a call-and-response interaction between singers and accompanists that had never existed in pop music. "The St. Louis Blues" doesn't just suggest improvisation, it demands it. And, with its predictable three-chord blues framework, the song practically provides a road map for how and where to improvise. This composition is the first step that popular songwriting took toward jazz.

The B strain of "St. Louis Blues" is sixteen bars long, and it is a minor-keyed tango ("St. Louis woman, wid her diamon' rings. . . ."). The tango was popular with dancers in 1914, and Handy wanted the habanera feel to add rhythmic variety to his blues. He had seen black dancers in Havana do the tango, and he knew that the rhythm was originally African (called *tangana*) and that it had been introduced to the Spanish by the Moors. It was a brilliant way to break up his tune and to head off potential monotony with the simplicity of twelve-bar melodies and few simple chords.

"The St. Louis Blues" allows for more variation in tempo and style than any other blues of its time. It sounds good whether it is taken as a dirge (as Bessie Smith did) or whether it is played brightly (as the ODJB did). It had reincarnations as a march (by Glenn Miller's Army Air Force band), as a boogie-woogie (by Earl Hines), and as a mambo (by the Richard Maltby Orchestra, in 1954).

There was originality in "The Memphis Blues"—blue notes, twelve-bar strains, and the first written-out "break"—but "The St. Louis Blues" is simpler and sturdier. "Memphis Blues" is harder to play and to remember than "St. Louis," and George Norton's lyric makes "Memphis" almost impossible to sing. "Jogo" had a memorable opening strain—which Handy adapted as the chorus of "St. Louis Blues"—but there is a melodic sprawl in it. It doesn't hang together as tightly as "St. Louis Blues" does, nor is there the same progression toward a resolute chorus. If, in 1914, one had heard every published blues there was, including Handy's first two, the conclusion would have been inescapable: "The St. Louis Blues" has it all. It is what is meant by "the blues."

Handy continued his exploration and adaptation of black song through the mid-teens. His next publication after "St. Louis Blues" was "The Yellow Dog Rag," issued by Pace & Handy in late 1914. This song was inspired by the black guitarist at Tutwiler, who sang of going "where the Southern cross' the Dog." The lyric tells of a woman's hunch that her lover has fled to Moorhead, Mississippi (where the Yazoo Delta railroad—Yellow Dog, in black slang—crosses the Southern railroad line).

In 1915 came Handy's "Joe Turner Blues," which, as Handy put it, "followed my frequent custom of using a snatch of folk melody in one out of two or three strains of an otherwise original song." It is an extensive revision of an old song about Joe Turney, the brother of a Tennessee governor, who framed blacks for minor crimes, then contracted them out as cheap farm labor around the state. Handy threw out the Turney story and made the Joe Turner character an aggrieved lover who is threatening to leave his sweetheart. ("If you don't b'lieve I'm leavin', count the days I'm gone. You will be sorry, be sorry from your heart....") His "Hesitating Blues" updates an old song with a reference to the telephone ("Hello, Central, what's the matter with this line? I want to talk to that High Brown of mine...."). Prince's Orchestra recorded "Hesitating Blues" in late 1915, and the record sold well into the following year.

There was still a bit of the bandleader in Handy, which came out in his "Hail to the Spirit of Freedom March" and in his "Shoeboot's Serenade"—a bluesy paraphrase of Schubert's "Serenade"—both issued in 1915. That same year, Pace & Handy began to publish compositions not written by the company's owners. Among the first were Al Morton's "Fuzzy Wuzzy Rag"—almost a note-for-note steal of Joplin's "Maple Leaf Rag"—and Will Nash's "The Snakey Blues." William King Phillips' "The Florida Blues" ("Rearranged by W. C. Handy") was issued in 1916. Handy made a tentative step toward ragtime in the first strain of his 1916 instrumental, "Ole Miss." The Pace & Handy catalog also listed "No Matter What You Do," a 1916 piece by William Grant Still (1895–1978), who was the company's arranger.

By 1917 the Pace & Handy company was doing well enough to justify expansion, so the firm opened a branch office in Chicago. Harry Pace was still climbing the corporate ladder as an insurance company executive in Atlanta, so it fell to Handy to organize the Chicago operations. Even though Handy's schedule was more flexible than that of his partner, he was still leading (and representing) bands around Memphis, so he had many projects of his own to juggle. The company would be centered in Chicago for only about a year, but it would be a very profitable year. A hit song of 1917 would finance their move to New York and secure their reputation as "The House of the Blues."

Pace & Handy issued blues by other writers in 1917 (Charles Hillman's "Preparedness Blues" and Douglas Williams' "The Hooking Cow Blues"), but Handy himself had the big one: "Beale Street Blues," which became his second most-recorded song after "St. Louis Blues." Earl Fuller's Famous Jazz Band got to it first, for Victor, in August 1917, and Prince's Orchestra recorded it next, for Columbia. In September 1917, through Harry Pace's business contacts in New York City, Handy got his own chance to record for Columbia. Pace raised enough money for Handy and eleven bandsmen to come to New York. Of course, Handy's first thought was to make a band of his regular players from Memphis. When several of his men refused to leave Memphis to make these recordings, it was the beginning of Handy's disillusionment with his home base. Most of the players in the group that Columbia called "Handy's Orchestra of Memphis" were recruited from Chicago.

Handy's Orchestra of Memphis was in the Columbia studio for four sessions, made from September 21–25, 1917. The eleven released sides from these sessions show that Handy still had a lot to learn about the record business. His instrumentation was more like an 1897 minstrel band's than like that of the small jazz bands that were sweeping New York. Handy's group included three violins, a cello, and a xylophone. In choosing his tunes, he passed up the chance to plug his own best work and his company's best copyrights. The first session yielded only one side, a slapdash version of the suspiciously Joplinesque "Fuzzy Wuzzy Rag." Over the next three sessions there came "Snakey Blues," "The Old Town Pump," a pop tune called "Sweet Child," a cover of the ODJB's "Livery Stable Blues," and a waltz called "Moonlight Blues," among others. The lone Handy composition was "Ole Miss." The recordings did not sell, and Columbia never asked Handy back into the studio.

However disappointing his recording debut had been, Handy knew he was ready for a larger professional base than Chicago. And he was tired of wrangling with his Memphis bandsmen and their employers over nickels and dimes. "Beale Street Blues" helped Handy decide what to do. In early 1918 Pace & Handy received a check for $1,857, royalties on the Earl Fuller recording of "Beale Street." It was enough to get him to New York. On Handy's first day in town, as he was making courtesy calls on music jobbers, he collected nearly $1,000 more from sales of "Beale Street Blues."

Handy took offices in the Gaiety Theatre Building at 1547 Broadway, and Pace & Handy opened for business. A hierarchy was formalized: Harry Pace (who gave up his insurance career in Atlanta to join his partner in New York), president; Charles Handy (the composer's brother), vice-president; W. C. Handy, secretary-treasurer; and J. Russel Robinson, professional manager. (Robinson would also occasionally represent the firm in contracts and licensing matters when Handy felt that a better deal could be made by a white negotiator.) William Grant Still was brought up from Memphis to head the arranging department, overseeing three copyists. Fletcher Henderson (1897–1952) was one of Pace & Handy's three on-staff pianists. Handy hired two pluggers, at $40 a week each.

The company had a hit almost immediately, with Eddie Green's "A Good Man Is Hard to Find," which had great sheet music sales prompted by Sophie Tucker's hit recording. With additional mechanical royalties from other Pace & Handy songs rolling in, the firm began its heaviest period of copyright acquisitions. Clarence Stout's "O Death, Where Is Thy Sting?" sold well for the company after Bert Williams recorded it in August 1918. A few white writers—Al Bernard, Marshall Walker, Madelyn Sheppard, and Annelu Burns—joined the Pace & Handy roster. Handy's five-year-old "Yellow Dog Rag" was renamed "Yellow Dog Blues," and with no other change to it, the song began to get recordings.

Most gratifying of all to Handy was the warm reception he received from the most important black bandleaders in New York. Will Vodery took Handy as his guest to the Coconut Grove on the New Amsterdam roof; Tim Brymn presented him to the New Amsterdam Musical Association; Ford Dabney introduced him at the Clef Club. He particularly hit it off with Jim Europe. The two Alabamans talked long into the night about the possibility of black military bands going overseas to entertain American soldiers in France. This outpouring of good will came to Handy, not because he was a fellow bandleader, but because he had written four blues—"Memphis," "St. Louis," "Yellow Dog," and "Beale Street"—that were in the repertoire of every dance band in New York. Handy had been in the city only a few weeks when he was invited to conduct a Clef Club Orchestra at the Selwyn Theatre on Forty-second Street. In February 1919 Handy conducted at the welcome-home concert for the black 369th Infantry "Hellfighters" Division at Carnegie Hall.

After about eighteen months in the Gaiety Building, Pace & Handy needed more office space. The company took over an entire building at 232 West Forty-sixth Street. Handy was busy in 1918–1919, but he wasn't doing much writing. His song "The Kaiser's Got the Blues," with lyrics by Domer C. Browne, was his only blues publication during this time.

As popular as the Handy blues were as instrumentals, there was some resistance to them as vocals. Harlem club audiences disliked Handy's lyrics, which were rooted in the small-town, hard-times South that many of them were trying to forget. And George Norton's lyric for "The Memphis Blues" meant nothing to Harlem. Gilda Gray was shimmying to "The St. Louis Blues" in her 1919 vaudeville act, and "Beale Street Blues" was featured by her in the *Shubert Gaieties* that year. But Handy's blues were mostly unsung.

Handy wanted them sung, though, and he took a singer named Viola McCoy to audition at seven record labels. There was no interest in recording her. Executives said that her diction was unintelligible and that nobody would buy the records. It would be left to Perry Bradford to break the studio barrier for blues vocalists when he talked OKeh into recording Mamie Smith in February 1920.

It seems odd that Handy did not record McCoy himself. He had his second recording session in the autumn of 1919, leading a group called Handy's Memphis Blues Band for Lyratone, but there are no vocals on the four sides. He at least scrapped the violins, cello, and xylophone, but this group of eleven men was still too large to sound like a contemporary jazz band. The best feature of these recordings was the cornet playing of Johnny Dunn. Dunn was the major blues instrumentalist in the city at the time and the first cornetist in New York to make the wah-wah sound that would typify dance arrangements of the 1920s. (Dunn's hard, thin tone reigned supreme in New York until the arrival of Louis Armstrong in 1924.) The tunes chosen for this session were all Handy standards: "Beale Street," "Joe Turner," "Hesitating Blues," and "Yellow Dog." He had by now learned to plug his own product.

When Mamie Smith made her historic first recording in early 1920, she sang a song published by Pace & Handy, Perry Bradford's

"That Thing Called Love," so the year began well for the company. But not long after this bright beginning, the company began to totter financially. Woolworth's, Pace & Handy's best customer since its earliest days in Memphis, closed the sheet music departments in all of its 600 stores, and Pace & Handy was stuck with hundreds of thousands of copies of unsold music. And many of the titles in the publisher's 1920 catalog would be hard to sell elsewhere.

The company had grown too fast, overextended itself, and acquired too many dud songs. A Pace & Handy ad in the Chicago *Defender's* issue of October 16, 1920, illustrates the problem. There are thirty songs listed in the ad—among them: "Pee Gee Blues," "Why Did You Make a Plaything of Me?," "The Insect Ball," "Louisiana Dip," "Sliding Fever," and "Manvolyne Waltz"—but there is only one good number on the list: Handy's six-year-old "St. Louis Blues." Staff members were fired to staunch the flow of money, and Handy began doing his own arranging and bookkeeping again.

Late in 1920, as financial problems grew more critical, friction developed between the founding partners. Harry Pace left Pace & Handy to form the Pace Phonograph Company, whereupon Handy reorganized and renamed his company. He appointed his brother Charles as president, and Handy Brothers Music moved back into the Gaiety Building, to smaller offices.

The Pace Phonograph Company—the first black-owned record company—began in January 1921, with Jack Nail (Harlem's leading real estate executive) and W. E. B. DuBois on its board of directors. Harry Pace named his record label Black Swan, after the nineteenth-century concert singer Elizabeth Taylor Greenfield, and rented offices at 257 West 138th Street. Black Swan took over studios and a pressing plant on Long Island. Pace hired Fletcher Henderson as his recording manager and William Grant Still as his music director. (Handy had laid both of them off.)

Pace wanted to record all kinds of music, not just blues, and the first Black Swan records featured the baritone C. Carroll Clark and the soprano Revella Hughes. Her recording of "Thank God for a Garden" was the company's first release. But the blues market that had been opened by Perry Bradford and Mamie Smith could not be ignored. Black Swan soon started to specialize in blues recordings. The company's slogan became "The Only Genuine Colored Record—Others Are

Only Passing For Colored." Black Swan's first and biggest hit came in the spring of 1921, with Ethel Waters' recording of "Down Home Blues," backed by "Oh, Daddy." Bessie Smith flunked her audition for Black Swan in 1921, but the company already had Ethel Waters and Alberta Hunter. For nearly two years, they would be enough.

Handy struggled to stay in business after Pace left. The blues publishing field was crowded by 1921, and the old master found himself in competition with Joe Davis, Clarence Williams, Jack Mills, Perry Bradford, and Irving Berlin's "race" division, Rainbow Music. Handy was $25,000 in debt, but instead of declaring bankruptcy, he determined to pay off his creditors and tough it out. He sold his house on 139th Street, and he borrowed money, mostly from Clarence Williams and Bill Robinson. He asked for credit—and got it—from printers and jobbers who had worked for him in better days. Looking for a novelty hit, he wrote a foolish pop song: "Who Was the Husband of Aunt Jemima (The Mammy of the Gold Dust Twins)?" Henry Troy wrote the lyric, and it was published by Handy Brothers in 1921. Then, Handy did what was, for him, unthinkable: he sold the copyright of one of his own compositions. His instrumental "Aunt Hagar's Children," written in early 1921, wasn't going anywhere, and he didn't have the resources to plug it. When Richmond-Robbins made him an offer, he took it. The new publisher fitted it with a lyric by Tim Brymn, and Alice Leslie Carter (accompanied by James P. Johnson's Jazz Boys) made the first vocal recording of the number (renamed "Aunt Hagar's Blues") in September 1921.

To add to his troubles, in the early 1920s Handy's eyesight began to fail. As a child he had had a schoolyard accident that had damaged an eye, and he had worked without goggles over vats of molten iron as a young man. He had ignored pains in his eyes for years, but he could ignore them no longer. A doctor slowed the progress of his blindness with medication, but the deterioration of his eyes continued. By the mid-1930s his eyesight would be gone.

While Handy Brothers struggled to right itself in 1922, Pace's Black Swan label grew rapidly. Pace had only one star singer, Ethel Waters, but her star continued to rise. In the fall of 1921, she made a promotional tour with the Black Swan Troubadours, directed by Fletcher Henderson, and by December, Black Swan was showing more than $100,000 in earnings from record sales in that year. In early 1922

Handy made four sides for Paramount—Black Swan's chief rival—with his Memphis Blues Band. By mid-1923, however, Black Swan began to falter. The competition for the race market was ruthless, and the major labels, especially Columbia and Paramount, could outproduce and underprice Harry Pace. The pinch was too tight, and in early 1924 Harry Pace sold the Black Swan catalog to Paramount and returned to the insurance business.

Handy was too busy digging himself out of his hole to take much notice of the demise of Black Swan. There was no instant hit that turned Handy Brothers around, but from 1923 through 1925 there were cumulative small successes that slowly reversed the company's low fortunes. Handy's reputation as the premier composer of blues was revived at the same time.

Over a period of eight months in 1923, Handy made fourteen instrumental sides for OKeh with a group called Handy's Orchestra. The "St. Louis Blues" that he recorded in March sold well enough to serve as a reminder that the composer was still around. In April 1923 he cut his Orchestra to four men to accompany Sara Martin on three tunes for OKeh. (These sides with Sara Martin were his only small-group recordings, as well as his only vocal accompaniments. They were probably done as a favor to Martin's mentor, and Handy's creditor, Clarence Williams.) Alberta Hunter had a successful 1923 Paramount recording, with Fletcher Henderson's Orchestra, of Handy's "Loveless Love," which she had introduced at Chicago's Dreamland Cafe within hours of Handy's writing the lyric in a Chicago barbershop in 1921. Ted Lewis had a big recording of "Aunt Hagar's Blues" in September 1923.

Best of all, Bessie Smith finally got around to Handy's blues in early 1925. The first Smith recording of a Handy number was, appropriately, "The St. Louis Blues," and it is one of the great blues performances of all time. It was made in Columbia's New York studio at Columbus Circle on January 14, 1925, with the accompaniment of two instruments, Louis Armstrong's cornet and the reed organ played by Fred Longshaw. There is a single chord from the duo as an introduction, then Smith sings the song once through at a funereal tempo. Her customary power is there, but she sounds dazed, as though she is reading from a suicide note that she has just written. Longshaw's stately country-church harmonium is under her like a hardwood floor, and Armstrong's cornet mutters in sympathy beside her. It was the most serious treatment that "The St. Louis Blues" had ever received, and Smith revealed the riches of the song as no one had done before. On May 6, 1925, Smith found the earthy humor in "Yellow Dog Blues," accompanied by Fletcher Henderson's Hot Six.

Handy's compositions were beginning to blend into their folk sources. His "Loveless Love" of 1921 added a verse and some new lyrics to an old song, "Careless Love," to make a blues without a "blue note" in it. His "John Henry Blues" of 1922 begins the John Henry story with an original verse then paraphrases the old folk melody in the chorus. His "Harlem Blues" of 1923 has an original thirty-two bar verse followed by a blues paraphrase of an old song, "Gotta Travel On." (The traditional opening line, "I've laid around and stayed around this old town too long," becomes, in Handy's chorus, "And since my sweetie left me, Harlem ain't the same old place. . . .") His "Atlanta Blues" of 1924 has as its chorus—and as its subtitle—"Make Me a Pallet on Your Floor." The blues that were getting the most action in the early 1920s were mostly rough-and-ready comic songs about busted love affairs, and Handy was going against the commercial tide in the composition of these folk-centered blues. Even though he was writing outside the mainstream, Handy got several recordings of each of these "folk blues."

By the mid-twenties, Handy Brothers had almost stopped buying copyrights. Part of the reason was the caution inbred in Handy after his firm nearly toppled under the weight of dead songs. But there was also a philosophical shift taking place in him. In 1920, when he was nearly fifty years old, he published his first arrangement of a spiritual, "The Rough, Rocky Road." From then on, spirituals and folk songs—such as "I'm Drinking from a Fountain That Never Runs Dry," "Steal Away to Jesus," and "Goin' to See My Sarah"—began to take an equal place with blues in the Handy Brothers catalog. By 1930, when his rediscovery as blues master was peaking, Handy was publishing more folk material than blues. He was doing more than disclosing his sources, he was offering the world what he felt were the real treasures of African-American song.

The most important event in American concert music in 1924 was George Gershwin's February 12 debut of his *Rhapsody in Blue*, commissioned by Paul Whiteman and played by the composer with the Whiteman band at Aeolian Hall. The *Rhapsody* provoked discussion far beyond questions of its musical worth. The concert was designed by Whiteman to show the great strides in popular music over the past several years—especially those made by the Whiteman band and its arrangers—and the *Rhapsody*, along with the rest of the Whiteman numbers, prompted much speculation about the nature of American popular music. What was "American" about American pop? The answer implicit in the *Rhapsody* was that the most "American" ingredient in popular music was the blues.

On November 23, 1924, as a rejoinder to the Whiteman concert, the bandleader Vincent Lopez produced another "American" concert evening. He didn't have a *Rhapsody* to premiere, but he could at least give his audience a precedent to the Gershwin work. The centerpiece of the Lopez event at Metropolitan Opera House was a symphonic arrangement, made by Handy, of one of his favorite folk songs, the "Gotta Travel On" theme that he had used in his recent "Harlem Blues." The piece was called *The Evolution of the Blues*, and Lopez led a sixty-five-piece orchestra in its debut. This Lopez concert led to the programming of other highbrow arrangements of Handy themes. (An important early recording of the symphonic Handy was Don Voorhees' "Fantasy on the St. Louis Blues," in an arrangement by William Grant Still, released by Columbia in two parts in the spring of 1927.)

Although Handy said that some of these arrangements "sounded to me like a farmer plowing in evening dress," the concert versions of his blues and folk songs that began to be heard in the late 1920s legitimized him—and his blues. The public began to think of him as the channeler, the bringer of the most distinctive "American" elements to American music. The construction of his lofty reputation was underway. Handy was beginning to be seen as someone above the workaday world of the pop music business, as someone serving a higher good. He had never hustled hard for recordings as Perry Bradford and Clarence Williams did, but recordings came to him now in great numbers. From

1930 until the end of Handy's life, "The St. Louis Blues" would be the most valuable copyright in the world.

A major factor in the Handy revival was the publication of his book, *Blues: An Anthology*, issued by Albert and Charles Boni in 1926. The *Anthology* was more than a collection of Handy Brothers hits; it was the first book to examine black secular music and its influence on pop and jazz. Handy, as editor, chose a generous sampling of his blues, of course, but he also included the folk songs and spirituals that had inspired them—or that might illustrate their origins. The introduction was written by Abbe Niles, a Wall Street lawyer who loved folk music. Niles had come to interview Handy the previous year and was impressed by the depth of Handy's interest in and knowledge of black songs. Handy was no scholar, but he could remember what he had heard and when and where he had heard it. He was fascinated by the structures of all kinds of songs, and he was still masterful at transcribing sounds that had stuck in his head thirty years ago. And for those who weren't interested in the genealogy of the blues, the book was simply great fun to play. In the era that had recently produced "Wop Blues," "Crazy Crossword Puzzle Blues," and "Susie's Got the Bluesies Again," the *Anthology* was a powerful reminder of what the classics were, where they came from, and how rich they could be.

The *Anthology* included some recent Handy blues—"Friendless Blues" and "Blue-Gummed Blues" were published for the first time there—as well as some recent pop songs that were blues-tinged, including Gershwin's "You Don't Know the Half of It, Dearie, Blues" and Kern's "Left All Alone Again Blues." Gershwin was so pleased to have his blues credentials validated by the master that, for the *Anthology*, he wrote out special breaks for the chorus of "You Don't Know the Half of It" that are not in the standard song sheet. Gershwin gave Handy an inscribed copy of the *Rhapsody* in 1926. The inscription read: "For Mr. Handy, whose early blues songs are the forefathers of this work, With admiration and best wishes. . . ."

Another new Handy song in the book was "Golden Brown Blues," with lyrics by Langston Hughes (1902–1967). In January 1926 Alfred Knopf issued Hughes' first poetry collection, *The Weary Blues*, and Handy had commended the spare, stripped-down verses as an "entirely original" use of the blues form. Hughes made a point of meeting Handy and introduced him to Carl Van Vechten, the white photographer and novelist who was a cheerleader for the Harlem Renaissance. From then on, Handy would be in Van Vechten's pantheon, on the short list of those who contributed the most to Harlem's cultural renewal. (In the year that the *Anthology* appeared, Handy became one of the few songwriters to have a pop song written about him, Willard Robison's "Page Mr. Handy.")

All the attention to Handy's music paid off handsomely. The four Handy classics—"Memphis," "St. Louis," "Yellow Dog," and "Beale Street"—kept getting new recordings and making new hits. Ben Pollack and His Orchestra made "Memphis" in 1927 and had a hit with "Yellow Dog" in 1929. Ted Lewis had a big recording of "Yellow Dog" in 1930. Alberta Hunter, accompanied by Fats Waller on organ, had a hit with "Beale Street" in 1927, and Joe Venuti and Eddie Lang's orchestra made a successful recording of it, with a Jack Teagarden vocal, for Vocalion in 1931.

The champ of them all was, of course, "The St. Louis Blues." Record buyers seemed never to get enough of it. Hits with the song were made by Louis Armstrong (in 1929), by Rudy Vallee and Cab Calloway (both in 1930), by Bing Crosby (singing with the Duke Ellington band, in 1932), by the Mills Brothers (in 1932), and by the Boswell Sisters (in 1935). And there were dozens of recordings that weren't hits. The song was heard everywhere, all the time. It was interpolated into the McHugh-Fields score for Lew Leslie's *Blackbirds of 1928*, and it was the highlight of a concert evening featuring black composers that Handy produced at Carnegie Hall on April 27, 1928. In 1927 the banjoist Eddie Peabody chose "The St. Louis Blues" for performance in one of the first sound shorts, a nine-minute film called "Eddie Peabody in Banjomania," and the song began its long string of interpolations in movies.

In 1929 Handy co-wrote (with Kenneth W. Adams) a short film scenario of his most famous song, and RCA Photophone bought it. Handy thought that Bessie Smith's record of the song was the best, so he suggested Smith for the lead. A director, Dudley Murphy, was chosen, and a forty-two voice choir was engaged. James P. Johnson was hired to play the piano with the jazz band, mostly members of the Fletcher Henderson orchestra, in the barroom scene. *St. Louis Blues* was shot at the Astoria Studios, on Long Island, in June 1929. The seventeen-minute film opens with Smith—playing a character called

"Bessie"—catching her boyfriend in a tryst with another woman. The boyfriend, enraged by the interruption of his lovemaking, throws Smith to the floor and storms out. She finds a bottle of liquor, drains it, and sings "The St. Louis Blues." In the second scene, Smith is drowning her troubles in a smoky bar (the other customers are the choir). After a brief dance number, the boyfriend enters, seemingly bent on apologizing to Smith. As they dance, he filches the bills that she has stashed in her stocking. With her money in his hand, he shoves Smith away and leaves. She clutches a drink and sings the title song again. The film was as successful as a musical short could be, which is to say that it was shown frequently over the next two or three years. It didn't make any of its creators rich, but thanks to W.C. Handy, Bessie Smith made her sole appearance on film.

Handy's transfiguration into cultural treasure began in the 1930s. He became a frequent lecturer in schools, colleges, and churches. He was invited to conduct radio orchestras on NBC and for WLS in Chicago. He occasionally appeared with the old vaudevillians assembled by Joe Laurie, Jr., for his touring nostalgia show, *Memory Lane*. The city of Memphis named a park for him in 1931.

The horn player and educator Willie Ruff remembers Handy's coming to his school in Muscle Shoals, Alabama, in 1937, when Ruff was in the fourth grade. He said that Handy—nearing sixty-five, and blind by then—stood alone on the stage of the auditorium of the black schoolhouse and coaxed a "sweet, singing sound" out of a muted trumpet as he played "Go Down, Moses" and "The Memphis Blues." Handy told the children to value their musical heritage. "Be proud of it and hold it up," Handy said. "Sing it with thanksgiving in your hearts and with pride and dignity in your voices."

Handy Brothers was publishing very little. Reissues of old songs appeared, but there were few new ones among them. The bassist Red Callendar applied for a job as copyist at Handy's company in the mid-thirties, and Handy listened patiently as the young man described his qualifications. Then he said to Callendar, "Son, I've got to tell you that this office is just a front to get me out of the house. I've been living off 'The St. Louis Blues' for the past twenty years."

In the late twenties major labels began to record blues talents in the South, in Memphis, Dallas, and Atlanta. Blind Lemon Jefferson (1897–1929) made his first recording in 1926, and Charlie Patton

(1887–1934) in 1929. The 1930s saw the blues of Robert Johnson (ca. 1912–1938) and Leroy Carr (1905–1935) issued on Vocalion. And John Lomax and his son Alan began to make the pioneering field recordings that would document the songs of bluesmen as well as those of convicts and laborers. If Handy was aware of or interested in these recordings of regional song, he never mentioned them in his talks.

In 1938 Jelly Roll Morton became enraged while he was listening to a radio program called *Believe It or Not*, on which W. C. Handy was identified as the originator of blues and jazz. Morton wrote a letter to *Down Beat* denigrating Handy, saying in part: "Mr. Handy cannot prove that he has created any music. He has possibly taken advantage of some unprotected material that sometimes floats around. I would like to know how a person could be the originator of anything without being able to do at least some of what they created." Handy's success had rankled the pioneer jazzman for years. Morton told anyone who would listen that he had met Handy in Memphis around 1908 and that he had asked Handy to play a blues. According to Morton, Handy's reply was that "blues couldn't be played by a band." Morton said that he had heard Tony Jackson playing the blues in New Orleans as early as 1905 and that he had begun to compose his own blues soon after hearing Jackson's. Whatever Morton was hearing or doing before 1912, Handy had beat him to the punch with his "Memphis Blues," and it was Handy's blues, not Morton's, that changed the way popular songs were made. Years later, Willie the Lion Smith would say in defense of Handy, "He heard the same Negro music that every other band instrumentalist, singer, banjoist or piano player heard early in this century; it was just that Handy had more talent for putting what he overheard into an original composition." The same year that Morton lit into him publicly, Handy made a series of folk-song recordings for the Library of Congress. For the first time, he accompanied himself on the guitar.

Also in 1938 Handy's second anthology appeared. This was *W. C. Handy's Collection of Negro Spirituals*, published by Handy Brothers. Handy produced an evening of "Negro music" at Carnegie Hall that was part of ASCAP's Silver Jubilee on October 2, 1939. The day after Christmas in 1939, Handy made his last commercial recordings, four sides for the Varsity label. There was a six-piece jazz band behind him as he sang and played the trumpet. He did "St. Louis," "Beale Street," and "Loveless Love." The only "new" tune in the set was his 1932 number, "Way Down South Where the Blues Began."

In 1940, Handy reclaimed his errant "Memphis Blues" for Handy Brothers. Under the provisions of the U.S. Copyright Act of 1909, protection was extended for a period of fifty-six years, but after twenty-eight years a copyright held by someone else could revert to the author of a work. It had been precisely twenty-eight years since L. Z. Phillips and Theron C. Bennett had cheated Handy out of "The Memphis Blues." Handy had been waiting to get his tune back, and he got it. The first recording of the song to pay off for its writer was the one by Harry James, which was made in 1942 and which sold steadily for two years. In June 1940 the NBC radio network devoted an entire program to Handy's work, the first such broadcast to be built around a black composer. Handy proudly placed "The Memphis Blues" among his standards to be played by the NBC orchestra.

In the summer of 1939, the Macmillan company signed Handy to write his autobiography. Handy chose Arna Bontemps as his ghostwriter. The old man was full of good stories, but he was not an easy collaborator. Bontemps wrote to Langston Hughes: "The Handy book is a headache. He jumps on my neck when I jazz it up; Troustine [Handy's lawyer and literary agent] screams when I fail to." However difficult it was, Bontemps caught Handy's voice, and *Father of the Blues* appeared in 1941. In his 1926 *Anthology*, Handy paid his respects to his folk sources and expressed a genuine modesty about his achievement; fifteen years later, he did the same. If the book's title seemed immodest, Handy honestly felt that he had earned it.

Handy tinkered at writing and publishing songs through the 1940s. There was not much to do in the office except keep an eye on the major copyrights. "The St. Louis Blues" alone was still bringing in over $25,000 a year. (Langston Hughes wrote to Bontemps that Handy was itching to sue the producers of the 1946 Broadway musical *St. Louis Woman* for copyright infringement, but he couldn't figure out what his grounds were. The show did not use any Handy compositions, and its title, although it was the most famous lyric phrase that Handy ever wrote, was not the title of Handy's song.)

On October 28, 1943, when Handy was about two weeks away from his seventieth birthday, he fell in a subway station and fractured his skull. His health was fragile by this time, and his recovery was slow. But after a long recuperation, he went back to his work as the goodwill ambassador for the blues. He performed in Billy Rose's Diamond Horseshoe club in 1947, and he made his rounds as a lecturer. (A recording of his 1945 appearance at the University of Michigan, during which he played the trumpet as well as spoke, was released on a com-memorative LP in the 1950s.) He kept in contact with his old competi-tors, Perry Bradford and Joe Davis. He wrote to Davis in March 1948: "By being seventy-four years old and so blind that I cannot see what the chicks look like, I have saved so much money, and it would be a plea-sure if you would tell me when and where we can dine together at my expense." In 1949 he supervised the reissue of (and the revised notes for) his 1926 *Anthology*, which was retitled A *Treasury of the Blues*.

Art Tatum (1910–1956) made an odd recording of "Aunt Hagar's Children"—interspersing "Black Coffee" into the Handy number—in 1949, and Coleman Hawkins (1904–1969) recorded six Handy songs in 1950. But the recordings that pleased him most in his old age were those made by Louis Armstrong for a 1954 LP called *Satch Plays W.C. Handy*. The Columbia recording is wonderfully loose, and its star, play-ing and singing brilliantly, swims in the Handy material. There is noth-ing reverential about the album. When Handy heard his advance copy, he wept with joy.

In 1954, after the death of his wife Elizabeth, Handy married his secretary, Irma Louise Logan. She moved into the Handy home at 19 Chester Drive, in Yonkers. Handy, already frail, suffered a stroke in 1955. He was confined to a wheelchair for the remainder of his life.

In 1956, although he was ailing, he granted an interview for a doc-umentary film, *Satchmo the Great*, produced by Edward R. Murrow and Fred Friendly. He wanted to show his appreciation to Armstrong, who had done so much to spread Handy's blues around the world. W.C. Handy died in New York on March 29, 1958.

In the year of his death, Handy got his own film biography, the grossly inaccurate Paramount release, *St. Louis Blues*, which starred Nat King Cole (1919–1965) as Handy. To show its subject's modernity, the film's poster said that it was "Based upon the Life and Music of W. C. Handy (Daddy of Rhythm and Blues)." The line could not have meant anything to young moviegoers, and it probably put off older ones. Pop music was changing rapidly in 1958, and an unlikely coalition of parents, music teachers, and jazz players was horrified by the simpleminded, "three-chord" rhythm and blues, and its stepchild, rock and roll, which seemed to be sweeping away everything that had come before. Perhaps the old guard should have seen the Handy poster as a warning. The three chords of rock and roll were the ones that W. C. Handy brought us. They were old when he found them, and they would last a long time.

PERRY BRADFORD

At the end of 1919, there were only three black singers who were known as solo recording artists: Bert Williams, Noble Sissle, and the baritone C. Carroll Clark. Williams had been at it the longest, and he had the largest output—fifty-nine sides made since his recording debut in 1901. Noble Sissle had made nineteen sides since his first, in 1917 (eight of these with Jim Europe's 369th Infantry Band). Clark had sung light classical selections for Columbia for about nine years, beginning in 1907, but only two of these were still listed in the Columbia catalog as of September 1919. The Dinwiddie Colored Quartet made some "Genuine Jubilee and Camp-Meeting Shouts" for Victor in the early century, as did

W. C. Handy and Perry Bradford

the Fisk Jubilee Quartet. The most prominent black band to record in the late teens, Wilbur Sweatman's, had not yet issued a record with a vocal by December 1919. The solo voice of a black woman had never been heard on a commercial recording.

By the end of 1920 the very nature of the recording industry had been changed by the persistence and ingenuity of a writer-publisher-promoter-hustler named Perry Bradford. He wanted his songs recorded by his singer, and, refusing to take a hundred no's for an answer, he finally got his way. His songs were a new kind of blues, flip and full of sass, and his singer was a black woman, Mamie Smith. Smith's first two recordings for OKeh went through the roof, awakening the industry to a huge market that was waiting to be tapped. The Bradford-Smith sides sold especially well, but not exclusively, in black neighborhoods. The industry's response to their success was to create a subindustry, of "race" companies and exclusively "race" series within larger companies, to feed a demand that it had never realized was there. Major artists— Ethel Waters, Bessie Smith, Alberta Hunter, among many others—had their careers jump-started by Bradford's popularizing of a singing style that they were already specializing in. A "black sound" seemed to be the key to getting hit records, so black musicians were brought into studios where their employment would have been unthinkable only months before. If Handy's blues seeped into the musical mainstream, Bradford's roared in like a tidal wave.

John Henry Perry Bradford was born at home in Montgomery, Alabama, on February 14, 1893. His father Adam was a bricklayer, and his mother Bella was a cook. When Perry was about six years old, the Bradfords, including daughters Bessie and Clara, moved to Atlanta. They lived in what Bradford called "a four-room shack" next to the city jail on Frazier Street. Bella Bradford was hired by the city to provide two meals a day to the prisoners: molasses and biscuits for breakfast, peas and cornbread for dinner. Perry and his sisters attended a private neighborhood school run by a woman named Molly Pope, then he spent three years at Atlanta University's prep school.

By age twelve or thirteen, Perry knew that schooling was not for him. His family was not particularly musical, but, with his mother's encouragement, Perry had learned to play the piano a bit by ear. He first played for dances at the university, but he soon began to schedule work in the tonks of the red-light district on Decatur Street, in addition to his prep school jobs. He also had some neighborhood renown as a cakewalker, winning several contests held at Ponce de Leon Park. Perry attended vaudeville shows when he could afford it, and he was especially impressed by the Whitman Sisters. He saw the Whitmans' act in 1906, and it helped to clarify his vague dream of a show business career. Their compact performance showed him what professional entertainers did, and made him want to do it, too.

In the fall of 1907 Allen's New Orleans Minstrels played in Atlanta, and when they left town, Perry Bradford went with them. His career as a minstrel lasted less than a year, but it was a year crowded with the adventures and travails of low-level black show business. There was a wild, week-long booking in New Orleans that coincided with the 1908 Mardi Gras. Bradford said that he met the pianist Tony Jackson during this time, as well as John-the-Conqueror and Snake Annie, two voodoo practitioners who told his fortune and gave him mojo charms. Bradford got caught cheating at craps while the minstrels' train was passing through Vinita, Oklahoma. He saw a beating coming, and he escaped by bailing out of the train car window. He said he walked the thirty or so miles from the northeast Oklahoma town into Kansas and, from there, he hoboed to Tennessee. He played in a Knoxville saloon long enough to get enough money together to go to Chicago. At the end of 1908, he was playing at Johnny Seymore's saloon, at Twenty-seventh and State streets, and was entering the piano contests organized by Charles Warfield.

In late 1908 or early 1909, Perry Bradford met the woman who would be his professional partner for ten years, Jeanette Taylor. They formed a song-and-dance act called "The Chicken Trust," and, billed as Perry Bradford and Jeanette, they began to work in vaudeville. Taylor was lithe and petite, and she was the better dancer of the two, capable of eccentric kicks and gyrations. Bradford played the piano and sang his specialty song, "Whoa, Mule!" and the two did comic crosstalk. As they traveled, Bradford picked up dance steps in local saloons and from other vaudeville acts and began to write songs about them. (Handy was picking up bits and pieces of folk music at the same time.) Bradford and Jeanette freshened their turn throughout the teens with variations on the Bull Frog Hop, the Possum Trot, and the Jacksonville Rounders' Dance.

The male-female, music-and-comedy act was a recent innovation in black vaudeville. There had been mixed dance teams since the 1890s, but they rarely sang, and never talked, on the stage. Bradford and Jeanette were one of the first talking acts, following in the fresh footprints of Butler May and his wife, who billed themselves as Stringbeans and Sweetie May. Another popular duo was Willie and Lulu Too Sweet, who, like Bradford and Jeanette, featured original songs in their act. The Too Sweets' numbers included "Keep It Up All the Time," "Mama Don't Allow No Easy Talking Here," and "I'm So Glad My Mamma Don't Know Where I'm At." In 1917 the pair who would make the most enduring double act, Jodie Edwards and Susie Hawthorne, were married on the stage of a black vaudeville house in Philadelphia. As Butterbeans and Susie, they would weather changing tastes in entertainment over decades, continuing to perform together until Hawthorne's death in 1963.

The importance of the double acts to the story of the blues lies in the tone and subject matter of their dialogues and songs. The Mays, Too Sweets, and Edwardses were married—and audiences thought that Bradford and Jeanette were married, although they probably were not—and their stage talk was designed to give the impression that the audience was listening to the bickering, complaints, threats, and sexual boasting of an earthy and long-suffering couple. When the blues came into vogue in the mid-teens—about the time that Perry Bradford was beginning to take his songwriting seriously—the double acts began to use blues songs. But they were closer in spirit to the marital sitcoms of vaudeville than to the sorrowful folk stories of the first blues singers. These "double-act blues" would be the kind that Perry Bradford would write all of his life.

In the summer of 1910 Bradford and Jeanette played New York for the first time. They were based in Chicago for a few more years, but after their success at Harlem's Lincoln Theatre in 1916, they shifted their touring to the Northeast rather than the Midwest and South. In 1916 Bradford self-published his "Lonesome Blues" during a stint in Philadelphia.

Bradford's self-published song was not a big seller, but it motivated him to write more and peddle harder than he ever had. In 1917 he placed an old dance song of his, "Scratchin' the Gravel," with Charles K. Harris in New York. Harris brought in Jack Yellen and Charlie Pierce to touch up Bradford's lyric, and the song became Bradford's first real commercial publication. Jeanette Taylor began to feel that Bradford was putting more work into his song-selling than into polishing and booking their act, and their relationship became strained. When Bradford assembled a short vaudeville musical, Sgt. Ham of the 13th District, in 1917, he hired a plump and pretty cabaret singer named Mamie Smith and offered to become her manager. Whether Taylor's jealousy of Smith was professional or personal, it was enough to split up Bradford and Jeanette. In early 1918 she teamed with a dancer named Seymour James—whom she would later marry—and left Bradford's orbit.

In the summer of 1918, Bradford and Mamie Smith were displayed to good effect in Bradford's Lincoln Theatre revue, *Made in Harlem*. Although Harlem audiences were still a bit standoffish about vocal blues, the hit of the show was Smith's rendition of Bradford's "Harlem Blues." He sold three numbers to Frederick V. Bowers in 1918: "Broken Hearted Blues" (made in the "St. Louis Blues" pattern, with a sixteen-bar strain sandwiched between two twelve-bar themes), "Lonesome Blues" (which Bowers probably did not know had been previously published by Bradford), and a dance song called "Stewin' de Rice." Bradford was becoming wise to New York now and was beginning to see how the publishing game was played.

1919 brought even more activity for the songwriter. Bowers published two more Bradford songs ("I'm Crazy About Your Lovin'" and "What Did Deacon Jones Do When the Lights Went Out?"), and in September the Ford Dabney band played his "Lonesome Blues" for Aeolian Vocalion, giving Bradford his first recorded number. Bradford's "That Thing Called Love" was issued by Melody Music, a small Harlem firm owned by Bud Allen. Bradford produced a new revue, *Darktown After Dark*, and he also revived *Sgt. Ham*. He wasn't a star and he wasn't earning much from his songs, but his name was getting around. He married Marion Dickerson and they settled into a $3-a-week room on West 138th Street. He was thinking, and hustling, all the time.

Bradford's hangout was the clubroom of the Colored Vaudeville Benevolent Association, at 424 Lenox Avenue. He spent his days there, playing the piano and picking the brains of show business veterans. He was planning an assault on the recording industry, and he sought their advice. Suppose a black writer (who wasn't much of a piano player) had these songs (which weren't hits) that he wanted to get recorded, and suppose he were managing a female singer (whom no one outside of Harlem had heard of) whom he wanted to sing them on records? He consulted with Bert Williams, Bill Robinson, and Rosamond Johnson. All were sympathetic, but no one knew exactly how to get a hearing for a female singer. Wilbur Sweatman reminded him of the time Sweatman had taken Jeanette Taylor to Columbia and had been told that the label was not about to conduct the "experiment" of adding vocals to the Sweatman records. And W. C. Handy had taken Viola McCoy to record companies with no success. Bradford didn't have the assets of star power or reputation downtown; he had only his nerve. He hit the streets.

Usually his "interviews" at record companies were with receptionists, and they lasted only long enough for them to tell him to get out. If he had the occasional contact with an assistant's assistant, the interview was not much longer. In January 1920, he thought he had a toe in Victor's door. A test recording was set up for Mamie Smith, with Bradford playing piano for her. To no one's surprise but Bradford's, Mamie Smith did not pass her test at Victor. When Bradford groused about his treatment to a group of songwriter friends, one of them, a white lyricist named William Tracey, spoke up. Tracey said that Bradford should go see Fred Hager, the recording manager for OKeh, and that Bradford should use his name to get in.

On a cold day in early February, Bradford walked from Harlem to a saloon at Fortieth Street and Eighth Avenue. He bought a beer, tucked away the free lunch that came with it, and braced himself to drop in on Hager. OKeh's headquarters were nearby, at 145 West Forty-fifth Street, and Bradford had been there many times before. At the sight of him, a secretary started to shoo him away. He yelled, "I have a message for Mr. Hager from Bill Tracey!" Hager heard this and came out of his office. Bradford had rehearsed his pitch and he made it quickly: there were millions of Negroes who would buy OKeh records if they could hear Negro voices on them; there was a great market for Negro songs and singers among Southern whites; Bradford was a published writer who had had a song recorded; he had some songs here that had gone over well in Harlem revues.

Hager was interested in the part about a Southern white market, and he offered to take a look at Bradford's songs. He liked two of them—"That Thing Called Love" and "You Can't Keep a Good Man Down." Bradford's bubble burst when Hager said that these songs would be just the thing for Sophie Tucker.

Hager sent Bradford to see Tucker and to show her the songs. Bradford went, but it was only a courtesy call. He knew that Tucker was already under contract to Aeolian Vocalion, and that she could not record for OKeh even if she liked the songs. He returned to Hager and leaned hard on him. He talked Hager into recording the black woman he had never heard of. A studio session was scheduled for February 14, 1920, Valentine's Day and Bradford's twenty-seventh birthday. He ran to tell Mamie Smith.

Mamie Smith had a strong contralto voice, but she was not really a blues singer. She was a show business pro, though, and she had been one since childhood. She was born Mamie Robinson in Cincinnati in 1883, and she was touring as a "pickaninny" in a white act, the Four Dancing Mitchells, by the early 1890s. She spent several seasons with Salem Tutt Whitney's Smart Set company, and when the Whitney show brought her to New York in 1913, Smith decided to stay after the run was over. Her first marriage, to a comedian named Sam Gardner, dissolved, and she married William "Smitty" Smith, a sometime singer. She made a reputation in Harlem singing pop songs in cabarets in the teens: at Barron Wilkins', Leroy's, and Digg's Cafe. She didn't have the power of the great blues belters, but Perry Bradford's songs didn't require it. She was a sweet-faced beauty,

Mamie Smith

brown-haired and heavy-hipped, with a lazy sensuality about her. The rougher-edged black singers of the mid-twenties would eclipse her, but Bradford's confidence in her was well-placed. She would not let him down. He knew that the door that had been so hard to open would not slam shut because of Mamie Smith.

Smith was accompanied on her first recordings by OKeh's house orchestra, a white group named for its leader, Milo Rega. Okeh's sales department did not show the same decisiveness in marketing the February 14 sides that Hager had shown in making them. The label of "That Thing Called Love" and "You Can't Keep a Good Man Down" read that the songs were sung by "Mamie Smith, Contralto." The company did not know what to do with the record—how many copies to press, where to distribute it, how to advertise it—so for several months, it did nothing. With no fanfare of any kind, the record was finally released in the summer of 1920. It started strong, with a burst of sales in Harlem, and it held steady. Perry Bradford kept an eye on his record's progress and he went around to Harlem record stores to make sure they were well-stocked with copies. He suggested that the stores put phonographs out on the sidewalks, so that passersby could hear the songs.

Bradford opened shop as a publisher by taking offices in the Gaiety Theatre Building—at 1547 Broadway, where Pace & Handy was located—in 1920. He could publish only one of the songs on the Smith record because he had sold the copyright of "That Thing Called Love" to Pace & Handy earlier in the year. Zez Confrey had made a piano roll of "That Thing Called Love" for QRS in 1919, so the song was known to Pace & Handy before Smith's record was released. The sale of this copyright probably financed Bradford's move into the Gaiety Building. The first publication of the Perry Bradford Music Company was, of course, "You Can't Keep a Good Man Down," with Sophie Tucker's picture on the cover

Bradford believed his record was doing well, but he didn't know what his mechanical royalties would be or when he would see them. In midsummer, he was offered a job as a singer in a black quartet on the tryout tour of a Shubert show, *Dearie*. There was nothing to do but take it. But before he left town, Bradford made one more pitch to Fred Hager, on Friday, August 7.

Hager was quick to see Bradford this time. OKeh was getting encouraging sales reports on the Smith recording. It was doing well in the South, the Midwest, Chicago, and Philadelphia. Bradford got right to his proposal: if a black woman singing songs by a black writer had met with such success, how much more novelty appeal might there be if the woman sang with a black band backing her? Hager asked him the name of the band. Bradford had no band, so he made up a name: "It's the Jazz Hounds." Hager laughed and said, "Mamie and the Hounds can bark next Monday morning at 9:30." The date was set for August 10, 1920.

There are two first-person, "eye-witness" accounts of what happened next, one by Perry Bradford and the other by Willie the Lion Smith. Each denies the other a role in the story. In Bradford's autobiography, he says that he spent Friday night rounding up musicians in various Harlem clubs and spent all day Saturday rehearsing them. They were, according to Bradford: Johnny Dunn, cornet; Dope Andrews, trombone; Ernest Elliott, clarinet; and Leroy Parker, violin. Bradford does not mention hiring a pianist, nor using one at the session. He says he rehearsed Mamie Smith from 4:00 P.M. Sunday until 2:30 Monday morning at Smith's apartment. Smith's mother kept them supplied with homemade hooch from the bootlegger next door, and they fell into a fitful sleep when their work was done. They awoke early Monday and took the subway to midtown Manhattan, where they were met by the band members on the street in front of the OKeh studio.

With the OKeh engineers shushing them, they ran through several takes of Bradford's "Harlem Blues." Someone on the OKeh staff mentioned that the song's title might limit the sale of the record. Bradford renamed it on the spot, calling it "Crazy Blues." The new title did not affect the lyric. After getting "Crazy Blues" down, they went on to "It's Right Here for You (If You Don't Get It, 'Tain't No Fault of Mine)," another Bradford-owned song, with lyrics by his wife, Marion Dickerson, and music by "Alex Belledna." The session lasted eight hours, and when it was over, Smith, Bradford, and the Jazz Hounds all went to back to Smith's apartment, "where Mom Smith was waiting with a heaping pot full of black-eyed peas and rice." Bradford says he went to OKeh the next day and helped Hager select the takes to be released, and that he left town with *Dearie* a few days later.

Willie the Lion Smith told a very different story. The pianist says that he was the first musician involved with "Crazy Blues," brought aboard at the request of Mamie Smith's husband, Smitty. The Lion was told that Mamie had "an audition" at OKeh and that she needed his coaching. They worked together for a day or so, then went to OKeh to make the tests, which were supervised by a company executive, Ralph Peer. Peer liked their music and told them to get a band together. The Lion knew more musicians than Mamie Smith did, so he assembled the group. He recalls bringing in Andrews, Elliott, and Parker, but says that Addington Major—not Johnny Dunn—was the cornetist. The four musicians that Willie Smith put together were all regulars in the house band at Leroy's, where he frequently played. They named themselves the Jazz Hounds, and they reported for their OKeh session on August 10. The Lion remembered "only Mamie, Ralph Peer, myself, and the band in the studio. I can't recall that Bradford was anywhere in sight."

The Lion supposedly coached the Hounds in their parts during the session, as the band and their singer stood around "a large megaphone-like horn." Smith remembered that they were paid $25 each for the day—and that they waited two months for their money.

As usual, the truth seems to lie somewhere in between. If the story were broken into halves, Bradford would have the more believable first half, and Smith the more believable second half. The August 10 session was indisputably the result of Perry Bradford's efforts—and of the success of his February recordings. And Bradford definitely had a hand in choosing the material to be recorded. The two Bradford songs were integral to the package that OKeh put together that day. If a pickup band such as Willie Smith described had had such a crucial opportunity come their way, they would have chosen better-known songs, or at least songs from a better-known writer. They would have given themselves the insurance of Handy numbers, or Chris Smith's, or Maceo Pinkard's. Composer credit to Perry Bradford would have meant nothing to a record buyer or to the OKeh marketing department. The Bradford songs were part of the risk taken in the studio that day, and they were there because Bradford put them there.

The recorded and printed evidence concerning the personnel is weighted toward Willie Smith's version. Bradford mentions no pianist in his account, but there is a barely discernible piano on the August 10 sides. The pianist plays no solos or breaks, so he cannot be identified by his technique, but it is unlikely that Bradford would have trusted his own piano playing in this important session. (Pops Foster said of him: "He was one of those old honky-tonk piano players that played with one finger." Eubie Blake said, "Poor Mule couldn't play.") The trombonist dominates the ensemble, and the bit of cornet that is heard doesn't have the acrid tone of Bradford's supposed cornetist, Johnny Dunn. The sheet music, issued by Perry Bradford shortly after the recording was made, pictures the four musicians whom Willie Smith named backing Mamie Smith, with the Lion himself sitting at the piano.

The recording of "Crazy Blues" hit Harlem like a thunderbolt. It had a sound unlike anything else in the record stores at the time. Mamie Smith's voice is recognizably "black," and her tones are wide and powerful. She doesn't wail exactly, but she certainly takes charge.

The Jazz Hounds' music is gutsy, full of growls and bent notes, and the "arrangement" consists only of the band's agreement on the structure of the tunes. There is improvisation as well as embellishment, and the whole thing is rough and loose-sounding. It was said that on a walk along any Harlem block in the autumn of 1920, one could hear the sound of Mamie Smith and the Jazz Hounds pouring out of cafes, and music shops, dance halls, and apartment windows. "That Thing Called Love" heralded the coming of vocal blues; "Crazy Blues" was their arrival.

Perry Bradford, in a stopgap against thievery, switched the structure of the recorded version of "Crazy Blues"—and also left out a twenty-four-bar strain—when he published it. The printed version is simpler than the one on the record, but it is still more complex than most pop songs of its time. The standard thirty-two-bar chorus in AABA form—four strains of eight bars each, with only two melodies among them—had pretty much taken hold in pop songwriting by 1920. The sheet music of "Crazy Blues" contains three melodic strains in ABC form. The A section is sixteen measures long, followed by a B section of twelve and a C (chorus) section of sixteen measures. The melody is busy, studded with blue notes and fairly rangy, making several reaches up to F in the key of B♭. Here is the printed lyric of the first verse and chorus of "Crazy Blues":

> *I can't sleep at night, I can't eat a bite,*
> *'Cause the one I love, he don't treat me right.*
> *It makes me feel so blue, I don't know what to do.*
> *Sometimes I sit and sigh, and then begin to cry.*
> *He went away and never said goodbye.*
>
> *I could read his letters but I sure can't read his mind.*
> *I thought he's loving me, and he was leaving all the time.*
> *So now I've seen that my poor love was blind.*
>
> *Now I've got the Crazy Blues, since my babe went away.*
> *I ain't got no time to lose, I must find him today.*
> *The doctor's goin' to do all that he can,*
> *But what he's goin' to need is the undertaker man.*
> *'Cause my love has been refused, so now I got the Crazy Blues.*

The alternate couplet for the second chorus is: "Goin' to do like a Chinaman, get myself some hop, Get myself a gun and shoot myself a cop." The mild-mannered Handy must have cringed the first time he heard it.

Bradford was touring with the ill-fated *Dearie* when "Crazy Blues" began to sweep New York. And he saw it in record stores everywhere on the road, too, so he knew it was selling well. (OKeh rather stiffly got into the spirit, identifying it on the label as a "Popular Blue Song.") It was doing so well that OKeh couldn't wait for Bradford to supervise another session with Smith and the Hounds. The company tracked him down by leaving a message at a Detroit music store where they knew he would go to promote his record. Bradford was asked to come back to New York at once. He gave his two weeks' notice to *Dearie* and left the show in early September in Wheeling, West Virginia. Bradford returned to New York and got the figures: in Harlem alone, "Crazy Blues" had sold over 75,000 copies (at $1 each) in its first month.

Bradford quickly planned two more sides for Mamie Smith and the Hounds to make on September 12: "Fare Thee Honey Blues" and "The Road Is Rocky (But I Am Gonna Find My Way)," both Bradford compositions, of course. Acting as manager for Smith and her band, Bradford booked them into Philadelphia's Gibson Theatre at $400 a week, then into Harlem's Lafayette at $500. Variety acts were added to fill out the show, and bookings in Pittsburgh and Washington, D.C., followed. About this time, Willie Smith left the Jazz Hounds and was replaced at the piano by Porter Grainger. Four more sides were made for OKeh in early November, with Johnny Dunn on cornet.

The composer-lyricist-producer of "Crazy Blues" was getting noticed within his industry, but he was still broke. He had signed with OKeh for two-cents-a-copy mechanical royalties, but late in 1920, he still hadn't seen any money. Eubie Blake remembered Bradford basking in glory in the Gaiety Building, then taking Blake aside to borrow a quarter for lunch. One day, after coming through with the daily quarter for Bradford, Blake went to an appointment downtown. When Blake returned to Harlem, he found a dazed Bradford sitting on a curb at 135th Street. He had a check in his hand for $100,000—his first royalties from "Crazy Blues." Since it was late in the afternoon, the banks were closed. Blake loaned him $1.25 to get some supper and take a cab home. It was a lifelong joke between the two men that Bradford never paid him back.

Riding on his successes for OKeh, Perry Bradford was the blues king of New York. The triumvirate of Bradford, Smith, and Johnny Dunn were making the hottest—and best-selling—recordings of the new music, and Bradford became known as the person to see on any blues-related matter. The bantam promoter was neither a handsome man nor a charmer of any sort, but that didn't matter now. He was no longer talking his way into strangers' offices. People were knocking on his door for a change, seeking his advice and help. His braggadocio, his tough talk, and his ever-present cigar were seen as colorful eccentricities, not as the trademarks of a pesky little man who wanted to tell white record executives how to run their business. He was a fixer, a supplier of talent. He found black acts for stage shows. He recommended singers for recordings, and he licensed his own songs to white acts who were nervy enough to sing them. (Cliff Edwards sang "Crazy Blues" in his act at the Winter Garden; Jimmy Durante wanted Bradford material; Mae West sent her maid, Bee Jackson, for copies of his songs.) He could afford the occasional generous impulse: he actually let Smith and Dunn record a non-Bradford song in January 1921 for OKeh: the Spencer Williams–Clarence Williams "Royal Garden Blues." Bradford was the guru of the blues, and he would soon be acting as de facto A & R man for half a dozen labels.

As busy as the Bradford offices were, all was not work at the Gaiety Building headquarters. At the close of the business day, Bradford's friends dropped by his office for drinks and food before beginning a nightly spree at Harlem rent parties and clubs. The fun-seekers varied in their numbers, but the fraternity usually included Fats Waller, James P. Johnson, and Andy Razaf. The bibulous group called itself the Joy Club, and they convened almost daily. Bradford came up with an appropriate motto: "When business mess up with pleasure, then cut the business and let the pleasure roll on." Any mail delivery might bring Bradford a check in five figures, so the Joy Club was secure in its sponsorship.

Bradford was soon to be the facilitator of another historic recording at OKeh. He had gone into the studio with Smith, Dunn, and the band, now called Her Jazz Hounds, to lay down Marion Dickerson's "Jazzbo Ball" and Bradford's "What Have I Done?" When the vocal sides had been made, Bradford suggested that the Hounds make some instrumental sides. Bradford's earnings for the label had put OKeh's executives in an expansive mood, so they agreed. On February 21, 1921, Mamie Smith's Jazz Hounds became the first black jazz band to make a commercial recording, playing two Bradford tunes, "That Thing Called Love" and "Old Time Blues."

Bradford's energy had its limits, however. He was still acting as booking agent for the stage appearances of Mamie Smith and Her Jazz Hounds, and the chore was getting him down. Smith was very demanding with her musicians, and Bradford was often called away from his other enterprises to deal with resignations and replacements within her band. Bradford turned over her management contract to a white manager named Maurice Fulcher, with the stipulation that Bradford receive $500 a week from any of Smith's theatrical engagements. Bradford would continue to manage her recording sessions. This relinquishing of control over Smith's stage appearances complicated a situation that was already more complex than Bradford knew. In addition to Fulcher, Smith's estranged husband ("Smitty") was also trying to act as her manager, as was her new boyfriend, an ex-waiter from Digg's Cafe named Ocey Wilson. This four-way tug on Smith's professional and personal lives eventually caused a rift with Bradford, abbreviating her big earning years and wasting a lot of her money.

Smith's success quickly inspired pretenders to her throne, as several other labels went after a piece of OKeh's blues market. The second blues singer to record was Lucille Hegamin, a beautiful woman with a rich, torchy voice, who made "Jazz Me Blues" and "Everybody's Blues" for Arto in November 1920. Then came Mary Stafford, who recorded "Crazy Blues" for Columbia in January 1921, before the company had made any royalty agreement with its composer. When Bradford went to the Columbia offices, he was told by an executive, who apparently didn't know much about the song or about Bradford, that Columbia shouldn't have to pay any royalties because the powerful company could "make the song a popular hit." Columbia sent Bradford a contract to sign the next day, with a clause that provided for the waiving of royalties. Bradford fired off his answer: "Please be advised that the only thing Perry Bradford waves is the American flag."

Bradford's financial success had been noted in the industry, as had Smith's and OKeh's. In June 1921 he was slapped with a lawsuit by

Frederick Bowers. Bowers claimed that all money from "Crazy Blues" was his, because it was the same song that Bradford sold him in 1918 as "The Broken Hearted Blues." (The chorus melody of "Broken Hearted Blues" is note-for-note the same as the middle section of "Crazy Blues," and they share two lines of lyrics.) Max Kortlander, of the QRS company, struck next, claiming that Bradford's licensing of the song "Wicked Blues" to QRS was void, because it, too, was "Crazy Blues." (The Kortlander claim was a stretch. The two songs share several rhythmic figures and a structural similarity in one section, but their melodies and lyrics are very dissimilar.) The legal wrangling went on for months, and late in the year, Bradford paid Bowers and Kortlander enough to settle both suits out of court.

Bradford kept an eagle eye out for infringement, too. When he heard Valaida Snow play at Philadelphia's Standard Theatre, she used a Johnny Dunn cornet figure from one of the Mamie Smith records. Bradford sprang from his seat and shouted at her, "You can't use that! That's copyrighted!"

The gulf widened between Bradford and Mamie Smith. Bradford booked an appearance for her at the Winter Garden—a stage job, and, technically, Fulcher's department—and Smith failed to show up. And Bradford had several run-ins with Ocey Wilson (including a violent one, Bradford claims). The breakup came in the summer of 1921. Bradford was assembling the talent for a musical called *Put and Take*, to be produced by Irvin C. Miller at Town Hall. When he asked Fulcher for Mamie Smith, Bradford was refused the services of the star he had made. Smith and Johnny Dunn went into the OKeh studio in August, without the blessing of Perry Bradford. They cut two non-Bradford songs, and the separation was complete. Mamie Smith would never work with or for Perry Bradford again.

Mamie Smith's stardom continued through the twenties. She was a hard worker, recording steadily until 1931 and trooping the United States annually with a new stage revue. She earned a lot of money and spent it lavishly. She wore a $3,000 cape made of ostrich plumes in her show, and she took it off to reveal a dress trimmed in ermine. She bought an apartment house, as well as a grand dwelling at 130th Street and St. Nicholas Avenue where she installed electric player pianos in several rooms. She dealt more in glamour than in the blues, but she always kept a top-notch band. Such stalwarts as Bubber Miley,

Coleman Hawkins, and Buster Bailey performed and recorded with her, and her comic support on stage included John Rucker, Eddie Anderson, and Dusty Fletcher. For dance specialties she hired Ida Forsyne and Dewey Weinglass.

Smith's last hit record came in 1923—"You've Got to See Mamma Every Night, or You Can't See Mamma at All." Her romantic entanglements continued. She married a producer named Jack Goldberg, but she kept seeing Ocey Wilson, who kept spending her money. She made a nine-minute musical short in 1929 called "Jail House Blues," but OKeh released none of the sides she made that year. Smith toured with the Fats Pichon orchestra in the early 1930s and made a tentative comeback in New York with a brief engagement at the Town Casino, an elegant club on Fifty-second Street, in 1936. In 1939 she made the first of four all-black feature films, *Paradise in Harlem*, in which she sang with the Lucky Millinder band. She was in *Mystery in Swing* in 1940, and she had starring roles in *Murder on Lenox Avenue* and *Sunday Sinners*, both in 1941. Her last film was a three-minute soundie, "Because I Love You," in 1943. When Mamie Smith died in a Harlem rooming house on October 23, 1946, she was alone, without much money and without Ocey Wilson.

Put and Take opened at Town Hall on August 23, 1921. Bradford published the songs by Spencer Williams (eight of them, the majority of the score), as well as two of his own that he put into the show ("Nervous Blues" and "Old Time Blues"). The musical ran for only thirty-two performances, and the score yielded no hits, but it did provide the occasion for Perry Bradford to meet his next singing discovery. In September 1921, when he left OKeh in protest over the company's "unauthorized" August sessions with Mamie Smith, he went to Columbia, taking with him a young showgirl from *Put and Take*, Edith Wilson. On September 15, Bradford supervised a Wilson session that featured Johnny Dunn's cornet. Columbia had stolen Dunn from OKeh when it was learned that OKeh had neglected to put him under contract, thereby putting two-thirds of the OKeh triumvirate back together. Dunn would work in various Bradford studio bands throughout the 1920s.

The "race label" trend was well underway by the time Bradford left OKeh. Black Swan had decided to specialize in blues in May 1921, and two months later, OKeh created an entire blues division with its "Original Race Records" series. Columbia's race series began in 1922, and in the mid-twenties Vocalion, Perfect, and Brunswick joined the game. The larger labels identified their "race" records by serial numbers. (OKeh's "race" numbers began at 8000, Columbia's at 14000, and Victor's at 23000 and—in a second Victor series—at 38000.) These numbers were sales guidelines for distributors and store clerks. The numbers told distributors not to place many of them in white stores and told clerks that white customers would not be interested in them.

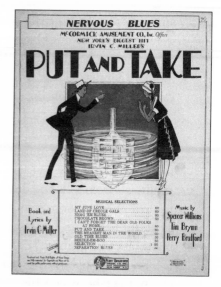

Put and Take

But the object of each label and series was to produce the kind of records that Perry Bradford had produced for OKeh in 1920. And to get the same kind of hits with them.

All labels needed female blues singers now. Among those making studio debuts in 1921 were Alberta Hunter (1895–1984), Trixie Smith (1895–1943), Edith Wilson (1896–1981), and Ethel Waters (1896–1977). Within two years the field would be joined by Ma Rainey (1886–1939), Bessie Smith (1894–1937), Ida Cox (1896–1967), Rosa Henderson (1896–1968), Sara Martin (1884–1955), Clara Smith (c. 1894–1935), and Eva Taylor (1895–1977). Even with the scores of lesser names added to their rosters, the studios' demand for blues singers outstripped their supply. Many of the blues women recorded under several pseudonyms each. Alberta Hunter was "May Alix," "Josephine Beatty," and "Helen Roberts." Ida Cox was "Velma Bradley," "Kate Lewis," "Julia Powers," and "Jane Smith." Rosa Henderson was the queen of pseudonyms, recording under no fewer than eight aliases. Sometimes the pseudonyms were used to sidestep contractual obligation to a particular label; sometimes they were merely a way of making more recordings (at $25–50 per side).

The floodgates were open. America went blues-crazy in the mid-twenties, and "blues" became a catchword, a handy label to hang on any song that had a trace of syncopation or a blue note in it. There were sad blues, joyful blues, topical blues, Broadway blues. In January 1925 a white band, Hitch's Happy Harmonists, recorded two classic rags for Gennett. Their titles were changed on the label to "Cataract Rag Blues" and "Nightingale Rag Blues."

Perry Bradford started more than a mere musical vogue. For the first time in the history of the music industry, recordings became more important than sheet music. There were hundreds of blues issued as song sheets, but the real money came from licensing and mechanical royalties—from rolls and discs and, later, from film use. The word "publishing" even took on a new meaning: it meant the acquisition of copyrights for licensing. The issuance of song sheets was an afterthought for many blues "publishers." And some of them issued no song sheets at all.

Bradford's publishing arm was strong in the early twenties, however. In 1922 he issued his own "Wicked Blues" and "Unexpectedly" (with a lyric by Jim Burris). "Unexpectedly" was one of Bert Williams' last recordings—made in October 1921—and the song was published around the time of his death. His photo on the cover of "Unexpectedly" gave his fans a last musical souvenir. Other writers' songs issued by Bradford that year included Spencer Williams' "Pensacola Blues" and "Birmingham Blues" by McCord and Matthews.

A song that he bought from writer Lem Fowler called "He May Be Your Man, But He Comes to See Me Sometimes" got Bradford into another legal jam. Lucille Hegamin made a popular recording of it in October 1922, and Bradford was anticipating about $10,000 in royalties. When the Hegamin recording hit Chicago, a cry went up from the Ted Browne Music Company there. Fowler had sold the same song to Browne only a few months earlier, and Browne had published it. Browne sued Bradford, and a court hearing in December revealed that Bradford had perjured himself in an affidavit concerning the case. It was reported that Bradford was tried for subornation in January 1923 and that he drew a jail sentence of four months.

If Bradford received such a sentence, he didn't serve much of it, because he was in the Columbia studios on February 14, 1923, making his first vocal recording, with Johnny Dunn's Original Jazz Hounds. It wasn't a great singing debut—he chanted the word "Hallelujah!" over and over as the band played "Hallelujah Blues"—but it was the kickoff to his most active years in the record industry. In April 1923, he assembled the first of the bands that he would call Perry Bradford's Jazz Phools, to accompany Lena Wilson on four sides for Paramount. The Jazz Phools bands, which recorded from 1923 to 1925, did not exist outside of the studios nor did any of the other Bradford bands. They were all ad hoc groups, organized on demand as occasions for recordings arose, and their personnel shifted over the years. Bradford was the guiding force behind most of the Original Jazz Hounds records as well as those of the Gulf Coast Seven, and he would also lead the Georgia Strutters, Perry Bradford and His Gang, and Perry Bradford's Mean Four. None of the Bradford bands was very prolific, but each usually featured top-flight players, and they made some of the scrappiest jazz of the era.

In 1923 Perry Bradford Music issued its first composition by James P. Johnson, "Worried and Lonesome Blues." Johnson had been a friend of Bradford's for several years, and their professional relationship would grow in the late twenties. Bradford championed Johnson by using him in the recording studio whenever he could and by issuing some of his most important pieces.

Also in 1923, Bradford began a second publishing company, Blues Music Company. (He would add a third imprint, Acme Music Publishing Company, to his enterprises in the late twenties.) Blues Music's first issues included Shelton Brooks' "If Anybody Wants a Real Kind Mama" and Gus Horsely's "Four O'Clock Blues."

Bradford's reputation was based on his being up to date, on knowing who the comers in jazz were and in getting them into the studio while they were still news. When the influence of Louis Armstrong began to be felt, soon after his first recordings in 1923, Bradford began to build his studio bands around hot cornetists. Bradford's own instrument, the piano, would not be important to his record sessions until the Johnson recordings of the late twenties.

Bradford supervised several dates with cornetist Johnny Dunn (1897–1937), and he had the occasional services of Bubber Miley (1903–1932) and Jabbo Smith (1908–1991). Bradford teamed Dunn and Miley on two 1924 Jazz Phools sides for Paramount. Then, in November 1925, Bradford put together a Phools session for Vocalion in which he presented the star of stars, Louis Armstrong (1901–1971).

Bradford gave his jewel a splendid setting: Armstrong was backed by Charlie Green on trombone, Buster Bailey on clarinet, Don Redman on alto sax, James P. Johnson on piano, and Kaiser Marshall on drums. The two sides featured Perry Bradford songs, of course, and Bradford himself sang them. They were two of his best, "I Ain't Gonna Play No Second Fiddle" and "Lucy Long." The result was hot stuff. Bradford's vocals are droll and deadpan; Bailey and Redman toss off fine solos; and Marshall moves an ordinary stop-time figure squarely into a Charleston rhythm in both numbers. Armstrong is busy and brilliant as accompanist and soloist. He is a gadfly, buzzing behind others' solos and stinging in his own. If the Phools had made no other recordings, these two would secure their place in jazz history.

One of the rare instances in which Perry Bradford let a musical trend get away from him occurred in 1926. He had revised his old vaudeville number, "The Jacksonville Rounders' Dance," in 1923 and made it into a song called "The Original Black Bottom Dance." His new song was performed by Ethel Ridley in an Irvin C. Miller show called *Dinah*, where it was heard by the Broadway impresario George White. Although the Black Bottom was having some vogue as a social dance in Harlem, Bradford neglected to publish the number or to include it in a record session. When the 1926 edition of *George White's Scandals* opened in June, the dancer Ann Pennington was shaking it to a new DeSylva, Brown and Henderson song called "Black Bottom." Bradford quickly published his number and recorded it with his Georgia Strutters in October, but the chance had passed. The Black Bottom that became famous was not Perry Bradford's.

Bradford pushed his songs with singers as well as with his bands. The Phools made two sides with Sippie Wallace (1898–1986) in 1925, and the Mean Four accompanied Alberta Hunter in early 1926. Louis Armstrong played and sang Bradford's old "Lonesome Blues" for OKeh in June 1926, and Bradford himself continued making vocal sides. Bessie Smith recorded several Bradford songs, notably "My Home Ain't Here, It's Farther Down the Road"—which she retitled "Dixie Flyer Blues"—and "I Ain't Gonna Play No Second Fiddle" in May 1925.

In 1927 Bradford began to increase his efforts on behalf of James P. Johnson. Bradford issued Johnson's "Snowy Morning Blues" and *Yamekraw: A Negro Rhapsody*, as well as "Toddlin'" and "Scoutin'

Around." (A Bradford folio called *Jazzapation* included these two Johnson stride pieces as well as two rags by Fred Longshaw and two piano numbers by Bradford.) Johnson's "Ebony Dreams" was issued by Bradford in 1928.

Bradford pushed for Johnson as he had pushed for no one since Mamie Smith. He was in a good position to help; he had had more of a recording career than Johnson at that point and had more contacts in the industry. In March 1927 Bradford got Johnson into the Columbia studios for piano solos of "Snowy Morning Blues" and Bradford's latest, "All That I Had Is Gone" (from his flop show *Black Bottom*). In February

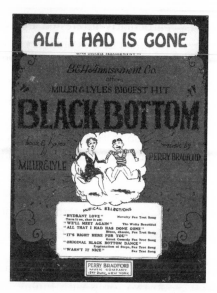

Black Bottom

1927 Johnson joined Perry Bradford and His Gang for two OKeh sides—"All That I Had Is Gone" and "Lucy Long"—and in March Johnson became an Original Jazz Hound for one session to make the same two songs for Columbia; in September Bradford sang with Johnson's Jazzers for Columbia. In October 1928 Johnson was featured with the Gulf Coast Seven, temporarily including Johnny Hodges (1906–1970), Barney Bigard (1906–1980), and Sonny Greer, on two sides for Columbia, a driving "Daylight Savings Blues" and "Georgia's Always on My Mind," in which Bradford's singing is so loose that he seems to be improvising rhymes like a rapper. The breaks and solos on the Johnson-Bradford sides sound more planned out than those on the Phools sessions of a few years earlier. But these late twenties records crackle with fun.

Bradford and Johnson began to write songs together. Their dance song "Skiddle-de-Scow" was used in the score of *Keep Shufflin'* in 1928. Bradford shares credit with Johnson on the set of five instrumentals called *Dixieland Echoes* that Bradford issued as a folio that same year. Despite their cliched titles—"Cotton Pickin'," "Liza Jane's Weddin'," and so forth-these pieces are based on folk themes. Johnson had explored this territory in his *Yamekraw* in 1927. Bradford was not particularly interested in folk material, and his contribution to the *Dixieland Echoes* numbers must have been slight if it existed at all. The folio was among the last publications of Perry Bradford Music. Bradford sold his catalog to Denton & Haskins in 1928—keeping his Blues Music and Acme imprints—and concentrated on writing and recording with Johnson.

Johnson and Bradford wrote the score for *Messin' Around*, a black revue that opened at the Hudson Theatre on April 22, 1929. The show was not successful, running only thirty-three performances, but several of its songs were published by Witmark. One of them, "Your Love Is All I Crave," was interpolated into a Warner Brothers film musical, *Show of Shows*, later that year. The Bradford lyric was overhauled by Al Dubin, and the song was renamed "Your Love Is All That I Crave."

In March 1929 Perry Bradford made his last recordings as a vocalist, on two songs with Jimmy Johnson and His Band. As busy as he had been during the 1920s, he had been without real hits since the Mamie Smith days. His interests were scattered. He had done many things well, but he had not written enduring songs. And he had never had a home base, a permanent job, at any label. He had made and seized opportunities for recordings, and he had plugged his product and his favorite musicians every chance he got. But he had not synchronized his writing, publishing, and recordings tightly enough or plugged his copyrights effectively enough to make hits of his compositions or his records. The distribution of his published music was scattershot at best. Perry Bradford Music published around 300 songs—about a third of them by Bradford—but the company's song sheets are not commonly found by collectors today. His concentration was centered on recordings, and his reputation would rest largely on the sessions that he organized.

And popular taste inevitably changes. As the small-band blues and jazz of the 1920s gave way to the big bands of the 1930s, Perry Bradford's decline began. If he was remembered at all in the industry, he was recalled as the producer of those old records that no one danced to any more. By 1930 the record-buying public hardly knew his name.

Bradford issued a few more James P. Johnson pieces in 1930 through his Acme and Blues Music imprints, but the distribution for these was even slighter than the Perry Bradford Music publications had received. He kept at it into the thirties, often using Johnson in his sessions, although Johnson too was beginning to be seen as something of a relic. Bradford was involved in the thirty-five Johnson recordings of 1939, but if jazz critic John Hammond had not been involved as well, the Johnson sides probably would not have been made. Precise credit hardly mattered, because most of these records were not released until years later.

Bradford had one more minor hit, and even this small success was not without its problems. An old song of Bradford's, "Keep a-Knockin'," was picked up by Louis Jordan (1908–1975) to record with His Tympany Five for Decca in March 1939. Jimmy Dorsey recorded it for the same label on December 5. About two weeks after the Dorsey session, Bradford, Eva Taylor, and Clarence Williams—working as a committee put together by the Colored Professional People of America—supervised the distribution of sixty-two Christmas turkeys to needy families in Queens. But in the summer of 1940, two of the three Samaritans were at each other's throats over the ownership of "Keep a-Knockin'." Bradford had neglected to copyright it until after the recordings were made, and, since it sounded to Williams like his old song, "My Bucket's Got a Hole in It," Clarence Williams claimed it. Bradford prevailed and kept his rights to "Keep a-Knockin'," but it got only a few subsequent recordings.

His stature in the music business dwindled through the early 1940s, and Bradford supervised his last record session on September 1, 1944. He produced four sides made by the Rod Cless Quartet, which featured James P. Johnson's piano, for the Black and White label. There were no new Bradford tunes to make and no old ones to revive. The two independent-label 78s were hard to find in stores.

By the mid-forties Perry Bradford needed a day job. He worked for several years behind a betting window at Belmont Park. He wrote a campaign song for Thomas E. Dewey and Earl Warren ("Good Times Are Coming") in 1948 and self-published it with a photo of the presidential candidate and his running mate on the cover. He began to promise—or threaten—a forthcoming autobiography that would tell the real story of the coming of blues and jazz. The standard accounts, especially the writings of Hugues Panassie and Ramsey and Smith's *Jazzmen*, infuriated him. *Jazzmen* did not even mention Bradford, and Panassie was almost as neglectful about his role. He released a few scraps of his story in the 1950s, but he could not find a publisher for the whole thing.

In 1965 his book, *Born with the Blues*, finally appeared, issued in hardcover and paperback by Oak Publications, a small press devoted to folk music. The book is a generally good-humored, stream-of-consciousness account of his career, and it included the words and music of eleven Bradford songs. There is some crankiness in it, and some settling of old scores. But by 1965 even jazz fans had forgotten that there were scores that needed settling. Perry Bradford died on April 20, 1970, in New York City.

As W. C. Handy's company was faltering in the early twenties, Perry Bradford's was rising, and Bradford remained a major force in the music business for about five years. Handy's revival snowballed in the late twenties as Bradford's career was declining. By the mid-thirties Handy's name had become synonymous with "blues," and the reputations of Perry Bradford and Clarence Williams shriveled under Handy's long shadow. The problem for Bradford lay in his writing. His songs had no staying power, and when their original recordings were forgotten, their day was over. His tunes never became standards. The Bradford songs are fun to hear, but they were ephemera, seldom rerecorded after their novelty wore off. There were no symphonic arrangements of Bradford songs, no Bradford evenings at Carnegie Hall, no all-Bradford programs on NBC. But the recordings matter a great deal. Hits or not, he got them, and wouldn't stop until he had them. And in doing so, he opened an industry that had been closed to black voices, black jazz, and black blues. He let us all into the Joy Club.

CLARENCE WILLIAMS

If Perry Bradford was a one-man mom-and-pop store in the blues business, Clarence Williams was its Kmart. As writer, publisher, plugger, accompanist, talent scout, radio performer, band leader, and supervisor of recording sessions, Williams dominated the blues industry in the 1920s. He was responsible for more published and recorded blues than Handy and Bradford put together. His publishing company owned around 1,500 copyrights; Williams got recordings for about half of them, and his name is on nearly a third of them. He issued over 400 song sheets and on more than 200 of these published pieces he is credited as composer, lyricist, or both. He played, sang, and/or conducted on more than 700 released recordings. He was a better businessman

Clarence Williams

than either of his rivals; he outplugged Handy and he out-hustled Bradford. His company remained vital after the blues boom was over, acquiring and issuing new pop songs and piano pieces into the 1930s. His business was his life. There are no funny stories about his wild spending or his uproarious partying. Williams was a close man with a nickel—and he needed his sleep. He had appointments to keep, and he kept them, by the hundreds.

Clarence Williams' name is on many good songs, usually sharing credit with a better songwriter. Every Williams hit comes with an implied question mark. Did Spencer Williams, Fats Waller, James P. Johnson, Chris Smith, or Willie the Lion Smith consistently run into problems in composition that could be solved only by the input of Clarence Williams? Probably not. Williams seems to have been the leading exponent of the cut-in, the composer *quid* for the publisher *quo*. Would the songs of Hezekiah Jenkins, Charlie Gaines, or Lucy Fletcher have ever seen the light of day without Williams' name on them as cocomposer and publisher? Again, probably not. The unknowns and the masters all struck their bargains with Clarence Williams for the same reason: he would publish their songs and then plug them every way to Sunday. His genius was for promotion, not composition.

Williams lived in an age of songwriting and performing giants, but he was not dwarfed by them. He could not write—or play—a "Carolina Shout" or a "Keep Your Temper," but he could publish them. He was not in the musical league of Armstrong and Bechet, but he could get them into the studio. He was only a so-so accompanist, yet he accompanied more singers on blues recordings than anyone else did, from stars like Bessie Smith and Sippie Wallace to unknowns like Margaret Johnson and Maggie Jones. Despite the ebullient personalities of Louis Armstrong and Fats Waller, the wallflower Williams logged more hours on radio in the 1920s than they did. In short, Williams could be outclassed in every creative department except one: the creation of opportunities—for himself, his songs, his friends, his blues.

There is still some question as to the year of Clarence Williams' birth. It has been variously given as 1893, 1895, and—on his death certificate—1898. Considering what we know about his early professional activities in New Orleans, and the responsibilities that his jobs there entailed, we should probably take the word of his wife, Eva Taylor. She said that Clarence Williams was born on October 8, 1893, in Plaquemine, Louisiana, a Delta town just southwest of Baton Rouge. His father was a guitarist and bass player in local bands. The Williamses were a poor family in a poor place, and their struggle for survival was hard enough for Dennis and Sally Williams to need their son's help. After a few years of elementary school, Clarence dropped out to go to work. His first job was carrying water for a railroad gang, and by age eleven or so, Clarence was a cook and bus boy at the Silver Brothers Hotel in Plaquemine.

When he was about ten, Clarence discovered the fun of playing at the piano. There were not many pianos in Plaquemine's black community, but Clarence knew where they all were. He was willing to walk several miles to any home that had one. He sang with his friends for tips on the street in front of the hotel, and he sang in the dining room when he was not clearing tables. He put together a little string band and took them "serenading"—going house-to-house, delivering music to the door of anyone who would give him a nickel or a few pennies.

There are two versions of the story of his leaving Plaquemine. One was that he went for a season with the Billy Kersands minstrel troupe at age twelve and never came back. Another was that thirteen-year-old Clarence was literally lured away by the music of the Buddy Bolden band when he heard Bolden play on an excursion boat. (If the Buddy Bolden story is true, it would support a birth year earlier than 1898 for Williams; Bolden was confined to a mental institution early in 1907.) However he got there, and even though he was too young to be there on his own, Clarence Williams was making his way in New Orleans by himself around 1906.

He gravitated to the Storyville district. His money came from shining shoes and from mending and pressing pants in a cleaners, and his delight came from the music that he heard. He took to hanging around Jelly Roll Morton (1890–1941) and Tony Jackson (1876–1921), the composer of "Pretty Baby." Their playing must have inspired him, because he sought out a piano teacher. He managed to take "about eight" lessons—the only music training he would ever have—at twenty-five cents apiece from a music store demonstrator, Mrs. Ophelia Smith. Around 1910 he began to play in wine rooms with his two-song repertoire, "Lovie Joe" and "Some of These Days." He couldn't compete for jobs with the New Orleans pianists, but he was good enough to travel to small-town Louisiana joints with a handful of other musicians and eke out a living. He played in whorehouses in Alexandria and Oakdale, and he recalled traveling as far as Houston in 1911, to play at a silent movie theatre.

Early in 1913, in New Orleans, Clarence Williams discovered his real talent: the ability to run things. He became the manager of a roughhouse cabaret on Rampart Street. He cleaned up the place by installing a bouncer to oust the layabouts and instituted a dress code—the requirement of a necktie—for patrons. The dive took in $1,500 during Mardi Gras week. He took over the management of the Big 25 club, at 135 Franklin Street, an unofficial headquarters for Storyville musicians, a loafing place and a waiting place for impromptu jobs. From there, Williams went on to run Pete Lala's Cafe, a huge, boisterous saloon, at the corner of Iberville and Marais, popular for its 4:00 A.M. happy hours, where a pimp and his stable of girls could relax after work. There were still a few out-of-town forays for Williams in the early teens, but he was a fixture in Storyville by then, known more as a club manager than as a musician. But in 1914, one of his occasional band jobs brought Williams into contact with the man who would be his partner in publishing.

A locally popular violinist, Armand J. Piron (1888–1943), was leading a sextet called the Olympia Orchestra, and he asked Clarence Williams to be his pianist. Piron had been born into a family of musicians; his father and two brothers played professionally. He had been seriously injured in an accident at age seven and was unable to walk for several years. During his recuperation he passed the time by learning the violin at home. By age twelve he could walk again, and he had attained enough skill to play the violin professionally. In his early teens, Piron played in several society ensembles, including the highly respected Peerless Orchestra, and he took charge of the Olympia in 1913, when the group's founder, Freddie Keppard, went on a vaudeville tour. Piron replaced Keppard with Joe Oliver on cornet, and, in addition to Piron and Williams, the 1914 membership included Sidney Bechet (clarinet), Louis Keppard (guitar), and Henry Zeno (drums).

Williams and Piron began to write songs, and they decided to create a publishing company in 1915 to issue them. Their association must have seemed unlikely to the musicians who knew them: the handsome, soft-spoken Piron, with his courtly Creole manners, and the pudgy, pushy Williams. But each had something that the other needed. Piron had a solid musical background; he could compose, notate, and arrange. Best of all, he had a band, a vehicle for plugging the Williams and Piron songs. Williams was short on the technical end of music, but he had an ear for what people were listening and dancing to—and he had the nerve of a burglar.

The new company opened its doors at 1315 Tulane Avenue and soon issued its first song, Williams' "You Missed a Good Woman When You Picked All Over Me." Piron's band plugged it incessantly, of course, and Williams waded into selling it the only way he knew how. He went door-to-door, as he had done in his "serenading" days in Plaquemine. He had a stack of song sheets with him, priced at a dime each. Sometimes he could make a sale merely by humming a little of his number out on the porch, sometimes he had to go inside to demonstrate it on the piano. He occasionally took Lizzie Miles around with him to sing it on streetcorners. Within six months of the song's issue, Williams had sold over 5,000 copies with his homemade hustle.

Williams began to cast a wider net. He badgered the local Woolworth's manager into placing the song in his music department. When Piron refused to take his band out of town to plug it, Williams put together duos and trios and hit the road himself. He told Sidney Bechet he was taking him on a vaudeville tour, and Bechet found himself playing in dime stores in East Texas, flogging Williams' song with the composer at the piano.

The publishing partners issued two more songs, their first collaborations: "I Can Beat You Doing What You're Doing Me" and, their local favorite, "Brown Skin" (the Williams & Piron name is not on the cover of the latter, but that of their distributor, Dugan Piano Company, is). Piron reluctantly disbanded the Olympia to devote more time to the selling of their three-song catalog. Williams and Piron booked themselves as a violin-and-piano team in vaudeville theatres. They played mostly in the Southeast but went as far away as Kansas City and into Michigan. When Williams and Piron played in Memphis, they met W. C. Handy, who helped them get copies of their songs into local stores. They hit it off so well with Handy that he asked them to tour for a while as a featured duo with the Handy band.

In 1916, Williams & Piron published its first number not written by its owners, Jimmie Cox's "Long, Long Time Before You See My Face Again." Williams' only piano rag, "Wild Flower," was also issued that year. The best news for the company was that the Victor Military Band recorded "Brown Skin," in a ricky-tick arrangement that was heavy on the woodblock. By 1917, Williams was beginning to wheel and deal with his dozen or so copyrights. He sold his "You're Some Pretty Doll" to Shapiro-Bernstein by mail. He went to Chicago to explore the possibilities of moving his publishing operations there, and while he was there, he sold his and Piron's "You Can Have It, I Don't Want It" to McKinley Music. He began to advertise his songs in the Chicago *Defender*. When a royalty check for $1,600 from the Victor recording of "Brown Skin" arrived, Williams could afford to make the move to Chicago. He didn't close the New Orleans offices of Williams & Piron, but in late 1918 he opened a branch in Chicago, along with a music store, at 3129 South State Street.

Piron wasn't so sure about the Chicago venture. As Williams was making his first explorations there, Piron went about his business in New Orleans, forming a new orchestra in 1917. In 1918, with a partner in each city, Williams & Piron issued numbers from both cities. In February 1919 Piron went to their Chicago headquarters—which he had never seen—to try to help with the growing business. It was the only time that Piron ever lived away from New Orleans, and the only time in his adult life that he was not a bandleader. He didn't like either condition. He gave it a good try, which lasted six months. In

September he returned to New Orleans, ready to phase himself out of publishing. Piron would continue to write, and to publish with Williams & Piron, but his decision to go home was the beginning of his separation from Williams. Williams charged on, now solely in charge of their company. In 1920 he acquired a second music store and moved the Chicago offices to larger quarters.

The collaborator who took Piron's place as a frequent songwriting partner was Spencer Williams. Williams and Williams (no relation) began to write together in 1919, and their first three songs—"I Ain't Gonna Give Nobody None o' This Jelly Roll," "Yama Yama Blues," and "Royal Garden Blues"—were all successful. Clarence Williams was not buying many songs during this time, but some of his acquisitions were choice. In 1919 he issued Lukie Johnson's "Don't Tell Your Monkey Man," and the next year, Tony Jackson's "I'm Cert'ny Gonna See About That." And in 1919 an amateur songwriter named Lucy Fletcher brought a lyric that she had written to Williams' State Street office and timidly showed it to the publisher. Williams looked it over and decided to write a tune for it and to change some of the words. The song was "Sugar Blues," and over the years it would prove to be his most valuable copyright.

"Sugar Blues" was issued in 1919, with the lyric credited to Fletcher and the music to Williams. Although Fletcher was desperately poor when she brought the song to Williams, and would have been the easiest of his collaborators to cheat, he seems not to have taken advantage of her. If Williams had bought the song outright, he probably would not have given her credit as cowriter. Her name meant nothing to the buyers of sheet music, yet it remained on the song in its various reissues. Williams may have actually paid her royalties from its sheet music sales and its many recordings. It is tempting to think that he did the right thing by Lucy Fletcher.

Clarence Williams' best and best-known songs are collaborations. He shares credit with several great songwriters of his day as well as with one-song writers like Lucy Fletcher. So it is hard to say what is characteristic of him as a composer. His songs with Fats Waller sound like Waller; his songs with Spencer Williams sound like the other Williams. The songs that bear his name alone are the least interesting of his publications. Was he a chameleon who took on the musical colors of his collaborators? Most likely he was a fixer-upper, someone who could supply a synonym to fix up a lyric and could supply a coda or a turn-around to fix up a tune.

Whether or not "Sugar Blues" is typical of his writing style, it is certainly typical of his publishing product. It is a pop song sprinkled with blues effects. Its form is simple: its verse is twelve bars long, and its chorus has sixteen bars, with a two-bar tag on the end giving it eighteen. There are blue notes in its melody, but they are decorations, not intrinsic to the harmonies of the piece. Here are the lyrics to the published first verse and chorus of "Sugar Blues":

> *Have you heard these blues*
> *That I'm going to sing to you?*
> *When you hear them, they will thrill you thro' and thro'.*
> *They're the sweetest blues you ever heard,*
> *Now listen and don't say a word:*
>
> *Sugar Blues,*
> *Ev'rybody's singing the Sugar Blues.*
> *The whole town is ringing,*
> *My lovin' man's sweet as he can be,*
> *But the doggone fool turned sour on me.*
> *I'm so unhappy, I feel so bad,*
> *I could lay me down and die.*
>
> *You can say what you choose but I'm all confused,*
> *I've got the sweet, sweet Sugar Blues, more sugar,*
> *I've got the sweet, sweet Sugar Blues.*

It hangs together somehow, and the effect is pleasing. But it doesn't have Handy's architecture nor Bradford's funkiness. The song became the theme of the wah-wah trumpeter Clyde McCoy, and he had two hit records of it (in 1931 for Columbia and in 1935 for Decca). McCoy's version of "Sugar Blues" is definitive; it is cute and it can still evoke a smile. But it is not playing the blues, it is playing around with them.

In 1919–1920 Clarence Williams sold a few more of his copyrights, including his three Spencer Williams successes, to Shapiro-Bernstein. His business was expanding, and he needed capital to put into it. He opened a third music store in Chicago, and he occasionally traveled to New Orleans to keep an eye on the Williams & Piron branch there. There was an unexpected boon of royalties from two 1919 recordings of "I Ain't Gonna Give Nobody None o' This Jelly Roll," the first by Wilbur Sweatman's band and the second by Ford Dabney's Novelty Orchestra.

The publishing company was thriving on all fronts. Inspired by the vocal blues boom set off by Perry Bradford, Williams unilaterally decided in 1921 to move Williams & Piron to New York. He set up shop in the Gaiety Building, which was already the headquarters of Handy and Bradford—and already known by Tin Pan Alley wits as "Uncle Tom's Cabin." He hired Tim Brymn as Williams & Piron's first professional manager.

In early 1921 Williams ran into a pretty singer/dancer whom he had previously met in Chicago. Her real name was Irene Gibbons, but her professional name was Eva Taylor. She was a St. Louisan who had been in show business since age three, when she had begun touring with Josephine Gassman and Her Pickaninnies. As a teenager she took up the "Russian" dancing style of Ida Forsyne and landed a job in an Al Jolson show, Vera Violetta. At the time she became reacquainted with Williams, Taylor was starting to get singing jobs in Harlem clubs. Williams and Taylor began to date, and on November 8, 1921, they were married at St. Benedict's Church on West Fifty-third Street. It was a solid professional, as well as personal, match. Taylor was smart, personable, and ambitious. She would be a reliable presence in the recording studio and a savvy colleague in Williams' publishing enterprises throughout his years in the business.

Williams wanted in on the blues craze that was sweeping New York. He temporarily shifted his efforts from publishing song sheets to placing recordings of his numbers. The recording studio was where the action was, and Williams knew there was a direct connection between hearing a song and wanting to buy it. It was a lesson that he had learned long ago, singing his first compositions on porches in black neighborhoods in New Orleans. Shortly after his arrival in New York, he placed a song ("Play 'Em for Mama, Sing 'Em for Me") with Katie Crippen, who recorded it for Black Swan. Daisy Martin sang it next, in April for OKeh. In September Trixie Smith sang "You Missed a Good

Woman When You Picked All Over Me"—to James P. Johnson's piano accompaniment—for Black Swan. And on October 11, 1921, Clarence Williams made his first recording, singing four numbers with a seven-piece band called Johnnie's Jazz Boys for OKeh. By the end of 1921 he had made seven sides as a singer, six of them Williams & Piron publications.

Williams shifted his plugging focus almost immediately after he and Eva were married. Because Taylor was better-known than Williams was, he began to accompany her as she sang his songs in clubs. In the late spring of 1922, Taylor went into the New York company of *Shuffle Along*—earning $45 a week—for the last of its run. She could have gone on the road with *Shuffle Along*, but Williams devised a revue called *Step On It* to feature himself and Taylor. He booked a summer route through cities in the Northeast and along the Atlantic coast. When their tour ended, Williams and Taylor came back to New York to find a performing opportunity and a business opportunity, each of which would be of enormous benefit to their careers.

The performing opportunity seemed inauspicious at the time. In August the singer Vaughn DeLeath took Taylor and Williams to a small radio station on Tenth Avenue and gave them a part in her musical program. Eva Taylor was the featured singer and Williams served as her accompanist on the local show. It was the beginning of Taylor's fifteen years as a radio artist. She would go from local to regional to national broadcasts, becoming the only black performer to have a radio career in the 1920s. She, not Williams, was the radio star, but Williams was usually in the studio with her, playing the piano, occasionally singing and bantering with Taylor, and choosing the latest Williams songs that needed radio plugs.

The business opportunity was not inauspicious at all. It was the chance to buy out Piron. A. J. Piron came to New York in September 1922 to sell his share of Williams & Piron to his partner, to be rid of the publishing company that he had never been wholeheartedly interested in. It is not known what the terms of the transfer were, but the deal gave Williams all of the Williams & Piron copyrights, plus several songs that were Piron's alone. Williams smelled a hit in one of the Piron songs, so he quickly renamed the firm the Clarence Williams Music Publishing Company and published "I Wish I Could Shimmy Like My Sister Kate."

"Sister Kate" had been copyrighted in Piron's name in 1919, and although the Piron orchestra had been playing it in New Orleans for several years, it had never been published. Louis Armstrong would claim all of his life that he had written "I Wish I Could Shimmy Like My Sister Kate," and he may have. New Orleans musicians were notoriously lax about copyrighting their material. Performance took precedence over publication in that city, and many fine tunes floated around for months or years before anybody set them down and claimed them. Some of the best New Orleans players were musically illiterate, and when they hummed their melodies to someone who could notate them, the stage was set for trouble. The notator could cut himself in as cowriter, could buy the song outright for a few dollars, or could switch around a few notes and claim a piece as original material.

Williams was managing Pete Lala's Cafe in the mid-teens when Armstrong was playing there. Armstrong's specialty piece was a smutty song called "Keep Off Katie's Head," and perhaps Williams called in Piron to take it down. He may have even offered Armstrong a few dollars for it. In any case, the usually large-spirited Armstrong held a grudge about it for decades. When Al Rose asked Piron about the song in 1939, he said, "that's not Louis' tune or mine. . . . That tune is older than all of us. People always put different words to it. Some of them were too dirty to say in polite company. The way Louis did it didn't have anything to do with his sister Kate." Whatever the genesis of "Sister Kate," it was the first smash hit of the Clarence Williams Music Publishing Company. It got a dozen or so recordings in 1922 alone, and it became a cornerstone of the Williams catalog.

In September 1922 Eva Taylor made the first of her scores of recordings with her husband as her accompanist, singing "New Moon" (by Williams and Joe Wolff) for OKeh. She was featured in a shortlived Nora Bayes show, Queen o' Hearts, on Broadway in October, and on Thanksgiving Day she went into the OKeh studios with Williams to record "Sister Kate" and another Williams song of disputed authorship, "Baby, Won't You Please Come Home?" (Charles Warfield, the Chicago pianist who claimed to have been cheated out of "I Ain't Got Nobody" by Spencer Williams, said that he wrote "Baby, Won't You Please Come Home?" Warfield's name is on the song along with Williams', so he must have sold it—however cheaply—to the publisher.) "'Tain't Nobody's

Business If I Do" (by Porter Grainger and Everett Robbins), another Williams publication of late 1922, also began to get recordings. Anna Meyers sang it first, with the Original Memphis Five, for Pathe Actuelle in October; and Sara Martin did it, with Fats Waller's piano accompaniment, for OKeh on December 1.

Clarence Williams, like Perry Bradford before him, began to act as "blues advisor" to several record labels. Because he was a better pianist than Bradford, he could maneuver more adeptly. Whenever an opportunity presented itself, Williams was instantly ready as an accompanist for whichever singer a recording director had in mind. He didn't have

to scout up a band as Bradford did. (Bradford made a few recorded accompaniments, but he generally preferred to leave the piano playing to someone else.) Five of Williams' six recordings of late 1922 were made for OKeh, and by early 1923 Williams was acting as OKeh's house man. His relationship with the label would soon be formalized when OKeh put him on the payroll as "race manager" for their blues series, a position he would hold for five years. It was during the "fringe time," when he didn't yet belong to OKeh, that Clarence Williams was instrumental in the discovery of the greatest of the blues singers, Bessie Smith.

Bessie Smith

Bessie Smith's first recording session was an epochal moment in popular music, and, as with the historic "Crazy Blues" session, there are conflicting accounts as to how it happened. Perry Bradford claimed that he was the first to shop Smith around to various labels, and that they had all turned her down because she was "too rough." Rumors have persisted that Smith made test recordings for the Emerson label as early as 1921, but no evidence except a newspaper blurb about these recordings has been found. A Philadelphia record shop owner claimed that he was the first to make contact with Clarence Williams on Smith's behalf. Williams said that he arranged a test session for her at

OKeh in January 1923, and Sidney Bechet said that he played on the session. There were no 1923 Bessie Smith recordings released by OKeh, and no masters have ever been found from this January date. Frank Walker, Columbia's director of race recordings, said that he heard Smith sing in 1917 in Selma, Alabama, and that, when blues fever hit Columbia in early 1923, he thought of her and sent Clarence Williams to find her.

It should be remembered that, no matter who discovered her, by early 1923 Bessie Smith was a star ready to happen. Smith was born in Chattanooga, Tennessee, probably on April 15, 1894—the date she gave on her marriage license application in 1923. Her family was dirt-poor, and she was orphaned by age nine. She sang for pennies on Chattanooga streetcorners as a child, and when her brother Clarence joined the vaudeville show run by Moses Stokes in 1912, he arranged an audition for Bessie. She joined the Stokes company, which included a husband-and-wife team, Gertrude and Will Rainey. Later in 1912, when "Ma and Pa" Rainey broke away from Stokes to form their own show, they took Bessie with them. Smith was on her own by the mid-teens, patching together a career and making a reputation throughout the South. Her main venue was Atlanta's "81" Theatre, and she could always pick up a week at the "81" after her stints with the Florida Blossoms company and with the perennial "Silas Green from New Orleans" show. In the late teens she began to play in the Northeast. She sang the blues at Philadelphia's Standard Theatre in 1921 and at Atlantic City's Paradise Gardens in 1922. She had moved to Philadelphia by 1922, and when Eddie Hunter's *How Come?* began its run there in January 1923, she joined the musical's cast as a featured singer. She had a Philadelphia boyfriend, a night watchman named Jack Gee, and she was not about to go back South. She knew she was good—audiences told her every night. She must have had her eye on New York.

However the match was made, Bessie Smith—escorted by Jack Gee—arrived in New York in early February 1923 and began rehearsing with Clarence Williams for her recording debut. On February 15, Smith and Williams walked into Columbia's Columbus Circle studios. Frank Walker recalled, "She looked like anything *but* a singer, she looked about seventeen, tall and fat and scared to death—just awful!"

With Williams dutifully plunking behind her, Smith tried nine times to get "'Tain't Nobody's Business If I Do" down, then took two shots at "Down Hearted Blues." (The second song was written by Alberta Hunter and Lovie Austin, and it was not a Williams publication. It was probably chosen because it was a number Smith already knew.) Nothing sounded satisfactory to the Columbia engineers, and Smith was plainly nervous. The session was mercifully aborted and rescheduled for the following day. Smith and Williams must have had a strategy meeting overnight and possibly another rehearsal. When they returned the next day, they had scrapped "'Tain't Nobody's Business" and substituted another Williams copyright, his own "Gulf Coast Blues." The new tune was laid down in three takes and "Down Hearted Blues" in three more. Bessie Smith had been caught on record. The world was about to learn who she was.

Bessie Smith would have more sensitive accompanists than Clarence Williams, but in a way, his simple octave-chord playing was just right for her first recordings. He stayed out of the way and let the power of Smith's voice carry the songs. His accompaniments were plain in the way that she was plain, and their heaviness complemented hers. There was nothing of Mamie Smith's or Ethel Waters' cabaret tinge to her. She liked her tempos slow, on the floor, and her dark voice filled all the spaces that slow tempos—and unimaginative pianists—leave. The market was flooded with blues singers by the time Smith made her first recordings, but she had a presence that the others didn't have. She had the largest soul—her sorrows sounded like great sorrows, and her pleasures were deep and lusty. You got a lot for your seventy-five cents when you bought a Bessie Smith record.

Columbia knew that it had someone special in Smith. Even before her first two sides were released, Walker got Smith back into the studio—with a small band put together by Clarence Williams—on April 11 to make four more sides, two of them Williams publications. Sometime soon after this second session, Jack Gee began looking over Smith's paperwork. He found that Smith was not under contract to Columbia, as she thought she was, but was under contract to Williams, who was acting as her manager. She was getting a flat fee of $125 per released song, and Williams was taking half of it, along with the mechanical royalties from any Williams publications that she recorded.

Williams had given her $375 of the $750 for her first six sides, and when his royalty cut eventually rolled in, he would make more from the Bessie Smith recordings than she had. Gee and Smith flew into Williams' Gaiety Building office for a showdown. One account has it that Smith beat up Williams while Gee stood by and watched. In any event, they left the Gaiety Building with a release from Smith's managerial contract with Williams and went directly to the Columbia offices to negotiate with Frank Walker.

Walker heard their story and saw his own golden opportunity. He put Smith under contract to Columbia—with himself acting as her manager in record matters—and promised her $1,500 a year against a flat fee of $125 per side, with a one-year option to renew at $150 per side. Walker dropped the standard artist's royalty clause, and in a sidebar, offered to copyright any of her compositions with his Frank Music Company. (Walker would soon create a subsidiary, Empress Music, Inc., to hold the Smith copyrights. Empress Music published nothing of Smith's, but it allowed Walker to collect all mechanical royalties from Smith compositions that were recorded.) In short, Smith got from Walker pretty much what she had had with Williams, a raw deal. But Smith and Gee were pleased about the new contract. Columbia's guarantee signified a commitment to keeping her, to making and releasing enough sides to get its money back.

Smith and Gee were married in Philadelphia on June 7. By midsummer, her "Down Hearted Blues" was being heard everywhere. The record sold 780,000 copies before the year was out. She had the world in a jug, the stopper in her hand.

Chastened by his experience with Smith and Columbia, Clarence Williams plunged into a frenzy of recording. He would make more than seventy-five sides during the remainder of the year, all of them at OKeh. Most of his OKeh accompaniments were for Sara Martin, whose career he was managing through the Clarence Williams Booking Agency, and he also played for Eva Taylor, Mamie Smith, and Esther Bigeou (c. 1895–c. 1936) that year. In April 1923 he made the first of his six piano rolls for QRS ("Sugar Blues"). In May he recorded the first of his handful of piano solos (his own "Mixing the Blues" and Artie Matthews' "Weary Blues"). Also in May he assembled the first of the bands that he would call Clarence Williams' Blue Five to record with Eva Taylor. The various Blue Fives, which would be Williams' basic studio unit, made fairly ordinary good-time jazz, and Sidney Bechet (1897–1959) would be a frequent member of their changeable personnel.

Williams' publishing business was booming now. In 1923 he issued "Baby, Won't You Please Come Home?" (with Eva Taylor's photo on the cover), George Thomas' "New Orleans Hop Scop Blues," and Fats Waller's first publication, an instrumental called "Wild Cat Blues" (with Williams credited as cowriter). Sidney Bechet replaced Tim Brymn as the company's professional manager, and Eddie Heywood was hired as an arranger. Williams' first child, Clarence, Jr., was born in March, and in August the Williamses bought a plot of land in Jamaica, Queens, to build a house on.

Armand Piron brought his New Orleans Orchestra to New York in late November 1923 to make some test recordings for Victor. While Victor executives were making up their minds about Piron's test, Clarence Williams snagged him. The first Piron recordings were done at a Williams session for OKeh in early December. Piron recorded fourteen sides for three labels (OKeh, Victor, and Columbia) during his ten-week stay in New York, almost all of them Williams publications. Williams acted as Piron's booking agent during the winter and placed his orchestra into the Cotton Club and into Broadway's premier dance pavilion, Roseland. And the publisher capitalized on the Piron recordings and dance-hall appearances by issuing several of the Piron pieces that he had acquired in 1922, the instrumentals "New Orleans Wiggle" and "Bouncing Around" and the songs "Kiss Me Sweet" and "Mama's Gone, Goodbye." "Mama's Gone" got recordings by Clara Smith, Viola McCoy, and Guy Lombardo and His Royal Canadians in 1924, and it would become, along with "Sister Kate,"one of Piron's standards in the Dixieland repertoire. Piron would not stay in New York, of course. He returned to his permanent post on the bandstand at Tranchina's Restaurant in New Orleans' Spanish Fort amusement park. But his visit had been a windfall for Williams.

In 1924 Williams published "Cakewalking Babies from Home" (credited to himself, Chris Smith, and Henry Troy), as well as one of his biggest successes, "Everybody Loves My Baby" (by Spencer Williams and Jack Palmer). The Williams company went international that year, signing with music distributors in London and Melbourne.

There were more recordings with Eva Taylor, and Williams accompanied Sippie Wallace and Butterbeans and Susie as well.

Clarence Williams preferred New Orleans musicians for his various recording ensembles, and in late 1924 he brought three of the city's giants into the OKeh studios. In September his old Olympia Orchestra compatriot, Joe Oliver (1885–1938), came to New York from Chicago. He had not come to see Williams, but Williams quickly arranged a record date for him. Williams' piano and Oliver's cornet backed Butterbeans and Susie on two sides for OKeh. In October Williams put Louis Armstrong and Sidney Bechet into his Blue Five for occasional dates made over three months or so. The first side they made together for Williams was "Texas Moaner Blues," which the two giants turned into a duel. They are obviously trying to outplay each other, and it is exciting to hear the challenges thrown and taken up in their solos. Williams used the two as he needed them after that, as accompanists for Virginia Liston (c.1890–1932), Eva Taylor, and Sippie Wallace. Williams ended the year at OKeh on December 17 with Armstrong and Bechet back with the Blue Five, romping through two tunes from the *Dixie to Broadway* score, "Mandy, Make Up Your Mind" and "I'm a Little Blackbird Looking for a Bluebird."

In 1925 Clarence Williams discovered stride piano. He couldn't play it but he could publish it. He issued James P. Johnson's "Carolina Shout" and Willie Smith's "Keep Your Temper" that year, and he included Smith's number in his company's first folio, *Negro Classics: Syncopated Piano Solos*. This collection of nine instrumentals also contained Fats Waller's "Oriental Tones" and Williams' own "Gravier Street Blues." The Johnson and Smith pieces were too hard for the average player, so they didn't sell well. Williams continued publishing stride for another year or so, issuing Johnson's "Jingles," "Eccentricity," "Keep Off the Grass," and "Scalin' the Blues" (all in 1926), but then dropped the style until the mid-thirties, when he made a serious commitment to issuing Willie Smith's work again.

Williams began to push Fats Waller as a composer. Having used Waller in the studio a few times, Williams knew Waller was a fine player, and he saw rich possibilities in Waller's writing. Giving himself credit as cowriter, Williams published Waller's instrumentals "Midnight Stomp" and "Old Folks Shuffle" and his songs "Charleston

Hound" and "Senorita Mine"—both from the revue *Tan Town Topics*, produced by Eddie Rector, who also cut himself in on the show's songs. The Waller-Williams song that got the most attention was "Squeeze Me," a 1925 Williams publication that was another occasion for hurt feelings.

The resentment over "Squeeze Me" was Andy Razaf's. He held his tongue for thirty years, but toward the end of his life, Razaf began to let it be known that he had written the lyric to the song. When Razaf's name did not appear on the published version, he joined the ranks of those disenchanted with Clarence Williams. (The bassist Pops Foster, who was Williams' cousin, called him "a real horse thief.") The interesting thing about all of the badmouthing of Clarence Williams is that no one seems ever to have backed up a complaint with a lawsuit. Whereas Perry Bradford was a lightning rod for litigation, no one ever took Williams to court. And, without exception, the complainers— Louis Armstrong, Sidney Bechet, Bessie Smith, Andy Razaf, Charles Warfield, Pops Foster—all wrote and published with Williams again and/or worked for him in the studio after the supposed malfeasance occurred. Did they all say, "Well, that's show business"?, or "Well, that's Clarence Williams"? Williams' company was not the only game in town for these major talents. They all wrote, published, and recorded elsewhere during and after their association with Clarence Williams. Long after he had retired from the business, Williams himself told Al Rose: "You understand I never stole anything. That's the way the music business worked in those days. If you couldn't get a piece of the copyright, it didn't pay to publish it. Songwriters understood that putting the publisher's name on it, along with his own, was part of the original deal." Clarence Williams did not originate the original deal.

The Clarence Williams enterprises flourished in the mid-twenties. Williams, Eva Taylor, and Clarence Todd formed a radio trio, and they appeared often enough on WGBS, the station owned by Gimbel Brothers, to justify promotional tours, stage revues built around them, and began recording together as a team. The publishing company expanded with the addition of a "classical department"—for the publication of spirituals and mood pieces—in 1926, and a branch office in Chicago, managed by Richard M. Jones (1889–1945), was opened that year. Clarence Todd (1897–1949) and a white songwriter, Will

Skidmore, served as professional managers during this time, and Joe Jordan was a staff arranger. Williams was heard on about sixty recordings in 1925 and more than seventy-five recordings in 1926, a decrease from his two hundred sides in 1923 and 1924. In October 1925 Louis Armstrong made his last recordings with Williams as leader, joining the Blue Five to back up two Eva Taylor vocals. In November, Frank Walker made a peace offering to Williams, asking him to return to the Columbia studios to play on two Bessie Smith sides. (It was his first association with Smith in two-and-a-half years.) Williams seized the moment by bringing two of his own songs, "New Gulf Coast Blues" and "Florida Bound Blues."

Bessie Smith's career had surpassed that of any other blues singer during her time away from Williams. She was one of Columbia's top-selling artists, and, like Mamie Smith, she had toured as the star of her own show, commanding upward of $1,500 a week for her stage appearances since late 1923. Fletcher Henderson and Fred Longshaw had been her two primary pianists on records since the rift with Williams, and each served her well. However resentful Williams was at losing his protégé, he could at least take comfort—and mechanical royalties—from the fact that she had made successful recordings of two of his publications, "'Tain't Nobody's Business If I Do" and "Cake Walkin' Babies from Home." Williams never fully regained the trust Smith had had in him in early 1923—Jack Gee saw to that—but he accompanied her occasionally after 1925. He capitalized on their détente best on March 5, 1926, when he brought four Williams publications, including "Squeeze Me," to a Smith session at which were all recorded. In November 1926 Columbia bought OKeh, thus consolidating Williams' status at two major labels.

The flurry of activity during this time made Williams' daily commute to and from Queens too difficult. The Williams family, now including a second son, Spencer, took a house at 236 West 136th Street. (They kept the Jamaica house and would return to it in the early thirties.) A Columbia publicity shot from this period shows a prosperous-looking Williams, contented but not quite smiling. He is wearing a business suit and round-rimmed glasses. His hair is the giveaway that he is in show business. It is shiny and straight, reaching for a pompadour. He looks to be both nerd and huckster.

Early in 1926 Williams began to experiment with his basic five-piece studio band. In January he made his first recording with his Stompers, not quite a big band but larger than the Blue Fives by the addition of second and third reeds, a second cornet, and a tuba. Soon after the creation of the Stompers, he tried a four-piece group, the Dixie Washboard Band. The substitution of a washboard for drums as a rhythm instrument created a loose, good-timey sound that must have reminded Williams of the "spasm bands" of his youth in New Orleans. He didn't continue in the big-band direction of the Stompers, but he stuck with the washboard. He found occasions to use it in ensembles of various sizes—his Blue Grass Foot Warmers, his Washboard Four, his Washboard Five—over the next few years. He

compounded the folksy effects by using more houseware—jugs and scrapers—as well as gourds and kazoos in several of his early thirties bands.

Bottomland

Among these various groups, Williams employed a lot of musicians. The trumpeter Charlie Gaines described the way Williams the contractor kept his supply: "He never engaged a man for specific dates. He had a stable of musicians on a weekly payroll. You might be called for several dates a day or maybe none for a week, but you received a standard sum of about eighty-five dollars each week. Williams had only one day to pay, and if you were out of town, it accrued on the next week's salary."

The focal point of Williams' activity in 1927 was the preparation and promotion of his only musical, *Bottomland*. The show was a vanity production, designed to show off the Clarence Williams Trio. Williams produced the play, wrote the book and lyrics—with various composers, including Joe Jordan, Spencer Williams, and Chris Smith—and conducted the theatre orchestra when he was not onstage with Taylor and Clarence Todd. *Bottomland* was a melodramatic affair, about a poor country girl who comes to the city to find her long-lost

friend and discovers that her childhood playmate has become an alcoholic nightclub singer. Critics complained that although *Bottomland*
aspired to drama, most of the dialogue consisted of song cues rather
than plot or character development. *Bottomland* opened at the small
Princess Theatre on June 27, 1927, and it ran for twenty-one performances. There were no hits from the show, but it was not for Williams'
lack of trying. Williams published nine of the *Bottomland* songs and
recorded them in dance arrangements and as vocals throughout the
summer. In June he temporarily named a recording unit His
Bottomland Orchestra. It was not until September that he gave up on
the *Bottomland* songs. The show was gone and, despite Williams' best
efforts, it was quickly forgotten.

In the early summer of 1928 Williams began heavily recording his
old New Orleans compatriot, Joe Oliver. Oliver had recently moved to
New York, and even though his protégé, Louis Armstrong, had surpassed him, Oliver was still a force in jazz. He had been publishing with
Melrose Music, a Chicago firm, and most of his recording before 1928
had been done in Chicago during a long residence there. Oliver needed money, and Williams put him to work. Their first recordings together were instrumentals featuring Oliver with the Blue Five and with
Williams' Jazz Kings. But as he had done so often with instrumental
giants—notably Armstrong and Bechet—Williams soon began jobbing
Oliver into vocal sessions, using him to back up singers who were less
interesting than their accompaniment (including Elizabeth Johnson,
Hazel Smith, Eva Taylor, and Williams himself).

Oliver had a new tune that he wanted to launch in New York, and
he showed it to Clarence Williams. It was "West End Blues," and
Williams immediately bought the copyright. Williams pulled together
a seven-piece band, including himself and Oliver, which he called King
Oliver's Dixie Syncopators, to give the number its premiere recording
for Vocalion on June 11, 1928. On June 28, Louis Armstrong recorded
"West End Blues" with His Hot Five for Columbia. The two records
appeared within days of each other, and, of course, comparisons were
made between them. Once again the precocious pupil outstripped his
teacher. The Armstrong version of "West End Blues" would be on anyone's short list of the best jazz recordings of all time, and the Oliver-
Williams recording was left in its wake. In the year of Oliver's death

Williams republished "West End Blues"—with himself credited as cowriter—and, as a bonus on the sheet music, he included a transcription of the "Trumpet Cadenza as Played by Louis Armstrong on OKeh Record No. 8597."

On July 2, 1928, Clarence Williams made his best solo piano recording. He dug out his 1916 "Wild Flower Rag" and gave it a deft and loving treatment. The piece must have sounded old-fashioned to record buyers of 1928, and, in the age of Johnson and Waller, it was. It has none of the surge or complexity of stride. "Wild Flower" is a sweet piece, jaunty and relaxed, simple as a stroll through a meadow. Williams' playing is gentle but rhythmically sure, flecking its three-over-four figures with grace notes. He sounds like a New Orleans club player trying the piano before the customers arrive.

Williams placed five more of his company's songs with Bessie Smith in May 1929. He and the guitarist Eddie Lang made a duo to accompany her on three sides—including "Kitchen Man"—and a week later Williams played with the five-piece band behind her on the vaudeville guitarist Hezekiah Jenkins' "I've Got What It Takes (But It Breaks My Heart to Give It Away)" and on the Jimmie Cox classic, "Nobody Knows You When You're Down and Out." Williams leaves the breaks and fills to cornetist Ed Allen.

One of the ways that publishers could acquire copyrights was to take advantage of a peculiarity built into the 1909 copyright law. Twenty-eight years into the fifty-six-year life of a composition's protection, a writer could reclaim his piece if he had second thoughts about its disposition to a particular publisher. (It was this interim stopgap that allowed Handy to reclaim his "Memphis Blues" after its duplicitous sale to Theron Bennett.) The idea was that composers and publishers would keep an eye on the calendar and make new deals with each other—or renew old deals—twenty-eight years after the original filing of a copyright. The loophole was that if no action was taken by publisher or writer during this hiatus—that is, if someone forgot to watch for this halfway point—a piece was up for grabs. It was in this way, in 1929, that Clarence Williams acquired one of his most famous numbers, the Dixieland standard "High Society."

"High Society" was written by Porter Steele in 1901, and copyrighted by Elmer J. Denton and published as a "March and Two-Step" by Brooks and Denton, of New York, that year. It was recorded in a crisp, Sousa-like arrangement by Prince's Band in 1911 and duly credited to Steele. The march caught on among New Orleans bands and became a staple of their parade repertoires. As jazz improvisation came into New Orleans music, it was only natural that everyone would tear into "High Society," a piece they all knew. King Oliver recorded it as "High Society Rag" in 1923, and Jelly Roll Morton recorded it in 1924. The piece took on new life as a jazz favorite. Any working New Orleans musician had to be able to play "High Society."

Although Steele was still alive and Denton was still in business in 1929, neither filed the paperwork to renew the tune. Clarence Williams pounced on it in May of that year. He filed for a copyright on "High Society" on May 13, and he recorded it in July with his Washboard Band, crediting the music to A. J. Piron. He recorded it as "High Society Blues" a year later with His Jazz Kings, crediting himself as composer. (To complicate the number's history, Melrose Music issued its version of "High Society" in 1931 under its own copyright, crediting the composition to Porter Steele and Walter Melrose. Melrose's edition uses two of Steele's four strains to make a Mortonesque "jazz" version of the piece. Williams seemed to take no notice of the Melrose version, and did not bring a lawsuit.) In the early 1930s there were a dozen or so instrumental recordings of "High Society," and Williams saw a chance to recycle the tune as a vocal. He chose the two best-known themes and put words to them. He published the result ("Music by A. J. Piron, Lyric by Clarence Williams") in 1933, with the Boswell Sisters' photo on the cover. When Williams reissued "High Society" in a folio in 1938, Steele had regained his composer credit, but Williams was still named as the song's lyricist.

The blues craze cooled in the late 1920s. Williams was released from his staff job at OKeh in 1928, and he began to record for several other labels. In a nonexclusive agreement, Williams was one of several artists—including King Oliver, Earl Hines, and Jelly Roll Morton—signed by Victor to a commitment of twelve to twenty-four sides per year. (His "exclusivity" to OKeh had not been total, but he had not done much moonlighting with other labels over the last five years.)

There was a tinge of desperation to the blues business now. A shifting market led to a change in the product. In the scramble for attention, several labels and artists began to deal in blues that bypassed the suggestive and went straight to the salacious. Hannah May and Sammy Sampson's "Pussy Cat Blues" ("You can play with my pussy but please don't dog it around. . . . "), Irene Scruggs' "I Must Get Mine in Front," and Bo Carter's "My Pencil Won't Write No More" exemplified the dirty blues trend of the early 1930s. Clarence Williams dabbled in smut a bit, singing "Wipe 'Em Off" and "The Dirty Dozen" with Lonnie Johnson for OKeh in 1930, and accompanying his and Henry Troy's "For Sale (Hannah Johnson's Jack Ass)" on Clara Smith's recording in 1931.

Early country artists were greatly influenced by the black blues of this period. Jimmie Rodgers created a persona that was equal parts outlaw and home boy, and the "outlaw" half was expressed in such songs as "High Powered Mama" and "Ground Hog Rootin' in My Front Yard." One of the first Rodgers imitators was Jimmie Davis, who began recording for Victor in 1929. Davis' sessions sometimes used black guitarists, and his Victor repertoire included "High Behind Blues," "Do-do-Daddling Thing," and "Organ Grinder Blues." Gene Autry's "Do Right Daddy Blues" says, "You can feel of my legs, You can feel of my thighs. . . ."

Bessie Smith, whose reputation was rougher than any other singer's when she began her recording career, didn't traffic in dirty songs nearly as much as others did in the early thirties. Williams made his last piano accompaniments for her in November 1931, when she sang "Need a Little Sugar in My Bowl" and "Safety Mama." Compared to the songs that were coming in the mid-thirties, such as Bessie Jackson's "Shave 'Em Dry" and Georgia White's "I'll Keep Sittin' on It," Smith's admission of "needing a little sugar in her bowl" seemed tame.

Smith's career was tottering by late 1931. Her mastery was universally acknowledged, but she seemed locked into a style of singing that was on its way out. The industry began to see her again as it had seen her in early 1923: she was too plain, too blunt, too countrified. She was serious business, and there was no cuteness in her. Bessie's life since 1923 had been a dual treadmill of recordings and stage appearances, and she had trooped all over the East and Midwest with her musicians, chorus girls, and dancers. Her show moved by private train, but by the mid-twenties her tours had become traveling brawls. She drank too much and fought incessantly with Jack Gee. When Gee stopped traveling with her, she began a series of affairs with chorus members of both sexes. She still called Philadelphia her home, but she was seldom there. She was a tough boss and a demanding performer. She took no nonsense from her troupe nor from the theatre owners who hired her. In 1927 in Concord, North Carolina, she faced down a pack of Klansmen who had come to disrupt her show, yelling obcenities at them until they fled.

In the mid-twenties Smith's recordings stood far above those of any other blues artist, in sales and in quality. She didn't favor a particular composer but chose her material from the spectrum of blues writers from Handy to J. C. Johnson. She could even bend pop material—such as "My Sweetie Went Away," "After You've Gone," and "Alexander's Ragtime Band"—to her will. And her own compositions, such as "Reckless Blues," "Backwater Blues," and "Young Woman's Blues," yielded some of her best recordings.

In April 1929 Jack Gee left Bessie for the last time. In May she suffered the embarrassment of being in Maceo Pinkard's abysmal *Pansy*, but in June she sang magnificently in her only film, the short *St. Louis Blues*. Although her billing was slipping, she kept trooping through the late twenties, listed at the middle or below on posters advertising variety shows at the Lafayette and the Apollo. Small labels and new singers were cutting into the blues market, and by 1930 Columbia was on the verge of bankruptcy. Smith was still singing well during this time, and she was writing well ("Poor Man's Blues," "In the House Blues," and "Long Road"). But her records were pressed in the thousands now instead of in hundreds of thousands. On November 20, 1931, after recording her last two sides with Clarence Williams, the ax fell: Frank Walker told her that Columbia was dropping her. She did the only thing she knew to do. She kept going with her stage shows, appearing wherever she could and taking the billing she could get. Her last recording session was arranged by John Hammond for OKeh in November 1933. There were four released sides and Smith was paid $150 for the day.

It would be a long climb back, but Smith was determined to make it. She worked up some current pop material for a stint at a Fifty-second Street club, the Famous Door, in February 1936. She did well there, but the engagement didn't entice anyone to record her. She took to the road again, shuttling around the South with a small troupe. Traveling apart from her company, driven from place to place in her old Packard by her current boyfriend, Richard Morgan, was her only star perk.

In the early morning hours of September 26, 1937, Smith and Morgan were traveling out of Memphis on Route 61, heading south to Clarksdale, Mississippi. A truck that had been parked on a narrow shoulder pulled onto the highway, and the Packard sideswiped it. The truck sped away. Dr. Hugh Smith, a Memphis surgeon who was traveling with a friend to get an early start on a fishing trip, came upon the scene of the accident. On the deserted road, Dr. Smith found a dazed Richard Morgan staggering about, and he saw Bessie Smith lying near the wreckage of her car, her right arm gone. Dr. Smith's friend found a house with a telephone and called an ambulance. By the time it arrived, Smith had lost too much blood. She died in the ambulance during the ten-mile ride to Clarksdale's black hospital. A white hospital was about the same distance away. There is no truth to the legend that Smith died because she was denied entrance to the white hospital. The ambulance driver, who was black, knew better than to take her there.

Radio helped Williams weather the changes in the music industry. Almost alone among publishers, he had seen the medium as an ideal method of plugging his product in the mid-1920s. Every network, as well as many local stations, had live orchestras on staff, and program schedules were studded with musical and variety shows. They all needed songs, yet most of Tin Pan Alley was as standoffish about radio as it had been about phonograph records a generation earlier. Williams and Eva Taylor always made time for radio, even when their publishing and recording schedules were hectic. WGBS was home base for Taylor, presenting her with the Clarence Williams Trio in a half-dozen formats. She worked almost as often at WOR (as "The Dixie Nightingale") and at WEAF. Taylor's was the only black voice heard in a coast-to-coast NBC broadcast on Christmas Day, 1929. She was featured in an NBC series called *Careless Love* in 1931, and the following year was a regular on WEAF's *Valspar Hour*, earning $350 a week. In 1934–1935 Taylor was all over the dial: on Wednesdays at noon on WJZ; on Thursdays at 6:45 P.M. on WEAF; on the Rye Crisp program on WJZ at 10:15 P.M; as soloist six times a week for eighteen weeks with the NBC Orchestra on WEAF's *Morning Glory Show*; on NBC's *Soft Lights and Sweet Music* program. Eva Taylor was not the best singer in town, nor was Williams the best musician, but they knew the power of radio for themselves and for their music company. In 1931, when many other publishers were closing shop, Clarence Williams left the Gaiety Building for new offices at 145 West Forty-fifth Street. He needed larger quarters.

Williams must have foreseen the coming of the big bands in the early 1930s, but he opted for supplying them with songs rather than putting out a big band of his own. Perhaps it is during this period, when the pressure to produce "all blues all the time" was off, that we may get an idea of what his personal tastes in music were. He took up the cause for James P. Johnson—as Perry Bradford had done earlier—and for Willie the Lion Smith. He published Johnson's "Modernistic" in late 1933 and Smith's "Finger Buster" in 1934 and "Love Remembers" and "Hot Things" in 1935. He issued a few of Smith's songs—with his own name attached—such as "Let Every Day Be Mother's Day" and "The Stuff Is Here and It's Mellow." Williams added his name to Smith's "Echo of Spring" in 1935 and to his "Harlem Joys" in 1937, but he issued these moody stride pieces, both of them unlikely to be published elsewhere. And Williams used both Johnson and Smith in the studio. They did not always get to shine in their Williams sessions—in his various jug bands, pickup orchestras, and washboard groups, and as accompanists for Williams' vocals—but he hired them when no one else would.

Williams' influence in the studios shrank in the mid-thirties. He made the first recordings of a new race series started by Decca in 1934, consisting of eight sides with his Alabama Jug Band with Willie Smith on piano. This didn't seem to be what Decca had in mind for its race numbers, and Williams was never asked back to the label. He went from a fifteen-side year in 1935 to no recordings at all in 1936. For the first time in many years, Williams wasn't on the lookout for new singers. Eva Taylor had made her last recording, one side in a brief reunion of the radio trio in May 1933. Williams played piano behind Josh White—recording under the name "Pinewood Tom"—on two sides for Banner in 1935 ("Black Gal" and "Milk Cow Blues"), and there were some odd orchestra-chorus dance arrangements of spirituals made for Lang-Worth in 1937. Williams mostly provided his own vocals during this time.

The last song that Williams seems to have really plugged was "I Can't Dance, I Got Ants in My Pants," written by the trumpeter Charlie Gaines. Williams heard of the song and went to Philadelphia, where Gaines and his band were appearing at the Club Dixie, to buy the rights. He got "I Can't Dance" for $100 plus transportation for Gaines and his sax player, Louis Jordan, to come to New York to make the song's premiere recording with the Williams orchestra in March 1934. Williams published the number, listing himself as composer and Gaines as lyricist. "I Can't Dance" didn't go far, nor did the old New Orleans folk tune, "My Bucket's Got a Hole in It," which Williams remembered and copyrighted in 1933. (He had claimed "Michigan Water Blues" as his own back in 1924.) He tried a few topical songs— "So Long, Huey Long," "Brown Bomber" (about the boxer Joe Louis), and "Peace, Brother, Peace" (inspired by Father Divine)—but with no success. He had a valuable backlog of copyrights, but their numbers weren't growing.

Williams issued James P. Johnson's "Over the Bars"—the new name of his 1917 "Steeplechase Rag"—and Willie Smith's "Rippling Waters" in 1939, but he was mostly recycling his copyrights in song folios during this time. He assembled collections built around Louis Armstrong, Fats Waller, and Clyde McCoy. He put out *Harry Carey's Western, Tropical and South Sea Island Songs*, as well as instruction books (*Learn to Sing*, *The International Drum Method*, and *How Your Play Can Crash Broadway*). In 1940 he issued his *Boogie Woogie Blues* folio, in which two of his twenties copyrights, "Cow Cow Blues" and "New

Orleans Hop Scop Blues," represented boogie. Clarence Williams Music was still prosperous, getting recordings of its material and signing with an Italian distributor in 1938. Williams went to New Orleans for Mardi Gras, taking Clarence, Jr., along to visit relatives and to see his adopted city. There was still much to celebrate when Williams played Santa—and sang "Santa Claus Blues"—at the company's office party that year.

Neighborhood schools and St. Benedict-the-Moor Roman Catholic Church in Queens had only to ask Williams and his family when benefit performers were needed for fund-raisers. His adolescent daughter Irene, who was the only one of the Williams children to go into show business, was an especially eager volunteer to sing for these causes. Mr. and Mrs. Williams sang "Baby, Won't You Please Come Home?" at the ASCAP Silver Jubilee in 1939. In 1940 Eva Taylor made a brief return to radio at WOR. That same year, rehearsing for retirement, Williams opened a shop in Harlem. He called it an "antique shop," but it was really a junk store. The only antiques were the Williams 78s in the back room.

The last commercial recording session for Williams was a reunion of the Blue Five, with Eva Taylor's vocals and James P. Johnson as copianist, on two sides for Bluebird in October 1941. The last publication was a trunk song, probably written years earlier, by Williams and Piron called "Mama's Got It" in 1942. It was time to go, but while he was still a working publisher, there was a favor to be done for an old friend. Armand Piron was ill in New Orleans, and he was worried about money. He asked Williams to help him get into ASCAP, because he needed the royalties that any of his live copyrights might bring. Williams piloted Piron's application through channels and Piron became an ASCAP member in 1942, the year before he died.

In early 1943 Decca Records made Williams an offer for his catalog, and Williams took it. The rumored price was $50,000—a bargain, considering the fact that Decca supposedly got over a thousand copyrights. Taylor said that Williams retained a third interest in the company and half-interest in his own compositions. He really was a shopkeeper now, sitting in a chair in front of his place in Harlem, easily accessible to the stray dogs that he loved to feed and to any jazz fans who happened to drop by. His name was seen on the *Billboard* charts in the late 1940s as composer of two hit vocal recordings by Johnny Mercer. Mercer rewrote the lyric to Williams' "You're Some Pretty Doll," renaming it "Ugly Chile," in 1946, and he had another success with "Sugar Blues" in 1947.

Williams moved his family to Brooklyn in the early 1950s. In case anyone had forgotten, he had business cards printed that identified himself as "The Originator of Jazz and Boogie-Woogie," giving his 717A Madison Street address. In 1953 he was seriously injured when he was struck by a taxi, but he recovered well enough to appear at the Town Hall benefit for James P. Johnson in 1955. Diabetes plagued his last years, causing him to lose his sight in the late fifties. He moved back to his old Jamaica neighborhood in 1959, and he died in Queens General Hospital on November 6, 1965.

Perhaps Williams' busy life is best remembered for its busyness. He didn't just send his songs to market, he took them, in every medium available to him at the time. For all his hundreds of recordings, he had few hit records of his own (Sara Martin's "Sugar Blues" and one or two others). He used the studio as an aural billboard to announce his publications and to demonstrate them to those who would have the hits with them. Willie Smith said, "Clarence was a great publisher. . . . In all fairness I want to point out that he was an inspiration to all of us. . . . He inspired and helped us to get our original compositions published"—and played—and recorded. As Smith pointed out, Clarence Williams was the first New Orleans musician to have any influence in the New York music industry. He knew how to get things done, and he knew a good song when he heard one.

J. MAYO WILLIAMS

In the mid-1920s, when blues and jazz and black singers were rejuvenating the record business, there was only one black record executive, J. Mayo Williams. During his long career, he worked at three major labels and a half-dozen minor ones. The blues talents that he discovered in Chicago were nearer the taproots of the music than were the Harlem club singers who constituted New York's first wave of artists. Mayo Williams was not a folklorist nor an archivist. He was out to make the most successful commercial recordings that he could. But during his tenure at Paramount, the company's roster contained the names of singers who would never have been recorded in New York. Williams was the first to record male blues singers extensively, and some of his male artists were first-generation blues performers. Several of them made their first records under Williams' supervision, after years of traveling the byways of the South where they—and the music—had come from.

J. Mayo Williams

Mayo Williams alone among 1920s producers stuck with the blues throughout the 1930s. As mainstream pop music changed, he helped to change the blues, to make the music commercially viable in the big-band era. The sound that he pioneered in the mid-thirties was the first step taken toward rhythm and blues. He walked a tightrope through twenty years of being the only black employee in his companies. He never expected much in the way of promotions and pay raises, and he never got much. His money mostly came from the shady sidelines of publishing companies that didn't publish and from songs that he didn't write which bore his name. He was usually on commission, betting that the royalties he received on his companies' products, as well as the copyrights and kickbacks from musicians that he hired, would add up to a living. He was good at what he did, and he lived very well. He stayed in for the long haul, from the days of making records by singing into cardboard horns to the days of *Billboard* charts and race radio. He steered the blues our way.

J. Mayo Williams was born in 1894 in Monmouth, Illinois, a small town west of Galesburg in the northwestern part of the state. His family was relatively well-off, and if it had not been for the influence of his mother, who loved popular music, he probably would have shared the general black middle-class disdain for the blues. His enjoyment of music was strictly that of a listener. He didn't play an instrument, and he knew little about music. Mayo was a good student in high school and an avid participant in athletics, especially football and track. His grades—and the intercession of an alumnus—got him into Brown University in Providence, Rhode Island, where football and philosophy were his main interests. He graduated in 1921, with a Phi Beta Kappa key and vague notions of a career in banking.

After graduation, Williams went to Chicago, where his mother was living. He played football for a season or two with the Hammond (Indiana) Pros, a black team that was then part of the NFL. His stint with the Pros allowed him to live at home with his mother in nearby Chicago. He halfheartedly investigated opportunities in banking, but the low starting salaries dampened his interest in the profession. He stalled for a time, running bootleg gin for various South Side nightclubs. A fraternity brother, Joe Bibb, started a radical weekly called *The Chicago Whip*, and he asked Williams to write the sports column. Besides running the *Whip*, Bibb also acted as a distributor for Harry Pace's Black Swan records. Bibb let Williams in on his sideline and made him a collection agent for Black Swan. In the summer of 1922, Williams noted the fact that a local company, Paramount, had begun a race series of its own. In the spring of 1923 he decided to investigate the possibility of working in the record industry.

With his curiosity about the business as his only credential, Williams made the train trip to Paramount's headquarters at Port Washington, Wisconsin, a small town on Lake Michigan, nearly a hundred miles north of Chicago, to apply for a job. He had no idea if a job existed or whether the company would consider a black applicant, so he thought it best just to drop in. Late in his life, he remembered the children who followed him as he made his way from the train station to the Paramount office. There was not a single African-American resident of Port Washington, and they were amazed to see a black face.

As inexperienced as he was, he talked a good line to the Paramount executives, who knew even less than he about the music business. He presented himself as a newspaper writer. Since none of them knew what the *Whip* was—much less knew of its militant editorial stance—the executives eagerly mistook Williams for someone with connections in the black press. When he left the office, he had a job. It was not exactly a job in the record business, but that would soon follow. Working for bosses who didn't know the territory would prove to be both a blessing and a curse to Mayo Williams in his years at Paramount.

Paramount Records was a subsidiary of the Wisconsin Chair Company. In 1888 the company's founder, Frederick A. Dennett, had bought a moribund sash and door factory in Port Washington, and by the mid-nineties he had made the beginnings of a furniture empire. He invested in Michigan timberlands to ensure his lumber supply, and he added various specialty products to his output, including spring mattresses, school furniture, and cabinets for Edison phonographs. He bought the Sheboygan Knitting Company and the Northern Couch Company to add to his enterprises in the new century. By the early teens, the phonograph cabinet business seemed to be a branch to bet on. Designers were learning how to hide the odd-looking tin horns of the talking machines inside the cabinets, and record-players were being sold as decorative furniture (in furniture stores). About half a million American homes had phonographs in 1914, and there were sixteen manufacturers to supply them with the instruments. By 1919 two-and-a-quarter-million homes had phonographs, and growth looked like a permanent condition to Dennett. The big three labels—Edison, Columbia, and Victor—were cranking out records, and the record industry was attracting investors from non-related sources. The Starr Piano Company began producing Gennett Records in Richmond, Indiana, in 1915, and the bowling ball manufacturer, Brunswick, began putting out records bearing its name in 1916. In 1917 Dennett followed suit: he converted his Northern Couch Company to the manufacture of "phonographs and phonographic records" and renamed it United Phonograph Corporation. United Phonograph called its two record labels Puritan and Paramount.

Throughout its history. Paramount Records always operated from the point of view of a furniture company. Its bosses were not especially interested in, and surely never listened to, its product. They saw records as a necessary evil, as the things that perpetuated the need for phonograph cabinets. They went into the record business without knowing anything about it, and they never learned. United Phonograph's top executives would always be chair people at heart. The person in charge of Paramount Records was Otto E. Moeser, a furniture-plant supervisor who rarely left Port Washington.

Moeser thought the company should have a New York presence, so he opened a Paramount Records office there in 1918 and put a mechanical engineer named Maurice Supper in charge. Supper was an excellent draftsman, and he designed Paramount's "eagle" label. The company leased its first recording studio, at 1140 Broadway. For a while the company was doing more shifting of personnel than making records, and in the first of many formal and informal organizational shuffles, Supper was summoned to Port Washington and named sales manager in 1919. The New York recording director's job was given to an Englishman, Art Satherley, who was Dennett's son-in-law.

A year or so into its operation, Paramount had a couple of the basics under control: they had made some records and had issued them. The biggest names among Paramount's first artists were two tenors, Billy Murray and Henry Burr. Both had been around since cylinder days. Each had sold a lot of records in his time, but neither sold much for Paramount. When the world was going mad for Al Jolson and the Original Dixieland Jazz Band, Paramount was offering the top artists of fifteen years earlier. And there was plenty of competition by the time Paramount entered the field. Besides the three giants, there was Emerson—a company that began in 1916 and shook up the industry by offering seven-inch discs that sold for twenty-five cents—as well as OKeh and Gennett.

Competition for the public's entertainment dollar came from other media besides records. An evening at the movies could be had for a quarter, and a piece of sheet music cost fifty cents. Dinner at a respectable New York restaurant could be had for sixty cents. The biggest Ziegfeld stars could be seen in the *Midnight Frolic* for two dollars. A three-minute record (designed for 50–100 plays) was usually priced at seventy-five cents. And in this time, when per capita income was $600 a year, a quality phonograph could cost anywhere from $125 to $750. The record business was dicier than Frederick Dennett ever dreamed it would be. There was profit to be made, but neither Dennett, his plant foremen, nor his in-laws knew how to make it. (Dennett died in 1920, but his foggy grasp of the record business remained firmly in place after his death.)

The Paramount pressing plant—a converted furniture factory—was located in Grafton, Wisconsin, eight miles southwest of Port

Washington, and it turned out a very shoddy product. It used cheap materials and it relied on the old-fashioned hand-stamping system to press its records long after most companies had gone to automated pressing. Paramount had the poorest sound of any seventy-five-cent record: thin, with erratic levels and, often, with scratches built in.

Despite the terrible quality of its work, the Paramount plant was given a contract in 1921 that the company's executives hoped would turn its losses around. Harry Pace, the New York businessman who was the first black owner of a record company, decided to farm out much of the pressing of his Black Swan records to the Grafton plant. Paramount executives were impressed by the amount of business they were getting from Pace during his boom year of 1922. The race business began to look attractive to them. So, without any more consideration or analysis than they had given to the making and selling of records in 1917, Paramount decided to get into the race market in the summer of 1922. The furniture men were committing to make records for consumers who could never afford the fine, cabinet-model phonographs they were trying so hard to sell. The race record audience usually heard its music on the cheap, portable players designed for camp use by soldiers during World War I. The company issued about twenty race records the first year, fourteen of those by Alberta Hunter. Hunter had defected from Black Swan to Paramount, and her "Down Hearted Blues," recorded in New York, gave the label its first minor hit.

The infusion of Black Swan money into the Grafton plant helped for a year or so, but Black Swan began to sink in early 1923. In the summer of that year, Harry Pace stopped all of his recording activities. Paramount was left holding carloads of Black Swan records and dozens of Pace's unpaid pressing bills. Pace was near bankruptcy. He offered Paramount the Black Swan masters and inventory to cancel his debts, and Paramount took them. Paramount was losing about $100,000 a year in the early twenties, and it had to go deeper into the business or get out. Literally by default, and in desperation, Paramount entered the race record business in a big way. With the addition of Black Swan's hundred or so masters to the fifty or so of its own, Paramount's 12000 series was suddenly a major player in the race business. (The actual sale of Black Swan to Paramount did not occur until April 1924. Paramount began issuing the Black Swan inventory under its own imprint in May of that year.) The Wisconsin executives had to put aside their personal tastes, hold their noses, and figure out how to record and sell the blues.

It was just at this time, when the company's own race series was flat and Harry Pace's outstanding debts were beginning to worry the Paramount brass, that J. Mayo Williams entered the Port Washington office. He was bright, he was black, he was handsome and well-spoken—and he knew newspaper people. It made great sense to take him on in some capacity. He wasn't a Dennett in-law or a chair man, so he couldn't be given executive status. And he was the wrong color to be listed among the Paramount officials in the annual report.

Maurice Supper had an idea of where to use Mayo Williams. Supper had timidly entered the publishing business in January 1923. He knew no more about publishing than he knew about records, but he knew that copyrights were valuable things to have, that you could make money two ways if you owned the songs that you recorded. In late 1922 Supper had lost the rights to Alberta Hunter's "Down Hearted Blues" when she sold it to Jack Mills. To prevent a hit from getting away again, Supper formed the Chicago Music Company, with himself as president, his wife as secretary, and his brother-in-law as "director." Supper never intended to publish the songs recorded by Paramount's race artists, but he wanted to own the rights to them. Inaugurating Chicago Music was one of the smarter moves made by a Paramount official of that time, and it was made as an afterthought, as Supper's personal venture. (Supper would later add cosmetics to his portfolio. He manufactured and sold a brand of hair straightener named for Black Patti.)

Chicago Music could employ Williams and let him work for Paramount in a position that was not in the organizational chain of command and was therefore not too visible. Williams was named "manager" of Chicago Music—a glorified clerical position—and was given a small salary to administer Supper's copyrights. Incidentally (and without salary), Williams would find talent for Paramount's race series, as well as arrange and supervise studio sessions. In return for his efforts at Paramount, Williams would receive one half of the two-cents-per-record-sold royalty that was allotted to the publisher of recorded songs. It was more of an opportunity than a job, but it was a place to begin. Within a few weeks of his hiring, Mayo Williams would be indispensable to Paramount Records.

Williams saw the big picture and saw his place in it. Because his real income—the informal, penny-a-copy royalty—depended on Paramount's selling records, he knew he must not trust his livelihood to the men who owned the label. He quickly insinuated himself into the process. He took charge of Paramount's record-making in Chicago, acting as an independent producer, and his bosses gladly stayed out of his way. (Art Satherly was still bumbling along in New York. Williams' Chicago successes would far outstrip Satherly's, and the New York office would close in 1928.)

Williams got the Chicago Music offices organized first. He rented space in the Overton Bank Building, at Thirty-sixth and State streets, and he hired Althea Dickerson as his secretary. She was bright and efficient, and she knew the Chicago music scene better than Williams did. Besides being a pianist and an aspiring songwriter, Dickerson owned a small record store and did some booking of acts for local theatres. She was a go-getter and plainly ambitious. Williams kept enough of his operations secret from her so that she could not go after his job.

He knew that Paramount's singers would be the source of songs for Chicago Music, so he never hired staff composers. He did need an arranger, though, and he hired Georgia Tom Dorsey (1899–1993) to transcribe songs—for the filing of copyrights—from records at $3 per lead sheet. On the rare occasions when a particular song was wanted for a Paramount artist, Williams would buy it outright for $50 or so. He could usually get a singer's own material for $5 to $20 a song at the end of a recording session. Artists rarely thought about the disposition of their copyrights, and by the time a song was committed to wax, the connection between selling the song to Chicago Music and getting one's record released was all too obvious to the performer. Williams' name is on surprisingly few Chicago Music songs as co-writer—about fifteen of the 700 or so songs recorded during his time at Paramount— but he often cleaned up the lyrics that singers brought him, to make *double entendre* out of single *entendre*.

Williams began scouting for singers. Maurice Supper allowed him to record anyone he wanted to, the only rule being that an artist must sell at least 10,000 records to qualify for a second recording session. He went to the Dreamland Cafe (where Alberta Hunter was a mainstay), the Deluxe Gardens, and the Grand Theatre. He saw enough over-produced stage shows to realize that many singers made their effect on an audience by their dancing and visual trappings rather than by their voices. He was looking for those who could hold an audience by their singing alone. For this reason, he frequented the Monogram Theatre, a rundown T.O.B.A. house on South State Street, that hired no elaborate acts simply because it couldn't afford them. Lovie Austin (1887–1972) was the pit pianist at the Monogram, and she often gave Williams tips on who was booked there and how they were doing.

Mayo Williams' first important find was Ida Cox, a woman who, he said, just "stood flat-footed and sang" at the Monogram. In June 1923 Cox and Lovie Austin went into the Paramount studio—which was even seedier than the Monogram—to record three sides: "Any Woman's Blues," "'Bama Bound Blues," and "Lovin' Is the Thing I'm Wild About." Cox's hard, clear voice and her blunt, cynical lyrics would be heard on nearly eighty sides during her six years of recording for Paramount, often accompanied by Lovie Austin and Her Serenaders, sometimes backed by the piano playing of her husband, Jesse Crump. Cox's records were steady sellers, and her successes included "Death Letter Blues," "Chicago Monkey Man Blues" (which became Jimmy Rushing's "Goin' to Chicago Blues"), and "Wild Women Don't Have the Blues."

Mayo Williams saw "race records" as being more than blues, and he diversified the Paramount catalog in ways that would never have occurred to Supper. The fine pianist Jimmy Blythe (c. 1901–1931) became Paramount's utility man in 1924, recording solos, accompanying singers, and playing with jazz groups and bands. Blythe's presence paved the way for other pianists, such as Cow Cow Davenport (1895–1955), Will Ezell, and Blind Leroy Garnett at the label. Williams first recorded Jelly Roll Morton and His Orchestra in June 1923 and got King Oliver's Jazz Band in for a side in December of that year. He used Freddie Keppard's Jazz Cardinals to accompany a singer in 1926. (Oliver and Keppard must not have hit the 10,000 mark in sales, because they were not asked back. Morton must have made it, because he recorded for Williams again in the spring of 1924.) Late in 1923 Williams began recording the spirituals of the Norfolk Jubilee

Quartet, a group whose tenure at Paramount would be longer than his own. Early in 1924 Paramount issued some burlesque sermons by "Elder Take It All," and in the summer of 1925 the label began to issue the real thing, three-minute sermons by the Reverend W. A. White. The

Ma Rainey

Reverend J. M. Gates, who came to Paramount in late 1926, would become the label's most prolific preacher, with a dozen recorded sermons.

Williams' most important discovery occurred in late 1923. He saw a homely woman, nearly forty years old and lately up from the South, adorned with gobs of jewelry and a mouthful of gold teeth, take the stage of the Monogram and mesmerize her audience. She was billed as Ma Rainey, and Williams had never heard anyone like her. She was born

Gertrude Pridgett in Muscogee County, Georgia, in 1886, and she had been singing the blues since the early century. In 1904 she married a vaudevillian, William "Pa" Rainey, and they had trooped the Southeast, playing under canvas. She became as big a name as a tent show performer could be, with a wide and loyal following. The Raineys took Bessie Smith into their troupe in the early teens, and they watched Smith's star rise steadily after she left them. The blues boom of the early twenties expanded Ma Rainey's professional horizons, and she began to make forays into the North as she had never done before. Williams knew he had a winner in Ma Rainey, and, without asking Supper's permission, he made an unprecedented show of faith in her by recording eight sides in her first session, in December 1923.

For all her tent-show garishness, Ma Rainey was closer to the roots of the blues than any other female performer of the 1920s. She sang about boll weevils, mining camps, moonshine, hoodoo, screech owls, and the corns on her feet. The banjo is prominent in most of her recordings with a band—often drowning out the piano—giving a rough, homemade edge to her sound. Her horns growl and grind after her phrases, and her band seems to be recorded at the same level as she. She is not jamming with them exactly, but she is one of them, giving out with abandon as they are. She stuck close to the old twelve-bar form, and one of her songs, "See See Rider," is the paradigm of country blues. Rainey recorded exclusively for Paramount, and her dark-brown contralto was heard on more than ninety sides. Her "See See Rider"—made in October 1924, with Louis Armstrong temporarily a member of Her Georgia Band—was the biggest of her many successful recordings. Within six months of her debut, Rainey was outselling everyone else on the Paramount roster. She was given her own "label," with her name at the top, larger than Paramount's, and her picture on it.

Ma Rainey's record label

In the summer of 1924 Mayo Williams produced the first hit record by a male blues performer, Papa Charlie Jackson, whom Williams had heard on a Chicago streetcorner. Jackson accompanied himself on the banjo, and Williams saw him more as a novelty act than as a blues singer. But Jackson had a success with his first record ("Papa's Lawdy Lawdy Blues" and "Airy Man Blues"), and he would have another the following year with "Shake That Thing." Jackson would grow into a surprisingly versatile performer at Paramount, mostly recording his own work but sometimes singing duets with Ida Cox and playing his banjo with various bands.

Williams' success with Charlie Jackson inspired other producers to record blues men, of course. Women blues singers always dominated the field, but male artists brought something new to recorded blues. Some would call the new element authenticity, others would call it amateurishness. The early male blues singers had no theatrical polish to them, because they had rarely played in theatres. Their milieu were the honky-tonks, barrelhouses, and street corners of the small-town

South. They were wanderers, and by necessity they played inexpensive and portable instruments—guitars, harmonicas, banjos. They hollered, they kept time by stamping their feet, they growled and rasped, they had idiosyncratic instrumental techniques or no technique at all. Many of them had streaks of poetry in their lyrics, but often their lyrics were unintelligible. Their recordings would be more important as captured folklore than as commercial entertainment. There is a primal sound to the blues men of the 1920s, as though they are singing to us from aeons ago. Indeed, they are a link to the dawn of the blues. Their music was rough and raw, and, with a handful of exceptions, they would never approach the sales or the crossover appeal of the blues women.

As word got out about Williams' position with Paramount, singers and musicians began to pester him. They wanted auditions and session work, wanted their songs published. He was offered bribes and given threats. Unknown singers plied him with the promise of sexual favors. (Williams was responsible for much of his own harassment. In his first year, he put a blurb—accompanied by his photo—into the Chicago *Defender* announcing himself as "manager of the Race Artists' Series" and asking for "suggestions and recommendations" on material and artists to be recorded.) Because he was badgered everywhere he went, he began to turn the scouting missions over to Althea Dickerson, and he affected a chilly reserve in his dealings with musicians. He didn't pal around with anyone he recorded.

Williams kept a tight rein on his sessions, too. He demanded that his performers rehearse before they got into the studio. Family and friends of performers were not allowed in. Drinking was permitted in the studio only until it affected performance. Two or three flubbed takes were enough to cancel a session forever. Paramount used the studio facilities of Orlando R. Marsh, an engineer who rented space in the Lyons & Healy Building on South Wabash Street. Marsh's recording operation was as primitive as Paramount's pressing plant in Grafton was. He used old recording equipment, and his studio's insulation was such that summer heat and winter cold played tricks on the delicate recording wax. (One session was lost because mice scratched the masters that had been left in a box overnight.) The studio's proximity to the el tracks made it often necessary to stop recording while the trains roared by.

Each session began with about a half an hour of testing to find the artist's and accompaniment's proper distances from the horn that caught the sound. (Marsh did not convert to electrical recording until late in 1926, a year after everyone else did.) Williams preferred to schedule only one session per day, and he hoped to get three or four songs down in as many hours. When the session ended, it was time for settling up with the performers. Most of the singers got a flat fee of $50-$60 per usable side, plus an extra $5 or $10 per composition turned over to Chicago Music. A featured accompanist got $10 per side, and other musicians got $5. After the performers left, Williams chose the songs to be issued and the cuts to send to Grafton. He liked a weak B side, because he didn't want two hits on the same disc.

The success of Mayo Williams' artists lent a prestige to Paramount that it had never had before. His batting average was high. More than half of the performers he took into the studio sold the requisite 10,000 records to qualify for a second session. After years of recording nonentities and has-beens, the label was coming alive. It was time to do something about marketing. In the first six months of the race series, before Williams arrived, sales strategies had been practically nonexistent. There were ads in the *Defender*, but nowhere else. The primary distribution method was to sell stacks of records to Pullman porters for seventy-five cents each, so that the porters would take them on their runs through the South and sell them for a dollar.

The company stepped up its sales efforts, running larger and more florid ads. With dime-novel graphics, a dozen typefaces, and drawings or photos of the stars, the *Defender* trumpeted the newest releases from Paramount: "Hear Ida Cox pray, plead and moan for her daddy to do her right. You can almost see the tears in her eyes—the ache in her heart—as she sobs this wonderful, pleading 'Do Lawd Do' Blues"; "It takes 'Ma' Rainey—the Mother of the Blues—to sing a hit like this. Hear her tell the shebas to leave her man alone—hear about what she's gonna do with a bulldog if her man don't quit foolin' 'round"; "Thousands of you know and love Chicago's noted pastor, Reverend William Arthur White. Ever since the old days when he was the 'boy evangelist,' he has been 'Preacher White' throughout the Middle West and South. Now, in his great Paramount Record No. 12302, *he solves the question of evolution*—the great religious topic that so stirred the country just a few weeks ago. Be sure to get this record—you'll never grow tired of it." Most of the ads contained coupons for ordering records from Port Washington.

Paramount hired door-to-door salesmen—part-time and working on commission—to place its records around Chicago. Otto Moeser noticed that his records sold particularly well in the South, so he hired jobbers to get them into more stores there: drugstores, dry goods stores, and furniture stores, as well as department stores and music shops. Paramount's star jobber was Harry Charles, a hunchbacked white man who had run the music department of E. E. Forbes Piano Company in Birmingham, Alabama. Charles loved black music, and when the chance came to tear around the South on Paramount's behalf, he took it. His territory covered thirteen states, and he wore out a car every three months. His first stop in any city was not at a store to be targeted but at a black neighborhood, where he hired young men to act out a little playlet that he had written as a sales tool. While Charles was pitching his product to a store owner, the young men whom he had enlisted would enter the store, waving cash and eager to buy Paramount records and only Paramount records. After such dramatic evidence of demand, Charles usually left a store with orders in his pocket. (Other labels had wily salesmen, as well. One of OKeh's jobbers got his company's records stocked in a St. Louis funeral home.)

Although Mayo Williams was never recognized as a company employee, he was recognized as the reason for the upswing in Paramount's fortunes. He was given a company car. Otto Moeser even came down from Port Washington to consult with him occasionally. (Moeser never went to Williams' office. He usually stayed at the Palmer House, and Williams had to use the freight elevator to get up to his room.) Williams' royalty income was mounting up, so Moeser gave him investment tips, which he took to his advantage. Williams reciprocated by ordering the furniture for his apartment from the Wisconsin Chair Company.

With Paramount finally on its feet after a seven-year struggle, the furniture men would make a series of decisions in 1924–1925 that would lead to its downfall. In the summer of 1924 Maurice Supper closed the Chicago Music Company. While Chicago Music had fulfilled its purpose as a repository for copyrights, it had also been used as a place to hide Paramount's profits on its race series from the tax collector. False reports had been filed, and Supper was getting nervous. He thought it wisest to shut Chicago Music and remove its paperwork from the prying eyes of auditors. The closing of Williams' "official" business made little difference to him. He was turning out lots of records and doing well on his royalties. If the restructuring had stopped there, Paramount—and Williams—could have continued to prosper.

But in early 1925, Supper left his position as sales manager to open a mail-order record business in Port Washington. (Supper was on salary at Paramount and he was peeved to learn that some of his jobbers, with their padded expense accounts, were making more than he.) Supper's job should have gone to someone who knew the record business—someone like Mayo Williams or Harry Charles. But of course, it did not. Arthur C. Laibly, a salesman for the Wisconsin Chair Company, was named to replace Supper. Laibly, who had played the violin in Cincinnati dance orchestras as a young man, was eager to take a hands-on approach to his new job. Laibly was given the dual post of Sales Manager and Recording Director. With Laibly's new title, the organizational gray area in which Mayo Williams had operated so well vanished.

Williams went on as he had before, heavily recording Paramount's surefire race artists, Ma Rainey, Ida Cox, and Charlie Jackson. But in late 1925 Arthur Laibly, bypassing Williams, planned a record session for a discovery of his own. The success of Laibly's new singer would shake the foundations of Mayo Williams' fiefdom at Paramount.

A Dallas record salesman, R. T. Ashford, wrote to Laibly, urging him to record a local blues singer named Blind Lemon Jefferson (1897–1929). Wishing to accommodate an important regional representative, and to sell a lot of records in Dallas, Laibly agreed to record the singer he had never heard. Jefferson was sent for, and early in 1926 he recorded four sides for Paramount in Chicago. One of these, "Long Lonesome Blues," took off like a shot when it was released in the spring. Laibly wanted more from Blind Lemon Jefferson. Jefferson recorded over a dozen sides in 1926, all of them in Laibly's sessions, and his sales leapt to levels previously achieved only by Ma Rainey and Bessie Smith. Laibly's dumb luck in finding Jefferson stunned Mayo Williams, and it weakened his footing at Paramount.

Blind Lemon Jefferson was the best entertainer as well as the most imaginative musician and singer of all the early blues men. He was the first of them to have a dazzling guitar technique. His single-note runs could be delicate or powerful, and his ideas for fills and breaks were inexhaustible. His rhythm was impeccable, and his agile voice was the perfect complement to his playing. It could swoop or stab or ride high over his busy guitar, lonesome as a train whistle late at night. Jefferson's songs were his own—infinite variations on ancient twelve-bar themes. His blues ran the gamut of country subjects, and they were shot through with humor. Jefferson's "Matchbox Blues" of 1927 was another huge seller, and by the end of that year, Jefferson was given Paramount's highest accolade, a bright yellow label with his picture on it. He was lured away briefly by OKeh, but he would return to Paramount to record up to the time of his mysterious death in late 1929 or early 1930. (Various stories say that he succumbed to a heart attack, froze to death on a Chicago street, or drank poisoned coffee. Paramount marked his passing by issuing a song called "Wasn't It Sad about Lemon?" with a sermon called "The Death of Blind Lemon" on the other side.)

The great success of Blind Lemon Jefferson caused Laibly to think of himself as a perceptive finder and producer of talent. Paramount put out the word among their jobbers in the South that more singer-guitarists like Blind Lemon Jefferson would be welcome at the label. Harry Charles, now off the road and running a talent agency in Birmingham, began to recommend singers to Laibly. Charles brought one of them— a singer he called "Bo Weavil Jackson" (no one at Paramount ever knew his real name)—to Chicago, and Laibly duly recorded him. Thus began a parade of Charles' clients—Lucille Bogan, Buddy Boy Hawkins, Cow Cow Davenport—into the Paramount studios at Laibly's behest. In early 1927 Harry Charles was hired to oversee and approve all of Paramount's race releases, at a two-cents-a-record royalty, a better deal than Mayo Williams had.

There was nothing for Williams to do but get on Laibly's bandwagon and search for his own country blues talent. His most promising discovery was a Floridian named Blind Blake (c. 1890–c. 1933), who made his first Paramount sides in the summer of 1926. Blake recorded frequently for Paramount, but his sales never approached Jefferson's.

Laibly was chipping away at Williams' power. In a gesture that was both canny and symbolic, he took Althea Dickerson as his own secretary.

In the spring of 1927, a disgruntled Dennett son-in-law, E. J. Barrett, came to Williams with a proposition that they start a record company to rival Paramount. Barrett had $30,000 seed money from Richard Gennett, whose brother owned Gennett Records. Williams was dissatisfied enough to accept Barrett's offer, but he could not risk everything by cutting his ties to Paramount. He decided to have it both ways, and he was so far out of the loop at Paramount by this time that he got away with it. Williams ran the new label, which was named Black Patti, out of his Paramount office. He hired his wife, Aleta, as his secretary, and Black Patti began by reissuing several dozen old Gennett sides. Only a handful of new records appeared on the label. The secret was hard to keep, and the sales of the old Gennetts were abysmal. By late summer Black Patti had folded, and, without the company's learning that he had ever been moonlighting for someone else, Mayo Williams went back to working full time for Paramount.

A few months after the collapse of Black Patti, Otto Moeser informed Williams that Paramount was putting him on straight salary, with no more royalties on records sold. It was more than a slap in the face, it was an economic comedown that Williams couldn't abide. Laibly had won. Williams resigned, and Moeser made him a cash payment to relinquish his interest in any songs owned by Chicago Music Company. Early in 1928 Mayo Williams left Paramount.

Paramount lasted a few more years under Arthur Laibly's stewardship. Ma Rainey made her last side in December 1928 and then returned to the tent-show circuit from which she had come. Ida Cox's career wound down, and she issued her last two sides for Paramount in 1929. The death of Blind Lemon Jefferson was a great loss to the company's roster. Laibly closed the New York and Chicago studios in a cost-cutting move and transferred his recording operations to the Grafton pressing plant in 1929. There were a few major talents found by Paramount's Southern scouts in the early 1930s—such as Charley Patton (1887–1934), Son House (1902–1988), and Skip James—(1902–1969)—but there were also many bad records made on the advice of Laibly's jobbers. In 1927 Laibly introduced a hillbilly series that never sold as well as the race series. But because Laibly liked them,

country artists eventually made up 50 percent of the company's catalog. The last record issued in Paramount's race series was made by a
black stringband, the Mississippi Sheiks. The series, and the label,
went out of business in August 1932.

J. Mayo Williams landed on his feet. He was snapped up by Jack Kapp,
who was the Chicago administrator of Brunswick's race series, which
was issued by its two-year-old subsidiary, Vocalion. The blues industry
was in for some heavy weather over the next few years, but in early
1928 Vocalion's prospects looked bright. At Paramount Mayo Williams
had introduced the gritty Chicago blues sound to the world, and the
world had bought it. He was brought to Vocalion to produce more of
the same. With State Street Music as his nonpublishing "publishing"
arm, Williams was ready to go.

Williams' first session to produce a hit at Vocalion was in
November 1928. Ma Rainey's pianist, Georgia Tom Dorsey, had
teamed with a guitarist named Hudson Whittaker (who was known as
"Tampa Red") to play with various small bands around Chicago.
Dorsey and Whittaker brought in a song they had written called "It's
Tight Like That" to be sung by Frankie "Half-Pint" Jaxon, accompa-
nied by Tampa Red's Hokum Jug Band. "Tight Like That" was a frisky,
sexy number with an irresistible scuffling beat. It caught on quickly and
remained popular through the winter of 1928–1929. McKinney's
Cotton Pickers put it out on Victor about three weeks after its first
recording by the Hokum band, and Jimmy Noone's Apex Club
Orchestra made it for Vocalion in late December. Clara Smith picked
it up in January 1929, and Tampa Red remade it as a guitar solo for
Vocalion. Of course, it was owned by State Street Music, so there was
no song sheet issued until it was sold to Melrose Brothers.

"Tight Like That" flirted with boogie woogie, and Mayo Williams'
next hit consummated the affair. The pianist Cow Cow Davenport
took the unusual step of recommending a rival to Williams. Davenport
had heard a flashy young player at the Monogram and thought that

Williams should record him. His name was Clarence "Pinetop" Smith (1904–1929), and he was boogie woogie personified. Williams auditioned Smith, then quickly set up a session for him at the Vocalion studios in the Furniture Mart building, at 623 South Wabash, in December 1928. Pinetop Smith would record only eight sides, all for Vocalion, in his brief studio career, but one of them, his "Pinetop's Boogie Woogie," would create a new genre of popular piano-playing. It was recorded several times during the mid-thirties, and it was the foundation of the boogie woogie craze of 1938–1939. It was not published until 1937, when Williams sold it to Melrose, but many ambitious players learned it from Pinetop's Vocalion recording long before the sheet music appeared. Smith immediately became the artist that Vocalion had the highest hopes for. Mayo Williams was waiting for him in the Vocalion studio on the afternoon of March 15, 1929, when Smith's wife came in to tell him that her husband had been shot and killed in a brawl at a Masonic Hall dance early that morning. Pinetop Smith had turned twenty-five a few weeks before his death.

Vocalion entered the new decade with a strong catalog. Bertha "Chippie" Hill (1905–1950) had recorded for the label in 1928–1929—often accompanied by Georgia Tom Dorsey—and the greatest of the country blues women, Memphis Minnie (1897–1973), began recording for Vocalion in 1930. Memphis Minnie, whose real name was Lizzie Douglas, was one of the few blues women to play guitar, and she often recorded with her husband Joe McCoy's Memphis Jug Band. Her "Bumble Bee Blues" and "Hustlin' Woman Blues" were frank and earthy in the Ma Rainey manner. The pianist-singer Leroy Carr (1905–1935) and his guitarist Scrapper Blackwell (1903–1962) began their long association with Vocalion in 1928. Tampa Red's Hokum Jug Band followed up "Tight Like That" with "She Can Love So Good" in late 1930.

It was during this period that Mayo Williams' name began to appear on record labels as cocomposer of one of the most enduring blues songs, "Corrine, Corrina." ("Corrine, Corrina, where'd you stay last night? Your shoes ain't buttoned, girl, don't fit you right.") The song is a folk blues—sometimes called "Alberta" or "Roberta"—and it had had several recordings in the 1920s. Blind Lemon Jefferson made it for Paramount in late 1926 as "Corrina Blues," crediting its composition to himself. On one of the few discs made for Williams' shortlived Black Patti label, Frankie Jaxon sang it as "Corrine." The Too Bad Boys' "Corrine, Corrina Blues" had no composer credit on their Paramount record of 1929, and James Wiggins' Paramount version of 1930 labeled it "Traditional." Jaxon sang it again for Vocalion in the summer of 1929, accompanied by Dorsey and Whittaker, as "Corrine Blues."

The mystery is not how Williams' name got on the song—he had had two chances at it, one at Black Patti and one at Vocalion—but how Bo Chatmon (1893–1964) came to be given cocomposer credit for it. Chatmon was a blues fiddler who had spent most of the 1920s share-cropping in Hollandale, Mississippi, and playing regionally with his family's string band. He was touring and recording with the Mississippi Sheiks by 1930—but not recording for Mayo Williams. Chatmon may have heard about Williams and brought him the tune when he came to Chicago. In any case, Chatmon and Williams claimed the folk song and copyrighted it. The first crossover recording of "Corrine, Corrina" was made by Red Nichols and His Five Pennies, with a vocal by Wingy Manone, for Brunswick in late 1930, and the Nichols version was popular through the spring of 1931. Cab Calloway (1907–1994) recorded it later in 1931, and the song got several more recordings during the decade. It was still thought of as folklore, but it was folklore with two composers' names on it. Mills Music bought it from Williams, and after Mitchell Parish, a staff lyricist, redid the words, published it in 1932. The song became a rhythm and blues standard in the 1950s, with Joe Turner's 1956 recording the most popular. "Corrine, Corrina" had fifteen weeks on the pop charts in 1961 in a revival by Ray Peterson.

Mayo Williams' successes at Vocalion came during a time when the race record business was in trouble. Corporations, producers, and investors had all become understandably timid as the Depression economy tightened its grip on the nation. Startups and expansion were out of the question; holding on became the order of the day. There had been about 500 race records issued per year in the late 1920s, but the figure would drop to about 150 a year by 1933. Cutbacks in the amount of product meant cutbacks in the number of people needed to make and sell it. The downward spiral was self-perpetuating. Race record producers saw radio as the cause of their woes, although there were no radio shows made specifically for black audiences. (And because of an agreement with the American Federation of Musicians, no radio shows were allowed to use recordings at this time. Radio stations could broadcast only live music, with musicians paid at union scale.) A study made in the mid-thirties showed that only 17 percent of black households owned radios, while 30 percent owned phonographs.

Victor merged with the enemy (Radio Corporation of America) in 1929, while smaller companies, like Broadway Records, simply folded. Vocalion would survive this dire time in the race industry, but Mayo Williams would not. The numbers game was not working for him. The fewer records issued by Vocalion, the fewer chances he had at earning royalty income. And it was not a good time to be job-hunting in the record business. Williams left Vocalion in 1931 to coach football at Morehouse College in Atlanta.

As the national economic funk had wounded the record business, the upswing in the economy helped to heal it. Victor had been saved by its alliance with RCA; Brunswick (and its subsidiary, Vocalion) was bought by Warner Brothers; and Columbia (and OKeh, the subsidiary it had bought in 1926) was taken over by the Grigsby-Grunow Corporation, manufacturers of Majestic radios. These three major labels all tiptoed back into the race business. Victor began its Bluebird series in 1932; Vocalion also stepped up its output around this time; and ARC-Columbia began recording new race numbers for release on OKeh in 1932.

The repeal of Prohibition in January 1933 brought a boom to nightclubs, black and white. The country wanted a drink without sneaking around to get it. Clubs had always been a source of recording talent—including during Prohibition—and now that they could operate openly, opportunities for singers and musicians quickly expanded. Fresh talent flooded the clubs, and industry people could go and hear them without running the risk of being harassed by the law. People began to talk about recording contracts again. A new and direct link between clubs and the record industry, the jukebox, came on the scene shortly after Repeal. The nickel-a-play machines provided music for honky-tonks and taverns that couldn't afford live players, and larger places used them for "intermission music" while the band was on its breaks.

The surest sign of an economic recovery in the record business was the startup of new companies and labels, and in the summer of 1934, a new player entered the game. The British firm Decca decided to invest heavily in an American subsidiary. The idea was to start big rather than to grow big. Decca executives knew that, with bankable stars and smart marketing, their company could grab the lion's share of the reawakening record business. Jack Kapp was hired away from Brunswick to effect the realization of Decca's American dream.

The biggest musical star of the early thirties was Bing Crosby, and Jack Kapp had steered his recording career at Brunswick since 1931. It took only a phone call from Kapp to sign Crosby as Decca's first artist. On August 8, 1934, in a Los Angeles studio, Bing Crosby made the inaugural recordings for Decca Records. Kapp would quickly add Guy Lombardo, the Boswell Sisters, and the Mills Brothers to his roster of stars, but Crosby would be Decca's mainstay for three decades. Kapp's marketing ploy was simple: Decca would undersell everybody by pricing its records at thirty-five cents each. No record company was ever launched as quickly and firmly as Decca. It was a success almost as soon as it began. Kapp was confident enough to diversify Decca's product almost immediately. He wanted a race division, and he hired J. Mayo Williams to run it. Williams was summoned from Atlanta, and his long tenure at Decca began.

In October 1934 Mayo Williams kicked off Decca's 7000 race series by recording Clarence Williams' Alabama Jug Band, with Willie the Lion Smith as pianist. He found new artists who had the old Chicago-country sound. Williams supervised the Chicago recordings of Bumble Bee Slim and Peetie Wheatstraw, and the race series had a minor hit with Kokomo Arnold's "Milk Cow Blues." Decca was having respectable sales with several of its country blues artists, but, although Williams had pioneered the sound, he saw that this was not where the action was any more.

Although the concept of swing had not fully flowered in 1934, the big bands had certainly arrived, and several of the best were on Williams' doorstep at Decca. In September 1934 the orchestras of Fletcher Henderson, Earl Hines, Jimmy Lunceford, and Chick Webb all made their first recordings for Decca (none of these artists were issued in the label's race series). Lunceford recorded for Decca for the next four years, and Louis Armstrong began his long association with Decca in October 1935. Record-buyers wanted to dance, as they always had, but they now wanted the flash and power of ten or more instruments to inspire them. They could shag a bit to the old-time blues songs, but to bring off a Lindy, some horns were needed. Mayo Williams began to think about meshing his blues with a band sound. For the first time in his career as a record producer, he created a studio band.

Williams' invention was a seven-piece group he called the Harlem Hamfats, which made its first recordings in April 1936. The Hamfats' center was the old blues-band core: two guitars (one doubling on mandolin), piano, and string bass. But the addition of a trumpet, clarinet, and drums gave the Hamfats a range and drive that the blues bands didn't have. Herb Morand was the trumpet player and nominal leader, and the lead guitarist and main vocalist was Joe McCoy. They were the first "jump band" in the modern sense, and they made their good-time dance music on nearly a hundred sides for Decca's race series from their inception until late 1939.

The Hamfats' repertoire, blues-based and full of fun, was all their own. They didn't cover anyone else's numbers, and no one covered theirs. The message, spelled out musically and lyrically, in all their songs was "Let's party!" Their first two sides were "Oh! Red" and "Lake Providence Blues," and their first big seller came four months later with "Let's Get Drunk and Truck." The Hamfats' records rolled out during the late thirties: "We're Gonna Pitch a Boogie Woogie," "Baby, Don't You Tear My Clothes," "Let Me Feel It," and "Hallelujah Joe Ain't Preachin' No More." Joe McCoy reworked his "Weed Smoker's Dream" as "Why Don't You Do Right?" Lil Green (1919–1954) was the first to record it—in April 1941—and Peggy Lee's 1942 version was Lee's first hit.

The Harlem Hamfats were very popular with black record-buyers, and the performer who paid the closest attention to the Hamfats was Louis Jordan. In the fall of 1938 Jordan was leading a four-piece band at the Elks Rendezvous, a Harlem club, where Dan Burley, a black reporter for the New York *Daily News*, heard him. Burley was an old friend of Mayo Williams' from Chicago, and he was knowledgeable about jazz. Burley advised Williams to record the Jordan band. Williams went to hear Jordan and liked his neo-Hamfats sound. He suggested to Jordan that he add a tenor sax and a string bass to his alto sax/piano/trumpet/drums instrumentation. Jordan agreed, and seeing a recording opportunity in the making, he rehearsed his expanded band to perfection.

Williams used the Jordan group first to back up vocals by Rodney Sturgis, a singer previously recorded by Decca, in late December 1938. After three Sturgis vocals had been laid down, Williams gave the studio over to Jordan's Elks Rendezvous Band. They knocked out "Honey in the Bee Ball" (the band's theme) and "Barnacle Bill the Sailor," both with Jordan vocals. As a singer, Jordan was a smoother article than Joe McCoy, but his band had the same hard drive and sunny eroticism that the Hamfats had. Jordan's first record sold well enough to justify another, and Williams called him back into the Decca studio in March 1939.

This time the band was called the Tympany Five—although there were six instruments, including Jordan's alto sax—and the tight, high-spirited party sound of Jordan was in full bloom. Among the six band recordings that day were "Keep a-Knockin'," "Doug the Jitterbug," and "At the Swing Cats' Ball." Jordan would be a Decca star for years to come, and his fast-shuffling, boogieish music would eventually be recognized as a precursor of rock and roll. If Jordan's sound contained the rock and roll gene, its DNA came from Mayo Williams' Harlem Hamfats.

Several of Williams' old Paramount artists recorded for him at Decca, including Trixie Smith in 1938 and Tiny Parham in 1940. Alberta Hunter recorded for Decca in August 1939—still complaining about her missing Paramount royalties from fifteen years earlier. The pianist Sammy Price was assisting Williams around this time, and Perry Bradford was also doing what he called "stooging for Mayo Williams." Bradford brought in several artists, including Rosetta Crawford and a back-up band that featured James P. Johnson, for sessions.

The Ink Spots had their first big hit for Decca with "If I Didn't Care" in early 1939. Although the Ink Spots were not on the race series, and technically not Williams' department, Jack Kapp must have asked him to handle a situation arising from the quartet's hit. The company had received a strong letter of complaint from Zilner Randolph, the writer of "Knock-Kneed Sal," which was on the B side of "If I Didn't Care." Williams answered Randolph's accusatory letter, which concerned his copyright disposition and royalty accounting, with some home truths about the record business: "Please be informed that this song by virtue of its merits was not recorded on that phase of the work solely . . . and it could have been left on the shelf as easily as it was selected . . . there isn't one person in a thousand that could tell you the name of the song that is on the other side of the 'If I Didn't Care' record. . . . I merely mention these things in order that you might know that songs just don't happen on records but are recorded because of some connections and contacts that different people have with the recording engagements and artists." In other words, be thankful that you got a recording, and take the royalties we send you.

Although he did not know it, Williams' days of snapping the whip at Decca were coming to a close. Louis Jordan, Williams' discovery and his best-selling artist, was moved from the race series into Decca's general catalog. Williams supervised the last of Jordan's race records (in April 1940), and he was still cutting himself in on Jordan's songs. (His name is on Jordan's "Rusty Dusty Blues"—also known as "Mama Mama Blues"—and "That'll Just About Knock Me Out." "Rusty Dusty Blues," a generic blues tune, bears Williams' name alone, and he may actually have written the lyric.) But Williams' autocratic ways would not do outside of the race division. There were rumors of his drinking, taking payoffs from songwriters to get their material to Jordan, of demanding kickbacks on the union-scale salaries of side men, and of hiring inexperienced side men who would be easier prey to his poaching on their salaries. It seemed to Decca executives that their race supervisor needed supervising, and in 1941 Milt Gabler was hired to oversee Williams' work.

In an interview with David Jasen, Gabler recalled Williams conducting his business in hallways after recording sessions, his Phi Beta Kappa key dangling from a chain across his vest as he haggled with singers over copyrights and explained deductions in pay to musicians. It must have wounded Williams when Milt Gabler was assigned to produce the Louis Jordan sessions that produced the Tympany Five's first crossover hits, "Knock Me a Kiss" and "I'm Gonna Move to the Outskirts of Town."

As Williams' position was under siege at Decca, he was being chastised in the jazz press for his dealings with an old Chicago ally, the pianist Cow Cow Davenport. Davenport had recorded for Williams at Vocalion in 1929 but had been sidelined by illness—and a prison term—for most of the 1930s. In May 1938 Davenport was ready to resume his career, and he contacted Williams, who gave him a Decca contract. In 1940 Davenport applied for membership in ASCAP, but was turned down because he did not have the requisite number of publications. Davenport complained in an open letter to *Down Beat* that the reason he did not have publications was that, like most Vocalion

J. Mayo Williams

artists, he had sold his work for peanuts to Mayo Williams' State Street Music, which never intended to publish them. Carlton Brown, a *Down Beat* writer, took up Davenport's cause and knocked Williams incessantly in his columns. Williams was embarrassed by the flap, but he did not offer Davenport his songs back. ASCAP finally relented and admitted Davenport to membership in 1946.

Seeing the handwriting on the Decca wall, Williams began to create small labels of his own.

He started Chicago Records and Harlem Records, but he couldn't sign artists above the level of Ann Graham and Bea Booze. In 1946, after his long phaseout at Decca was complete, Williams became a founding partner of Sunrise Records. Sunrise was the brain child of Duke Ellington (1899–1974) and Ellington's best friend and personal physician, Dr. Arthur Logan. Ellington himself did not record for Sunrise, and the label folded within a few months of its creation.

Soon after the collapse of Sunrise, Mayo Williams sold his State Street Music copyrights to Leeds Music and moved back to Chicago. A couple of songs with his name on them were rhythm and blues hits in the 1940s. The first was "Fine Brown Frame," which is credited to Guadalupe Cartiero and Williams. Arthur Prysock sang the sly little number with the Buddy Johnson Orchestra in 1944, and Nellie Lutcher made it a hit again in 1948. One of the big hits of 1949 was "Drinkin' Wine, Spo-Dee-O-Dee," credited to Williams and Granville "Stick" McGhee (1918–1961). Stick McGhee and His Buddies gave the Atlantic label its first big hit when "Drinkin' Wine" made Number Two on the R&B charts; Wynonie Harris made it to Number Four, and Lionel Hampton made it to Number Thirteen. The song, celebrating wine as the fuel for a good party, was revived by Jerry Lee Lewis in 1973.

Williams began yet another small label, Ebony Records, when he returned to Chicago. Ebony issued a new version of Charlie Jackson's "Shake That Thing," but it didn't sell. Muddy Waters recorded for Williams before his years at Chess began in 1950, but Waters' career was moving too quickly for him to stay at the tiny label.

Williams kept business hours well into his seventies. He wasn't doing anything really, but his South Side office was a good place to visit old friends and to charm young amateurs who came to audition for him. The president of Ebony Records died in Chicago on January 2, 1980, after a long illness.

Mayo Williams was surprisingly modest with his last interviewer. He didn't go on about his Paramount discoveries and their changing the sound of the blues. He didn't proclaim himself a forefather of rock. He didn't think it remarkable that he had survived fifty years in a tough business. He was proud of one thing, though. He said, "I've been better than 50 percent honest, which in this business is pretty good."

CHAPTER 7

"IF YOU'VE NEVER BEEN VAMPED BY A BROWN SKIN"

•••••••••••••••••••••••••••••••••••••

Black Theatre Composers of the 1920s

THE MUSICAL THEATRE OF THE 1920S WAS star-driven in a way that ours is not. Nowadays the show itself is the star, the play is really the thing. The most successful musicals of recent times have been those with sweeping plots and/or spectacular effects, with their casts often hidden under animal suits, masks, and makeup. Many of our leading musical actors could take the subway home from work every evening without being recognized.

We think of the musical show as a complex entity made of many technical and artistic ingredients, all mixed by a director or choreographer to make a unified experience that is the mixer's vision bearing the mixer's stamp. Only a few times in a given season—usually in revivals—do we see stars being stars. There is something intrinsically old-fashioned about a musical that relies on someone's taking the stage and putting over some songs. In the 1920s, the star was the reason people went to the musical theatre.

Having only a handful of bankable musical theatre stars, we can hardly imagine a time when there were dozens. But there were dozens in the early twenties: new stars (Eddie Cantor and Marilyn Miller), old stars (George M. Cohan, Eddie Leonard, Raymond Hitchcock), and the already ageless Jolson. One-shot revues were built around stars (*Elsie Janis and Her Gang*; *The Ed Wynn Carnival*), and there were annual editions of revues presenting a parade of names disporting in follies, gaieties, scandals, hitchy-koos, and passing shows. Stars made musicals that weren't revues look like revues. Plots might stop at any point for sketches or jokes by the comic lead. Scores could always be padded to include songs that leading performers brought with them. If Al Jolson came to your town touring in *Sinbad* in 1920, you wanted to hear "Swanee," even though the song was not a part of the Sigmund Romberg score. And by god, Jolson gave it to you. Neither Jolson, his audiences, nor his producers were concerned about the integrity of *Sinbad's* score nor any possible hurt feelings on Romberg's part. (In fact, *Sinbad* was made up more of interpolations than of original music. By 1920 there were ten or so Jolson hits that audiences wanted to hear, and none of them were by Romberg.) The unified musical was not yet a gleam in Oscar Hammerstein's eye. Un-unified musicals let the stars loose and let the customers literally call the tune.

The musical had grown up a bit since the early century, however. There were fresh writing talents at work, and several of the new composers obviously had great gifts. Even though they wrote to serve similarly mindless plots, they didn't all sound alike. People began to speak of "Gershwin shows," "Youmans shows," and "Rodgers shows," as they had not spoken of "Sloane shows" or "Luders shows" a generation earlier. The old reliables—Romberg, Victor Herbert, Jerome Kern, and Irving Berlin—were still pitching, too. The job of composers and directors was not to present a cohesive aesthetic vision nor to comment on the times—except in the lightest of satirical ways—but to gladden customers with songs and dance numbers, to assemble packages of delight to be delivered by stars.

In the late teens, when black music in the forms of blues and jazz were the rage on the dance floor and around the phonograph, there were no black musicals on Broadway. There had not been one, in fact, since S. H. Dudley's touring show, *His Honor the Barber*, made its two-week stand at the Majestic in 1911. In a star-centered musical world, there was still only one black "crossover" stage star: Bert Williams, who had been co-opted by Ziegfeld since 1910. And there were only three black composers whose names were known to the general public: James

Reese Europe, Will Marion Cook, and W. C. Handy. (Europe died in 1919, and neither Handy nor Cook was writing for the theatre.)

Without the names of stars and composers to trade on, the prospect of black musicals taking root on Broadway seemed unlikely. But in 1921 a pair of black songwriters created a show that was appealing enough to plant them there. Their show had no stars of the Jolson-Cantor magnitude, but it had delights in abundance. And producers, black and white, would try for years to replicate it. These succeeding attempts to catch its combination of pep, speed, and hot dancing yielded many riches. Black shows produced enduring songs, changed show dancing forever, and presented the magic of black performers to Broadway audiences throughout the 1920s.

NOBLE SISSLE AND EUBIE BLAKE

The history of musical theatre is, to a great extent, the story of trends and fads, each of which began with a single, momentously successful show. From *The Black Crook* to *Company* and *Cats* (with *Clorindy*, *The Merry Widow*, and *Oklahoma!* among the turning points along the way), the theatrical landscape has been altered by hit shows that

demonstrated new ways of making a musical. Producing on Broadway has always been an expensive proposition, and, producers have generally favored the tried-and-true over the experimental. Only the innovative hit prompts imitation; the innovative flop does not.

Broadway producers were not seeking black musical projects in 1921 any more than they had been twenty-three years earlier, in the summer of *Clorindy*. Black writers and casts had been absent from the Broadway stage for a decade, and the chance of their return was slight. But, as had happened in 1898, a producer looking for a gimmick decided

Sissle and Blake

to present a black show and got more than he bargained for. A Baltimore saloon pianist and a society band singer, working as a composer-lyricist team, seized their chance and ran with it. Eubie Blake and Noble Sissle created one of the most profitable shows of the 1920s, and, in doing so, they changed the face of Broadway.

James Hubert Blake was born on February 7, 1883, at 319 Forrest Street, in his parents' house in Baltimore, Maryland. Both of his parents had been slaves in Virginia, and, at the time of Eubie's birth, John Sumner Blake was working as a stevedore and Emily Johnston Blake was a laundress. Eubie was the only one of their eleven children to survive past infancy.

Eubie's musical life started at age six, when a persistent salesman talked his mother into buying a pump organ for a dollar down and twenty-five cents a week. Emily Blake wanted Eubie to learn to play hymns, and she found a neighbor who was a church organist to teach him. Eubie was an apt pupil, but he couldn't let the hymns stand as written. He tricked them up with syncopation and flurries of notes that horrified the Baptist soul of his mother. When he began to pick out pop songs and marches by ear, he left church music behind forever. His constant practicing produced great strength in his hands, and his fingers grew so long that they looked deformed. When Emily Blake and her adolescent son boarded a streetcar, she often told him, "Double up your fingers, you look like a pickpocket."

At age fifteen (around the time that he dropped out of school), Eubie found work playing in a local whorehouse run by a white madam named Aggie Shelton. His job was kept secret from his parents, but not for long. There was much remonstration when they discovered his shameful employment, but this was muted somewhat when it was learned that every week he was bringing home about ten times more money than his father. In 1901 John and Emily Blake felt modified relief when Eubie chose a lesser evil by leaving Aggie Shelton's to join a medicine show. The following year he was buck dancing and playing the organ in a touring revue, In Old Kentucky, which was briefly in residence at New York's Academy of Music on Fourteenth Street.

By 1905 Eubie had become a contender for piano jobs in the black resorts and saloons of Atlantic City. Competition was fierce among players, and only the flashiest of them worked regularly. Eubie listened to his rivals and borrowed from their effects. But he also had his own arsenal of tricks—including stinging octave runs with his right hand and a descending "wobble-wobble" bass line—and he began to compose pieces to show them off. One of his earliest compositions was an aggressive and extremely difficult number called "Sounds of Africa," which he devised in 1899. It was the first truly urban rag, and he would make a piano roll of it in 1917. The roll bore the title it has been known by ever since, "The Charleston Rag."

For three years, from 1907 to 1910, Eubie was the "house man" in charge of the music at Baltimore's ritziest black hotel, the Goldfield, which was owned by the lightweight champion, Joe Gans. It was his first steady job, and he took satisfaction in the security he had attained in a fly-by-night profession. Blake finally had enough money to think about getting married, so he wooed and won a local beauty, Avis Lee. One month after their wedding (in July 1910), Joe Gans died and the Goldfield Hotel soon hit the skids. The rock-solid job vanished, and Eubie became an itinerant musician again.

Eubie had made a reputation at the Goldfield, however, so he got work in the best of the black clubs in Atlantic City as well as those in his home town. He began to frequent Harlem clubs—not as a player but as a listener—and what he heard amazed him. The young sharks who were beginning to gather there were taking popular piano playing to unheard-of heights with their proficiency and invention. Blake resolved to keep pace with them, and, by intense listening and practicing, he did.

Eubie composed several new rags for his repertoire, but as yet, he had had nothing published. Luckey Roberts (1887–1968) was the most formidable player of the Harlem school, as well as the only one to have connections with publishers. Roberts took Blake to the Joseph Stern Company to demonstrate his compositions in 1914, and Stern bought two of them, "Chevy Chase" and "Fizz Water." The published rags were simplified for use by amateur players, but they were Blake's first in print. Again, Blake seemed set on a professional course: he would continue to play clubs and he would occasionally publish his ragtime. In May 1915 he accepted a temporary job as pickup pianist with Joe Porter's Serenaders, who were to entertain at Baltimore's Riverview Park. Porter had hired Noble Sissle, a young man from Indiana, to sing with the band, and literally within minutes of Sissle's meeting Blake, at the Serenaders' first rehearsal, both of their lives took a new direction.

Noble Lee Sissle was born on July 10, 1889, in Indianapolis, Indiana. His father, George Andrew Sissle, was a Methodist Episcopal minister, and his mother, Martha Angeline, was a public school teacher. All six of the Sissle children were expected to excel, and Noble was the one who enjoyed excelling in a public way. He sang solos at his father's church, and he won a school prize for declamation when he was twelve. In 1906 the family moved to Cleveland, where Noble attended Central High School. (He was one of six black students among the 1,500 there.) Noble's high school years were interrupted by his working at various jobs—he would not graduate from Central until he was twenty-one—but he always came back and participated in everything that school had to offer: oratory, athletics, glee club, yell squad. In 1908 he took a summer job with the Edward Thomas Male Quartet, singing spirituals and hymns on the Chautauqua circuit around the Midwest. After graduation, Noble joined Hann's Jubilee Singers and sang in cities as far away as Denver and New York.

In 1913 Noble's father died, and his mother moved back to Indianapolis. In the fall of that year, Noble entered De Pauw University at Greencastle, Indiana, but he lasted only a semester there. In January 1914 he enrolled at Butler University in Indianapolis, where he sang with the school's dance orchestra. He was working as a waiter at the Severin Hotel when the manager asked him to organize an orchestra for the dining room. Noble assembled a twelve-piece group and featured himself as its singer. In order to look like a musician, he held a bandolin—a fad instrument of the day, which was equal parts banjo, mandolin, and snare drum—and occasionally pretended to play it. He had never trained as a singer, and he couldn't play an instrument, but he had style, polish, and pep. His hotel band was a great success. He left Butler to pursue a singing career, and one of his first solo engagements took him to Baltimore in May 1915.

The chance meeting of the eighth-grade dropout and the fellow he would always call "the college man" was show-business fate at its best. Eubie Blake knew of Sissle, not as a singer but as a lyricist. (Somehow Sissle had managed to get a song into the Tutt-Whitney touring musical of 1913, *The Wrong Mr. President*. He wrote "My Heart for You Pines Away" with Russell Smith, and Seidel Music of Indianapolis had published it. Sissle probably did not know of Blake's two published rags.) Blake suggested that they try writing songs together, and Sissle quickly agreed.

Although neither knew the other's capabilities, they made a perfect team. Blake's musical gifts were far greater than Sissle's, but Sissle was driven by ambition as Blake was not. He was handsome and charming, a go-getter, a cheerleader for whatever he was involved in. Blake was six years older than Sissle, married for five years, and pretty much settled down. His professional aim in 1915—and throughout his life—was simply to keep working. Sissle wanted to get somewhere and to get there fast. Without Sissle's prodding him, Blake would probably have never left Baltimore.

Within a week of their meeting, they completed a song called "It's All Your Fault," and Sissle talked their way into a backstage audition for Sophie Tucker at Baltimore's Maryland Theatre. She wanted the song for her act, and, because Tucker sang it, a local company, Maryland Music, wanted to publish it. Sissle and Blake were encouraged by the sale of their first song, and they resolved to write together as often as they could, although each had a living to make as a performer.

Sissle began to pick up singing jobs at society events, one of which was a private party in Palm Beach. A New York woman who heard him there was impressed by his fine tenor voice and excellent diction, and she thought he would do well with Jim Europe's Society Orchestras in New York. She gave him a letter of introduction to Europe, and Sissle gratefully took it. He had not seen the saloon side of show business, as had Blake, and he didn't want to see it. He wanted what Jim Europe had: the mingling, the money, and the prestige of playing for the elite.

In 1916 Sissle took off to introduce himself to Jim Europe. Europe hired him as a singer for his Society Orchestra organization, and Sissle quickly expanded his role to become Europe's administrative right-hand man. Europe's confidence in Sissle was such that, when Sissle recommended Blake as a pianist for the Society Orchestras, Europe sent for him. Blake's confidence in Sissle was such that he and his wife Avis picked up and moved to New York when the call came. He quickly proved his worth as a pianist, and Europe began to send him out as a conductor. Blake's legendary ability to rehearse a band was honed during his time with Europe. The standards for the Society Orchestras were high, and Blake became adept at putting snap and polish into Europe's pickup ensembles on short notice.

The Europe-Sissle-Blake combination lasted only a few months. In September 1916 Europe enlisted in the army, and Sissle quickly followed him into service. Blake, a slacker at heart, stayed behind to run the Society Orchestras and to keep the Europe organization going while the leader was away. Sissle sent Blake long letters from France, often enclosing song lyrics for Blake to set to music. In Sissle's absence, Blake formed his first vaudeville act, pairing with a barrel-chested comic singer and drummer named Broadway Jones. Blake had no ambitions for the act; it was only a way to make money until his partners returned. The three had plans to write for the musical stage together.

The theatre dream was put aside when Europe and Sissle got back in February 1919, because the military band that Europe had led in France with Sissle's help was now famous. People had read about the black 369th Infantry Regiment—about its brave exploits and its crackerjack band—and they wanted to hear the music that had accompanied the Allied victory. Europe's manager, a hard-nosed, foul-mouthed Irishman named Pat Casey, thought the "Hellfighters Band" should capitalize on its notoriety. Casey set up recording sessions for the band in early March. Then, within a month of the Hellfighters' return, he sent the band out on a heavily booked schedule of concerts in the Northeast and Midwest. Sissle went along as featured singer. In May, after an exhausting but highly profitable ten weeks on the road, Casey added a return booking in Boston on the way back to New York. During the intermission of the band's Mechanics' Hall concert, a band member attacked Jim Europe with a knife. Europe died in Boston's City Hospital a few hours later, and Sissle and Blake's grand scheme of using the Europe organization as a launching pad for Broadway died with him.

Europe's musical empire was thrown into disarray by his sudden death, and Sissle and Blake might have drifted apart if it had not been for the intercession of Pat Casey. Casey wanted to manage them as a performing team, and he had enough clout to book them immediately on the Keith-Orpheum vaudeville circuit. They could skip the obligatory years at the bottom and start near the top. They fashioned a "class act," along the lines of Cole and Johnson's but with more pizazz. Looking very dapper, the tuxedo-clad pair bounded onto the stage of Poli's Theatre in New Haven in the early summer of 1919 in their first appearance as "The Dixie Duo." Their next booking was at the Harlem Opera House; then, after only a few weeks in vaudeville, Casey decided that they were ready to scale the pinnacle, the Palace Theatre in New York.

Sissle and Blake went with Casey to the manager's office at the Palace to close the deal. Because the act was new, the Palace manager offered them some tips on how to improve it. Blake told a *Penthouse* interviewer nearly sixty years later:

> This guy says to Pat, "Tell you what we'll do. We'll get grotesque clothes for 'em. All ragged. And we'll have a piano on stage, in the box. . . . Now Sissle and Blake come on in these ragged clothes. And Blake says, 'Hello dere! Wha'. . . wha' dat?' And Sissle scratches his head and says, 'I dunno wha' dat is. Wha' is dat?' So then Blake inches up on the piano, lookin' scared, and he says, 'I'm . . . I'm gwine touch it. Look out!' And he hits one note and he says, 'Why, dat's a pie-anna!'"
>
> Now the most ridiculous part is that he wanted me to sit down and play the piano. That was supposed to be the joke. So Pat Casey says to him—well, I can't say it 'cause you're tapin' this. But I tell you, that man *cussed.*
>
> Then he says, "You want Sissle and Blake? . . . Well, if you want Sissle and Blake, you're going to take 'em in tuxedos and they're not going to act like that. Now if you don't want 'em, I'll sell 'em to the Shuberts."

The theatre manager backed down, and on July 4, 1919, the Dixie Duo went into the Palace. As would often be the case in their early vaudeville years, they started their Palace engagement as the second act on the bill (a weak position), then worked their way down. They moved to later spots because audiences wanted to see them featured, and because other acts did not want to follow them. The Dixie Duo was dynamite, and it would never occur to another manager to present them as clowns.

Sissle and Blake created one of the great vaudeville acts of the 1920s, and they inspired many imitators, among them, Layton and Johnstone and the white team of Al Bernard and J. Russel Robinson, performing as "The Dixie Stars." The premise was bone-simple: Blake played and Sissle sang. But the package was wrapped tight—no jokes, no patter, no digression. Their material was fresh, and it was all their own. They opened with a blast of "Gee, I'm Glad That I'm from Dixie," then went into "Ain'tcha Coming Back, Mary Ann, to Maryland?" or "Baltimore Blues." Next came the centerpiece of the act, a medley of war songs: "On Patrol in No Man's Land" and "All of No Man's Land Is Ours." Sissle was not a dancer, but, as actors say, he moved well. The war songs set him in full motion. As Blake made bugle calls and cannon fire on the piano, Sissle picked his way across an imaginary battlefield, lurching to duck Blake's artillery and charging on to victory as he sang. In their big ballad, "Pickaninny Shoes," Sissle yearned for his childhood days, holding up a pair of invisible baby shoes and making the audience see the shoes that weren't there. Their closer was the tender and raggy "Good Night, Angeline," sweetened by Blake's singing a harmony line to Sissle's tenor melody.

The team signed to publish with the Witmark brothers, who issued about a dozen of their vaudeville songs. The agreement gave Sissle and Blake $25 a week each, plus two-cents-a-copy on sheet music, as well as mechanical royalties. As they had started at the top in vaudeville, so they started at the top with their publishing. Unlike most black songwriters of the 1920s, Sissle and Blake would not bounce back and forth between Clarence Williams and Joe Davis. They would not publish exclusively with Witmark, but there were always major publishers to issue their work. Julius Witmark sponsored their memberships into ASCAP in 1922, and years later Blake would say of his publishers, "They're fine people. . . . The Witmarks always did right by us."

The vaudeville act attracted the attention of record companies, too. Sissle had recorded more than Blake before 1920, but now they were in demand separately and together. Blake played in the studio band that accompanied Sissle on ten or so sides for Pathe in 1920, but the electricity of their vaudeville act was not caught until the piano-vocal sides they made for Emerson, which were released early in 1921. They separately lent their names to orchestras for recordings in the early twenties—Noble Sissle's Sizzling Syncopators and Eubie Blake and His Orchestra—but the duo sides, with Sissle's clarion voice soaring over Blake's romping piano, were their best.

In the summer of 1920 Sissle and Blake played an NAACP benefit at the Dunbar Theatre in Philadelphia, and it was there that they met Flournoy Miller and Aubrey Lyles. Miller and Lyles were a rising comedy team who, like Sissle and Blake, had their sights set on musical theatre. They had patched together a libretto from pieces of their vaudeville acts, and they were looking for a score. Aubrey Lyles approached the songwriters and found them amenable to a collaboration. Vague promises were made to work together some time in the future. Sissle and Blake thought no more of the meeting until, a few months later, Lyles found them in New York and told them that Miller

Sissle and Blake, *left and right*
Miller and Lyles, *top and bottom*

and Lyles' manager, Al Mayer, had secured an audition with a Broadway producer, John Cort. Cort wanted to hear songs. Sissle and Blake had not yet written anything for the show, so they demonstrated their vaudeville material to Cort. He sat silently through a couple of numbers, but when the team presented a new ballad, "Love Will Find a Way," he was won over. He said he would produce a Miller and Lyles show, with music by Sissle and Blake.

The winning over of John Cort was a qualified victory. Cort had had a couple of bad seasons, and as much as he wanted to produce the show that would become known as *Shuffle Along*, he was nearly broke. A few investors were rounded up to make an organization called the Nikko Producing Company, so there was at least some startup money. But expedience would be the watchword in the creation of the show and its score.

The Miller-Lyles libretto told a story of small-town high jinks in a three-way race for mayor of "Jimtown." Miller and Lyles played two of the candidates, co-owners of a grocery store, where each dipped into the communal till to finance his campaign. The third candidate was

Shuffle Along

the handsome "Harry Walton," played by Ralph Matthews, and Sissle played Harry's campaign manager. The ingenue was Gertrude Saunders, and the leading lady was the beautiful Lottie Gee. Blake was to conduct the orchestra from the piano in the pit. As for the chorus, there would be as many "Happy Honeysuckles" and "Syncopating Sunflowers" as the payroll could stand.

John Cort booked a shabby rehearsal hall on 138th Street, and his son Harry went scrounging for costumes. Harry remembered that the clothes from Eddie Leonard's *Roly Boly Eyes*, an "old South" musical produced by his father in late 1919, were still in storage. Because the musty, sweat-stained castoffs could be had for nothing, Cort decided they'd be perfect for his new show. The plantation look was not what *Shuffle Along*'s creators had in mind, but because it would be on view all evening, Sissle and Blake wrote songs to fit it ("Bandanna Days," "Old Black Joe and Uncle Tom," and "Kentucky Sue"). The producers were in a hurry to get their show up, so most of the songs came from Sissle and Blake's vaudeville act. The act itself was thrown into the second half, listed in the program as "A Few Minutes with Sissle and Blake." Blake stepped away from his conducting chores to join an out-of-character Sissle on stage for several numbers, from the old war songs to "Baltimore Buzz."

A 1916 Sissle and Blake song called "My Loving Baby" was overhauled for *Shuffle Along*. Sissle's chorus lyric was kept almost intact, but Blake wrote a new melody for it. The result was a waltz called "I'm Just Wild About Harry," but Lottie Gee refused to sing the song unless it was converted to a one-step. Blake reluctantly agreed to put it in a peppier tempo. The number that everyone was worried about was "Love Will Find a Way." It was the climax of a love scene, and no one knew how white audiences would take to black characters expressing serious passion in song. But then, no one was sure of anything as *Shuffle Along* staggered out to begin its tryout tour.

The show's first booking was in Trenton, New Jersey, and from there the company played one-nighters in town halls and movie houses in Burlington, Pottstown, any place that would have them. At each stop the hope was that the take would be sufficient to get them to the next one. Salaries were often deferred, but most of the actors stuck with the show. They made it to the Howard Theatre by the kindness of a railroad company president who had seen the show and liked it enough to give them all free fares to Washington. When *Shuffle Along* arrived in New York, the Nikko company was $18,000 in debt. The theatre that Cort had rented for the show was not even a theatre. Daly's Sixty-third Street was a rundown lecture hall, far from the Broadway district, with neither stage nor orchestra pit. After some hasty carpentry, *Shuffle Along* opened at Daly's on May 23, 1921.

Shuffle Along took New York by surprise as few shows have ever done. It was far greater than the sum of its ragtag parts, and early customers spread the word that there was something wonderful going on at Daly's. Somehow, during weeks of duress, *Shuffle Along*'s creators had made an evening of nonstop fun. The critics trailed in, finally, and their reviews praised it as "an infection of amusement" "filled with liveliness and good humor," "a breeze of super-jazz blown up from Dixie." Everything worked: the roughhouse (but clean) comedy of Miller and Lyles, the snappy dances, all the songs. The 1100-seat house began to sell out the range of its tickets, from the $2 orchestra to the fifty-cent second balcony seats. Audiences were integrated, and the show did repeat business with patrons of both races. By the fall of 1921, *Shuffle Along* was taking in $13,000 a week (against a $7,500 break-even). The show ran more than fourteen months at Daly's, before it took to the road. *Shuffle Along* toured for two years, and at one point there were three national companies out at the same time. In its various editions the show would gross more than $8 million for the Nikko company.

Every black show of the decade would be measured against the standard of *Shuffle Along*, and—until Blake's *Blackbirds of 1930*—all would be found wanting. *Shuffle Along*'s distinctive features were its teamwork—the sheer collective energy demonstrated by everyone from the leads to the "Honeysuckles" and "Sunflowers"—the streamlined jazz dancing of its gorgeous, bobbed-haired chorines, and the cleverness of the rich and varied Sissle-Blake songs. Although Sissle's lyrics tended to wordiness, Blake's melodies were good enough to disguise the fact.

There were punchy, high-spirited numbers ("Bandanna Days" and "I'm Just Simply Full of Jazz," as well as the hit of the show, "I'm Just Wild About Harry"), the delicate and rhythmic "In Honeysuckle Time," the bluesy "Daddy, Won't You Please Come Home?," and the sexy "I'm Craving for That Kind of Love."

The problematic ballad "Love Will Find a Way"—which audiences cheered every night—is unlike anything else from a black show of the time. This is because Blake alone among the black writers of the 1920s thought of himself as a theatre composer. Others wrote songs for shows; Blake wrote scores. He had loved theatre music since he was a teenager, and he had great respect for the writing of it. His musical heroes were the operetta composers who were popular in his youth: Leslie Stuart (who wrote the score for *Floradora*, the hit of the 1900–1901 Broadway season), Victor Herbert, Franz Lehar, and Cole and Johnson. Like his idols, Blake was a long-line melody man and not afraid of sentiment. His love songs have a theatrical passion and range not found in those of Fats Waller or James P. Johnson. Their ballads flirt, but Blake's are declarative, and musically bigger than anyone else's. Syncopation is the pulse of his show music, but melody is its heart. His "Gypsy Blues" is a patter song built on the chord structure of Herbert's "Gypsy Love Song," but "Love Will Find a Way" is the real thing. It is as strong and graceful as Herbert at his best. Ragtime was what the public wanted from Blake in his later years—and he was showman enough to oblige—but he was proudest of his theatre music.

The success of *Shuffle Along* paid off handsomely for its creators. Noble Sissle was given an exclusive contract to record for Emerson, and Eubie Blake made records as accompanist for Alberta Hunter and novelty singer Irving Kaufman as well as for Sissle. (Blake and Kaufman, in the Emerson studio in September 1921, were the first interracial pair to make a recording.) Blake also recorded with his orchestra and as a piano soloist. Witmark published twenty of the *Shuffle Along* songs, an unusually large number to be issued from a single show. Even replacement cast members benefited from their association with *Shuffle Along*. Florence Mills and Paul Robeson received their first attention in New York when they took over roles at Daly's, and Josephine Baker's career began with her joining the first touring company as a chorus dancer.

One of the Nikko investors, John Scholl, asked Sissle and Blake to contribute a dozen songs to *Elsie*, a white show he was producing at the Vanderbilt Theatre. *Elsie* opened on April 2, 1923, and lasted forty performances. There was nothing remarkable about *Elsie* or its score—which was filled out with songs by Monte Carlo and Alma Sanders—but Witmark published eleven of the Sissle-Blake numbers.

In the same month that *Elsie* opened, Sissle and Blake were seen on Broadway in another medium: a piece of their vaudeville act on sound film. Lee DeForest, the radio pioneer, had patented a system of recording sound on film stock, and to demonstrate its effectiveness, he filmed six prominent variety acts. In the short Sissle and Blake segment, called "Snappy Songs," the team sang "All God's Chillun Got Shoes" and their own "Affectionate Dan." DeForest's Phonofilm of vaudeville stars was shown at the Rivoli Theatre, but it was shrugged off as an impractical novelty by the film industry.

In September a Sissle-Blake song was placed in a British revue, *London Calling*. The score was mostly by Noel Coward, but the first song ever performed by Coward and his costar Gertrude Lawrence was Sissle and Blake's "You Were Meant for Me." The number was staged by Fred Astaire, a friend of Coward's who happened to be in London during rehearsals.

Of course, it was expected that the quartet who created *Shuffle Along* would collaborate on another show, but Miller and Lyles wanted no part of it. The comedians were resentful that, given the royalties from touring companies and sheet music, as well as the mechanical royalties from their own and others' recordings of the *Shuffle Along* songs, Sissle and Blake were making more from *Shuffle Along* than they were. When George White asked Miller and Lyles to star in his upcoming *Runnin' Wild*, they left their implicit partnership with Sissle and Blake. (And they took their characters with them. Miller and Lyles played "Steve Jenkins" and "Sam Peck," the feuding grocers of *Shuffle Along*, in *Runnin' Wild*, which opened in October 1923.) Soon after their split with Miller and Lyles, Sissle and Blake were signed by the veteran producer B. C. Whitney, who promised them he would spare no expense in making their next project "the aristocrat of colored shows."

Whitney came through on his promise. The show was originally called *In Bamville*, but its title was changed to *The Chocolate Dandies* after its tryout tour. It was the most lavishly produced musical that either Sissle or Blake would ever be involved in, and its score remained

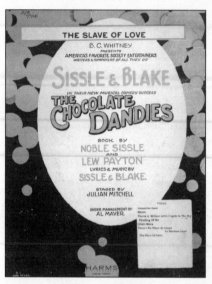

The Chocolate Dandies

Blake's lifelong favorite. The story was even thinner than that of *Shuffle Along*, involving the residents of a fanciful town that seemed to be interested only in horse-racing and romance. The comedy was more whimsy than farce. There was a long dream sequence in which the leading comedian imagined that he was president of a bank, and there was an elaborate wedding finale. A horse race was staged by having three real horses run on a treadmill. The show had a cast of 125, twice as many performers as *Shuffle Along*, and the scenery and costumes were stunning. Noble Sissle and Lew Payton (the comic lead) wrote the book. Blake was conductor and music director. The leading roles were played by Sissle, Payton, Lottie Gee, Ivan Harold Browning, Valaida Snow, and Elisabeth Welch. Josephine Baker was a featured chorus girl, and much of the comic thunder was stolen by a newcomer, Johnny Hudgins. Sissle and Blake's interpolated act was called "In Their Studio," and it was placed where vaudevillians wanted to be, next to closing.

The Chocolate Dandies opened at New York's Colonial Theatre on September 1, 1924, after a five-month tryout tour. Critics generally admitted to having a good time, but some of them agreed with Ashton Stevens in his Chicago *Herald and Examiner* review: "This show seems to suffer from too much white man; it is both sophisticated and conventional. . . . There is too much so-called politeness, too much platitudinous refinement and not enough of the racy and the razor-edged. There is, in a word, too much 'art' and not enough Africa." In other words, a black show should keep its music and humor on the boisterous level of *Shuffle Along*. To try anything else was to overreach, to put on airs. It was the kind of criticism that would dog black shows for years.

The Chocolate Dandies ran for 96 performances—compared to *Shuffle Along's* 504—followed by a tour of about thirty weeks. Overhead was too high and customers too few. The show ran only six weeks above break-even. Two of Blake's best ballads, "Dixie Moon" and "Jassamine Lane," were forgotten after the collapse of *The Chocolate Dandies*. Sissle and Blake spent the summer of 1925 back in vaudeville.

In September Sissle and Blake, with their wives, Harriet and Avis, sailed on the S.S. *Olympic* for an eight-month European tour that had been booked for them by the William Morris Agency. They were wildly popular in the variety houses of Scotland and Ireland, as well as in England. They shared music hall bills with British favorites, and they played the Kit Kat Club and the Metropol Club in London. They were asked to record ten sides for a British company, Edison Bell Winner, near the end of their tour. Two of these EBW recordings are among their very best: a loving treatment of a *Chocolate Dandies* ballad, "You Ought to Know," and "I Wonder Where My Sweetie Can Be," which features Blake's raggiest accompaniment to Sissle's singing.

Sissle enjoyed it all so much that, without telling Blake, he rebooked the same tour that they had just finished. Blake, in rare defiance of a Sissle business decision, balked. He wanted to go home. Sissle's action provoked the team's only serious argument, but when they both cooled down, the repeat bookings were canceled, and the partners and their wives left London as planned. On their way back to the United States, in the spring of 1926, they stopped over in Paris to see one of the sights—their ex-chorus girl, Josephine Baker, who was now the queen of Parisian music hall.

The four had had a fine time and had been treated well everywhere they went, but Blake was not enamored of postwar Europe. He had evidently veered off the visiting star's usual rounds of nightclubs and concert halls. He told the Baltimore *Sun* shortly after his return: "My advice to all American Negroes is to stay away from Europe. . . . No matter what happens or what the conditions may be in America, they can be nothing like the deplorable conditions that exist in London. I have seen thousands sleeping in the streets, bread lines with human beings standing four abreast and other distress that I hate to remember."

Sissle and Blake set into a heavy vaudeville schedule. Sissle, who had always been a persnickety traveler, seemed to be having a worse time than usual on the road. Finally, in the early summer of 1927, he came out with it. He told Blake that he wanted to go to the upcoming American Legion convention in Paris. Blake reminded his partner that they had eleven weeks of vaudeville commitments left. Nobody could think of going anywhere for a long time. Sissle said he was going any-way. Blake asked him, "When you comin' back? You gonna stay over there?" Sissle took a moment without saying anything, then he left the room. With no more discussion, and with no contingency plan, the preeminent black songwriting and performing team of the 1920s broke up. Sissle went to Paris, but before he left, he recorded ten sides for OKeh in July. Rube Bloom was his accompanist.

Blake tried to sort out what had happened. He knew that Sissle's wife Harriet had been a thorn in the partnership. She had considered Blake a mere piano-player, good enough in his way but undeserving of 50 percent of their earnings. She thought that another pianist could be found, and she urged Sissle to find someone who would work cheaper. And Blake knew that Sissle was enamored of the society entertainer's world—especially as that world existed in Europe, where princes, duchesses, and barons dropped into night clubs, played drums with the band, had drinks with the singers. The wonder was that Sissle hadn't left sooner.

Eubie Blake got busy, rebuilding his career and rethinking his life with-out Sissle. He tried a songwriting collaboration with the lyricist Henry Creamer, but nothing came of it. He teamed with Broadway Jones again, this time to assemble an eighty-minute tab musical called *Shuffle Along, Jr.* Jones, Blake, and their cast of eleven, including six chorus girls billed as "The Panama Pansies," trooped the show for a full season on the Keith-Orpheum circuit.

Europe's welcome to Noble Sissle was as warm as he had hoped it would be. He began his expatriation as a successful solo act in British music halls, accompanied by Harry Revel at the piano. He placed a Sissle-Blake trunk song, "Old Noah's Ark," for use in a stage prologue to a 1927 silent film, *Uncle Tom's Cabin*, which was shown at the London

Pavilion. (If Blake ever saw the published song sheet, he must have flinched. It bore the legend "Arranged by Noble Sissle.") In Paris Sissle met Cole Porter, another songwriter who had come a long way from Indiana. Porter urged Sissle to form a band and assured him that he could get the band booked to play for floor shows at one of his favorite hangouts, the elegant Café les Ambassadeurs, on the Champs-Elysées. It was not long before the Noble Sissle Orchestra was in residence there. The cafe's advertisements for its house band quoted endorsements from Bill Tilden, Baron Rothschild, Irene Castle, Jascha Heifetz, and Peggy Hopkins Joyce. Sissle was making himself at home abroad.

Eubie Blake's first project in 1930 was a favor for a friend. John Scholl, the *Shuffle Along* investor who had recommended Sissle and Blake to write *Elsie*, asked Blake if he would write a few numbers with his son, Jack Scholl, an aspiring lyricist. Scholl told Blake that Will Morrissey was producing a revue for a club called the Folies Bergere, and that Morrissey would probably use some of his son's songs if Blake's name were attached to them. Blake agreed to try some songs with the young man, and the Folies Bergere revue, which opened in April, featured a minor hit called "Loving You the Way I Do," with music by Blake and lyrics by Jack Scholl. (Will Morrissey's name is also on the published song.) In August, Morrissey's revue—now called *Hot Rhythm*—opened at the Times Square Theatre for a short run. "Loving You the Way I Do" was sung in the show by Revella Hughes. Blake's three songs for *Hot Rhythm* were his first to be heard on Broadway in five years. His next show would be a much bigger deal.

Eubie Blake was approached by the producer Lew Leslie, who wanted Blake to write the score for his next *Blackbirds* revue, with Andy Razaf as lyricist. Leslie's first *Blackbirds*, a London production of 1926, featured songs by four white writers, and the most successful edition of the show, that of 1928, was built around songs by Jimmy McHugh and Dorothy Fields. Leslie had used occasional interpolations by black songwriters over the years, but he had never trusted an entire score to a black composer and lyricist. Blake was eager to write for Broadway again, and, on being assured that Shapiro-Bernstein would publish the show's songs, he signed on for *Blackbirds of 1930*. He was given a $3,000 advance by Leslie, and he agreed to write twenty-eight songs.

Despite his reputation as a cheapskate and an obsessive tinkerer with his shows, Leslie was always able to hire major talents for his *Blackbirds*. His 1930 cast featured comedians Flournoy Miller, Mantan Moreland, and Broadway Jones; the dancing stars were the Berry

Brothers and Buck and Bubbles; and the primary singers were Ethel Waters and Minto Cato. J. Rosamond Johnson did the vocal arrangements, and Cecil Mack assembled a choir for the show. Blake was the orchestra conductor as well as musical director.

Blackbirds' tryout tour began at Brooklyn's Majestic Theatre on September 1, 1930. The show got great reviews in the Brooklyn papers, the general opinion being that anything that looked and sounded as good as this *Blackbirds* was bound to be a hit on Broadway. Then Leslie stepped in to fix what wasn't broken. He called midnight rehearsals—

Blackbirds of 1930

after performances that had evoked cheering—to cut, to reorder, to restage. He fired so many performers that the show never had two consecutive weeks with the same cast. Although *Blackbirds* was doing good business, the producer began to withhold royalties from the songwriters. As the *Blackbirds* company left for Boston, they knew they were in for a bumpy ride.

Blackbirds of 1930 opened in New York on October 22 at the Royale Theatre, to first-night acclaim and enthusiastic reviews. But Leslie's erratic management decisions, and his nervousness about money, aborted what should have been a successful Broadway run. For some inexplicable reason, Leslie abruptly closed the show after sixty-one performances and announced that he was taking it on the road again. *Blackbirds* was packed up and moved to Philadelphia. Sometime during the next jump, from Philadelphia to Newark, Leslie abandoned the enterprise. He disappeared, leaving his company stranded. They straggled back to New York, knowing that the chance was lost for *Blackbirds of 1930*. Leslie would not be back, and no other producer would take over the troubled show.

Of all those involved with *Blackbirds of 1930*, only Eubie Blake and Andy Razaf profited from the bitter experience. Their score yielded hits and—even better—standards. Blake stretched himself for *Blackbirds*, and several of his songs have no precedents in his earlier work. One of these is the rousing pseudospiritual "Roll, Jordan." It is more complex in structure than anything else of Blake's, with no less than eight melodic themes in various lengths of from four to twenty bars. "Roll, Jordan" starts high and goes higher, elevated to ecstasy by Blake's surging gospel rhythms and Razaf's sanctified-church recitative. It is one of the most thrilling pieces of show music ever written. Another song that is not typical of the composer is the suggestive "My Handy Man Ain't Handy No More," for which Blake's music was as funny as Razaf's words. "That Lindy Hop" and the Latin-flavored "Doin' the Mozambique" show Blake perfectly at ease with two dance rhythms that were new to him.

As always in a Blake score, the ballads were something special. The bittersweet harmonies and graceful melody of "You're Lucky to Me" combine to make an undercurrent of emotion beneath a calm surface. The most enduring *Blackbirds* song—and Blake's second most profitable number after "I'm Just Wild About Harry"—was "Memories of You." The tune is a paraphrase of Edward MacDowell's 1896 piano sketch, "To a Wild Rose," but Blake's song climbs to melodic heights far beyond its model's. There is pain, as well as sweetness, in "Memories of You." Although its range makes it difficult to sing, there is nothing arty about it. It is just a gorgeous song that is musically large enough to hold a fervent passion.

Eubie Blake did not get the theatre offers that should have come after his work for *Blackbirds*. The Depression economy hit Broadway investors hard, and its first casualty was the black musical. Although Blake had written a white show in 1923, it never occurred to anyone that he might write another one. As Sissle had done when he was at loose ends, Blake took up the conductor's baton. He formed an orchestra for studio work in early 1931, and in September of that year Eubie Blake and His Orchestra were in the pit for *Singin' the Blues*, a musical melodrama with Jimmy McHugh–Dorothy Fields songs that ran five weeks at the Liberty Theatre. In 1932 Blake and his orchestra appeared in two films, *Harlem Is Heaven* (an all-black feature starring Bill Robinson) and "Pie, Pie Blackbird" (a Warner Brothers short that featured the Nicholas Brothers dancing to Blake's music). Although many theatre writers with less experience and fewer hits were summoned to work writing for films, Blake was not called. His neophyte lyricist, Jack Scholl, was among those who began Hollywood careers during this time.

Sissle's orchestra was more successful than Blake's, playing long stints and return engagements at fine clubs and hotels in Paris, Monte Carlo, Deauville, Glasgow, and London. In late 1931 Noble Sissle and His Orchestra came to New York for an open-ended engagement at the Park Central Hotel. The group was also featured on CBS radio broadcasts. Sissle still wrote lyrics occasionally, and his 1932 song "Hello, Sweetheart, Hello" (music by J. Russel Robinson) was published by DeSylva, Brown & Henderson.

In late 1932 the idea was hatched to reunite Sissle and Blake for a Broadway revue to be named—tritely—*Shuffle Along of 1933*. Flournoy Miller signed on to write the libretto and to star. (Aubrey Lyles had died in August 1932.) Sissle and Blake wrote an entirely new score, and Mantan Moreland and Edith Wilson were set to costar with Miller. The spark was gone from the Sissle and Blake collaboration, however. *Shuffle Along of 1933* opened at the Mansfield Theatre on December 26, 1932, and it barely made it into 1933. It closed after its seventeenth performance.

The failure of the show hardly broke Sissle's stride. His orchestra made a Vitaphone short called "That's the Spirit" in 1933, the year that it began to tour extensively in the United States. In 1934 he wrote and produced *O Sing a New Song*, an elaborate pageant celebrating Negro history, which was staged at Soldier Field in Chicago. (He met and encouraged a young choreographer, Katherine Dunham, during the preparations for this event.) The Music Corporation of America took over the booking of Sissle's orchestra in 1935. His featured singer in the mid-thirties was Lena Horne, and she recorded with the Sissle orchestra in 1936. In 1938 Sissle began his long association with lyricist-showman Billy Rose. Rose had opened a nightclub called the Diamond Horseshoe, and he kept the Sissle orchestra in residence for floor shows and dancing for nearly five years. Sissle was involved in several professional organizations during this time. He was particularly active with the Negro Actors Guild, which he had founded and led as its first president in 1937.

Blake's career was spotty. He was doing a little arranging for Handy Brothers Music, a little writing with Andy Razaf, turning out club revues for flat fees. He was occasionally called by Shapiro-Bernstein to act as a tune detective. The company wanted to make sure that their acquisitions weren't old melodies with new titles. Blake listened to their prospective buys to see whether he could identify them. (He said the one that stumped him was the British hit, "Red Sails in the Sunset." Blake was sure he had heard the tune before, but he couldn't place it. Convinced that if Blake couldn't remember it, no one else could, the company issued the song.)

Blake had long since disbanded his orchestra, and he had made no recordings since 1931. He had a handful of publications in the late thirties, including four songs from *Swing It*, a show produced by the WPA Variety Theatre wing at the Adelphi Theatre in July 1937. He enjoyed working with the *Swing It* lyricists, Milton Reddie and Cecil Mack, but their songs went nowhere. One of his 1936 Handy publications, a meandering instrumental called "Blue Thoughts," probably depicted Blake's state of mind during these years.

In 1939 a low time in Blake's life got lower. His wife Avis died of tuberculosis. Even though he had been a bit of a womanizer in the twenties—and had had a long affair with Lottie Gee—Avis had stuck by him in good times and bad, and he had always come back to her. Without Avis, and without any projects to take his mind off her, the nights were very long at his house on West 138th Street.

When the chance came to write with Andy Razaf again, Blake jumped at it. Irvin C. Miller was producing a revue called *Tan Manhattan*, to go into rehearsals in late 1940, and he wanted Blake and Razaf to do the score. Miller had big plans for *Tan Manhattan*, and he chose Avon Long, Nina Mae McKinney, and Flournoy Miller to lead his cast. The show had brief runs at the Howard Theatre and at Harlem's Apollo in early 1941, but Miller did not have the resources to make the dreamed-of leap to Broadway. The Blake-Razaf score included the swingy "I'm a Great Big Baby" and a march called "We Are Americans Too." The best of the *Tan Manhattan* songs was a moody ballad originally named "I'll Take a Nickel for a Dime." Under a new title, "I'd Give a Dollar for a Dime," the song was taken up by Joe Williams in the late 1950s, and it has been a standard of the saloon repertoire ever since.

Sissle and Blake both led USO troupes during World War II. Sissle organized an orchestra to play at bases in Europe, and he took Flournoy Miller and Ivan Harold Browning overseas with him. Blake was afraid of flying, so his show—usually featuring Edith Wilson—played hospitals and training camps in the United States that he could get to by train. The military shows were exhausting, and there were a lot of them, but both men—Sissle in his mid-fifties, Blake over sixty—stayed with the USO throughout the war years.

After the war Sissle returned to the Diamond Horseshoe, and Blake got married. The bride was a widow named Marion Gant Tyler, who had been a secretary at Northrup Aircraft Company in Los Angeles and had also worked in that capacity for W. C. Handy. If one could pinpoint the date of the turnaround in Eubie Blake's life, it would be his wedding day, December 27, 1945. The newlyweds moved into Marion's house on Brooklyn's Stuyvesant Avenue, and Blake began to use his famous line, "I got the coop with the chicken."

Marion Blake took firm charge of her husband's business affairs. Her first priority was a successful campaign to upgrade his ASCAP rating, and Blake settled into what he thought would be a serene retirement. His improved status with ASCAP would matter a great deal in 1948. The theme song of the Truman campaign was "I'm Just Wild About Harry," and it was used thousands of times, with each play bringing payment to its writers. The sheet music was reissued with Truman's photo on the cover.

Blake quickly grew bored with his inactive state, and he began studies for a music degree at NYU in 1946. In 1950, the year of his graduation, there appeared a book that would send him off on another, entirely unexpected career. This was *They All Played Ragtime*, by Rudi Blesh and Harriet Janis, and it reminded the music world that one of ragtime's living masters, Eubie Blake, was still around, and was ready to play. Audiences and record companies rediscovered him. The ragtime revival that Blesh and Janis began would keep Eubie busy for the rest of his life, cramming his calendar with dates for concerts, television appearances, and recording sessions. But before Blake's renaissance got rolling, he and Sissle tried Broadway one more time.

The show was called *Shuffle Along of 1952*, and every possible wrongheaded decision was made in its preparation. The melodramatic story by Flournoy Miller and Paul Gerard Smith—about the return of a soldier who was thought by his wife to be dead—would have seemed dated thirty years earlier. The script was tailored to a star (Pearl Bailey), who withdrew from the cast after a stormy and demoralizing rehearsal period. Worst of all, the producers did not trust Sissle and Blake to write the score. Their songs were thrown out one by one, to be replaced with numbers by Floyd Huddleston and Joseph Meyer. By the time the show opened at the Broadway Theatre, on May 8, 1952, Huddleston and Meyer had more songs in the score than Sissle and Blake. Reviews were brutal, and *Shuffle Along of 1952* lasted only four performances. The experience did more than break the hearts of Sissle and Blake. It embarrassed them, and it obliterated what was left of their reputations as theatre writers.

Sissle retired to Tampa, Florida, but Blake's old age was deferred by his busy schedule on the ragtime and media circuits. In 1968, at the live recording session of *The Eighty-Six Years of Eubie Blake* LPs in the Columbia studios, there was one last glimpse of the team's magic. Blake played as Sissle sang "It's All Your Fault," then the two ripped into a dazzling medley of songs from *Shuffle Along*. The songs and the performances shone like old gold.

Blake saw Sissle for the last time on a visit to Florida in 1974. Sissle was frail and his mind was going, but his son, Noble Jr., persuaded a reluctant Blake to make a videotape of the act with his old partner. Sissle hardly knew where he was, but Blake's music led him through it. The piano intros and fills of fifty years ago stirred Sissle and reminded him of lyrics that he had long forgotten. When the taping was over, Sissle doddered again. He died in Tampa on December 17, 1975.

In September 1978 a revue of Blake's songs called *Eubie!* opened on Broadway. His songs held up, of course, and the show was successful. Blake was very proud of it, and he attended many performances, often leaping onto the stage to play and sing with the cast. His new career as a ragtime pioneer was in full swing, and he took every opportunity to plug the show in his concerts and interviews. But Broadway was a very different street from the one that Sissle and Blake had known in the 1920s. Among *Eubie!*'s neighbors on the musical stage that season were a murderous barber and the residents of a Texas whorehouse. Sissle and Blake's brand of entertainment, as sunny as it was, was not what the new Broadway was about. Eubie enjoyed his return to the main stem, but he knew it was only a visit. There would not be a *Eubie! II*. When the show closed, the old man marked it and moved on. He was over ninety now, but he still had work to do.

Blake was lauded in his old age with doctorates, portrait busts, biographies. He was a lively and charming ghost from another musical era, and he was a tireless performer. He kept his act fresh with new compositions and an unending stream of stories about long-dead characters he had known. He told of attending prizefights with George M. Cohan, of marching in parades alongside John Philip Sousa, of being arrested for having a bottle of whiskey in his pocket in Toronto during Prohibition. He gave longevity tips to Johnny Carson, he played on *Saturday Night Live*, he issued ten LPs of his work on his own record label. He had his eye on the calendar as he galloped toward his centennial.

Only the death of his wife Marion, in the summer of 1982, made him falter. His last winter was a rough one, but willpower kept him alive. He was too weak to attend any of his hundredth-birthday celebrations, but no somber announcement cast a pall over the parties for him. Five days after honoring his bargain with his fans, on February 12, 1983, Eubie Blake died in Brooklyn.

HENRY CREAMER AND TURNER LAYTON

The story of the six-year collaboration of Henry Creamer and Turner Layton is that of a team out of sync. Creamer was serious about theatre, and his long apprenticeship in the profession made him the most likely of all his contemporaries to succeed at it; Layton was a gifted pianist and composer who saw the theatre as a place to promote pop songs. When the going got tough, Layton got out. They had their chances, their shows, their hits—but there was always something that kept it from coming together for them. At various times they needed smarter producers, bigger publishers, or better first recordings of their songs. Yet, for all of their near-misses in the theatre, theirs is not a hard-luck story. They had big songs and a few of these became standards. They simply never made the parlay of hit songs from hit shows.

Henry S. Creamer was born June 21, 1879, in Richmond, Virginia. His family moved to New York when he was a child, and he completed his education in the city's public schools. After graduation from high school, Creamer took several front-of-the-house theatre jobs, as usher, program seller, and house manager. He may have been working in some such capacity in a vaudeville house that hosted Williams and Walker's *The Policy Players* or *Sons of Ham*, because it was during this time that he met the songwriter Tom Lemonier, who had songs in both shows. Creamer and Lemonier began to write songs together, and in 1906 Lemonier's vanity firm, Archer & Lemonier, issued three of their collaborations, the first lyrics by Henry Creamer to see print: "All Wise Chickens Follow Me," "Dinah, Come Kiss Your Baby," and "I Wonder How the Old Folks Are at Home." Lemonier had had a hit in 1905 with "Just One Word of Consolation," so Creamer's association with him was a good start.

The young lyricist found work as a stage manager in vaudeville houses, and, drawing on his skills as an eccentric dancer, he began to help various acts as a director. By mid-1907 he was well enough known in black theatrical circles to be hired as colyricist (with Lester A. Walton) for *The Oyster Man*, an Ernest Hogan show with music by Hogan and Will Vodery. The star and the score of *The Oyster Man* got good notices when the show began its New York run in November 1907, but illness forced Hogan to withdraw from the show during its tour in early 1908. Even though the show's run had been abbreviated by the loss of its star, Witmark issued several of its songs, including "Yankee Doodle Coon," "Within the Shade of Morro Castle," "Contribution Box," and "When Buffalo Bill and His Wild West Show First Came to Baltimore"—all with lyrics by Creamer.

In late 1908 Creamer and Silvio Hein got "That's the Doctor Bill" into Marie Cahill's show *The Boys and Betty*. The following year Bert Williams collaborated with Creamer on "That's a-Plenty," and the star sang it in *Mr. Lode of Koal*. One of Williams' numbers in his first *Follies* (in 1910) was his and Creamer's "Chicken." In the spring of 1910 Creamer's standing in the inner circle of black show business was confirmed by James Reese Europe's asking him to become a founding member of the Clef Club. Creamer performed a dance at the club's first fund-raiser in May, and in October he and Tom Lemonier sang a medley of their songs at the Clef Club's "Second Grand Musical Melange and Dance Fest." Creamer wrote "Clef Club Chant" for the autumn evening's closing number.

Creamer and Will Vodery teamed again for a theatre score in 1912, S. H. Dudley's *Dr. Beans from Boston*, which played in Washington's Howard Theatre and in Atlantic City. A few numbers were published from the show. The team tried again with songs in *The Boys from Home*, another show which never reached New York. Undeterred by his two flops, Creamer put on another theatrical hat in late 1912, becoming a producer-director. Along with Will Marion Cook, Alex Rogers, and the actor Charles Gilpin, he organized the Negro Players Company. The aim of the stock company was to create a new kind of musical, more intimate than the spectacles designed for Broadway audiences, with meatier, more realistic parts than existed in the musical farces that were the standard fare for black performers.

The first production of the Negro Players was a musical playlet called *The Traitor*, with music by Cook and lyrics by Creamer and Rogers. *The Traitor* ran for a tense week at Harlem's Lafayette Theatre in March 1913. Cook was argumentative about every creative decision made by his collaborators, and the production was in constant turmoil because of their infighting. A final blowup led to the early closing of the show and to Cook's withdrawal from the company. Creamer and Rogers felt pressure for the Negro Players to come up with something viable to follow *The Traitor*, so they quickly went to work preparing a second production. This was an odd half-musical called *The Old Man's Boy*, a backstage story with more drama than music. Creamer contributed lyrics, and he acted and directed as well. *The Old Man's Boy* had a tryout run at Philadelphia's Casino Theatre in May 1913, then came back to its home base, the Lafayette, in June. By August, when "Rogers and Creamer's Negro Players and the Dancing Demons" were featured doing a syncopated waltz at the annual Frogs' Frolic, *The Old Man's Boy* was planning a tour of the South in hope of making up for its losses in Harlem. However, by the end of 1913 the Negro Players Company had disbanded.

Creamer's recent shows had been unlucky, but he was doing better with his songs. Bert Williams recorded "I Certainly Was Going Some" (by Creamer and Will Vodery) in January 1913, and the song was one of three by the team to be published by Waterson, Berlin & Snyder. Creamer had two published songs written with Jim Europe in 1912, and one of them, "I've Got the Finest Man," was recorded by Ada Jones.

When Lester Walton decided to produce his 1915 musical, *Darkeydom*, he asked Henry Creamer to write the lyrics to music cocomposed by Jim Europe and Will Marion Cook. Creamer's anticipation of collaborating with Europe overrode his dread of working with Cook, and he accepted the assignment. Walton had grand dreams for *Darkeydom* and he staged it on a huge scale. But the show was a financial disaster for its producer and an artistic disappointment for its writers. After a poor week at the Howard in Washington and a few slow weeks at the Lafayette, Walton pulled the plug on *Darkeydom* in late November 1915.

Henry Creamer had worked at theatre for nearly ten years, and he had hands-on experience in every aspect of putting on a show. But he had not had critical success since his first musical, *The Oyster Man*, in 1907. And among his two dozen or so published songs, he had had no real hits.

Not long after the collapse of *Darkeydom*, Creamer met a vaudeville pianist named Turner Layton. Layton was fifteen years younger than Creamer and not particularly interested in the theatre—nor had he published a song before their meeting. Creamer was probably the one to suggest that they write together. After a succession of flops with three of the best-known black composers—Vodery, Cook, and Europe—the chance to write with a talented unknown must have looked like a fresh start to him. Some sources say that they formed a vaudeville team, but whether or not this is so, they did begin to collaborate on songs. Creamer steered their material toward the theatre, and, during their six years together, they contributed songs to nine shows and wrote two full scores. Layton's tunes put a zip into Creamer's lyric writing that was not there before. The old pro was yanked from the Ernest Hogan era into the jazz age.

John Turner Layton, Jr., was born on July 2, 1894, in Washington, D.C. His father was a respected educator who taught vocal music in the District's schools for years. In 1895 he was appointed director of music for the city's colored schools, the position he held until his death in 1916. The senior Layton was also active in church music, as choir director of Washington's Metropolitan AME Church for forty years, and he was a founder of the city's Samuel Coleridge-Taylor Choral Society. He had several hymns published in the 1897 edition of the AME hymnal, the first edition to include music as well as lyrics. (One of these, "Jesus, Lover of My Soul," is still used in Protestant services.) The conservatory-trained father was delighted when his son showed an aptitude for music, and he gave the boy many hours of instruction at the piano.

J. Turner Layton

After Turner, Jr.'s high school graduation, he enrolled in the Dental School at Howard University. He stayed for a year or so, but playing the piano interested him more than his studies did. Probably without his father's blessing, he left Washington for New York to seek work as a musician. He was a good sight reader, and this skill served him well as a pianist in James Reese Europe's various Society Orchestras. In the year of his father's death, he met Henry Creamer.

Creamer knew his way around show business much better than Layton did. He even had a few strings to pull with publishers and producers. The pair had not been writing together very long when Creamer got one of their numbers, a dance song called "The Bombo-Shay," into *Follow Me*, a Shubert revue that opened on Broadway in November 1916. Remick published the song—with a cut-in credit given to Henry Lewis—in early 1917, and it was the first of their sixty-five or so songs in print. They soon began publishing with Broadway Music, and the firm would issue their numbers almost exclusively for three years. Creamer's friendship with Bert Williams was a plus for the new team. Williams sang two of their songs—"Everybody's Crazy 'Bout the Doggone Blues But I'm Happy" and "Unhappy"—in the 1917 *Ziegfeld Follies*, and he recorded their "Twenty Years" in September of that year.

The song that would become Creamer and Layton's hardiest perennial was being heard everywhere except New York in 1917. *So Long,*

Letty, a Shubert musical that had only a middling run in New York in late 1916, was proving to be very popular on the road. In early 1917 a new song was interpolated into the score of the touring show: Creamer and Layton's "After You've Gone." It was a hit with audiences, but it was not available in sheet music or on recordings. When Broadway Music finally issued the song in 1918, *So Long, Letty* was defunct, so it was printed with an ordinary cover, without a star's photo or a mention of the show. The first recordings of "After You've Gone" didn't help it either. The old-timers Henry Burr and Albert Campbell got to it first, and they issued their bland vocal duet in late 1918. This was followed by indifferent recordings by Marion Harris and Billy Murray a few months later.

The song was good enough to survive its stumble into the market-place, however. Although this jazz standard was not in band books during most of the Jazz Age, Bessie Smith's 1927 recording marked its rediscovery. Other hit recordings of "After You've Gone" were made by Sophie Tucker (in 1927), Paul Whiteman (in 1930), and Louis Armstrong (in 1932). The song was the first to be recorded by the Benny Goodman Trio (in 1935), and it remained a staple of Goodman bands, trios, and quartets for years. It took ten years for "After You've Gone" to enter the pop pantheon, but it remained there for decades.

"After You've Gone" is one of those solidly built songs—like "Some of These Days" and "St. Louis Blues"—that sounds good at any tempo. Its chorus is compact, only twenty measures long, but it is harmonically busy, shifting chords with every measure. The first four notes of the chorus melody are the same as those of "Peg o' My Heart," and there is a built-in break in measures seven and eight ("You'll miss the dearest pal you've ever had"). Creamer's lyric is simple, giving natural vowel stresses to the syncopations in Layton's sinuous tune. The words contain no slang or dialect, and because syncopation was ubiquitous in pop song by 1917, there is nothing to mark it as a "black song." The team's first names were dropped from their credits on song sheets early in their publishing career, and music store customers probably did not know who "Creamer and Layton" were.

Songs poured out of them in the late teens, and Broadway Music kept publishing them. One of their best was a 1917 song, "Sweet Emmalina, My Gal," enhanced by Layton's rich harmonies. Al Jolson chose their "I'll Sing You a Song about Dear Old Dixie Land" for inclusion in

Sinbad, and Bert Williams recorded their "Oh! Lawdy" and "It's Gettin' So You Can't Trust Nobody." With the exception of one published song—Creamer's lyric for Will Tyers' instrumental "Maori," in 1918—their partnership was exclusive.

Early in 1920 the chance came to do a full score for a Broadway musical. The Georgia-born actor Charles Coburn and his wife Ivah decided to produce (but not star in) a show called *Three Showers*, and Creamer and Layton were hired to write the music. The plot's premise was that if you make a wish on a day with three showers, your wish will come true. The style of the show was "Broadway rural," with farmers and farmerettes capering about in pastel overalls and calico dresses. Creamer and Layton's score was more sophisticated than the nonsense going on around it, but the show, which opened on April 5, 1920, lasted only forty-five performances at the Harris Theatre. Charles K. Harris published sixteen of the *Three Showers* songs, but there were no hits among them. *Three Showers* was the first white show with music by black writers since the Cole and Johnson era, but its ineptness made it less than historic.

In 1921 Creamer and Layton had a minor hit with a strange concoction called "Dear Old Southland." It is a verseless song that uses the melody of "Deep River" as its main theme and "Sometimes I Feel Like a Motherless Child" as its bridge. Except for a bit of rhythmic tweaking at the ends of lines, Layton's tunes are note-for-note the same as his models'. Creamer's lyric is a collection of old-South clichés, allusions to the Swanee shore, Mammy Jinny, and singing pickaninnies. "Dear Old Southland" is a throwback to the "refined" coon ballads of a generation earlier, and its popularity must have lain in the fact that everyone already knew and loved the melodies from which it is made.

Creamer and Layton made their only recording in April 1921, a pair of vocal duets for Black Swan ("I'm Wild about Moonshine" and "It's Gettin' So You Can't Trust Nobody"). Early in 1922, Charles and Ivah Coburn called on them again, this time to supply three songs for a play with music called *Bronx Express*. Coburn won praise for his portrayal of a sweet-natured buttonmaker in the sentimental drama, but no one noticed the songs.

Probably frustrated by so many theatrical dead ends, Henry Creamer decided to produce his own show to feature Creamer and

Layton music. The trials that lay ahead for Creamer's revue would rend his partnership with Turner Layton.

Creamer planned to capitalize on the slowly growing popularity of a song that the duo had written two years earlier, a bright number called "Strut, Miss Lizzie." The Original Dixieland Jazz Band had recorded it first, in December 1920 in a medley with "Sweet Mamma,"and it got several vocal recordings in early 1921, including one by Lucille Hegamin. Van and Schenck had sung it in the 1921 *Ziegfeld Follies*. Creamer put together a one-man organization he called the Creole Producing Company and began choosing material and personnel for a revue that would feature the song. He chose Joe Jordan as his musical director, and he hired Cora Green and Hamtree Harrington to star. He decided to put himself and Layton in the show, doing an act in outright imitation of Sissle and Blake's. He set to work on the score with Layton, and they had particularly high hopes for one of the new numbers, "Way Down Yonder in New Orleans."

Gilda Gray was set to sing Creamer and Layton's "Come Along" in the 1922 *Ziegfeld Follies*, and their "In Yama Yama Land" was going into an April revue called *Some Party*. Creamer was confident about both songs, so much so that he was depending on the royalties from them to launch his own production. However, "Come Along" did not make the hoped-for hit in the *Follies*, and *Some Party* folded after seventeen performances. Neither of Creamer's songs in these shows received recordings, and there would be no start-up money for *Strut Miss Lizzie* to be had from them.

Ziegfeld was using a new slogan, "Glorifying the American Girl," that year, so Creamer touted his upcoming *Strut Miss Lizzie* as a show "Glorifying the Creole Beauty." However, Creamer was undercapitalized before he began, so he borrowed $1,600 from the publisher Jack Mills. And he started looking to rent a theatre. The only landlord who would bargain with Creamer over such a small-potatoes production was the burlesque impresario Billy Minsky. For a piece of the show, Minsky agreed to house it in his National Winter Garden Theatre, a seedy *palais du strip* on Second Avenue near Houston Street. *Strut Miss Lizzie* opened there on June 3, 1922.

Creamer quickly saw that the remote East Village location would sink his show, and he knew that he needed to be in the theatre district.

Still without resources, he cut another deal with Minsky. For $2,500 of each week's gross, Minsky would move the show uptown to the Times Square Theatre on Forty-second Street, another Minsky-managed

Strut Miss Lizzie

property. After two weeks of poor business on Second Avenue, *Strut Miss Lizzie* came to Broadway, opening at the Times Square on June 19.

The critics' reactions to *Strut Miss Lizzie* were generally positive, and audiences especially liked the title song and "Way Down Yonder in New Orleans." The show was no earth-shaker, but it was an entertaining example of what was by then called a "speed show," a black revue full of upbeat music and flashy dancing. The reviews gave a glimmer of hope to the show, and Creamer seized on it. He decided to make a stand. He borrowed $1,500 from Arthur Lyons, a vaudeville agent, to pay the first week's salaries. In

return he gave Lyons the royalties on ten of the *Strut Miss Lizzie* songs until the debt was paid. With Creamer in desperate straits now, Minksy and Lyons advanced him more money in exchange for 75 percent of the show's profits. Creamer's debts were now eating into his net as well as his gross. His two creditors installed themselves in the box office to watch over the take and get first dibs on anything that came in.

Creamer had to break the grip that Minsky and Lyons had on his ticket sales, so in late June, he moved the show again, this time to the Earl Carroll Theatre on Seventh Avenue at Fiftieth Street. The price of his freedom was Carroll's high rent: $3,400 a week. Creamer's cast had been taking IOUs instead of salaries, and when he posted a closing notice after one week at Earl Carroll's, his actors formed a cooperative to try to save the show. However, the spiral of financial woes widened. Lyons sued Carroll for stealing his show; the actors sued Lyons for withholding their salaries. When *Strut Miss Lizzie* finally ended its agony after two weeks at Earl Carroll's, the shell-shocked troupe was presented with a bill from Lyons for $159. Props and costumes were hauled away by marshals, to be held against *Strut Miss Lizzie*'s morass of debt.

Among the salvage from the show were its two best songs. "Strut Miss Lizzie" and "Way Down Yonder in New Orleans" both went into *Spice of 1922*, a July revue at the (uptown) Winter Garden. "Strut Miss Lizzie" is a toddling tune with a streetwise lyric about watching a pretty girl who knows she's fetching. Layton's melody quotes the old "Hoochy-Koochy" dance, and there is a driving, rhythmic patter section between choruses. ("Go down the street, by the school, pat your feet, you steppin' fool. Strut your stuff, use your 'kerch,' trot your tootsies by the church. Through the alley, dodge the cans, shake Miss Sally's pots and pans. Cool your dogs we're comin' thru, get set for Lenox Avenue.")

"Way Down Yonder in New Orleans"—like "After You've Gone"—didn't get the recordings it deserved when it was new. It is so strongly rhythmic that it is impossible not to swing when singing it. The twenty-eight bar chorus has an interesting structure, with a catchy dual stop-time phrase. ("Stop! Oh, won't you give your lady fair a little smile? Stop! You bet your life you'll linger there a little while.") Although it is rarely sung, there is a tango-tempo patter section that paraphrases "La Paloma." The Dixie Daisies had the first recording of "Way Down Yonder in New Orleans," in October 1922 on Cameo, and Gene Fosdick's Hoosiers and the Cotton Pickers got to it a few months later. The Paul Whiteman orchestra recorded it in February 1923, but the first hit did not come until the 1927 Frankie Trumbauer recording that featured Bix Beiderbecke's cornet. The song was used in several feature films in the thirties and forties, and Frankie Cannon put it on the hit parade again in 1960.

The nightmare experience of *Strut Miss Lizzie* destroyed the Creamer-Layton team. Layton was not a partner in Creamer's Creole Producing Company, and he must have been horrified at his lyricist's wheeling and dealing with their copyrights and profits to keep the show afloat. There were a couple of Creamer and Layton songs issued in 1923—"Down by the River" and "Whoa, Tillie, Take Your Time"— but these were holdovers that had been sold to publishers earlier. (Edythe Baker made a delightful piano roll of "Down by the River," and Paul Whiteman's Virginians recorded "Whoa, Tillie.") By the end of 1922, Turner Layton was teamed with a singer named Clarence "Tandy" Johnstone for vaudeville dates, and Henry Creamer had already published a half-dozen songs with various composers, all of them white Tin Pan Alley veterans.

Creamer found a new theatre project right away. He was hired as colyricist (with Ben Harris) for a show called *How Come?*, with music by Will Vodery. Bessie Smith was briefly in the *How Come?* company during its tryout run in Philadelphia, but she had left the cast by the time the show opened at Broadway's Apollo Theatre on April 16, 1923. The show ran only five weeks, but Goodman-Rose issued several of its songs. Creamer placed songs in revues—*Innocent Eyes*, Ed Wynn's *Grab Bag*, *Gay Paree*—over the next few years, but *How Come?* was his last full score until 1929. His major collaborators during his freelancing years in the mid-twenties were James F. Hanley, Lew Pollack, and Harry Warren.

Turner Layton placed one of his songs ("Easy Goin' Man," with lyrics by Darl MacBoyle) into *Runnin' Wild* in 1923, but he published only a handful of songs after his rift with Creamer. His teaming with Tandy Johnstone was a success, and the two became favorites at society parties. A photo on a 1924 song sheet shows the pair in white tie and tails, the distinguished-looking, gray-haired Johnstone leaning on a baby grand piano smiling at the handsome young Layton, whose hands are suspended over a chord.

In February 1924 Layton and Johnstone made their European debut in an extravagant revue at the Empire Theatre in Paris. They shared a bill with the continent's biggest stars: Maurice Chevalier, Little Tich, the beloved clown Grock, Yvette Guilbert, and Raquel Meller. (Also featured on the gigantic stage of the Empire were a forty-horse equestrian act, Powers' Musical Elephants, and Winstone's Mermaids and Seals.) The Americans made a solid hit, and in the late summer they went from Paris to London's Coliseum Theatre. British audiences, including the royal family, loved their combination of polish and sentimentality, and in the mid-twenties they owned London as Josephine Baker owned Paris. Layton and Johnstone never came home, but Layton kept in touch with their American fans through the occasional columns he sent for publication in the Chicago *Defender*. The duo were fixtures in London's largest variety halls for ten years. They were often heard on BBC radio in the early 1930s, and they recorded dozens of sides for the Parlophone label.

Henry Creamer plugged away, more a figure of Tin Pan Alley now than of the Broadway stage. He placed a couple of songs into Eddie Dowling's *Honeymoon Lane* in 1926, and one of them, "Jersey Walk" (written with Dowling and James F. Hanley), had a small success in its recording by Fred Waring's Pennsylvanians. Earl Carroll took "Alabama Stomp," by Creamer and James P. Johnson, for his 1926 *Vanities*, and the song was popular enough to carry over into the next edition of the show.

Creamer and Johnson wrote a major hit in 1926, but, like Creamer's other hits, it was slow in taking off. It was a graceful little soft-shoe song called "If I Could Be with You One Hour Tonight." Eva Taylor and Clarence Williams recorded it first, in early 1927, but it did not become popular until Louis Armstrong's August 1930 recording. Creamer and Johnson wrote two unproduced musicals—*Geechee* and *Chicago Loop*—in 1926, and they managed to get three of their songs into *A la Carte*, a short-lived revue of 1927.

Creamer also worked briefly with Eubie Blake in 1927, but none of their songs were published. (Blake liked Creamer, even though he "talked like a Sunday school teacher.") Creamer's lyrics were featured in *Keep Shufflin'*, the successful black revue that opened at Daly's Sixty-third Street Theatre on February 27, 1928. His words were mostly to James P. Johnson's music, but Creamer's name is also on *Keep Shufflin'* songs written with Con Conrad (the show's producer), Will Vodery, and Clarence Todd. The best-received of the Creamer and Johnson songs in the score was "'Sippi."

On January 7, 1929, *Deep Harlem* opened at the Biltmore Theatre. It was the most ambitious of Henry Creamer's shows, and it was his biggest failure. *Deep Harlem* was presented by two

George Washington Bullion Abroad

brothers, J. Homer Tutt and Salem Tutt Whitney, pioneer producers of, and performers in, black stock shows. For years the pair had barnstormed the country with their Smart Set productions, mostly musicals and farces, such as *George Washington Bullion Abroad*, *Bamboula*, and

Oh, Joy. And now the old-timers had made it to Broadway, mounting as expansive a pageant of African-American history as they could afford. The story began with the selling of an African tribe into slavery, then followed the descendants of that tribe through generations in America from Savannah, Georgia, into contemporary Harlem. The music was written by Joe Jordan, and the lyrics were by Homer Tutt and Henry Creamer (who also directed). *Deep Harlem* was ripped to shreds by the critics, who scoffed at its tatty scenery and its "grotesque" story. It was too different, too serious, too African. New York reviewers and audiences wanted

The Lady Fare

brownskin vamps and peppy dancing, not *Deep Harlem*. The show closed after its eighth performance.

There was not much left of Henry Creamer's career. He had a song in a black film of 1929 called *Feelin' Blue* ("Dreary Night," with music by Peter DeRose), and there were three Creamer-Johnson songs in another film, *The Lady Fare*, that year. The last Creamer lyric for the stage was "Flower of a Day," an English adaptation of a Spanish song used in a 1930 play called *Dishonored Lady*. Henry Creamer died in New York City on October 14, 1930.

In 1935 the Layton-Johnstone act was destroyed by scandal. Tandy Johnstone was named as co-respondent in the divorce action of a white English couple, and he fled to New York, where he would die in obscurity in 1953. Layton continued as a solo performer in England, and he remained popular long enough to become one of the first variety stars of BBC television. He retired from music in the mid-1950s and spent his last years running his own pub in Bury St. Edmonds, in Suffolk, England. Turner Layton died in London on February 6, 1978.

JAMES P. JOHNSON

In the *Ziegfeld Follies of 1922* there was a song by Louis Hirsch, Gene Buck, and Dave Stamper called "It's Getting Dark on Old Broadway."

Its lyric is a crude comment on the increasing number of black entertainers in midtown cabarets. ("It's just like an eclipse of the moon, Ev'ry cafe now has the dancing coon. . . . Yes, the great white way is white no more, It's just like a street on the Swanee shore.") Gilda Gray sang it, while a trick of lighting put the line of beauties behind her into temporary blackface. There was only one black show on Broadway when the 1922 *Follies* opened—*Shuffle Along*, nearing the end of its run—but by the time the next *Follies* premiered, in October 1923, Broadway had seen *Put and Take*, *Strut Miss Lizzie*, *The Plantation Revue*, *Liza*, and *How Come?* None of these black shows had scenic wonders like the *Follies*, their books and sketches were as

James P. Johnson

silly as anything in the operettas of the time, and their stars were generally unknown to white audiences. But all of them, including the flops, had something to offer that white shows didn't have. Critics called it "zest," "snap," or "verve"—and what they meant was jazzy music and hot, energetic dancing. These became the trademarks—and finally the trap—of black shows.

Three days after the 1923 *Follies* opened at the New Amsterdam, *Runnin' Wild*, the musical that embodied the frenzy of the Jazz Age, came to Broadway. The score, by James P. Johnson and Cecil Mack, contained a number called the "Charleston," and the first four notes of its chorus are all that have ever been needed to conjure the era for succeeding generations. It went BAM/BAM! BAM/BAM!, much as the twenties did, and the dance that it inspired kept black choreographers and dancers busy on Broadway throughout the decade.

James Price Johnson was born on February 1, 1894, at his parents' home in New Brunswick, New Jersey. He was the son of a mechanic and a maid who were known throughout black New Brunswick for their lively neighborhood parties. James' mother Josephine provided the dinners for these affairs, and her guests provided the music for dancing. Most of them were country people from the South, and they brought their guitars, mandolins, and jaw harps along to accompany the reels and ring-shouts that they learned in their youth. James had been playing the family's piano since he was about four, but on party nights he just watched and listened. The rhythms of the exuberant dancing that he saw stayed in his head all of his life. The Johnsons moved to Jersey City in 1902, and James began to hear a kind of music that was new to him, the rags and pop songs that wafted from the saloons there.

When James was fourteen, his family moved again, this time to "San Juan Hill," a rough neighborhood in the west Sixties in New York City. New York offered a great variety of music, from street organs to symphonies, and James took it all in. He was serious about ragtime by now, and he worked hard to master everything by Scott Joplin (1868–1917). In 1911, around the time the Johnsons moved to Ninety-ninth Street, James found that he could earn a little money playing in West Side dance halls and silent movie theatres. By age twenty he was a familiar (and highly competitive) player at Harlem rent parties. The pay was small at these at-homes which charged admission, but food and drinks were free to musicians. And they attracted the best pianists in Harlem, which is to say the best popular pianists in the world. The Harlem players were friends as well as rivals. James P. was an intimate of Luckey Roberts and Willie the Lion Smith (1897–1973), and he met Eubie Blake when he went to hear Blake play at a club in Newark. Each of them was a showier player than Johnson, but showmanship was all that he lacked. His mind and his fingers were nimbler than anyone else's.

Like most of his contemporaries, James P. Johnson was interested in songwriting but not particularly interested in nor committed to the theatre. Indeed, there was little reason for black composers to consider the profession in the teens. The opportunities that existed were for players, not writers. For most black musicians, a show was just another place to play or conduct a band, on a par with but no more important than a cabaret or a dance hall, something to take if one could get it. A few hardy souls, like Tutt and Whitney, ground out stock shows for black audiences every season, and these usually featured music written by their producers.

Johnson's first theatre work was typical: as bandleader for a short-lived farce called *What's Your Husband Doing?* in 1917 and as music director for the Smart Set's tour of *My People* the following year. During this time he was making his money from his piano rolls and club jobs, and he was practically living off the food at rent parties. His first publications came in 1917 when F. B. Haviland issued three of his songs, all with lyrics by Will Farrell. The first of them, "Mama's Blues," became fairly well known, and, although the songs brought him no royalties (they were sold outright), he acquired the cachet of publication. Johnson married a club singer named Lillie Mae Wright in 1917, after a three-year courtship.

By 1920 Johnson's renown as a pianist had surpassed even that of Harlem's original powerhouse, Luckey Roberts. The vehicles for Johnson's growing reputation were his hand-played piano rolls. He made his first rolls in 1917, and he made more of them than any other Harlem pianist (a lifetime total of fifty-four, compared to Roberts' five). Johnson's rolls influenced a generation of young players, who studied the movement of the player piano keys as closely as they listened to the music. Just when it seemed to his imitators that Johnson had taken syncopated thinking to its limit in the late teens, he took it farther in the early twenties by conceiving an entirely original genre, a super-complex kind of ragtime that became known as "stride."

The definitive stride composition is James P. Johnson's "Carolina Shout." He made it first as a piano roll in 1918, and it was a dazzling showpiece even then. But when he made his second roll of the number in 1921, he added syncopated countermelodies to the left hand, in effect doubling the syncopation of an already tricky rag. His right hand skittered across the keys, as it had in the 1918 version, but in 1921 he laced the melody with flashes of harmonies in thirds, giving a bell-like effect to his playing. "Carolina Shout" became the test piece for all urban ragtimers, the number that hotshots had to know. Few amateur players could master it, indeed most could not even parse it out at the piano. There was no profit in publishing unplayable rags, so "Carolina Shout" was not available in sheet music form until 1925, in a small printing issued by Clarence Williams. Stride was enormously influential, but there was no money in composing it. During the time he was conceiving the most sophisticated of all popular piano music, Johnson was making his living as an accompanist for blues singers and was still taking his dinners at rent parties.

In late 1922 Johnson served as music director for a show called *Plantation Days*. Its producers had booked the show to play in several northern and Midwestern cities, with a stop at Harlem's Lafayette Theatre as their last. If all went well at the Lafayette, rumor had it, the show would go from there to London. The star of the revue was the comic song-and-dance man Eddie Green. One of Johnson's songs, "Ukelele Blues," was used in the show, along with three unauthorized tunes lifted from *Shuffle Along*. *Shuffle Along*'s producers filed an injunction to remove the Sissle and Blake songs from *Plantation Days*, and the legal action delayed the opening at the Lafayette by more than a month. After a one-week run at the Lafayette in early April 1923, the *Plantation Days* company sailed for London.

When they arrived, they found that their show was not to be produced in its entirety but was to be compressed into a twelve-minute segment performed during a Gershwin musical, *The Rainbow*, which was already running at the Empire Theatre. Johnson had met George Gershwin about three years earlier, when both were piano roll artists for the Aeolian company. Gershwin greatly admired Johnson's playing and had gone to Harlem many times to hear him. The two socialized a bit in London, but they never wrote anything together, as some have claimed. Despite some racial hostility from the British cast of *The Rainbow* and the fact that their show had been truncated to almost nothing, *Plantation Days* was a step up from the level of theatre that Johnson had done before. It was almost worthwhile.

The next show job for James P. Johnson was another stopgap, as music director for *Raisin' Cain*, at the Lafayette in July 1923. But while he spent his evenings leading the *Raisin' Cain* cast through the Donald Heywood-Jo Trent score, he was spending his days working on the songs for the show that would be his biggest hit.

Probably on the recommendation of George Gershwin, Johnson was hired that summer by George White to write the score for an upcoming Broadway project. White was a self-taught hoofer who had danced in several Broadway shows in the teens, including two editions of the *Ziegfeld Follies*. When he began his own revue series by launching the first *George White's Scandals* in 1919, he lured away Ziegfeld's dancing star, Ann Pennington, to join his cast. Ziegfeld tried to head off any competition from his former employees by wiring White an offer of $2,000 a week if he and Pennington would come back to the *Follies*. White's reply was to wire Ziegfeld an offer of $3,000 a week if he and Billie Burke would dance in the *Scandals*.

White prospered as a revue producer from the beginning. His shows were not as grand as Ziegfeld's, but they had better scores, better dancing, and a lively, low-class tone. In 1920 White's coup was to sign George Gershwin as his *Scandals* composer. (Gershwin wrote five *Scandals*, and in 1925 he was succeeded by DeSylva, Brown and Henderson as White's composers. From the mid-twenties on, the *Scandals* would regularly best the *Follies* in reviews and at the box office.) After the 1923 *Scandals* opened successfully on June 18, White turned his attention to the show that he had in mind for the fall.

Being a dancer himself, White appreciated the innovations that black show dancers and choreographers were bringing to Broadway. The more expensive mainstream Broadway shows of the time invariably seemed dull in comparison to even the skimpiest black revues or musicals. There had been a few black solo dancers to get attention— U.S. "Slow Kid" Thompson in *The Plantation Revue*, Eddie Rector in *Liza*, Johnny Nit in *How Come?*—but the chorus was really the dancing star of any black show. No matter how fast or intricate the steps, they were executed with relaxation and spontaneity, often by dancers who were singing at the same time. Bits of black show dance—wings, tap steps, and clogs—had been taken up by white dancers, but there was no white chorus that attempted to do fast combinations of these steps in precision. George White wanted the dancingest show Broadway had ever seen, and he hired choreographer Elida Webb (1895–1974), celebrated for "the prettiest legs in Harlem," to create it.

The show that would contain all the dancing was *Runnin' Wild*, which began its tryouts at the Howard Theatre in Washington on August 25, 1923. Miller and Lyles were the comic leads, and the featured singers were Adelaide Hall, Revella Hughes, and Elisabeth Welch. The plot was on the vaudeville-skit level, with the Miller and Lyles characters pretending to be mediums in order to bilk their neighbors in Jimtown. Business was good in D.C. and in the Boston run that followed. By the time *Runnin' Wild* opened at New York's Colonial Theatre on Broadway at Sixty-second Street on October 29,

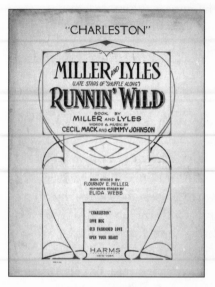

Runnin' Wild

George White knew he had something. Audiences loved the show, and it ran for over 200 performances (a 100-performance run was considered a hit in the early twenties). A touring company extended the show's life into 1926, and in 1928 a *Runnin' Wild* company took London by storm.

The *Runnin' Wild* score by Johnson and Cecil Mack was full of good numbers. There was the sweet and flirty "Love Bug" and the high-kicking "Ginger Brown." The big ballads were "Open Your Heart" (one of Johnson's rangiest tunes) and "Old Fashioned Love," with its hymnlike harmony. There was a "Juba Dance" sequence and a "lazy man's dance" (including slow-motion splits) performed by Tommy Woods and George Stamper.

Best of all, there was the "Charleston." James P. Johnson's "Charleston" was not the first heard on Broadway—*Liza* had a Charleston number and *How Come?* had two—but it was the definitive one. Elisabeth Welch sang the song, then the stage was given over to a group of chorus boys billed as the "Dancing Redcaps." The pit band dropped out, and the energetic, knees-and-elbows dance was done to the bare accompaniment of hand-clapping and foot-stamping. As the chorus beat out more complex rhythms, the Redcaps danced more frenetically. The effect was electric. Johnson's tune was as hard-edged and angular as the dance itself, and none of the dozens of Charlestons written after his displaced it for a minute. Oddly, critics didn't seem to notice the first-nighters going wild for it. No reviews mentioned the number—most bet on "Old Fashioned Love" as the show's hit—but as the run continued, the "Charleston" became so popular that it was used as the finale of both acts of the show.

Six of the Johnson-Mack songs from *Runnin' Wild* were published by Harms. The "Charleston"'s popularity lasted so long after the show had closed that a second edition was issued with no mention of *Runnin' Wild* on the song sheet. This "Charleston" had a bright red cover and instructions on the back—with four photos of a couple's feet—for learning the dance. The directions were written by Oscar Duryea, identified as an "American Authority on Modern Dance" from the Ballroom of the Hotel des Artistes in New York City. Duryea cautioned, "Discretion should be used as to how pronounced the CHARLESTON 'kick up' and 'toddle' movements are made for ballroom dancing." The *Runnin' Wild* company, with no discretion in their kick up or toddle, had given the decade its favorite workout.

Keep Shufflin'

The success of *Runnin' Wild* brought Johnson more theatre projects in the mid-twenties. He was music director for Will Marion Cook's *Negro Nuances*, a series of concert musicals presented at the Lafayette in 1924. In December 1925 Johnson and Cecil Mack wrote the score for *Moochin' Along*, a book musical with a libretto by Jesse Shipp, also at the Lafayette. Johnson's 1926 collaboration with lyricist Henry Creamer gave them a pop hit, "If I Could Be with You One Hour Tonight," but their revue songs, in the 1926 *Earl Carroll's Vanities* and in a 1927 show, *A la Carte,* were not successful

If the royalties on Johnson's theatre songs were erratic, his studio fees were not. In February 1927 he made the first of his fourteen recordings as accompanist for Bessie Smith, and he would be a mainstay of Perry Bradford record sessions for the next several years. Johnson's own best-selling record was his "Snowy Morning Blues," a piano solo issued by Columbia in the spring of 1927.

When Con Conrad asked Johnson and Creamer to write the score for a new Miller and Lyles musical, Johnson suggested that the job be shared with his young protégé and constant companion, Fats Waller, and Waller's lyricist-partner, Andy Razaf. Conrad's backer, the gangster Arnold Rothstein, agreed to this two-composers/two-lyricists division of labor, and work began on *Keep Shufflin'*. The show opened at Daly's Sixty-third Street Theatre in late February 1928, and it moved downtown to the Eltinge Theatre on Forty-second Street on April 23. As he usually did for his shows, Johnson played the piano in the pit and conducted the orchestra. Although the score of *Keep Shufflin'* was strong and the dancing was good, Miller and Lyles' lowbrow antics were beginning to wear thin. The show managed 104 performances, and it had a brief tour in the fall. The Johnson-Creamer songs that were most successful were "Give Me the Sunshine" and "'Sippi," both published with Con Conrad's name added to their credits. The real reason to attend *Keep Shufflin'* was to hear the Johnson-Waller intermission duets, when they played brilliant four-hand stride variations on "'Sippi" at two pianos in the orchestra pit.

Shortly after the show moved to the Eltinge, Johnson missed an event that would certainly have helped his career. W. C. Handy had planned a Carnegie Hall concert to present a survey of African-American music, from spirituals to works by contemporary black composers. Handy wanted Johnson to be the piano soloist with a thirty-piece orchestra in the premiere performance of Johnson's "Yamekraw," which was subtitled "A Negro Rhapsody." Johnson had completed the piece in 1927, and Perry Bradford had published it as a piano solo that year. The chance to present "Yamekraw"—orchestrated by William Grant Still—in such a setting was a composer's dream.

But Miller and Lyles refused to let Johnson take the night off from *Keep Shufflin'* to perform in his Carnegie Hall debut. (The pair may have been acting out of spite. Their relationship with Johnson had been cool after he had questioned their bookkeeping in figuring his royalties from the *Runnin' Wild* tour.) Since there was no arguing with Miller and Lyles, Johnson suggested Fats Waller as his substitute at Handy's Carnegie Hall evening. On April 27, 1928, Waller played "Yamekraw" in Johnson's stead. The dual concert debuts, Waller's and "Yamekraw"'s, were both well received.

"Yamekraw" was James P. Johnson's first concert work, and it has remained his most popular over the years. Perry Bradford, in a foreword to his publication, called it "A genuine Negro treatise on spiritual, syncopated and 'blue' melodies. . . . expressing the religious fervor and happy moods of the natives of Yamekraw, a Negro settlement situated on the outskirts of Savannah, Georgia." The piece is about eleven minutes long, and it is an odd patchwork of tunes and tempos. The main themes are a spiritual ("Every Time I Feel the Spirit"), two Perry Bradford songs ("Sam Jones Done Snagged His Britches" and "You Can Read My Letters But You Can't Read My Mind"), and three Johnson melodies ("Brothers and Sisters," "Mississippi Roustabouts," and "We Are Leaving for Yamekraw"). There is a lot going on in "Yamekraw," but none of it is developed. It has a cluttered feel, as though Johnson were more interested in melodic variation than in cohesion. It was considered an important work during the 1930s, however, and it was featured on radio by several orchestras. In 1930 Warner Brothers made a nine-minute Vitaphone short

Messin' Around

called "Yamekraw" based on the piece, but Johnson was not involved with the making of the film. In 1938 "Yamekraw" was used as the overture to Orson Welles' "voodoo" *Macbeth* in the Federal Theatre Project production at the Lafayette Theatre. Johnson himself finally recorded it, for independent record producer Moses Asch, in 1944. (Asch later issued it on his Folkways label in the 1950s.)

Perry Bradford wrote the lyrics for Johnson's next musical, *Messin' Around*, which opened at the Hudson Theatre on April 22, 1929. The show starred Cora LaRedd and Bamboo McCarver, and it was one of the many attempts to make another *Shuffle Along*. No other black musical had come close to matching Sissle and Blake's paradigm of fun, and the trite imitations of it had become tiresome over the years. And the recent advances in musical theatre made during the late twenties made the *Shuffle Along* clones look even thinner.

The Broadway musical had not turned serious by any means, but several shows had proven that there were satisfactions beyond those of watching pretty girls and vaudeville comedians. The 1927 season brought *Rio Rita*, *A Connecticut Yankee*, *Funny Face*, and *Good News*—all accessible, mainstream musicals and all of them hits—each of which was assembled with care and craft unknown even five years earlier. The idea was dawning that musicals could be *about* something and still be fun.

When *Show Boat* appeared in December 1927, the expectations for the Broadway musical were changed forever. *Show Boat* had it all—great score, big themes, engaging story line, handsome production—and it raised the stakes irrevocably. If a trivial book musical made it to Broadway, its triviality was all the more noticeable after *Show Boat*. And there was competition for black shows even in the pep department. The slick and brassy *George White's Scandals* introduced hot new dances ("Black Bottom" and "Pickin' Cotton") and catchy new songs ("Birth of the Blues" and "Lucky Day") and presented them all with the socko energy that was the *Scandals* trademark.

Black book musicals of the late twenties were in an artistic bind. They were not novelties any more, yet novelty was all they had to offer. Their stock in trade was flash and speed, but these were no longer enough. There had been too many shows built around the misadventures of low comics, too many slapdash plots, too many digressions to accommodate specialty acts. But although black shows needed to grow up, audiences and critics wouldn't let them. The shows that tried to break the mold by presenting something more sophisticated (such as *Chocolate Dandies*) or more serious (such as *Deep Harlem*) were financial failures. Any deviation from the *Shuffle Along* formula was considered overreaching—unnatural and arty. So, during the maturation of mainstream musicals, the black book musical remained in artistic kindergarten.

The compromise, of course, lay in the revue form. If music and dancing were all that Broadway audiences wanted from black shows, the revue was the way to give it to them. There were successful black revues over the years, but after 1930's *Brown Buddies*, there was not another successful book musical by black writers for decades—until Melvin Van Peebles' *Ain't Supposed to Die a Natural Death*, in 1971.

Messin' Around had some good songs by Johnson and Bradford ("Put Your Mind Right on It," "Skiddle-de-Scow," and "Your Love Is All I Crave"), but some of its other ingredients typified the desperate search for novelty in black shows. Bamboo McCarver's big number was a dance performed on roller skates. And the centerpiece of the evening was a boxing match that pitted Aurelia Wheedlin against Emma Maitland. They were billed as "the only two licensed female boxers in America," and the second act stopped while one pummeled the other to the floor. The stunts couldn't save *Messin' Around*, and the show ran one month.

Johnson's next project was the June production of a short film, *St. Louis Blues*, which starred Bessie Smith. Johnson played a pianist in a barroom scene, and he led the band, which was billed as "James P. Johnson's Orchestra." Late in 1929 he collaborated on a musical with Flournoy Miller called *A Great Day in New Orleans*. It had a short run at Philadelphia's Pearl Theatre, but it never came to New York.

Revues were where the work was now, so Johnson worked on revues. In March 1930 *Kitchen Mechanics' Revue*, with music by Johnson and lyrics by Andy Razaf, was the new floor show at Small's Paradise, a Harlem club. By late June, Johnson was leading a band called the "Syncopators" in *Fireworks of 1930*, an elaborate revue starring Mamie Smith at the Lafayette. That summer Johnson's "Rumba Rhythm" was used in *Earl Carroll's Vanities*.

Flournoy Miller produced *Sugar Hill*, a book musical with a score by Johnson and Jo Trent, which opened at Broadway's Forrest Theatre in late December 1931. It was another Miller and Lyles knockabout, and it closed after eleven performances. The next revue was Johnson's most successful: *Harlem Hotcha*, which began as a Connie's Inn floor show in September 1932 and moved to the Lafayette Theatre in March 1933.

In 1932 Johnson wrote the best of his concert works, *Harlem Symphony*. The symphony has four movements, and the themes in each are explored much more fully than those in "Yamekraw." It is program music of a very high order, describing the subway ride to Harlem from Penn Station, a spring day in Harlem, a night club, and a Baptist mission. The "Baptist Mission" theme is an old hymn, "I Want Jesus to Walk with Me," but the other melodies are original. The bustling "Subway Journey" takes the listener through Jewish and Spanish neighborhoods before arriving at 135th Street. "Night Club" suggests the high-kicking ponies in a Harlem chorus line, and "April in Harlem" is tender and melancholy. "Subway Journey" and "April in

Harlem" were used as ballet music at the Lafayette Theatre in 1937, and the Brooklyn Civic Orchestra presented the premiere of the entire *Harlem Symphony* at the Brooklyn Museum in 1939. "April in Harlem,"

AINTCHA GOT MUSIC

Harlem Hotcha

the only part of the work to receive publication, was issued in 1944.

Johnson was the only one of the Harlem piano giants to produce much symphonic writing. The 1930s was a belt-tightening decade for black composers, and Johnson's commitment to concert music had its economic price. He was earning his money from his radio appearances with Eva Taylor, royalties on 1920s songs, and a dwindling number of recording sessions. But even though performances and publications of his serious work were few, he kept writing for the concert hall. His "Jassamine Concerto" was completed in 1934, but only one movement was published—the second, retitled "Blues for Jimmy," in 1947. Also in 1934, he devised his "American Symphonic Suite," a three-part fantasy on "The St. Louis Blues," but not even W. C. Handy was interested in seeing to its publication. His 1935 *Symphony in Brown* went unpublished and unplayed. He tried it all—tone poems, string quartets, sonatas—and much of his work was so long neglected by the musical establishment that it was lost. Only the Brooklyn Civic Orchestra championed him, giving the first full evening of his concert work, with the composer at the piano, on March 8, 1942.

In the decade when he should have been writing in Hollywood, Johnson had only two film credits. The first was a brief on-camera appearance in *The Emperor Jones* in 1933. Johnson is a pianist again, and not even a featured one. He is seen playing "The St. Louis Blues" under dialogue in a party scene. (He is sometimes credited with the film's score, but the music for *The Emperor Jones* was written by J. Rosamond Johnson.) And in 1936 he got a song—"Mister Deep Blue Sea," with lyrics by Gene Austin—into a Mae West film, *Klondike*

Annie. The use of his and Ted Koehler's "There's No Two Ways about Love" in *Stormy Weather* in 1943 completes Johnson's film résumé.

Johnson's appearance in John Hammond's "Spirituals to Swing" concert at Carnegie Hall in December 1938 brought him more attention than he'd had in a long time. But the "swing connection" threw the attention out of focus. After the Hammond evening, Johnson was more often presented as a pioneer jazzman than as a show composer or as a master of stride piano. Instead of bringing theatre projects or retrospectives of his work, his new fame mostly brought him band jobs.

On December 30, 1938, *The Policy Kings*, Johnson's last musical of the thirties, opened at the Nora Bayes Theatre. The score by Johnson and lyricist Louis Douglass got good reviews, and several of the songs were published, but critics

The Policy Kings

and audiences were uneasy with the show's comic treatment of Harlem gangsters. In the same words they had used about other shows ten years earlier, reviewers mentioned enjoying the "dusky steppers" and not enjoying the "uninspiring" comedians. *The Policy Kings* could sustain only three performances. In 1940 Johnson and Langston Hughes collaborated on a one-act opera called *De Organizer*, which received one performance at Carnegie Hall during an International Ladies Garment Workers Union convention. The following year Hughes submitted *De Organizer* to CBS radio for consideration, but a network executive sent it back, saying it was "too controversial for us." Johnson's score and Hughes' libretto are lost.

Johnson suffered a stroke in August 1940, and his recuperation was slow. He spent nearly a year and a half puttering about his house on 108th Avenue in St. Albans, Queens, before he felt up to working again. In early 1943 he came back, leading bands in Fifty-second Street clubs and taking the occasional piano gig. Fats Waller's death, in December 1943, hit Johnson almost as hard as the stroke had. He moped at home for several months, finally coming out of his mourning to record eight Waller songs for Decca in April 1944. In 1945 Johnson was honored at two New York concert evenings of his work, one at Carnegie Hall in May and the other at Town Hall in October.

In 1947 Johnson's *Meet Miss Jones* (with libretto and lyrics by Flournoy Miller) had a brief run at the Experimental Theatre in

Harlem. And there was one more try at commercial theatre. This was *Sugar Hill*, revised from the 1931 production by the man who produced both versions, Flournoy Miller. The show rehearsed in Harlem and opened at Los Angeles' Las Palmas Theatre on July 12, 1949. Reviews were good, but there was no interest in optioning it for a film or in transferring it to Broadway, and the show closed after three months. In 1951 Johnson was paralyzed by another stroke, and there would be no more writing or playing for him.

Sugar Hill

At the time of Johnson's death in Queens, on November 17, 1955, his name was generally unknown outside of musical circles. He had created a new kind of ragtime, had written pop hits, and had written concert music in more forms than any of his contemporaries. As a stride player, he had no equal. None of these achievements translated into celebrity for him. His name does not spring to mind even when we hear the "Charleston." His solo piano recordings, which awed his piano-playing contemporaries, went unappreciated by the record-buying public. But his music is all still there, on song sheets and on CDs, waiting for us. Johnson's treasure chest contains an amazing array of gems, many of which would still shine if they caught the light.

FATS WALLER

The decade that began with one black stage star ended with nearly a dozen whose names could go up in lights on Broadway marquees. They were not thought of as leading men and leading ladies, but as singers and dancers. Their celebrity had been earned in revues, not in book shows. No one knew or cared whether they could act, but everyone knew that they could deliver the goods as entertainers. The first black luminary after Bert Williams was Florence Mills, whose career was cut short by her death in 1927 at age thirty-two. Among the distinctive talents who followed Mills to stardom were singers (Ethel Waters, Adelaide Hall, and Edith Wilson), bandleaders (Cab Calloway and Duke Ellington), and song-and-dance men (Bill Robinson and Buck and Bubbles).

By 1930 the era of the black book musical was over. As had happened twenty years earlier, when the first vogue for blacks on Broadway had passed, there was a decline in the number of productions—and successes—of black shows. The most-produced black show composer during this lean time was the hapless Donald Heywood (1901–1967), who contributed scores and songs to seven Broadway productions, none of them hits. (Two of Heywood's opening nights were disastrous. At the first performance of *Africana*, in 1934, as Heywood was poised to conduct his orchestra in the overture, a man in evening clothes ran down the aisle and attacked him with a crowbar. On the opening night of *Black Rhythm*, in 1936, the theatre had to be cleared after someone threw stink bombs in the house.) Because revues offered a straight shot of what audiences wanted most from black performers, they thrived in the marketplace longer than did musical plays. The most successful songwriter during this Indian summer of great black revues was Fats Waller.

If there were a career to be had by a black show composer after 1929, Waller would have had it. Because there was not, he left theatre writing. Waller did a bit of performing in both of his Broadway revues, but because he was not yet used much as a singer, he was underused. He made his first vocal recording in 1931, and he began a radio career the following year. In the mid-thirties, he was the most dependable hit-producer among Victor's recording artists, and by the end of the decade, he was the most popular black performer in the world. Because his fame was rooted in recordings and radio, it was hardier than that of those who to tried to write for and perform in a separate and barely existent black theatre.

Africana

Like the rest of his writing, Waller's theatre songs came in a hurry, practically improvised under pressure of assignments and deadlines. And in the theatre, as in the recording studio and at the radio microphone, his talent never failed him. However hurriedly he wrote, he invariably produced songs worth hearing. His two Broadway revues and his one book show were all successful, making him the only one among his contemporaries to bat a theatrical thousand.

Thomas Wright Waller was born on May 21, 1904, in his parents' apartment on Waverly Place, in Manhattan's Greenwich Village. His father Edward, who owned a small trucking business, was a man who took his churchgoing seriously. His various good works on behalf of Harlem's Abyssinian Baptist Church became so time-consuming that, soon after Tom's birth, he moved his wife and five children uptown to be nearer the focal point of his life.

A passion for music grew in Tom, in much the same way it had grown for James P. Johnson and Eubie Blake: beginning with hymn-centered study at home, followed by the discovery of pop music, then by experimentation at the piano, then by veering off the course of his music lessons to immerse himself in the joys of syncopation. His father disapproved of it all (even the hymns on the organ) until, at around age ten, Tom became proficient enough to play the harmonium to accompany the passing of the hat after Edward's sermonizing on Harlem street corners. As Johnson and Blake had done before him, Tom dropped out of school in his early teens to pursue a musical career however he could.

The tall, chunky youngster—already known as "Fats"—ingratiated himself with Maizie Mullins, the organist at the Lincoln Theatre, a silent movie house on 135th Street. Mullins let him play in her stead occasionally when she took a break, and he became enthralled with the powerful sound he could produce from the huge instrument. When Mullins quit in 1919, the Lincoln's manager offered the job to Waller. Because he was hidden away in the orchestra pit, the audience could not see that the weaver of musical motifs for Charlie Chaplin and Blanche Sweet was the neighborhood deli's errand boy, still in short pants.

Fats Waller

Waller's mother died in 1920, and he began spending more time away from his family's apartment to escape the ceaseless rows with his father. He roved Harlem in search of company, food, and piano music, and he was on an easy quest. The neighborhood's perpetual rent parties provided all three in abundance, and Fats' sunny charm made him welcome everywhere. After hearing James P. Johnson's piano rolls at a friend's house, he became an admirer of Johnson's playing and did his best to emulate it. When his friend offered to introduce him to Johnson, Fats was dumbstruck. The meeting of Waller and his hero was duly arranged, and Johnson spent an afternoon coaching him at the piano. The bond forged that day between the shy master and his clownish pupil would last the rest of Waller's life. Fats worked hard at getting Johnson's technique down, and his proficiency was soon great enough to impress his teacher's other disciple, the cantankerous Willie the Lion Smith. Johnson, Smith, and the teenaged Waller became inseparable—a hard-drinking, hard-partying club of three members, the musketeers of stride. When Waller married Edith Hatchett in 1921, the club carried on as usual. He spent more time carousing with Johnson and Smith than he spent at home.

One change that came with Waller's marriage, however, was a need for more money than he was making by playing for silent movies. Johnson and Smith threw a few cabaret jobs his way, but, after Edith became pregnant, even this extra income was not enough. Clarence Williams used his influence at OKeh on Fats' behalf. In October 1922 Waller made his first recordings, piano solos of "Birmingham Blues" and "Muscle Shoals Blues." OKeh began using him as an accompanist for blues singers, and within a year or so, other labels, including Paramount and Vocalion, were hiring him in the same capacity. When Waller began to compose music, Clarence Williams was the first to buy his work. Williams issued his first instrumental publication, a rag called "Wild Cat Blues" (with Williams credited as co-composer), late in 1923, as well as Waller's first published song, "In Harlem's Araby" (with lyrics by Jo Trent), in the summer of 1924.

James P. Johnson's contribution to the Waller finances was an introduction at the QRS Company, the leading maker of piano rolls. In March 1923, Fats cut his first roll, Spencer Williams' "Got to Cool My Doggies Now," which was followed by nine more QRS rolls that year. No single musical activity brought him a good living—he got $50 each for his piano rolls, and he sold his songs outright, usually at about the same price. It all added up, but it didn't add up to much. Edith filed for a divorce in 1923, and her alimony payments were as unpredictable as her household allowance had been.

In 1924 a press agent named "Captain" George H. Maines took on the herculean job of managing Fats Waller's career. Maines had heard Waller at a new Harlem club, Connie's Inn, and he saw Waller's potential as the Compleat Entertainer. Johnson, Smith, and Roberts might be more inventive players, but Fats was funny. He sang bawdy songs, he made outrageous comments as he accompanied other singers, he carried on conversations with his fingers and his audience as he played, and he pursed his lips and rolled his eyes in mock ecstasies over the music he was making. Maines would spend eight years trying to put his client on a sensible professional path, and he helped Waller a great deal. But as he and the three managers who succeeded him would learn, Fats Waller was generally unmanageable.

Waller's talents were vast, but so were his appetites, for food, drink, and fun. He was driven by a hedonism that knew no bounds, and he sold his gifts cheaply for ready cash. His recordings were aimed at the urban race market (that is, Harlem), yet his target audience could hear him in person at practically any hour of the day or night, performing without pay at rent parties and clubs as long as the free food and liquor kept coming. When he was strapped for money, he would rush to QRS and offer to undercut his already low asking price to make a piano roll. He made frequent rounds to Tin Pan Alley offices, selling songs anonymously and outright for a few dollars each. If process servers were after him, he would bolt from any employment—no matter how lucrative—to skip town.

Waller's day job in the early twenties was as organist at the Lafayette Theatre, a large movie-and-vaudeville house managed by Frank Schiffman. When Schiffman decided to produce his own stage revue at the Lafayette in early 1926, he asked Waller for songs, providing the opportunity for Waller to sidle into show writing. Waller had published a bit with Spencer Williams by then, and he selected a few of their trunk songs as his contributions to *Tan Town Topics*. (Spencer Williams was in Paris with *La Revue Negre* during the preparation of Schiffman's show.) The two Waller-Williams songs that got the most attention were "Charleston Hound" and "Senorita Mine." Both were published by Clarence Williams, with his name appended as cocomposer, and the show's star, Eddie Rector, named as colyricist. Schiffman was pleased enough with *Tan Town Topics* to try another revue later in 1926—and to ask Waller for more songs—but his *Junior Blackbirds* was not as successful. With his career on a feeble upswing, Waller was married again that year, to a pretty girl named Anita Rutherford, whom he had met at a luncheonette.

Even though *Tan Town Topics* was hardly known outside of Harlem, Waller's fame began to spread beyond the boundaries of his neighborhood. There were four Waller piano rolls issued by QRS in 1927, which was also the heaviest year for Waller recordings up to that time (with nearly twenty sides for Victor as organist and pianist, and about ten sides for various other labels as accompanist for blues singers). His name was on ten publications that year, most of them instrumentals. He put together the show band for the 1927 summer revue at the Lafayette, *Brown Sugar*. He had so far published only one song with Andy Razaf, but because of their close friendship and their intensive song peddling together, they were already thought of as a songwriting team.

Waller's mentor, James P. Johnson, recommended him to producer Con Conrad to share the composing chores for *Keep Shufflin'*. Waller naturally asked for Razaf as his lyricist and, together with the team of Johnson and Henry Creamer, they set to work on the Miller and Lyles musical. In mid-February 1928, *Keep Shufflin'* had a brief tryout at Gibson's Theatre in Philadelphia, where its advertising promised "90 of the World's Most Dazzling Beauties" as well as "The Peppiest Cast of Colored Performers Ever Assembled." By the time the show opened at Daly's Sixty-third Street on February 27, it was polished to a high gloss.

James P. Johnson conducted the *Keep Shufflin'* orchestra, and sitting among the players were—as the program noted—"on the white keys 'Fats' Waller" and "behind the bugle Jabbo Smith." Of course, Johnson played ("on the black keys") as he conducted, and the dual pianos of Johnson and Waller, combined with the blazing cornet of Smith, made the orchestra pit the focal point of *Keep Shufflin'*. Reviewers rarely mention show bands, but they mentioned this one in their enthusiastic notices. Because their playing was proving to be the highlight of the evening, Con Conrad asked Johnson and Waller to remain at their posts during intermission and provide some more. Their nightly two-piano improvisations on the Johnson-Creamer song "'Sippi" were the most popular feature of the show. Only the most confirmed smokers left their seats. The music deserved recordings, and it got them. On March 27, 1928, a four-piece group called the Louisiana Sugar Babes went into the Victor studios in Camden and made delightful takes of two songs from *Keep Shufflin'*: "'Sippi" and the Razaf-Waller "Willow Tree." The Sugar Babes were Johnson (piano), Waller (organ), Jabbo Smith (cornet), and Garvin Bushell (reeds)—the core of the *Keep Shufflin'* orchestra.

Waller left *Keep Shufflin'* in June, well before its 104-performance run ended. He had made his presence felt on Broadway as composer and as performer, but he was, as usual, hurting for cash. His wife Anita was pregnant with their second child, and his first wife Edith was pressing him for back alimony, so when a better offer came, to play the organ for four months at Philadelphia's Grand Theatre, he took it. When Broadway saw Waller next, about a year later, his name would be on one of the greatest revue scores of all time.

This festival of Waller-Razaf songs was called *Connie's Hot Choco-lates*, and it was produced by the Immerman brothers, George and Con-nie, owners of Connie's Inn in Harlem. The Immermans wanted two simultaneous versions of their show, one on Broadway, the other uptown at their club. (Waller was late in coming to the project, because he had spent the winter of 1928–1929 in jail for nonpayment of alimo-ny.) The schedule was too hectic even for the agile talents of Razaf and Waller, so they brought in a third writer, a pianist named Harry Brooks (1895–1970), to help them. We cannot know the exact dynamic of the new writing team, but it is generally believed that Brooks wrote the verses of the songs, Waller the choruses, and Razaf the lyrics. Whatev-er their method, they produced more than a dozen fine songs.

A recollection by jazz pianist/arranger Mary Lou Williams provides a snapshot of Waller at work under pressure:

> Naturally it was a great day for me when some musicians took me across to Connie's Inn on Seventh Avenue to meet Fats, working on a new show. The way Waller worked was anything but slavery.
>
> The OAO (one and only) sat overflowing the piano stool, a jug of whiskey within easy reach. Leonard Harper [the director] . . . said, "Have you anything written for this number, Fats?" And Fats would reply, "Yeah, go on ahead with the dance, man." Then he composed his number while the girls were dancing. . . . Meanwhile, he bubbled over with so many stories and funny remarks that those girls could hardly hoof it for laughing.

Hot Chocolates had its tryout in May 1929 at the Windsor Theatre in the Bronx, before opening at the Hudson Theatre, on West Forty-fourth Street, on June 20. As soon as the curtain fell at the Hudson, the cast dashed uptown to do a late-night performance at Connie's. (The Immermans occasionally scheduled a "midnight matinee" at the Hudson, giving the cast some three-performance days.) The club edi-tion of *Hot Chocolates* was a tab show, shorter and looser than the Broadway version, and it featured Waller more prominently. Waller's performance at the Hudson was at first confined to hot licks on the piano in the orchestra pit, but about six weeks into the run, he joined Edith Wilson and Louis Armstrong—a new addition to the cast—on stage in a feature billed as "A Thousand Pounds of Rhythm."

The show's big song was "Ain't Misbehavin'," and it was served up several ways throughout the evening. It was introduced as a boy-girl duet by Paul Bass and Margaret Simms, then reprised at intermission in a scalding trumpet solo and scat vocal by Louis Armstrong, then used as a departure point for the comic asides of the "Thousand Pounds of Rhythm." For all its lightweight charm, "Ain't Misbehavin'" is musically sturdy enough to stand just about any treatment given to it. (Dizzy Gillespie would write of it in his autobiography, *To Be or Not to Bop*: "The bridge in 'Ain't Misbehavin'.' Where did [Waller] get that from? I haven't heard anything in music since that's more hip, harmonically and logically.") The song got hit recordings within weeks of *Hot Chocolates'* premiere, and it has been making ordinary singers sound hipper ever since.

Most of the *Hot Chocolates* numbers were used as dance specialties, and critics paid more attention to the dancers than to the tunes they were dancing to. The eight-man dance chorus was called the Bon Bon Buddies, and the sixteen female chorus dancers were the Hot Chocolate Drops. Both choruses were used liberally in the show, in their own features as well as to back solo dancers. The Lolita-like Baby Cox scored with "Say It with Your Feet" and "Dixie Cinderella." Paul and Thelma Meers did "The Waltz Divine," and Paul Meers became "That Rhythm Man." There was Louise Cook as the "Goddess of Rain," doing what one critic called "just such a dance as grandfather used to sneak off and see at the county fair." Margaret Simms and the Hot Chocolate Drops demonstrated "That Snake Hip Dance," and the entire company explored the intricacies of "Off Time" in the finale. The only serious moment in *Hot Chocolates* came in the bleak "Black and Blue," which surprised the show's creators by consistently winning encores amid the high-energy frivolity that surrounded it.

Like most revues, *Hot Chocolates* varied its material from time to time, adding and subtracting numbers and changing its personnel. Cab Calloway and Louis Armstrong were late arrivals to the cast, and among the Razaf-Waller song additions were "Redskinland" and "Poolroom Papa" (described by a reviewer as "one of those songs which are supposed to mean two things, but which only mean one").

Hot Chocolates was a triumph for Waller and Razaf, racking up 228 performances, an especially impressive feat for a show opening in June in the days before air conditioning. There were four big-selling record-ings of "Ain't Misbehavin'" in the summer of 1929: Louis Armstrong's, Leo Reisman's, Gene Austin's, and Ruth Etting's. In September Irving Mills and His Hotsy Totsy Gang made "Ain't Misbehavin'" for Brunswick, with rhythm provided by the tapping feet of Bill Robinson. Waller also had a pop hit that summer: "I've Got a Feeling I'm Falling" (written with Billy Rose and Harry Link) was successfully recorded by Gene Austin, with Waller himself as pianist in the studio band.

Waller and Razaf should have been set for life from the publication rights and mechanical royalties yielded by "Ain't Misbehavin'" alone. But about three weeks into the show's run, the *Hot Chocolates* copy-rights were sold along with seven other Razaf-Waller songs to Mills Music for $500. The disastrous deal hurt Razaf more than Waller in the long term, but its immediate effect was to break the momentum of their partnership. They could not afford to wait for the worthwhile projects that would have surely come to them after *Hot Chocolates*. With a half-dozen hits between them, they were broke. They could not be choosy about what they would work on next.

So the next Waller-Razaf project was a small one, three songs for *Load of Coal*, the fall revue at Connie's Inn. The *Load of Coal* score was mostly made up of *Hot Chocolates* songs, and although the new songs were all winners—"Honeysuckle Rose," "My Fate Is in Your Hands," and "Zonky"—they were overshadowed by the popular holdovers from the preceding show. ("Honeysuckle Rose" was particularly slow to take off. It would not become a staple of the jazz repertoire until the mid-thirties.) "My Fate Is in Your Hands" had a hit recording by Gene Austin in late 1929, and "Zonky" was recorded by McKinney's Cotton Pickers in February 1930. By the time the *Load of Coal* songs were mak-ing their way into record shops, their creators were punching a time clock in Joe Davis' publishing office at 1658 Broadway.

It was probably Razaf's idea that they turn to Davis during their economic crunch, because he was the publisher who was then issuing most of Razaf's songs. Davis had previously issued only three Fats Waller publications—an orchestration of "Alligator Crawl," a piano piece called "Meditation," and a song composed with Spencer Williams. Although Davis had cheated Razaf on "S'posin'," their rela-tionship had not curdled because of it. While the larger publishers were scrambling to make alliances with film studios, Davis was concentrating on his business in New York. He was buying songs, many of them from black writers, and issuing and plugging them as he always had. He was not the most prestigious publisher in New York, but he was the one who offered them jobs. They might have bargained their way into a better firm, but they were timid about bargaining now. It was their bungled bargaining that had got them into the mess they were in.

Davis wanted Waller-Razaf songs, of course, but he did not intend to use the writers exclusively as a team. He set Razaf to work making lyrics for instrumentals that he had in his files, and he also issued new Razaf songs written with Paul Denniker, Alexander Hill, and Spencer Williams. Davis had the right of first refusal on any Waller songs, too, and, with Waller on the premises, he had a brilliant in-house demonstrator of his company's products. Waller could make anything sound good, and Davis knew it. When vocalists and bandleaders dropped by to hear the latest Davis numbers, Fats was called on to put them over. To keep Waller in his cubicle from ten to five, Davis gave him a weekly salary, royalties on his published songs, and two bottles of liquor a day. Despite the liquid perks at the Davis office, Waller was not totally a company man. He continued to peddle his songs to other publishers while he worked for Davis, placing several of his numbers with Santly Brothers and Southern Music.

Waller's time in the Joe Davis office lasted about nine months, ending in the summer of 1930. Davis reaped only one big hit from Waller during his tenure there, "Blue, Turning Gray Over You" (with a lyric by Razaf), issued in late January 1930 and recorded first by Louis Armstrong on February 2. Because Waller went where the wind blew him, it was inevitable that he would leave his job with Davis. (And in leaving Davis, he was also leaving Razaf. They would write together off and on during the 1930s, but they would never again be a working team.) Davis occasionally published Waller's work over the next several years, issuing several of the major piano pieces that may not have been published elsewhere: "African Ripples," "Clothes Line Ballet," "Alligator Crawl," "Effervescent," and "Viper's Drag." However, Waller escaped the stigma of being known merely as a "Davis writer." In his haphazard way, he was headed for bigger things.

The immediate occasion for Waller's leaving Davis' office was a job in Chicago, playing piano and organ at the Regal Theatre in August

1930. But he kept his ties to Harlem, and especially to Connie's Inn, contributing a song called "Rollin' Down the River" (with a lyric by Stanley Adams) to Connie's spring revue, *Spades Are Trumps*. In the fall of 1930 the Immermans installed an organ for Waller to use in his frequent stints there.

In December Waller was hired as the pianist for a new radio show, *Paramount on Parade*, a fifteen-minute amalgam of music and chatter (mostly about women's fashions) heard on WABC, a CBS owned-and-operated station, on Mondays, Wednesdays, and Fridays at noon. The show proved popular enough to expand to thirty minutes and to extend for another thirteen weeks after the first thirteen were over. Waller's talents as writer and pianist were well known, but there was a piece of his talent that the public did not know. The missing piece would be revealed in recording sessions in March 1931, and it would be the bedrock of his stardom. The world was about to hear Fats Waller sing.

Joe Davis claimed credit for Waller's discovery as a singer, and he may have earned it. He had encouraged Waller to sing on the WABC show—and, of course, to sing Davis-owned songs—and he had tried to peddle him as a singer to Victor. Waller himself didn't think much of his voice. He saw his singing as a vehicle for demonstrating songs and nothing more. He had sung on a Victor recording in 1927 ("Red Hot Dan," with Tom Morris and His Hot Babies), and no one had paid much attention. But Davis had seen Waller's vocal salesmanship work its magic on the singers and bandleaders shopping for songs in the office. Professionals usually walked out with music under their arms after Waller had sung to them. There was no reason that Waller vocals could not sell records.

Waller and Alexander Hill (1906–1936) had placed a song called "I'm Crazy 'bout My Baby" with Davis in February 1931, and Davis believed he could get a hit with it. The recording made by King Oliver and His Orchestra on February 18 was going nowhere, so Davis decided to give the song another push, this time with a Waller vocal. He shopped the idea to Frank Walker, Columbia's recording manager. Walker had recording dates scheduled for Ted Lewis on March 5 and 6, and he suggested that Waller be featured with the Lewis band. It was an odd pairing—the cornball Lewis with the hipster Waller—but Davis (and Waller's manager, George Maines) okayed it.

On March 5 Waller sang "I'm Crazy 'bout My Baby" with the Lewis band behind him. The following day, Lewis permitted him two more vocals, "Dallas Blues"—during which Lewis could not resist talking over a Waller piano solo—and "Royal Garden Blues." The records were not hits, but they did what they were supposed to do: they pleased Frank Walker. On March 13 Waller was called back into the Columbia studios to make his first piano/vocal recordings, "I'm Crazy 'bout My Baby" and—another Joe Davis publication—Alexander Hill's "Draggin' My Heart Around." "Crazy 'bout My Baby" sold well, but it would take a while to find the right instrumental complement for the Waller voice. Columbia recorded him with Jack Teagarden's band, and Banner Records, a Columbia subsidiary, put him with Jack Bland and His Rhythmakers (an Eddie Condon group). But after some professional and personal detours in the early thirties, Waller would bring into the Victor studio the perfect background for his vocal stylings: a kickass little band called "His Rhythm."

Within days of the demise of the *Paramount on Parade* program in June 1931, Fats Waller was back as a radio regular, this time on a show called *Rhythm Roundup*, which featured the Claude Hopkins band. In the fall Waller organized a band to replace the Fletcher Henderson Orchestra at Connie's Inn, and winter found him in late-night residence at the Hotfeet Club, at 142 West Houston Street in Greenwich Village. The Hotfeet was a lively little joint with a band and enough of a floor show to keep its customers drinking its bootleg hootch until dawn. The pay was pretty good for a Depression-era dive: $25 a night, plus tips that might go as high as $30.

Early in 1932 Waller found time to write with Andy Razaf again. Their "Keepin' Out of Mischief Now" was recorded by Louis Armstrong in March, and they contributed "Stealin' Apples" to Connie's spring revue, Hot Harlem. ("Stealin' Apples" was not published until 1936, and its classic Benny Goodman recording came in 1939.)

In the summer of 1932 Waller's friend and fellow bon vivant, Spencer Williams, talked him into going to Paris. Tin Pan Alley legend has it that they holed up in Williams' apartment for two days and wrote over two dozen songs to pay for their trip. (If this is true, they sold many more songs than were published. Only a few Waller-Williams songs were issued at this time.) The news of Waller's imminent departure came as an unpleasant surprise to Captain Maines. He had no time to arrange any work for Waller in Europe, and he must have disapproved of his client's using his songs for scrip to take a vacation. (Louis Armstrong also went to Europe that summer, but he left with a full schedule of bookings in England.)

Waller and Williams partied their way across the Atlantic on the *Ile de France*, accepting the food and drink sent over to them by fans who recognized them on the ship. After several riotous—and expensive—weeks in Paris, Waller was ready to go home, but he didn't have any money left. He wired a publisher friend, Saul Bornstein, for the return fare. Without telling Williams where he was going, Waller left him sitting in a restaurant and sneaked away to board the train to the ship that would take him back to New York.

Waller returned to find his manager ready to quit the business. George Maines was ill—and no doubt exasperated with his scamp of a client—and he passed the reins of Waller's management to Marty Bloom. Bloom quickly saw that corralling Waller was more than he could handle, and he turned the "harmful little armful" over to his friend Phil Ponce, who would prove to be the best manager Waller ever had.

Ponce was a songwriter himself (and the father of the singing Ponce Sisters), and although his songs were not as successful as Waller's, he knew his way around recording and publishing better than Maines and Bloom had. He believed in Waller's talent, and he devised a strategy to make him a star. Waller had been recording regularly since 1929, but his recordings had not yet delivered the entire package of his charm as a performer. Except in his solo piano recordings (which had not sold well), there was as yet no identifiable Waller sound. He had been heard with too many ad hoc, one-shot groups like the Louisiana Sugar Babes, Condon's Rhythmakers, and the Little Chocolate Dandies, who convened for a studio session or two only to disband as soon as the day was over. Even his debut as a vocalist was not a "Fats Waller record," it was a "Ted Lewis record." His radio experience had been equally vague. On various shows, he had noodled away under conversation, (anonymously) subbed for the organist Jesse Crawford, and accompanied the singing of Andy Razaf. Ponce knew that this was not good enough. He wanted Waller's radio work and his recordings to advertise each other, and he wanted both to sound like Fats Waller.

Ponce went after radio first. He got his client a guest appearance on a show that originated from WLW, a Cincinnati station with one of the largest transmitters in the Midwest, whose programs could be heard over the central and southern United States as well as in much of Canada. As Ponce had hoped it would, Waller's guest shot went well enough for the WLW management to want to build a show around him. Waller, his wife Anita, and their two sons moved to Cincinnati in the fall of 1932, and WLW began to assemble the personnel for *Fats Waller's Rhythm Club*. Ponce had secured a two-year contract for Waller with WLW, and although Waller would leave the show after about sixteen months, the *Rhythm Club* was Waller's finishing school. It built his confidence as a singing entertainer, broadened his repertoire, and won him fans in places he had never heard of.

Fats Waller's Rhythm Club was the centerpiece of WLW's Saturday night schedule, airing at 9:00 P.M. There was a (white) house band to back up the star, as well as a vocal quintet called the Southern Suns for Waller to sing and joke with. The announcer was Paul Stewart. A few weeks after the premiere program, a young and pretty singer/pianist named Una Mae Carlisle made such a hit in her guest appearance on the Christmas show that she was asked to join the *Rhythm Club* regulars. About six months into the run, the Southern Suns were replaced by a male quartet who became known as the Ink Spots. The show gave Waller wide latitude to choose material, sing, make medleys, and make fun. *Fats Waller's Rhythm Club* was enormously popular from the beginning, and WLW began to send Waller and his company around the Midwest for personal appearances in RKO theatres. (The Clarence Page band usually substituted for the white studio band on tour.) WLW often aired remote broadcasts of the *Rhythm Club*'s stage show from the various cities in which it played.

At Waller's suggestion, WLW created another show for him. He wanted to do a late-night program of organ music, but he didn't want his name attached to it. The show, which aired from 1:00–1:30 A.M. daily, was called *Moon River*, and its audience of lovers and insomniacs never knew that the organist who coaxed the soothing music—mostly Bach, folk songs, and romantic ballads—out of WLW's giant Wurlitzer was none other than the Master of the Revels at the *Rhythm Club*.

Waller had a falling out with Phil Ponce about his WLW contract, and he returned to New York early in 1934. His months with the

Rhythm Club had taught him much about himself as a performer, and meeting the demands of daily and weekly radio had focused him, made him sure of his sound and of the musical setting for it. He trusted his singing—and the comic value of his spoken asides—as he never had before, and he knew that a swingy, unpretentious "bar band" would inspire him. Ponce landed an exclusive contract for Fats with Victor— a contract that George Maines had tried for but couldn't get—giving Waller $100 per usable side and a 3 percent royalty on sales. On May 16, 1934, at 1:30 P.M., Waller walked into Victor's Studio No. 2 in New York—barely on time, as always—to begin making recordings under his new contract. He had five young men with him, the first ensemble to be known as "His Rhythm." Fats Waller and His Rhythm would make more good small-band jazz sides than any other group in the 1930s, and the outpouring of swing began with their first session.

Waller and His Rhythm made four sides that day, all featuring Waller vocals and all studded with free-wheeling improvisation by Fats and his side men. The personnel on the first session were Herman Autrey, trumpet; Ben Whitted, clarinet; Albert Casey, guitar; Billy Taylor, string bass; and Harry Dial, drums. (The makeup of His Rhythm varied somewhat over the years, but the group remained surprisingly stable for a studio band. Autrey and Casey played on almost all of the Rhythm sides for eight years. The reed man Gene Sedric became a Rhythm mainstay at their second session, in August 1934. Slick Jones became the regular drummer in 1936. Charles Turner was the primary bassist until 1938, when he was replaced by Cedric Wallace.) Whatever the personnel, most of the Rhythm records were hot and, whatever the tempo, they all swung like mad. The various Rhythm men caught the Waller spirit, that unlikely combination of ease and drive in his playing, and his playfulness inspired their own. The records by Waller and His Rhythm still bubble with life nearly seventy years after they were made, and they are the least dated of all 1930s jazz.

The first Rhythm session was typical in its hotness, and it was also typical in the material chosen for recording. The four songs laid down that afternoon included one piece of clever songwriting (James P. Johnson and Andy Razaf's "A Porter's Love Song to a Chambermaid") and three wisps of Tin Pan Alley chaff ("I Wish I Were Twins," "Armful o' Sweetness," and "Do Me a Favor"). Waller finds the musical juice in all of them, and he treats each with fervor and unsatiric fun.

The hottest of the four songs is, in fact, the lamest tune, "I Wish I Were Twins." There is not much kidding around with lyrics, as there would be in later records, but Waller's exhortations to his soloists are sprinkled throughout the songs—to Autrey: "Aw, swing it, gate"; to Casey: "Plunk 'em, plunk 'em"—along with assorted "yeahs" and "ahs" of encouragement. At the end of "Do Me a Favor," Waller makes his only extended ad lib of the day. He says, "Listen, honey, have you got a dollar-ninety? 'Cause I got the dime. We might as well go on out of here and find the parson. Ha-*ha*!"

Writers have criticized Victor for allowing Waller to record so much dreck, but because he never rehearsed for his sessions and never drew up lists of what he wanted to record, it was to be expected that publishers would push songs at him. If Waller was without ideas, publishers and A&R men were not. If there was not a new "Honeysuckle Rose" or an "Ain't Misbehavin'" on tap, why not do "I Love to Whistle" or "Your Socks Don't Match"? Many of the more than sixty big-selling records that Waller had with the Rhythm featured songs that would have got nowhere near the hit parade without him. He did not need to dig for gold; he was an alchemist.

In the early thirties the American Federation of Musicians began to relax its ban against playing records on the radio. The thinking in the twenties had been that radio music should come from live musicians only, and every station should keep a house band or two, as well as various solo performers, on its staff. Besides benefiting the musicians who were hired for radio work, the "all-live" policy benefited the record industry by forcing those who wanted to hear records to buy them. As the Depression deepened, radio stations began to let their in-house musicians go, and record sales began to decline. The A F of M decided that half a loaf was better than none. Perhaps the record industry could be shored up if radio stations were allowed to play records; perhaps radio play should be seen as "free advertising" for the record industry rather than as "giving it away."

In 1932 Al Jarvis at KJWB in Los Angeles began to design programming around the playing of records on the air. In 1935 Martin Block at WNEW in New York began filling the time between bulletins from the Lindbergh kidnaping trial, which lasted from January 2 to February 13, by playing recorded dance music. The dance records attracted more listeners than the trial, and Block's *Make Believe Ballroom* was born. The station soon copied Block's daytime idea to create an all-night record program, Stan Shaw's *Milkman's Matinee*, which made WNEW the first station to play records around the clock. Record-playing hosts were known as "disc jockeys," and they quickly became a major force in the music business. They chose the records to be played, and their choices mattered a great deal to the industry. It turned out that the A F of M's new policy was not just wishful thinking: radio play really did promote record sales.

Nobody benefited more from this new interaction between radio and records than Fats Waller. Hearing Waller in one medium made you want to hear him in the other. His records were three-minute packages of his ebullient personality, and his radio shows were pure fun. He recorded a lot, so there was always something new to sell, play, and talk about on radio. He was the best interview a DJ could wish for. His line of jive was unending, and he could schmooze with an audience of millions as easily as he could with one record spinner in a dingy sound booth. Within weeks of his returning to New York in early 1934, Waller was given his own twice-a-week show on WABC, on Mondays and Saturdays. And he was a frequent guest on other shows: on Morton Downey's *House Party, Saturday Revue, Harlem Serenade,* appearing with Ukulele Ike every other Sunday. In late 1934 there were no fewer than six Waller records on the newly instituted *Billboard* charts. This was not a coincidence.

With the records-radio combination working smoothly, Phil Ponce turned his eye to Hollywood, getting spots in two feature films for Fats Waller in 1935. The first was an RKO picture called *Hooray for Love,* which starred Ann Sothern and Gene Raymond. The film's songs were by Jimmy McHugh and Dorothy Fields, and Waller's small role as a bailiff who has come to evict a girl from her Harlem apartment was merely an excuse for him to sing and play. Waller spies her piano out on the street and goes over to try it. As he launches into "I'm Livin' in a Great Big Way," Bill Robinson walks up, joins Waller in some patter, then dances to the number. The sequence was shot in one afternoon in March, and Waller made $500 for the day. In late summer, Waller returned to Hollywood for another one-song sequence in another Jimmy McHugh musical, 20th Century Fox's *King of Burlesque,* the first film to star Alice Faye. In a concert setting, Waller, at a grand piano in his white tie and tails, tosses off "I've Got My Fingers Crossed." The two films did not make Waller a movie star, but they proved that he had joined the small number of black musical performers popular enough to be hired in white Hollywood. Attesting to his mainstream popularity, a 1938 Disney cartoon short called "Mother Goose Goes to Hollywood" caricatured Waller, along with Cab Calloway and the Andrews Sisters.

A three-year streak of record hits for Waller and His Rhythm began in early 1935. "Believe It, Beloved," "Lulu's Back in Town," and "I'm Gonna Sit Right Down and Write Myself a Letter" came in the spring, and his biggest record of that year, "Truckin'," came in late summer. Victor was reaping such a boon from Waller that sessions were scheduled for him as often as the company could pin him down. He sometimes made two sessions a month, rarely going more than two months without a recording date. And Victor got a lot out of Waller's studio time. Most artists would go in for a three- or four-hour session in hope of getting (at most) four usable sides. Waller made a party of it, sitting at the piano with his bottle of Old Grand-Dad and a glass nearby, running once or twice through whatever tune was thrust in front of him, laying down a take or two, then moving on to more drinks and to more songs. There were often eight or ten usable sides from a few hours with Waller, and seldom were there fewer than six.

Although the Waller-Rhythm records were slapped together, there is nothing superficial or half-hearted about the performances. Waller could take tunes that he had never seen, unerringly find whatever musical worth they had, and then layer interesting things onto them. He never comps or fakes chords under his singing or behind the solos of the Rhythm. He knows the harmonies and he plays them, decorating, adding, filling in. He made only casual and hasty acquaintance with his material, but his playing and singing were always clean and bright.

There was mockery in Waller's thin, sinuous voice, and he sent up many a poor lyric just by uttering it. If a song was hopelessly dopey, his savage instinct for parody kicked in. He attacked it in a burlesque "concert-baritone" style and ad libbed wicked asides at the end of lyric lines. ("If It Isn't Love" was one of the first to be mutilated in this way, in November 1934.) He recorded his own songs—mostly his standards—but they were not his biggest hits. He made "Fats Waller songs" out of "You're Not the Only Oyster in the Stew," "Christopher Columbus," "Your Feet's Too Big," and "'Tain't Good (Like a Nickel Made of Wood)," among many others. He forgot most of the studio songs as quickly as he had learned them, and he was sometimes caught short by a request for one of his hits that he didn't remember. One tune that he had to relearn was "I'm Gonna Sit Right Down and Write Myself a Letter." When a fan asked for it after it had been on the *Billboard* charts through the summer of 1935, Waller didn't know it. He had played it once in the studio, and he never expected to have to play it again.

Early in 1938 Phil Ponce became ill and retired, and Ed Kirkeby, who had been assisting Ponce in his office, took over as Waller's manager. Like Ponce, Kirkeby had seen long service in the music business. He had managed two popular 1920s bands, the California Ramblers and the Memphis Five, and he had represented the Pickens Sisters in the early 1930s. He had been a bandleader himself—of Ted Wallace and His Campus Boys—in the late twenties, and on his first day as an A & R man at Victor, in June 1935, the first artist he supervised was Fats Waller. Kirkeby was knowledgeable enough, but he didn't have Ponce's sensitivity to Waller. And he never had as broad a career vision for him.

Kirkeby found Waller's personal finances in chaos (their usual state), with his client behind in alimony payments, car payments, and back taxes. His answer to Waller's money problems was more work, not better work. Because big bands were dominating the charts, he thought that Waller should have one, so he assembled a unit and booked an extensive tour. Waller was tired of the road long before Kirkeby took over his management, and for the previous year or so he had shown his irritability by canceling dates or by simply ordering his driver to "head for the Holland Tunnel" if his tour route took him within a few hundred miles of New York. Waller's reputation as a no-show made him hard to book, and his cancellations had resulted in several heavy fines from the A F of M—another payment he was behind in.

In the spring of 1938 Waller gamely set out on Kirkeby's string of one-nighters with an expanded band, including two highly superfluous piano players. The tour was a bad idea in every way. Waller's fans understandably expected his live music to sound like his records, and it didn't. Theatre owners didn't buy much advertising for him, because they had heard from other owners that Waller might not show up. The large troupe was very expensive to keep on the road, and when Waller skipped out on a date in Durham, North Carolina, their fate was sealed. All their succeeding dates were cancelled. They limped back to New York, with Waller as frazzled and broke as he had been when the tour began.

Kirkeby was relentless about the big band idea, however. In April 1938 Waller went into the Victor studio with a thirteen-man "Rhythm and Orchestra." None of the eight sides made that day sold well, and Kirkeby began to see the error of his ways. Although he would some-times add the occasional extra player—and the occasional unnecessary vocalist—to Waller's basic studio group, the big-band Rhythm would not be tried again for four years. If Kirkeby couldn't sell Waller as a bandleader, he would sell him as a solo. In May, while Waller was floundering through another tour of the South and Midwest with a too-large band, Kirkeby was making arrangements for him to tour the British Isles as a single for ten weeks at $2,500 a week.

The tour was a series of triumphs for Waller. He was fawned over by the public and the press everywhere he went, and his ten weeks in Europe would be the most satisfying experience of his professional life. At his first performance, in the Empire Theatre in Glasgow on August 1, the audience went wild when Waller made his entrance wearing a kilt. When he sat down at the piano and swung "Loch Lomond," he had them in knots. After a program of his own songs and many of his Victor hits, there were ten curtain calls. His reviews were splendid, and he spent the rest of the week in Glasgow basking in the company of the Scots. (He had only one request of his waiters and hosts: "Don't be vague. Gimme some of that fine John Haig.") On August 8, Waller repeated his success at London's Palladium. He spent the next five weeks zigzagging from one major London variety house to another, often playing two nearby halls on the same evening.

Waller also got to do some recording in London that summer. He made six sides for HMV, with a group called His Continental Rhythm, on August 21, and a week later he played the organ to accompany the singing of his expatriate friend Adelaide Hall at the company's Abbey Road studios. He visited his old collaborator Spencer Williams, who was living in England, and they wrote a few songs together during his stay.

Kirkeby had set aside two weeks in mid-September for Waller to play in Scandinavia, and as he darted from city to city in Norway, Denmark, and Sweden, he tried to avoid the menacing-looking Nazi soldiers on the German trains he rode. Danish reporters, who were thrilled to interview such a luminary, let him pontificate on every musical and nonmusical subject. Waller let it be known that he was very religious ("back home in New York I never miss a service in my father's old church"), that he loved the classics ("my greatest joy is to play a figure of Bach on the organ"), and that he saw little hope for symphonic jazz ("[It] is nonsense. Jazz can't be symphonic."). After Scandinavia there was another flurry of London appearances, including several on BBC radio and one on BBC television. Waller and his manager were back in New York, where Kirkeby had more work lined up, by early October.

In an effort to boost the sales and prestige of its subsidiary, Bluebird, Victor moved several of its major artists, Fats Waller among them, to the lower-priced label. Waller's first Bluebird session, on October 13, produced his last big hit, "Two Sleepy People." He completed the year with three months at the Yacht Club, on Fifty-second Street, his longest gig ever in one place. That winter, the Wallers moved from Morningside Heights to St. Albans, Queens. They already knew some of their neighbors there: the families of James P. Johnson, Clarence Williams, and Count Basie.

In March 1939 Ed Kirkeby made the odd decision to take Fats Waller to London again. His British fans were glad to see him, of course, but it was too soon to go back. He interrupted his music-hall schedule almost as soon as it began for more sessions at HMV. In June, Waller recorded his only extended composition, "London Suite," a set of six mood pieces describing areas in the city he so enjoyed visiting. There was less attention paid to him in the London press this time, and after a few weeks of lukewarm shows, some of them in half-empty houses, Kirkeby decided to cut the tour short and go home. They had not earned enough for return-trip tickets, so Kirkeby wired John Hammond for a loan.

Waller had to work hard to make up for the time and money lost on Kirkeby's second London venture. His touring commitments for the next year or so were heavy, and the club jobs and radio shows that were interspersed among them never lasted long. In 1941, when he should have been making movies, Waller made four "soundies"—films played by dropping coins into a kind of jukebox with a screen attached—each of which was three minutes long.

And he wasn't writing much. In 1941 Waller published two songs—his fewest number in any year since 1924—and a folio of instrumentals, *Fats Waller's Piano Antics*. Also in the stores that year was a folio of "his" arrangements called *Boogie Woogie with Fats Waller*. Waller hated boogie woogie and refused to play it, so it is unlikely that he arranged this boogie collection for Mills Music. He was everybody's guest on radio, but at the height of his fame, he didn't have a show of his own.

The person who decided to get Fats out of his professional rut was not Ed Kirkeby, but a young jazz fan named Ernest Anderson, who was a copywriter in an advertising agency. Anderson had haunted Harlem clubs since the early thirties, and he was sometimes allowed to sit in with his trumpet at rent parties. He had come to know many musicians through his weed-smoking friendship with Eddie Condon, and it was Condon who introduced him to Waller. During one of their late-night talks in November 1941, Waller reminisced about the great music and the musicians he had heard at Carnegie Hall. He was in particular awe of Vladimir Horowitz, and he warmly recalled the times he had heard Horowitz from a second balcony seat. Anderson was surprised to hear such talk from Waller, and he was struck by Waller's veneration for Carnegie Hall and its classical artists. Almost in passing, Anderson asked Waller if he'd like to play there. Waller beamed at the unlikely thought and said, "Oh, how I'd love to!" A few days later, without telling or asking Kirkeby or Waller, Ernest Anderson went to the management office at Carnegie Hall, put down a $600 deposit and secured a date on which to present Fats Waller in concert. He chose a Wednesday evening, January 14, 1942.

Waller became nervous when he heard what Anderson had done, but he was enthusiastic, too. Eddie Condon agreed to act as music director for the evening, and Kirkeby stayed out of the way. Press releases were written and distributed, and Paul Smith made a poster design—the famous silhouette of an enormous, perfectly round Waller playing a tiny grand piano. Condon planned a six-part program to show the range of Waller's talents: he would begin by playing several of his songs on the piano; then spirituals on the organ; a blues improvisation with the trumpeter Hot Lips Page; the premiere of his *London Suite*; a Gershwin medley on the organ; and finally a jam session with a small band—Condon on guitar, John Kirby on bass, Gene Krupa on drums, Bud Freeman on tenor sax, Pee Wee Russell on clarinet, and Max Kaminsky on cornet. As a nod to the classics, Waller would improvise on a theme by Elgar at the organ and would play "Variations on a Tchaikovsky Theme" at the piano. Without much promotion in the New York press, over 2,000 tickets were sold.

Before the concert, well-wishers crowded the Toscanini Suite, which served as Waller's dressing room. Libations flowed and Waller's jitters escalated. He drank, he circulated, he chatted edgily. About twenty minutes past the 8:30 starting time, Anderson pried Waller away from the party and steered him down the stairs to the stage. As Fats stepped into the light and acknowledged the welcoming applause, Anderson realized that he was drunk. He faltered as he sat down at the Steinway, then, departing from the printed program immediately, he launched into "I'm Gonna Sit Right Down and Write Myself a Letter." Then he remembered that he was supposed to be playing his own compositions, so he segued into "Honeysuckle Rose." He was not playing badly, but he had obviously forgotten the order of music. He abandoned the Waller-songs part of the program, and went to the organ. The audience was expecting to hear spirituals, and they did hear a bit of one before Waller slid into "All That Meat and No Potatoes." The laughter that greeted this number addled him further. He began to play Gershwin's "Summertime." He fumbled with the Elgar, then Hot Lips Page came out to rescue him. Their duet went well, and they hurriedly left the stage for an intermission.

The fifteen-minute interval stretched to nearly forty minutes. Waller realized that disaster was in the making, and he drank heavily while he changed clothes. Anderson herded him back onto the stage to begin his *London Suite*. He played a bit of "Bond Street," then he strayed into "Summertime" again. Somehow he made it to the small-band segment of the program, and the presence of the other musicians buoyed him. They lit into "Honeysuckle Rose," and Waller did his best playing of the evening. After a ragtag "Star Spangled Banner"—the standard finale of wartime concerts, and the only piece on the program that Waller did not know—the ordeal was over. The press was kinder than it might have been. Reviewers said that Waller was a fine entertainer, but they also said that he had no business at Carnegie Hall.

On July 13, 1942, Fats Waller made his last recordings with His Rhythm, four sides for Victor, one of which featured a vocal by the

Stormy Weather

Deep River Boys. On July 30, Waller made his last commercial recording of any kind. Accompanied by Victor's "First Nighter" Orchestra, Waller sang an Irving Berlin song called "That's What the Well-Dressed Man in Harlem Will Wear," to be released in an album of songs from Berlin's all-soldier show, *This Is the Army*. On August 1, the American Federation of Musicians struck the recording industry, forbidding its members to work in the studios until there was an industry-wide agreement by record companies to pay the union royalties on records sold. The strike paralyzed the industry for thirteen months. During the strike, Waller made V-Discs for broadcast to military personnel, and there were some acetates of his radio performances (issued on LPs years after his death). But the romps with His Rhythm were over. No one knew how long the strike would last, so Kirkeby disbanded the Rhythm and began selling Waller as a solo artist again. He sometimes sent Waller out on tour to play with local pickup bands to avoid the expense of carrying a band of his own.

A plum fell into Kirkeby's lap early in 1943, when Irving Mills called from Hollywood. Mills, the brother of publisher Jack Mills, was working as a producer for 20th Century-Fox. He wanted to make an all-black film called *Stormy Weather*, and he wanted to feature Waller in it, along with Bill Robinson and Lena Horne. The plot was mostly a series of setups for musical numbers, and Waller was promised two of them. In a scene set in a cabaret, Ada Brown sings "That Ain't Right" (by Irving Mills and Nat Cole), and Waller accompanies her at the piano. He accompanies her vocally as well, answering almost every one of her lyric lines with a funny remark. ("Tell these fools anything, but tell me the truth. . . . Beef to me, Mama, beef to me, I don't like pork no-how. . . . Suffer, excess baggage, suffer. . . .") The crowd of extras representing the club patrons calls for another number, and Waller plays and sings "Ain't Misbehavin'." He wrote a new song, "Moppin' and Boppin'," for the film, but it was hidden under dialogue.

While Waller was in Hollywood, Ed Kirkeby was fishing to get him a role in a Broadway show. Kirkeby talked up Waller to producer Richard Kollmar, who was preparing a new musical called *Early to Bed*. Kollmar seemed amenable to the idea of casting Waller, and he asked Kirkeby to bring him back to New York as soon as shooting was finished on *Stormy Weather*. When the three finally met, Kirkeby learned that Kollmar didn't as yet have a composer for *Early to Bed*. He urged Kollmar to hire Waller, and he reminded him of Waller's big revue hits of the late 1920s. Kollmar agreed to give Waller a try, and he offered him a $1,000 advance. Kollmar's librettist and lyricist

Early to Bed

was George Marion, Jr., a veteran writer of film musicals, who whole-heartedly approved of Waller as composer. Waller worked at home in St. Albans, writing tunes to Marion's words, which were sent to him from Hollywood.

By the time rehearsals began for *Early to Bed*, it was decided that Waller should give up his acting role in the show to concentrate on the score. Waller knew that this was his chance to reestablish himself as a composer, and he took his work seriously. The story was slight—and slightly smutty—concerning a bordello on the island of Martinique operating under the guise of a school for girls. *Early to Bed* was Waller's only book musical, and he rose to the occasion. Inspired by Marion's literate lyrics, Waller wrote some of his most sophisticated and graceful melodies. The big song from the show was a ballad, "Slightly Less Than

Wonderful," which contains the longest melodic arcs in all of Waller's songwriting. "This Is So Nice" and "There's a Man in My Life" were also popular for a while, and the comic highlights were "When the Nylons Bloom Again" and "The Ladies Who Sing with a Band."

The only blot on Waller's happy return to the theatre was an ugly incident that happened during the show's tryout in Boston. Kirkeby had made reservations for Fats and Anita Waller at the hotel where the all-white cast was staying, and Waller was the guest of honor at a late-afternoon cocktail party at the hotel on the day of his arrival. Waller was happy and excited about the show, and he charmed the local politicians and press who had come to the party to meet him. But when he and Anita went across the lobby to check into their room, the desk clerk took a look at them and claimed that no reservation had been made. Kirkeby, who witnessed the incident, was furious at the obvious racism behind the clerk's action, and he demanded to see the hotel manager. The manager held firm and backed his clerk. The composer with his name in lights above the Shubert Theatre was turned out into a Boston street because of his color. Kirkeby called all over town and finally secured a room for Waller in a third-class hotel, from which he commuted to the Shubert to do his final polishing on the score.

Waller was deflated but not defeated by the Boston incident. *Early to Bed* had a successful opening at New York's Broadhurst Theatre on June 17, 1943. Although some critics were put off by the show's risqué premise, *Early to Bed* was proclaimed a fine summer entertainment. Waller was proud to be back on Broadway, and he never missed a chance to mention the show and to play his new songs in his radio appearances. (The recording ban was still in effect, so the *Early to Bed* songs got only radio plugs.) *Early to Bed* made money for Kollmar and it pleased its customers. And it made theatre people look at Fats Waller as a songwriter again. It should have been the start of a new—and easier—career for Waller, but it was to be his last show.

Instead of capitalizing on the success of *Early to Bed* by pitching Waller to write for another producer, Kirkeby sent him out for personal appearances again. Waller also made himself available for military shows, service hospitals, and bond drives in the cities where Kirkeby's tour schedule took him, often doing several free shows a day before the one show that he was paid to play. The only easy money that came to

Waller after *Early to Bed* was for the use of his photos in print ads for Royal Crown Cola.

In November 1943, Waller and Kirkeby arrived in Los Angeles, not to make a movie but to install Waller for a residency of several weeks at a club called the Zanzibar Room. He played for hours every night, soaked with perspiration while sitting under a powerful air-conditioning vent. He caught the flu, which necessitated ten days in the hospital, and he was still weak when he returned to work. He ground out his nights at the club, and he spent his last days in Hollywood tearing around to radio studios. Everyone wanted one more guest shot before he left town. The day after he fulfilled his obligation to the Zanzibar's owner, he fell exhausted into a berth on the Santa Fe Chief, which was to take him back to New York. On December 15, 1943, Waller lost the endurance race that he was running. While the train was stopped in Kansas City early that morning, he died of bronchial pneumonia.

Although he had three successful shows, Waller was never taken seriously as a theatre writer. But it was theatre, the medium from which he had slipped away in the late twenties, that brought him back. In 1978 an explosion of Waller songs hit Broadway in the form of a revue called *Ain't Misbehavin'*, which was conceived and directed by Richard Maltby, Jr. With its bright five-person cast, Luther Henderson arrangements, the Walleresque piano of Hank Jones, and the evocation of a Harlem club in the thirties, *Ain't Misbehavin'* caught its subject better than any other composer revue ever has. The show delighted audiences for 1,604 performances, and it belatedly installed Waller in the pantheon of American songwriters. His music was still hip and full of fun, and *Ain't Misbehavin'* let a new generation take him to its heart. Kids who had never known of Fats Waller could tell by listening: he was the kind of person who brightened rooms just by walking into them. One could do worse, couldn't one?

SOURCES

●●●●●●●●●●●●●●●●●●●●●●●●●●●●●●●●●●●●●

PROLOGUE

Charles Neider, ed. *The Selected Letters of Mark Twain*. New York: Harper & Row, 1982.

James M. Trotter. *Music and Some Highly Musical People*. Boston: Lee and Shepard, 1881.

CHAPTER 1

Tom Fletcher. *100 Years of the Negro in Show Business*. New York: Burdge, 1954.

Dr. Kelly Miller. "The Negro 'Stephen Foster'," *Etude* (July 1939).

Al Rose. *Eubie Blake*. New York: Schirmer Books, 1979.

CHAPTER 2

Eddie Cantor. *My Life Is in Your Hands*. New York: Harper & Brothers, 1928.

Randolph Carter. *Ziegfeld: The Time of His Life*. London: Bernard Press, 1974.

Ann Charters. *Nobody: The Story of Bert Williams*. New York: Macmillan, 1970.

Tom Fletcher. *100 Years of the Negro in Show Business*. New York: Burdge, 1954.

James Weldon Johnson. *Along This Way*. New York: Viking Press, 1934.

Edward B. Marks. *They All Sang*. New York: Viking Press, 1934.

Al Rose. *Eubie Blake*. New York: Schirmer Books, 1979.

Henry T. Sampson. *The Ghost Walks: A Chronological History of Blacks in Show Business, 1865–1910*. Metuchen, N.J.: Scarecrow Press, 1988.

Eric Ledell Smith. *Bert Williams*. Jefferson, N.C.: McFarland, 1992.

(HAPTER 3

Duke Ellington. *Music Is My Mistress*. New York: Doubleday & Company, 1973.

James Weldon Johnson. *Along This Way*. New York: Viking Press, 1933.

Al Rose. *Eubie Blake*. New York: Schirmer Books, 1979.

Isidore Witmark and Isaac Goldberg. *From Ragtime to Swingtime*. New York: Lee Furman, 1939.

(HAPTER 4

Roy Carew. "Shepard N. Edmonds," *Record Changer* (December 1947).

"Gotham-Attucks Company," *American Musician and Art Journal* (October 23, 1908).

(HAPTER 5

Reid Badger. *James Reese Europe: A Life in Ragtime*. New York: Oxford University Press, 1995.

Duke Ellington. *Music Is My Mistress*. New York: Doubleday & Company, 1973.

Patrick O'Connor and Brian Hammond. *Josephine Baker*. Boston: Bullfinch Press, 1988.

Sophie Tucker. *Some of These Days*. Garden City, N.Y.: Garden City Publishing Company, 1945.

(HAPTER 6

William Francis Allen, Charles Pickard Ware, and Lucy McKim Garrison, eds. *Slave Songs of the United States* (1867). New York: reprint by Dover Books, 1995.

Bruce Bastin. *Never Sell a Copyright*. Chigwell, England: Storyville, 1990.

Perry Bradford. *Born with the Blues*. New York: Oak Publications, 1965.

Stephen Calt and Gayle Dean Wardlow. "The Paramount Story," *78 Quarterly* (nos. 3, 4, 5, 6, and 7).

Pops Foster. *Pops Foster*. Berkeley: University of California Press, 1973.

Milt Gabler. Telephone interview with David A. Jasen. March 24, 1997.

W. C. Handy. *Father of the Blues*. New York: Macmillan, 1941.

Alan Lomax. *Mr. Jelly Roll*. New York: Duell, Sloan, 1950.

Charles H. Nichols, ed. *Arna Bontemps–Langston Hughes Letters, 1925–1967*. New York: Dodd, Mead & Company, 1980.

Paul Oliver. *The Story of the Blues*. Philadelphia: Chilton Book Company, 1969.

Al Rose. *I Remember Jazz*. Baton Rouge: Louisiana State University Press, 1987.

Willie Ruff. *A Call to Assembly*. New York: Viking Penguin Books, 1991.

Nat Shapiro and Nat Hentoff. *Hear Me Talkin' to Ya: The Story of Jazz by the Men Who Made It*. New York: Rinehart, 1955.

Willie the Lion Smith, with George Hoefer. *Music on My Mind*. New York: Doubleday & Company, 1964.

CHAPTER 7

Eubie Blake. Interview with Richard Ballad for *Penthouse Magazine*, vol. 5 (March 1974).

———. Interview with Gene Jones and "Ragtime Bob" Darch. April 21, 1982.

Robert Kimball and William Bolcom. *Reminiscing with Sissle and Blake*. New York: Viking Press, 1972.

Al Rose. *Eubie Blake*. New York: Schirmer Books, 1979.

Nat Shapiro and Nat Hentoff. *Hear Me Talkin' to Ya: The Story of Jazz by the Men Who Made It*. New York: Rinehart, 1955.

Laurie Wright. *Fats in Fact*. Chigwell, England: Storyville, 1992.

SELECT BIBLIOGRAPHY

●●●●●●●●●●●●●●●●●●●●●●●●●●●●●●●●●●●●●●●

Abbott, Lynn, and Doug Seroff. "'They Cert'ly Sound Good to Me': Sheet Music, Southern Vaudeville, and the Commercial Ascendency of the Blues," *American Music* (Winter 1996).

Albertson, Chris. *Bessie*. New York: Stein & Day, 1972.

American Musician and Art Journal. New York: 1906–1914.

ASCAP Biographical Dictionary. American Society of Composers, Authors and Publishers, 1966.

Badger, Reid. *James Reese Europe: A Life in Ragtime*. New York: Oxford University Press, 1995.

Bastin, Bruce. *Never Sell a Copyright*. Chigwell, England: Storyville, 1990.

Boardman, Gerald. *American Musical Theatre*. New York: Oxford University Press, 1978.

Bradford, Perry. *Born with the Blues*. New York: Oak Publications, 1965.

Brown, Scott E. *James P. Johnson*. Metuchen, N. J.: Scarecrow Press, 1986.

Calt, Stephen, and Gayle Dean Wardlow. "The Paramount Story," *78 Quarterly* (nos. 3, 4, 5, 6, and 7).

Charters, Ann. *Nobody: The Story of Bert Williams*. New York: Macmillan, 1970.

Davin, Tom. "Conversations with James P. Johnson," *Jazz Review* (June–July, 1959).

Fletcher, Tom. *100 Years of the Negro in Show Business*. New York: Burdge, 1954.

Godrich, John, and Robert M.W. Dixon. *Blues and Gospel Records, 1902–1942*. Chigwell, England: Storyville, 1969.

Handy, W. C. *Father of the Blues*. New York: Macmillan, 1941.

Harris, Sheldon. *Blues Who's Who*. New Rochelle, N.Y.: Arlington House, 1979.

Jablonski, Edward. *The Encyclopedia of American Music*. New York: Doubleday & Company, 1981.

Jasen, David A. *Tin Pan Alley*. New York: Donald I. Fine, 1988.

Jasen, David A., and Trebor Tichenor. *Rags and Ragtime*. New York: Seabury Press, 1978.

Johnson, James Weldon. *Along This Way*. New York: Viking Press, 1933.

Kimball, Robert, and William Bolcom. *Reminiscing with Sissle and Blake*. New York: Viking Press, 1972.

Lord, Tom. *Clarence Williams*. Chigwell, England: Storyville,1976.

Marks, Edward B. *They All Sang*. New York: Viking Press, 1934.

Meeker, David. *Jazz in the Movies*. New Rochelle, N.Y.: Arlington House, 1977.

Morgan, Thomas L., and William Barlow. *From Cakewalks to Concert Halls*. Washington, D.C.: Elliot & Clark, 1992.

Music Trade Review. New York: 1899–1933.

Record Changer. New York: 1942–1957.

Riis, Thomas L. *Just Before Jazz*. Washington, D.C.: Smithsonian Institution Press, 1989.

Rose, Al. *Eubie Blake*. New York: Schirmer Books, 1979.

Rust, Brian. *The American Dance Band Discography, 1917–1942*. 2 vols. New Rochelle, N.Y.: Arlington House, 1975.

———. *Jazz Records, 1897–1942*. 2 vols. New Rochelle, N.Y.: Arlington House, 1978.

Rust, Brian, with Allen G. Debus. *The Complete Entertainment Discography*. New Rochelle, N.Y.: Arlington House, 1973.

Sampson, Henry T. *Blacks in Blackface*. Metuchen, N.J.: Scarecrow Press, 1980.

———. *The Ghost Walks: A Chronological History of Blacks in Show Business, 1865–1910*. Metuchen, N.J.: Scarecrow Press, 1988.

Shapiro, Nat, and Nat Hentoff. *Hear Me Talkin' to Ya: The Story of Jazz by the Men Who Made It*. New York: Rinehart, 1955.

Singer, Barry. *Black and Blue: The Life and Lyrics of Andy Razaf*. New York: Schirmer Books, 1992.

Smith, Eric Ledell. *Bert Williams*. Jefferson, N.C.: McFarland, 1992.

Southern, Eileen. *Biographical Dictionary of African-American and African Musicians*. Westport, Conn.: Greenwood Press, 1982.

———. *The Music of Black Americans: A History*. New York: W. W. Norton, 1983.

Toll, Robert C. *Blacking Up: The Minstrel Show in Nineteenth-Century America*. New York: Oxford University Press, 1974.

Waller, Maurice, and Anthony Calabrese. *Fats Waller*. New York: Schirmer Books, 1977.

Whitburn, Joel. *Pop Memories, 1890–1954*. Menomonee Falls, Wis.: Record Research, 1986.

Witmark, Isidore, and Isaac Goldberg. *From Ragtime to Swingtime*. New York: Lee Furman, 1939.

Wohl, Allen. *Black Musical Theatre*. Baton Rouge: Louisiana State University Press, 1989.

Wright, Laurie. *Fats in Fact*. Chigwell, England: Storyville, 1992.

INDEX OF SONG TITLES

· ·

Numbers in italics refer to extended treatments of indexed items.

GENERAL INDEX

• •

Numbers in italics refer to extended treatments of indexed items.

THE AUTHORS

. . . .

David A. Jasen is an internationally recognized authority on ragtime, early jazz, and popular song. He is the author of numerous books, including *Tin Pan Alley; Recorded Ragtime, 1897–1958;* and *Rags and Ragtime: A Musical History* (with Trebor J. Tichenor). He has edited several collections of ragtime-era sheet music and produced numerous CD reissues of early pop song and ragtime recordings. He is Professor of Communication Arts at the C. W. Post Campus of Long Island University.

Gene Jones, from Olla, Louisiana, is an actor and music historian. He has written monographs on Tom Turpin and the Original Dixieland Jazz Band and is the author of *Fables in Slang*, a ragtime revue based on the writing of George Ade. He has appeared in Broadway and off-Broadway shows, and his voice is heard in several of Ken Burns's epic documentaries, including *The Civil War, The West,* and *Lewis and Clark*.

Gene Jones   *David A. Jasen*